Special Str Development for All Sports

Picture, Paolo Bona

Special Strength Development for All Sports
by Louie Simmons
Writer: Louie Simmons
Editor: Doris Simmons and Martha C. Johnson
Covers and layout: Scott D Web Graphics®
Printer: Action Printing, Inc. Wisconsin
Copyright © Westside Barbell, Louie Simmons 2015
No part of this book may be reproduced in any form or by any means without the prior written consent of the publisher. Except of the brief quotes used in reviews.
Disclaimer:
The author and publisher of this material are not responsible in any manner whatsoever for any injury that may occur through following the instructions contained in this material. The activities may be too strenuous or dangerous for some people. The readers should always consult a physician before engaging in them.

Foreword

This book is intended for the serious coach and athlete. You'll learn while reading it that the Westside System is a combination of the former Soviet Union system, the Bulgarian system and the Westside Conjugate system. Brought together and refined, the result is the Westside System, which brings you a sophisticated method to reach the zenith of your sport.

Soviet sports scientists and the information they collected from their programs and then provided in magazine articles and books made it possible for me to learn about their techniques and perfect my own. Scientists such as Zatsiorsky, Verkhoshansky, B. Tabachnik, P. Komi, Dr. Matveyev, Dr. Bondarchuk, Bosco, Berger, Vorobyev, Romanov, Schmolinsky, and many more – too many to list – played a role in my own strength education.

A special thanks to Dr. Mel Siff, a great friend and supporter. I write this book in his memory and with deep affection for Mel and what he taught me over the years.

TABLE OF CONTENTS

Foreword	iii
Table of Contents	v
Dedication	xvii
Introduction: The Conjugate System	**1**
Things to Ponder	2
Training Methodology	3
Repetition Method	4
Reasons for Small Special Exercises	4
Selection of Exercises	5
Training in Intensity Zone	6
Explosive Strength (Trained at fast velocities)	6
Speed Strength (Trained at intermediate velocities)	6
Dynamic Method	6
Maximal Effort Method (Trained at slow velocities)	6
Training Intensities	7
Percent of Speed Strength Day	8
The Sprint	8
The Plan	8
Maximal Mechanical Power (Trained at one-third of maximal velocities)	10
Muscular Endurance	11
A Method of Increasing Muscular Dynamic Endurance	11
Posterior Chain Training	12
Two Methods	12
Non-Motorized Treadmill	13
Power Sled Walking	13
Wheel Barrel Sprints	14
Sumo Deadlift	14
Belt Squat/ Belt Squat Walk	14
Walking with Medicine Ball	15
Pulling Workout Plans	15
Chapter 1: The Role of Strength in Sports	**19**
Special Strength	19
Concentric Strength	20
Eccentric Strength	20
Static Strength	20
Speed Strength	21
Reactive Strength	21
Starting Strength	21

TABLE OF CONTENTS

	Over Speed Eccentrics Plus Optimal Eccentrics	21
	Strength Speed or Slow Strength	22
	Eccentric Strength	23
	Eccentric Unloading	25
	Assisted Eccentrics	26
	Optimal Eccentrics	28
Chapter 2:	**Endurance**	**33**
	Endurance is the Ability to Counter Fatigue	33
	Squat on a Box	33
	General Endurance	35
	Explosive Muscular Endurance	37
	Second Style	40
	Endurance Summary	41
	Emotional Stress	41
Chapter 3:	**Conjugate System**	**45**
	A Final Note	47
Chapter 4:	**Contrast and Reactive Methods**	**51**
	Chain Work	52
	Weight Releasers	54
	Weight Releasers Workouts	54
	Maximal Eccentric	54
	Bands over Bar Method	55
	Band Resistance for Running	57
	More about Bands	57
	Static Overcome by Dynamic Method	58
	Relaxed Overcome by Dynamic Effort	58
	A Ratio of Bar Weight & Band Tension for Different Special Strength Development	59
	Combinations of Resistance Methods	59
	Virtual Force Effect	59
Chapter 5:	**Periodization – Division into Training Periods**	**63**
	Periodization by Percentages	76
	How to change volume at the same intensity zone	85
Chapter 6:	**General Physical Preparedness**	**89**
	Special Physical Preparedness	89
	The Box Squat of Kettlebell Swings	92
	Box Jumping	94
	1. Max Effort Jumping	96
	2. Dynamic Method	97
	3. Sub-Maximal Effort Method	98
	Interval Method	98
	Kneeling Jumps	98
	Jumping with Barbell	98
	Conjugate System of Jumping	98
	Posterior Development	99

TABLE OF CONTENTS

Non-Motorized Treadmill	100
Power Sled Walking	100
Wheel Barrel Sprints	100
Sumo Deadlift	101
Belt Squats	101
Belt Squat Walking	101
Walking With Med Ball	101
Sled Work for Runners	102
Power Sled Walking	102
The Sled Workouts	103
Sled Time Intervals	104
Points of Importance	105
For Longer Distance	105
Sled Work for Football and Hockey	105
Power Walking with Resistance	107
Indian Clubs	107
Bike Riding	107
Do you lack GPP?	107
Training of Powerlifters	108
Powerlifting Introduction	108
Lifting Technique	108
Squat	109
Technical Tips	109
Bench Press	110
Technical Tips	110
Deadlift	111
Technical Tips	111
Reasons for Failure	112
Squat	112
Bench	113
Flatting out on bench	113
Bench Tips	113
Reasons Deadlifts Fail	114
Box Squat	115
Box Squat Technique	115
Box Squat Bonuses	116
Box Squatting Summary	117
Weight Training for Throwers	117
Explosive Power	117
Maximal Effort Method	119
Deadlift Max Effort Workouts	120
Power Snatch and Power Clean	120
Push-Jerk from Front and Behind Neck	121
Good Mornings	121

TABLE OF CONTENTS

Bench Press	121
Specific Shot Exercises	122
General Exercises	122
Mobility	123
Dynamic Method	123
Maximum Mechanical Power	123
Squatting	124
Optimal Lifts	124
Three-Week Wave	125

Chapter 7: Olympic Lifting **133**

Volume and Intensity Zones	133
Max Effort Day	134
Isometric Work	135
Accommodating Resistance	136
Special Pulls	137
Lightened Method	137
Eccentric Work	137
Things to Ponder	138
Reasons for Failure	138
A Multi-Year Plan	139
Weight Lifting Programming	141
Comparing the Soviet System to the Bulgarian System	142
Ten Consecutive Workouts	143
Weight Room Programs	145
1. Maximum Effort Method	146
2. The Repetition to Near-Failure Method	147
3. The Dynamic Method	147
Basic Training Methods-Explosive Strength	147
Nine-Week Wave with Weight Releasers with a 500 Squat Max	148
Lightened Method	148
Sample Workouts	149
Nine-Week Wave with 600 Max Squat	149
Explosive Training for Bench Pressing	149
Example: 405 Max Bench Press	149
More Speed Benching	149
Speed Bench with Weight Releasers	150
Lightened Method Benching	150
Example: 315-Pound Max Bench	150
Speed Work for Pulling	150
Speed Deadlift 400-Pounds Max	150
Sample Week Wave for a 500-Pound Max	152
600 Max	152
Second Wave Three-Week Speed Strength	153
Two-Week Circa-Max Wave 800-Pound Max for the Very Strong	153
Speed Bench Three-Week Wave	153

TABLE OF CONTENTS

	Examples of max effort day:	154
	A 10-week wave cycle	154
	Max Effort Workouts	155
	Bench max effort workouts	160
Chapter 8:	**Training For Combative Sports and Arts**	**163**
	Introduction	163
	Building Blocks to Mastery	164
	Keep Records	164
	Level I: Components of General Physical Preparation	165
	Cardiovascular Endurance	165
	How to Train for Cardiovascular Endurance	165
	Summary	166
	Basic Exercises for Muscular Endurance (The Shingitai "Six-Pack")	166
	1. Neck Bridge	166
	Build The House From The Basement Up	168
	2. How to Perform Hindu Squats	169
	Want To Lift Your Opponent?	170
	3. Glute-Ham Raises	170
	Glute-Ham Raises with Tubing	173
	4. Sit-Ups	173
	5. Push-Ups	173
	6. Pull-Ups (Overhand Grip)	174
	How to Avoid Slumps in Your Training	175
	Secret Training Methods of the World's Best Athletes	175
	Exercises to Substitute for Those in Your Basic Program	176
	More Championship Strategies When Your Progress Stalls	177
	Five Methods of Exercising For Complete Development	177
	Basic Exercises to Prevent Shoulder Injuries	179
	Shoulder Exercises with Tubing or Expanders	179
	The Russian Dumbbell Shoulder Routine	179
	The Five-Minute Dumbbell Drill	183
	Guidelines for the five-Minute Dumbbell Drill	183
	The Mother of All Sets	184
	The Value of Physical Work	187
	How to Use Other Sports and Games to Develop General Speed	188
	Now, Let's Start Putting the Levels Together	190
	General Physical Preparation (GPP) or "Accumulation Phase"	190
	Directed Physical Preparation (DPP) or "Intensification Phase"	190
	Specific Physical Preparation (SPP) or "Transformation Phase"	191
	Optimal Surplus: The Key to Reliable Performance	192
	Louie Simmons, The Great Guru Of Powerlifting	192
	Optimal Surplus in Judo	192
	General Physical Preparation	193
	No Weak Links in the Chain	193
	General Physical Preparation (GPP) in the Former Soviet Union vs. the U.S.	196

TABLE OF CONTENTS

What the Experts Say Regarding GPP 196
Train like a Decathlete 197
To Be a Champion You Need Balanced Development 197
Developing Specific Endurance with Circuit Training 198
Research On Elite Judo Athletes at the U.S. Olympic Training Center 199
Training Secrets Of South Korea's 1984 Olympic Judo Team 200
Shingitai Beginners Circuit 202
Shingitai Intermediate Circuit 203
Shingitai Advanced Circuit 204
Aerobic vs. Anaerobic Endurance 205
Aerobic Endurance 205
Anaerobic Endurance 205
Interval Training 206
Interval Training Program Using a Throw 206
Alternative Interval Training Programs 207
    Four One-Minute Rounds 207
    Ten 30-Second Rounds 207
    Six 30-Second Rounds 207
Specific Physical Preparation: Secrets of Developing Speed 209
Mind and Spirit as a Factor In Speed 210
Skill as a Factor in Speed 210
Physical Training to Improve Speed 211
To Weight Train, Or Not To Weight Train? That Is The Question 211
Methods of Developing Speed Outside of Practice (Off the Mat): 212
Jump Training (sometimes called "plyometric" training) 212
    1.   Jumps Up Stairs 212
    2.   Box Jumps 213
    3.   Various Hops and Jumps On a Flat Surface 213
    4.   Hindu Jump Squats 213
    5.   Wide-Narrow Jump Squats 213
Summary and Guidelines For Speed Development 214
Weight Training For Maximum Strength And Speed 215
Maximum Strength Day (Monday) 215
Keep It Short And Sweet 215
Speed Day (Friday) 216
Why Box Squats? 216
Accommodating Resistance 216
How To Choose Assistance Exercises 217
What a Weekly Training Program Might Look Like 217
    MONDAY: Maximum Strength Day: Lower Body and Torso 218
    TUESDAY: Conditioning and Assistance Work 218
    WEDNESDAY: Maximum Strength Day: Upper Body 218
    THURSDAY: Assistance Work 218
    FRIDAY: Maximum Speed Day 219
    SATURDAY: Conditioning and Assistance Work 219

TABLE OF CONTENTS

SUNDAY: Active Rest	219
Lower Body Exercises	220
Box Squats (variation 1)	220
Box Squats with Chains (variation 2)	221
Box Squats with Bands (variation 3)	222
Box Squats	222
Zercher Squats	224
Leg Curls with Tubing	225
Torso Exercises (Low Back, Abs, and Sides)	226
Back Raises	226
Back Raise With Twist	226
Goodmornings	227
Goodmornings/Squat Variation	228
Reverse Hypers	229
Side Sit-Ups	230
Russian Twists	231
Side-To-Side Leg Raises	232
Vertical Bar Twists	233
Incline Sit-Ups	234
Upper Body Exercises	235
Hindu Push-Ups	235
Ring Muscle-Ups	236
Ring Push-Ups	237
Horizontal Pull-Ups	238
Rope Climbing	239
Four-Way Neck Exercise with Band	240
Hand and Forearm Exercises	241
Grip Training	241
Wrist Roller	243
Wide Wrist Roller	243
Total Body Exercises	244
Squat Thrust with Push-Ups And Pull-Ups Added	244
Medicine Ball Work	245
Barrel Lifts	246
Total Body "Chain Reaction" Exercises	247
Clean Pulls	247
Dumbbell Power Cleans	248
Throwing and Takedown Exercises with Tubing	249
Climb Around Your Partner	251
Partner Carries	252
Exercises To Transform Your Off-the-Mat Conditioning Into Fighting Shape	253
Partner Assistance Exercises	253
1. Partner Jump Squats	253
2. Partner-Push Ups/Grip Fighting (or Hand-Fighting)	254
3. One Leg Hop and Drive/One Leg Throws	255

TABLE OF CONTENTS

	4. Throw Your Partner and Drag Him Back Up	256
	How To Use Partner Assistance Exercises To Improve	256
	Weak Points In Your Technique	256
	More Partner Pulling Exercises	256
	Kettlebells	258
	Abnormal Training Methods For Abnormal Results	260
	How's This For An Abnormal Training Method?	265
	Level III Peaking Phase: A Tricky Business	266
	Super Compensation	267
	A Word Of Caution	267
	Two-Week Unloading Period	268
	A Few Closing Remarks	269
Chapter 9	**Sports Nutrition and Hydration**	**271**
	Protein	271
	Anabolism and Catabolism	273
	Amount of Protein an Athlete Should Consume	273
	Quality of Protein	275
	Protein Sources	275
	Protein Supplementation	276
	Timing	277
	Carbohydrates	278
	Carbohydrates and Muscle Contractions	279
	Carbohydrate and Intensity	279
	Types of Carbohydrates	280
	Types of simple sugars:	280
	How to Choose Type of Carbohydrate	281
	Carbohydrate Oxidation and Intake	282
	Carbohydrate Digestion	282
	Carbohydrate Super Compensation	283
	Too Many Carbohydrates?	283
	Glycogen Depletion	283
	Fats	284
	Essential Fatty Acids	286
	Several Different Types of Omega-3 Fatty Acids	286
	Good Fats	287
	Unhealthy Fats	287
	Fat Intake	288
	Hydration	288
	Hydrating Optimally	289
	Hydration Facts	290
	When to Hydrate with Water and When to Use Sports Drinks	290
	Electrolytes	292
	Water Cutting	293
	Diuretics	294
	Saunas and Whirlpools/Jacuzzi	295

TABLE OF CONTENTS

	Post Water Cut Rehydration	295
	Rehydration	296
	Alternatives for Water Retention	297
Putting it All Together		297
Using Macro Nutrients Properly		298
Waving Food Intake		298
Endurance Athletes - Meal Plan		299
Strength Athletes - Meal Plan		301
Example of a Permissible Clean Food List		303

Chapter 10 Restoration and Recovery Methods 307
- 1. Anabolic Steroids 307
- 2. Therapeutic 308
- 3. Mental Recovery 309
- 4. Small Workouts 310
- A Neuromuscular Therapist's View of the Reverse Hyper™ 311
- The Iliopsoas, the "Hidden Prankster" 313
- Other Anatomical Considerations 314
- Muscle Fiber Considerations 315
- Up for Debate: 315
- Curved and Wrapped Muscle Path Considerations 317
- Muscular Function and Biomechanics 317
- Functions of the Psoas at the Hip Joint 318
- Functions of the Psoas at the Spinal Joints 318
- How Does the Psoas have the Ability to Both Flex and Extend the Lumbar? 319
- The Psoas Creates Movement Segmentally 319
- Psoas Function as a Spine Stabilizer 320
- How Does the Psoas Stabilize the Spine? 320
- Psoas Contraction and Spinal Compression 320
- The Psoas' Effect on Spinal Alignment 321
- Psoas Conclusion 321
- Biomechanics and Function of the Psoas in Open Chain and Closed Chain 322
- Biomechanics of the Psoas's Antagonists When Performing the Reverse Hyper 325
- The Reverse Hyper: Therapeutic Exercise for Individuals with Low Back Pain 325
- REVERSE HYPER® 327
- Feet, Ankle, Knee and Hip Recovery 327
- Shoulder Rehab 328
- Examples and Views from Strength Coaches Around the World 329
- A Better Approach to Spinal Health Recovery and Performance 331
- The Uniqueness of an Atlas Subluxation 331
- Conclusion 332
- Pain Described 333
- "Mechanobiology and Diseases of Mechanotransduction" 341
- ARP Wave Therapy 346
- The Secret of ARP Wave 346
- How the Practitioner uses ARP wave 347

TABLE OF CONTENTS

The RECAST Approach to Strength Training for Short Track Speed Skating	348
Rugby Training Using the Westside Barbell Conjugate Method	352
Training Collegiate Athletes For Maximal Results	357
The Benefits of Sled Dragging	366
Conjugate System Is Program Cornerstone	367
Strength Matters in MMA	369
What does Westside's ART Specialist Say?	369
Soft Tissue Injuries	369
Injury Cycle	370
Tissues that are Compressed Together	371
The Phases of Remodeling of Soft Tissue Healing	372
Phase I - Inflammation	372
Phase II - Regeneration	372
Phase III - Remodeling	372
Treatment of Soft Tissue Injuries	373
The goal of ART treatment	373
What ART Treatment is like	373
Other Restoration Thoughts	374
Track Notes—Sled Work for Speed Development	375
Contrast Method	375
Chapter 11 Age and Long-Term Planning	**379**
Age and Weight Training	381
The Dynamic Method	383
Maximal Effort Method	383
Repetition to Near-Failure Method	383
The Optimal Lifts	385
Selected Bibliography & References	**387**

Dedication

I would like to dedicate this book to my readers. So thank you to all who will read this book, coaches and athletes alike.

I have always been inspired by reading books. One such book is *Jonathan Livingston Seagull* by Richard Bach. The book tells of a seagull trying to dive at speeds never before approached by a seagull. He would constantly lose control while trying a new personal speed record and crash into the sea. The elder gulls warned Jonathan that he would be banned from the flock if he continued his reckless behavior, which they finally did. Having flown at more than 200 miles per hour (mph), Jonathan was getting old, but no gull could stay with him, or so he thought. As he sat on a lonely beach after flying 273 mph, he said to himself, "A new record, but there must be limits." However, an elder gull, Chiang, said perfection doesn't have limits. The next few words changed my athletic career forever. Chiang said perfect speed is being there. In an instant, Chiang vanished and appeared at the water's edge fifty feet away. Then, he vanished again and in the same millisecond stood at Jonathan's side.

To me perfect speed meant once I touched the bar, the lift is complete. As I grow older I realize that now my goal must be to pass on what I have learned to be the truth about training and how to teach perfect speed to others.

Thanks to all I have had contact with over my lifting and learning career.

LOUIE SIMMONS

INTRODUCTION

The Conjugate System

INTRODUCTION

The Conjugate System

Merriam Webster defines conjugate as

    A. Joined together, especially in pairs

    B. Acting or operating as if joined

    C. Having features in common, but opposite or inverse in some particulars

The conjugate system was first experimented with in 1972 by the renowned Y.V. Verhoshansky. The experiment consisted of 20 to 45 special exercises. Large exercises, meaning with barbells, and small exercises, referring to back raises, calf raises, ham glute raises, belt squats and so forth, were included. Seventy highly qualified weight lifters were involved in the experiment. Afterwards one lifter was satisfied and the rest wanted more exercises. After that time the conjugate system has played a great role in the development of high-skilled weight lifters and athletes around the world. When done properly, it causes training to be controlled: optimal, energy sources, maximal, trainability, periodization, and evaluation. While the conjugate system means several things, it is the entire concept of the Westside system. To avoid accommodation, special exercises that are similar in structure to the classical lifts are used to increase strength and perfect form. However, it includes using special means, such as rubber bands and chains to make it increasingly more difficult while performing the lift. To raise qualitative motor abilities Westside realized that special exercises would increase the bench press, mainly the close grip. But what would increase the close grip bench press? Extensions, dumbbells, barbell pushdowns, and the like are used. The Goodmonings produced great results for Westside, but as soon as progress slowed, we realized that we must constantly raise our Goodmornings. How? Small special exercises: back raises, Reverse Hypers ™, glute/ham raises and inverse curls.

Correct periodization is the key to being your best on contest day. Severe workouts can be done every 72 hours. One is based on speed strength where high volume and moderate bar intensity is used for a fast rate of force development. For clarification, it is done on Friday. Monday is max effort day, the volume with the barbell is always less than 50 percent of Friday's barbell workout, but the intensity is plus 100 percent with 95 percent of the time on special barbell lifts, rack or box pulls, and a variety of Goodmonings or special squats. That's how we accomplish new records. Our small special exercises consist of 80 percent of the total volume while the large barbell work is only 20 percent. By doing this we constantly raise our weaknesses while allowing our lifters or athletes to use their special strengths to the upmost without injuries. This system also builds a very high degree of work capacity. The main aspect of our periodization is a three-week wave on speed or explosive strength day. With a combo of weight and band it represents 75 percent, 80 percent and 85 percent in a three-week wave. Our average weight is 80 percent for speed strength. A constant rotating of bars to avoid accommodation or change from band to chain or both will make it impossible to fully adapt to training. This ensures constant progress.

All of this makes it possible to beat our special records in training during our circa-max phase followed by our delayed transformation phase to ensure new records on contest day. Because strength is measured in three velocities, you must train all three during a weekly cycle: explosive strength (fast velocity-jumping speed strength); intermediate velocity (75 percent to 85 percent speed strength and strength speed); and slow velocity max-effort.

The Westside conjugate system makes it possible to become more explosive, build acceleration and absolute strength that can be monitored each week while raising work capacity with GPP blending simultaneously with SPP. The author has been using the conjugate system since 1970 while working out with no partner. He made new exercises to avoid boredom, plus making it possible to break a new special exercises each week. Some coaches and lifters are confused about the complexity of all the switching of special strengths and special exercises, but the authors see all sports as a conjugate system. A pitcher constantly changes the type of pitch he throws to produce a strike-out. A football coach uses a series of plays from running to passing to complete a successful drive. A boxer uses several combinations of punches at different speeds to lay traps for his opponent. Is each example not a conjugate system? Not so complicated after all, is it?

Things to Ponder

When training a track and field athlete, there is one common denominator: injuries are abundant — from muscle tears, to overstressed ligaments and tendons, and of course, stress fractures. This is from not maintaining a strong base of special exercises for not only the muscles, but also for increasing ligament and tendon hypertrophy. The latter can prevent soft tissue injury, while contributing to a greater effect on the stretch-shortening cycle for reversible muscle action.

Many sports sciences follow a block style of training supported by A.P. Bondarchuk, or Yuri Verkhoshansky and his work on long-term block organization and long-term adaptation to strength and sport skill. Through the transfer of exercises ranging from general, specific, and competitive events, it was concluded that it does one no good to be strong in the wrong exercises. This concept was thoroughly thought out by Bondarchuk and many others who have developed the world's best in track and field.

The basis of strength conditioning is to improve strength and conditioning simultaneously. The strength coach must understand the events to further special strength development or special strength preparation from explosive strength.

The athlete must choose a proven track coach, and the track coach must choose a proven strength coach. Not an ex-athlete or a bodybuilder, but a strength coach who understands how to distribute the proper selection of exercises, volumes and intensities. Most importantly, this strength coach should understand special strengths and their velocities.

The coach must understand each event that comes easily for the athlete, and what events are most challenging. The most challenging events must be given periodically in training the event skills. Is it a technique problem, a lack of understanding for the event's demands, or is it a strength defect in a particular muscle? As a coach, understand each athlete's mental and emotional state. Correspond with the strength coach to improve lacking muscle groups, and for the development of explosive strength while raising absolute strength. The jumping up to and off of boxes must be calculated carefully according to their physical qualities. Know when the interval weight training should be done in a weekly plan, and when speed strength and max effort should be used. Train optimally — more is not better — one must recover from workout to workout. For the athlete to be at their best on meet day, you must know how to distribute the slow (heavy) weight training and the fast (light) training to produce a short-term delayed transformation.

If you are using a program that is five or even 10 years old, your athletes will only produce the results that were done five or ten years ago. This is unsatisfactory.

Finally, the coach must be responsible to fulfill the athlete's potential.

A coach relayed once to me that an athlete was only average but "tried hard." Yet, after being introduced to a qualified strength coach, they excelled, tapping into the hidden potential the athlete possessed. The skill coach must be on a par and above the athlete's full potential he or she will achieve, as the multi-year training system is fulfilled. An athlete must have great desire, as a coach must have the ability to increase his knowledge by learning from previous athletes and personal experiences.

The second common denominator is a failure to maintain techniques in the jumping and throwing events. This should not happen after a wide base for General Physical Preparedness (GPP) is established. Technique must be polished to perfection. This is where I disagree with long-term block periodization. GPP and Special Physical Preparedness (SPP) must blend seamlessly together.

After track season is completed, there is a time period where no jumping or throwing is practiced. A weight training program has begun, but no sports technique is integrated while training for explosive power, speed strength and strength speed while technique is totally neglected. Now, the competition season is starting and the once perfect technique is now flawed and not allowing the increase in power and strength to contribute to new records in the throwing and jumping events. While it may be true that block one can contribute to block two, block one cannot carry its work in to block three. This does not work with weight training or powerlifting nor does it work in track and field. One must use the conjugate system of throwing and jumping simultaneously into the special strength development phase, such as standing long jumps, seated long jumps, kneeling jumping, jumping over an obstacle of some type, jumping with band resistance, throwing medicine balls, Kettlebell throws, kneeling throws with left, right and both arms for distance or height with different apparatuses.

This can be done flowing the conjugate system for special exercises and using a three-week pendulum wave style for organizing the max effort method, speed strength wave and jumping waves. By thinking it out, the Westside system will enable one to perfect form in the very technical track and field events while raising all special strengths, as well as raising your level of physical preparedness.

As you will learn later in this book, the Westside training system has managed to combine three methods (accumulation, intensification, and leading into transformation) into multiple three-week pendulum waves, the staple of Westside.

Training Methodology

As Dr. Verkhoshansky was busy discovering the conjugate system in 1972 at the Dynamo Club, your author was mixing many special exercises to avoid accommodation through max effort work. However, it wasn't until 1982 that Westside started to understand the need to exchange high-volume/ low-to-moderate intensity, for low volume/ max intensity every 72 hours. Since then, we also gained an understanding of how to distribute special strengths, and learned what velocities they are trained.

Westside has found that both injuries and lack of progress can be directly related to stress. It can be an adversary that you cannot defeat. It can be money, relationships, job business, but it can never be between the coach and the athlete. You must be on the same page 24/7. Athletes can be moody, but never a coach. The coach has a great responsibility to his or her athletes, and must be willing to seek help from specialty coaches, sometimes making it necessary to set an ego aside at all costs for the success of the sportsman.

Repetition Method

This system is measured by the amount of reps to failure of five, eight, ten, and so forth, commonly done with a barbell. This can be dangerous if the athlete has a muscle imbalance, for instance, in the lower back; the same risk of injury is also imminent for underdeveloped hamstrings. Westside recommends higher reps — up to 20 reps with 25 percent to 30 percent of a one rep maximum (1RM). The purpose is to build hypertrophy in the posterior chain. Belt squats, deadlifts (sumo style), power clean, or snatches are much safer.

As you recall, the Westside system uses a ratio of 20 percent classic lifts, and 80 percent special exercises. Biomechanically, no two athletes are built the same. That is precisely why a squat or press with a barbell does not insure the athlete will develop the same physically, although in today's sports world you have model athletes for particular sports event. But if one's upper leg is one inch shorter, or the torso is two inches longer, a multi-joint exercise will work differently on the two individuals.

Reasons for Small Special Exercises

Train a large muscle group like the hips or hamstrings first, then finish them off by working a particular hip muscle or the lower back with extensions. I hope you see our philosophy; as you know, an extreme workout can occur every 72 hours, small workouts 12 hours to 24 hours apart. The Russian strongman Valya Dikul even advocates when the legs are tired to ride a bike. The normal restoration time between different training loads:

EXTREME	72 hours
LARGE	48-72 hours
SUBSTANTIAL	24-48 hours
MEDIUM	12-24 hours
SMALL	12 hours

Remember, it is best to do the largest exercise first, then three to four special exercises. For increasing jumps, use heavy weights, but maintain .6 m/s up to .8 m/s. This will excite the central nervous system (CNS), causing a contrast method when using light or no resistance when doing jumping exercises.

Again, the Westside system calls for an example using a close grip bench to increase a regular bench. But how can we increase the close grip bench? Simply complete some tricep extensions or push downs with a variety of reps, bars, and accessory handles.

This should clarify our methods of training, the only scientifically proven methods.

Selection of Exercises

My friend and esteemed associate, Sakari Selkäinaho, has said, "It does no good to be strong in the wrong exercises." That is also what Anatoliy P. Bondarchuk expands on in volumes one and two of *Transfer of Training in Sports* (2010) This is a must, as no amount of training can be wasted during any period of, or while organizing, one's training.

When faster running times is the goal, you must be careful not to add any unnecessary mass. A sprinter's goal is to gain explosive power and absolute strength, but not added muscle mass, except in the regions where it biomechanically causes one to run faster. This means the calves, hamstrings, hips, glutes, spinal erectors, and abs as well as the arms, lats, and upper back.

You may think of squatting, cleaning, snatching and deadlifting initially, but special exercises are actually used at a ratio of 80 percent special to 20 percent barbell. Westside is a private facility, but has produced more than 75 800-pound squatters, with 19 being over 1,000 pounds, and two more than 1,200 pounds. Their training consists of 80 percent special and 20 percent barbell exercises, as calculated by Joe Lasko, who used 1) our strongest men, 2) women who squat at least 430, 3) a heptathlete, and 4) U.F.C. fighters Kevin Randleman (a former U.F.C. heavyweight champ) and in 2012, Matt Brown (who won six fights in a row at 170 pounds). I hope this is proof enough!

If a sprinter can squat 400 pounds, or her total volume is 4,800 pounds, then her Reverse Hyper™ volume in the same workout is roughly 20,000 pounds. This would be considered isolation work for the hamstrings, glutes, and hips — the muscles that can contribute greatly to squatting, and yes, to running. This is in fact the transfer of training in sports.

A 600-pound squatter has a total of 7,200 pounds; the Reverse Hyper™ volume is 28,000 pounds, about four times the squat volume. For squatting, the bar speed should be roughly .8 m/s for speed strength development. By adding inverse curls as a major special exercise as well as 200 leg curls each day with 10-pound to 20-pound ankle weights, the volume is great for the hamstrings, while at the same time thickening the ligaments and tendons that store elastic energy for the stretch reflex. Of course, many forms of shock training with massive bar weight should be included, as well as plyometric (bounding, drop jumps, and jumping with the resistance such as ankle weights, weight vest, Bulgarian bags, kettlebells, and combination of all) twice per week. Light barbell squats at 30 percent of kettlebell squat and very light weight with rubber band tension also can be included.

I have mentioned exercises with weights, jumping in many forms, and of course, running exercises. The system I am suggesting requires the athlete to reduce some of the running and replace the total work volume with special strength exercises. If more running makes a sprinter faster, then they look like a marathon runner. That is certainly not the case. Special exercises make it possible to increase a barbell max or reduce sprinting time.

When doing a multi-joint exercise, different athletes will not use the same percentage of strength potential in a particular muscle group. Some may use their lower back more, while some might use more upper or lower hamstrings. This is precisely why special exercises must be used; the weakest muscle group will be strengthened to ensure a reduction in injury-inducing muscle imbalances that may delay and impede progress if left unaddressed.

Training in Intensity Zone

When the goal is to train a special strength quality, one must know at what velocity that strength is trained.

Explosive Strength (Trained at fast velocities)

Explosive strength is trained at a fast velocity, which includes training at 30 percent of a 1RM or jumping. Explosive strength can be defined as the ability to rapidly increase force (Tidow, 1990).

Speed Strength (Trained at intermediate velocities)

It is noted that 780 superior Olympic weightlifters use 50 percent of the barbell lifts with 75 percent to 85 percent. This is speed strength and is trained at intermittent velocity. This information is taken from the works and studies of A.D. Ermakov and N.S. Atanasov (1975). Westside uses combination methods of training. This means 50 percent to 60 percent bar weight plus 25 percent band tension at the top.

Dynamic Method

The two special strengths are trained with the Dynamic Method. When training for explosive strength that requires light weight at high velocity, it is impossible to attain Fmm. This is why the dynamic method is not used for a maximal strength, but to improve and increase a fast rate of force development and explosive strength. This is a high-volume training day.

Maximal Effort Method (Trained at slow velocities)

Completed 72 hours after dynamic day, this is the most superior method for improving both intramuscular and intermuscular coordination. The athlete has now adapted to the stress on the central nervous system and muscles. This method of training brings out the greatest strength gains. Westside recommends single reps after a warm up to hold volume as low as possible. The goal is maximum intensity and/or a new personal record.

Two or three reps build strength endurance. While training a two or three rep record, you will always conserve yourself to complete the third rep. One rep max limits muscle mass to a minimum, so there is no unnecessary weight gain.

The max effort workouts are done by rotating a carefully chosen list of roughly eight exercises using mostly barbells, although a very heavy sled, wheelbarrow, or strongman yoke can also be included. The barbell exercises should be close in nature to the five classical lifts; rack pulls, high pulls, and all types of Goodmonings. A wide variety of squatting with specialty bars and an assortment of box heights and foot placement also can be used. As max strength goes up, so do all special strengths, including endurance of all types.

Training Intensities

Let's take a look at the ratio of speed strength squatting to working. An all-time max looks like this:

A 600-pound squatter's training volume is 7,200 pounds as a mentioned by using a three-week wave. The barbell weight is 50 percent, 55 percent, and 60 percent at .8m/s for 12x2 at Week 1, 10x2 at Week 2, and 8x2 at Week 3 (or 360 pounds x 10 sets x 2 reps = 7,200 pounds). To avoid bar deceleration and increase over-speed eccentrics, add 25 percent band tension at the top of the lift. With band shrinkage in the bottom, 10 percent is added to the bar. Here is the graph:

BAR WEIGHT	BAND TENSION	TOTAL PERCENT
50%	25%	= 75%
55%	25%	= 80%
60%	25%	= 85%

This all fits within the research on sets and reps conducted by A.S. Prilepin in 1974, and the 1975 data of A.D. Ermakov and his colleague, N.S. Atanasov.

Now, we know the total volume of a 600-pound squat is 7,200 pounds. But how does it relate to max effort day 72 hours later, after a warm-up with small weights, say, 315 pounds? Let's add up the total poundage to reach a 600-pound max:

WEIGHT x REPS	VOLUME
365x2	730
405x2	810
455x2	910
500x1	500
560x1	560
605x1 (PR)	605
VOLUME TOTAL:	**4,115 POUNDS**

PERCENT OF SPEED STRENGTH DAY

The barbell should be at 30 percent to 40 percent for explosive strength at fast velocity. Speed strength would be 75 percent to 85 percent at intermediate velocity. With strength speed (or slow strength), the barbell moves at a slow .4 to .5m/s velocity. There is also isometric training as well, which is, of course, trained at zero velocity.

The Sprinter

A 60-meter sprinter first must master correct running form. I recommend breaking running movements into small segments. This is exactly what Dr. Nicholas Romanov has purposed in the training essays and the *Pose Method books* (2001). It is pure physics and biomechanics: one must overcome the effect of gravity and learn how it can assist you while running. If speed-stride rate and stride length are the keys, Peter Weyand PhD, a bio mechanist in human locomotion, has discovered many interesting things. A paper published in the *Journal of Biomechanics* (1987) found that as little as one-tenth of the force is used horizontally at a constant speed. The other nine-tenths is applied vertically, if correct biomechanics is utilized. Here is where track coaches and science disagree. I take the side of science: greater ground force, not faster leg movements is the key. As discussed in the *Journal of Applied Physiology*, our goal is to increase power and strength with minimum increase in mass or body weight. Big is not strong; strong is strong. A 300-pound man can never compete with a 150-pound man while doing pull-ups for instance. Why? Large men do not have great relative strength. As weight training is introduced into the sprinter's program, one must reduce the amount of running, so as not to over train. It is true as an athlete gets better, the total volume must go up as well. However, train optimally, not minimally or maximally. This is backed by a study by Leena Paavolainen entitled "Explosive strength training improves 5K times by improving running economy and muscle power" (1999). She used two groups of well-trained 5K or longer runners. The two groups were close in performance. The group that added explosive-strength training reduced their total running by 32 percent. After nine weeks of training, the two groups were tested and the non-explosive strength trained group showed no improvements, while the weight-trained group showed great improvements.

Much of what I have just discussed is in Barry Ross's fine publication "*Underground Secrets to Faster Running*" (2005). I commend him on his years spent in the gym and perfecting what he found and improving on it. But how does one become stronger while maintaining speed and acceleration?

The Plan

Many think that as you become stronger you become slower. By examining basic physics and mathematics, this is not the case at all. Our female athletes will move their training weight on dynamic day at the same speed as our men. How? By training at the same percent of a 1 rep max and by doing the exact amount of sets and reps and the exact total amount of lifts, but more important the bar speed is 0.8m/s on average. Here lays the key to power training. Westside uses the most optimal weights for speed strength with barbell training by implementing a barbell weight of 50 percent, 55 percent, and 60 percent in a three-week wave with 25 percent band tension at lockout. This makes 75 percent, 80 percent, and 85 percent at lockout. These percents are used 50 percent of the time for speed strength training as suggested by the studies of A.D. Ermakov and N.S. Atanasov in 1975 with 780 high-skilled

Olympic weight lifters. At the bottom of the squat band tension is reduced to 100 pounds. By band shrinkage this represents 60 percent, 65 percent, and 70 percent. This is slightly above the normal 30 percent or 40 percent for explosive strength. However, with the overall speed eccentric caused by the bands pulling one down, a virtual force effect is present; a force that is there, but not recognized. Example: one can walk on thin ice, but cannot jump on the same thin ice without going through the same ice. Why? Over speed eccentrics.

400-Pound Max Squat

Percentage	Weight	Reps	Lifts	Band Tension	Volume
50%	200 lb.	12x2	24	25%	4,800 lb.
55%	220 lb.	12x2	24	25%	5,280 lb.
60%	240 lb.	10x2	20	25%	4,800 lb.
Bar Speed is 0.8 m/s avg.					

450-Pound Max Squat

Percentage	Weight	Reps	Lifts	Band Tension	Volume
50%	225 lb.	12x2	24	25%	5,400 lb.
55%	250 lb.	12x2	24	25%	6,000 lb.
60%	270 lb.	10x2	20	25%	5,400 lb.
Bar Speed is 0.8 m/s avg.					

500-Pound Max Squat

Percentage	Weight	Reps	Lifts	Band Tension	Volume
50%	250 lb.	12x2	24	25%	6,000 lb.
55%	275 lb.	12x2	24	25%	6,600 lb.
60%	300 lb.	10x2	20	25%	6,000 lb.
Bar Speed is 0.8 m/s avg.					

550-Pound Max Squat

Percentage	Weight	Reps	Lifts	Band Tension	Volume
50%	275 lb.	12x2	24	25%	6,600 lb.
55%	300 lb.	12x2	24	25%	7,200 lb.
60%	330 lb.	10x2	20	25%	6,600 lb.
Bar Speed is 0.8 m/s avg.					

600-Pound Max Squat

Percentage	Weight	Reps	Lifts	Band Tension	Volume
50%	300 lb.	12x2	24	25%	7,200 lb.
55%	330 lb.	12x2	24	25%	7,920 lb.
60%	360 lb.	10x2	20	25%	7,200 lb.
Bar Speed is 0.8 m/s avg.					

As you increase the squat max by 50 pounds your volume is increased by 600 pounds. A 400-pound squatter cannot train with a 450-pound percent plan. That would cause the bar speed to be too slow and reduce force. But how can one increase your squat during the training cycle? By special exercises and max effort day that is trained 72 hours later. Science tells us that.

What if as you become able to increase your maximal effort, this method makes it possible to recruit the most muscle units? This would make it possible to squat, let's say, 1,000 pounds. This may take two to three seconds to complete concentrically, but by increasing the rate of force development using the dynamic method to exert the maximum amount of strength in the shortest possible time. Explosive power or explosive strength in theory is much like increasing the max amount of strength by the maximal effort and shortening the time. To display it through a second method, explosive strength work with light weight 30 percent of a 1 rep max or jumping up or down on and off of boxes. This may seem somewhat hard to comprehend when working with a body weight sport. The true founder of shock training, Dr. Yuri Verkhoshansky, would use extremely heavy weight resistance as a contrast to jumping, bounding, and depth jumps or for the development of explosive strength and speed training, both fast velocity and slow velocity.

Let's examine Hill's equation of muscle contraction. Velocity training's relationship to maximal muscular performance is fully understood by realizing that motion velocity decreases as external resistance increases. Yuri Verkhoshansky found when using maximal weight, force is attained when velocity is small. The opposite is true when velocity is maximized; the resistance is close to zero. This clarifies why heavy weights are used for max strength and no resistance for max velocity training.

Maximal Mechanical Power (Trained at one-third of maximal velocities)

Maximal mechanical power requires different motor abilities. The Westside system uses a third proven method. Speed strength and accelerating strength by using bar weight ranging from 50 percent, 55 percent and 60 percent in a pendulum wave lasting three weeks. We eliminate bar deceleration by adding bands to the bar for accommodating resistance; for speed strength 25 percent band tension at the lockout. This makes the total at the top 75 percent, 80 percent and 85 percent. This represents 50 percent of the weight training for speed strength. Because of band shrinkage, the bottom weight with bar weight and band tension is at 60 percent, 65 percent and 70 percent. The bands also add over-speed eccentric for a greater stretch-reflex. To increase kinetic energy (KE), velocity is better than adding mass. This system makes it more advantageous to find the perfect weight at the top and bottom, something bar weight cannot do. The weight would be too heavy in the bottom and with just band tension the weight would be too light in the bottom. You must use a combination of both. See combination method and training in *Supertraining*, (Siff, 2003, P 409).

As you can see Westside uses fast velocity through jumping, bounding, depth jumps, intermediate velocity, speed strength squats, presses, pulls and slow velocity max effort in a weekly, monthly and yearly to multi-year plan. If you are a strength coach, you must know what velocity builds what special strength.

Muscular Endurance

A sprinter must start as fast as possible, gain top speed, and hold it as long as possible. The longer top speed is maintained the less deceleration occurs. How can we eliminate decelerating? By developing general and dynamic endurance.

First, let's define endurance. Endurance is the ability to work through fatigue while maintaining a high work capacity and without diminishing technique. What causes fatigue? Low physical work capacity along with a lack of cardiovascular fitness. Raising maximum endurance is directly connected by increasing maximal strength. For example, an athlete that has a max bench press of 675 pounds can do more reps with 225 pounds than an athlete whose max bench is 450 pounds. Why? Simple math: 225 is 33 1/3 percent of 75 pounds while 225 pounds is 50 percent of 450 pounds. A model athlete should always do more reps with a smaller percent of a 1 rep max, just like raising max strength to increase more barbell lifts with sub maximal weights. Let's examine how to increase dynamic endurance that ultimately helps reduce the deceleration phase at the end of most races.

Endurance must be raised by working not only at different intensities of an athlete's sporting event, but also using special strength exercises with weight sled, non-motorized treadmill, walking belt squats and pushing a wheel barrow. These special devices can be used with different loads for different distances and several combinations of additional resistance such as weight vest, ankle weights, hand weights and Kettlebells. This raises muscular strength endurance while also raising cardiovascular fitness. While many sports experts believe that walking has no benefit to increasing sports performance, I have found that walking with a heavyweight vest plus ankle weights and hand weights can greatly increase general fitness and raise work capacity. There are many types of endurance training and methods. For all running distances, I prefer the interval method using belt squats, belt squat walk, non-motorized treadmill, power sled walking, and wheel barrow. You must keep records for distance, weight, time, or repetitions for time. This means 60 meter, 100 meter, and 200 meter times are based off 60 meter resistance work. 100 meter power walking requires 400 meter times. Example: An athlete who had an 800 meter time of two minutes 14 seconds, power walked 400 meters in two minutes 30 seconds. She reduced the 400 meter power walking to two minutes 14 seconds and ran a 400 meter in two minutes ten seconds. High repetition leg curls, Reverse Hyper® work, inverse curls and the like greatly increase endurance and add thickness to the ligaments and tendons for a greater storage of kinetic energy.

A Method of Increasing Muscular Dynamic Endurance

An experiment with a 16-year-old female sprinter and male all-national decathlete champion should be of interest to sprinting and running coaches. Coaches commonly have their men and women who decelerate badly at the end of their races run 100 meters to 200 meters longer than their specialty. This, of course, produces less force per step and diminishes the running form. One can only produce so much force in a fatigued state. Our experiment called for the 16-year-old sprinter to power walk for 60 yards as powerfully as possible. With a sled weight of 45 pounds she covered the distance in 22 seconds. While adding weight on each trip she covered the distance in 17 seconds with a sled weight of 120 pounds. Her counterpart, a 27-year-old national decathlete champion had similar results. With 135-pound sled weight, he covered the distance in 17 seconds. The time came down while adding weight until the sled weight was 250 pounds. His power walk time was 11 seconds on the last two trips, but adding weight until an optimal weight was utilized. The force production was increased for eliminating deceleration. This is a positive method at any distance as proven by having the 16-year-old cover a distance at 12 seconds. After the first 12 second powerwalk on the balls of the feet, a distance was established with a sled weight of 90 pounds. She managed to add 20 feet in the 12-second power-walk, but by adding 25 pounds more to the sled she increased the distance another eight feet. This is the most superior method to eliminate much of the deceleration phase.

I hope this method of improving force development is easy to comprehend. If one runs a 400 meter or 800 meter and has a bad deceleration phase, and the coach without examining physics or science has his runner go an extra 200 meters, he must know that force production goes down even more as the athlete runs even slower regardless of the effort the athlete exerts. (See power sled walking, page 13)

Posterior Chain Training

Improve your work capacity while eliminating deceleration to maintain sports conditioning and increase posterior strength. The following special means are superior to all others. This is where coaching and science have conflicts.

The coach's coach probably made him run further to correct the need to eliminate deceleration when he was an athlete as well. However, science would tell a different story. When one slows down, they are producing less force production at the end of the race than at the start of the race. If the sprinter's force is diminishing, running longer would only lead to less and less force until the sprinter could run no further, producing zero force.

To correct this, power walk with a weight sled with the optimal amount of weight or resistance. Walk on the heels first for posterior development or on the balls of the feet to combine power into technique. Remember to experiment to find the optimal weight. Too light and small force is produced; too heavy and you will lose velocity.

Two Methods

First, time the athlete in the 100 meter, 200 meter, 400 meter then, pull a sled in that time frame. If one can add weight and cover the same distance, they have eliminated deceleration.

Next, have the athlete pull a sled for the time of the race. If their time in the 400 meter is 22 seconds, pull a set weight (remember use the optimal weight) for 22 seconds. As you continue, they should cover more distance on each proceeding trip.

This will indeed eliminate deceleration through science.

The work priority for a sprinter is roughly acceleration 65 percent, max velocity maintenance 18 percent, and reduce deceleration 12 percent.

Non-Motorized Treadmill

Walk, don't run, with heels striking first. This will resemble a partial glute/ham raise. Long strides are best to build the primary sprinting muscles. Warning! Do not duplicate your running form; the treadmill is to develop muscles. There are many varieties to use. First, hook rubber bands around your ankles or thighs. The band attachment is at the end of the treadmill. Walk as powerfully as possible; this builds the thighs, hips, abs and glutes. Interval training is the key.

For the 60 meter, walk for 10 seconds with 30 second rest intervals. The averages sets are 15 to 25, depending on your level of preparedness. For the most powerful athletes, add five to ten pound ankle weights along with the bands. A strong band should always be attached to the waist through a weight belt. One can add a weight vest as well. This combination builds general fitness power and dynamic endurance. For the 100 meter sprinter use 15-second walks with 40 second rest intervals. For 400-meter sprinters power walk for 60 seconds with 90-second rest intervals. For 800-meter sprinters power walk for two minutes and 30 seconds and try two minute 30 second rest intervals. A 1,600-meter runner will power walk five minutes with five minute rest intervals. The amount of work sets will depend upon the athlete's level of preparedness. Rotate some type of resistance that includes bands or weight. This will eliminate the principle of diminishing returns, also known as accommodation, a general law of biology.

POWER SLED WALKING

For those in good climates, use power walking with a weight sled attached to a weight belt around the waist, long strides with heel touching first. This will feel much like walking on a non-motorized treadmill. Each step is a start, the sled should jerk with each step. Also, this will almost eliminate deceleration. For sprinters up to 200 meters, power walk for 60 meters and use up to five 45- pound plates, keep the power walking up to 25 seconds. Walk with 90 pounds, 135 pounds, 180 pounds and 225 pounds, keeping records of each weight. Also, add ankle weights, weight vest, or both on some workouts. The heaviest sled walks should be done on Monday. For absolute strength, Wednesday drop 30 percent of weight and add trips for strength endurance. Use a lighter weight on Friday for a warm-up or restoration. For acceleration, men sprint with 50 pounds and women 25 pounds on grass, preferably, to eliminate shin splints.

For the 400-meter, pull a distance that last 60 seconds. For the 800-meter pull two minutes 45 seconds to start, for example with a sled. Use three plates to break records. Always walk on your heels with long strides. As the sled times are reduced, so should your running times.

For the 1,600 meter, power walk for five minutes and use at least three different weights as well as some ankle weights or weight vest at times. The amount of work sets must be established by your fitness level. One third of all power walks should be on the balls of your feet. For acceleration men sprint with 50 pounds and women 25 pounds on grass, preferably, to eliminate shin splints.

WHEEL BARREL SPRINTS

Interchange weights of the wheel barrel with at least three different weights. As with the other special means, keep records at each distance with each weight. You must sprint as fast as possible on the balls of your feet.

The wheel barrel works best for distances up to the 800 meter. Pushing a wheel barrel for four minutes can be very taxing. Don't let an exercise drill take more out of you than you get out of the drill. A big advantage a wheel barrel can give to the athlete is balance and stability that comes from controlling the wheel barrel by holding on to the handles. This builds the entire body, especially the oblique's that play a great role in all sports activities. Anytime you must grip an object tightly you bring forth many muscles, causing a greater and more intense workout.

SUMO DEADLIFT

A sumo deadlift is a wide stance deadlift pushing your feet apart to activate the hips and glutes to the fullest. High reps are in order. How many reps can you do in 30 seconds with 135 pounds or 225 pounds or how many reps can you do in 60 seconds with 135 pounds or 225 pounds. You must always increase your one rep max. Use rack pulls with the plates three inches, six inches, and nine inches off the floor for max effort method. Again, when griping a barbell many more muscles are utilized. The deadlift sumo style can be more effective then squatting. Always use a relaxed eccentric phase. This creates a relaxed, overcome by a dynamic action very similar to sprinting.

BELT SQUATS/BELT SQUAT WALKING

Westside uses two methods for belt squats. One is belt squatting to a soft box, i.e. foam on top of a hard box using a fast, relaxed, eccentric phase while exploding concentrically for a predetermined time. Always go about 25 seconds longer than your 60-meter or 100-meter time and five seconds longer than your 200-meter and 800-meter. Exercise 10 seconds longer than your 1,600-meter time. Always count the reps and try to increase reps inside the pre-determined time period. Only add weight when you feel comfortable. For strength endurance, one rep per second for 60 seconds is recommended.

The second method is to simply walk in the belt squat machine. One minute up to five minutes and longer can be done depending on your race time. Walk forward for glutes and backwards for quads. By pushing out to the sides the hips are activated to the max. This is absolutely the fastest way to increase the entire legs and hips plus glutes. This exercise is at the top of our list, especially in bad weather/climates.

WALKING WITH MED BALL

Walking while holding a 20-pound to 100-pound med ball against the upper stomach with the arms will build the abs, but most importantly, will correct proper leg swing motion. No more knock knees, which cause numerous injuries that should never occur.

By doing the special exercises large and small, your sports performance will go up as your injuries are eliminated.

Pulling Workout Plans

Power clean and power snatch from the hang can be placed into the programming to replace some jumping for explosive power. You must use the hang style to create a stretch reflex for reverse strength. Reversible muscular action is constantly used in many sport skills. This is also called the reversible action of muscles. The reps must be minimal because as force and power increases, energy expenditure is lessened.

Run a three-week wave going from 40 percent, 45 percent, and 50 percent then pendulum back to 40 percent to insure explosive power is maintained. If possible, use a small amount of band tension over the bar. Alternate power hang snatch to power clean then back to a form of jumping.

Example Plan

Power Hang Snatch

200 max

Percent	Weight	Reps	Lifts	Volume
40 %	80 lb.	6 x 3	18	1,440
45 %	90 lb.	6 x 3	18	1,620
50 %	100 lb.	6 x 3	18	1,800

Power Hang Clean

300-Max

Percent	Weight	Reps	Lifts	Volume
40 %	120 lb.	6 x 3	18	2,160
45 %	135 lb.	6 x 3	18	2,430
50 %	150 lb.	6 x 3	18	2,700

Sumo Speed Pulls
400-Max

Percent	Weight	Reps	Lifts	Volume
40 %	160	6 x 2	12	1,920
45 %	180	6 x 2	12	2,160
50 %	200	6 x 2	12	2,400

Now let's examine jumping workouts of a wide variety, jumping onto boxes of different heights and with an assortment of weights on the ankles, weight vest, kettlebells and combinations of all three. Establish records of all sorts. As well as jumping off knees with many sorts of resistance; barbell, kettle bell, Bulgarian bag jumping, barbell jumps 30 percent to 40 percent. See Explosive Strength Development for Jumping (2014) and Explosive Power DVD and GPP DVD. The examples below are guides to follow in a rotating pendulum wave periodization throughout the year. Use optimal rest periods. Be aware of depth jumps. They are for more advanced athletes who can squat a minimal of two times bodyweight.

CHAPTER 1 - THE ROLE OF STRENGTH IN SPORTS
Special Strength

CHAPTER 1 - THE ROLE OF STRENGTH IN SPORTS
Special Strength

Strength is measured at varying velocities. Explosive strength is fast velocity; speed strength is intermediate velocity; and strength speed is slow velocity. Consequently, isometrics are trained at zero velocity.

Strength is a term that is mostly related to how strong an individual is, but what does that mean? Simply put, strength is the ability to overcome or counteract external resistance of different loads with various rates of speed. In most sports explosive strength is essential.

What is explosive strength? It is the ability to rapidly increase force. The faster it's increased, measured in time, the greater the explosive strength (Tidow, 1990). How is it developed? Because resistance must be minimal, the simplest method in developing explosive strength is jumping rope, which can start at any age. Young boxers and wrestlers use it for conditioning and coordination, plus timing. For example, bounding over hurdles of varying heights, one-leg and two-legged multi jumps are tried and proven methods. In 1957, Dr. Y.V. Verkhoshansky was watching a triple jumper and was amazed by the rebounding ability exhibited on the take off after each landing. This was perhaps the beginning of his vast study for shock training. Another means for explosive strength is depth jumps with or without a rebound because they play a very large role in concentric and eccentric strength development. Jumping upward onto a predetermined box height increases explosive strength. Jumping resistance of some form can be incorporated that may include hand and leg weights, weight vest, or dumbbells.

Jumping upward from off the knees is excellent, and a barbell can add resistance. Remember the speed from which an individual moves depends on external resistance. All of this training is designed to increase the stretch shortening cycle or commonly known as reversible strength; refer to the jumping chapter.

A strength coach should not duplicate the actions that occur on the playing field in the weight room. This is Special Physical Preparedness (SPP), and only General Physical Preparedness (GPP) force should take place. Many of the players I have worked with say they practice too much and have too much contact in practice, reducing their abilities on game day.

If a football coach's mentality is to train more and more, an over exertion of physical and mental ability can occur. Hopefully, strength coaches can learn to train smarter, not harder. Repeating the same activities leads to accommodation, which causes a decrease in response of a biological object to a continued stimulus. In training, the stimulus is physical exercise (Zatsiorsky, 1995). By doing the same speed exercises, an individual develops staleness in the Central Nervous System (CNS). (Kurz, 2001). To avoid this stagnation, the Conjugate System should be implemented because it rotates exercises, training intensities and volume. This system includes changing the rhythm and frequency of sports tasks. Because of the short duration of most exercises and drills for explosive strength, maximal force cannot be attained, which is fully explained by the Hill equation for muscle contraction in Mel Siff's *Supertraining* (2003).

Football is an explosive, high velocity sport. Short work, (for example, a four to seven second play, meaning an average playtime interrupted by 40-second rest intervals) tends to produce fast twitch motor units. The work for football should duplicate this. When running gassers or longer distances, an athlete is truly specializing in developing slow twitch motor units. These muscle units are training the athlete to be slow and conserve muscle contraction, which is all wrong. The players know it, and complain about it, but the coach dismisses it as laziness. This happens in high schools, college, and pro teams. For example, training for a football game, not a marathon, is exercise specificity. Ball games of all kinds utilize reactive strength.

Concentric Strength

Raising weight concentrically without an eccentric phase first builds a powerful start. This develops starting strength where maximal force can be generated in the first 300 milliseconds. This works for a powerful start after a long snap count, for instance. Wilson's study stated that top athletes can hold the stretch reflex for two to four seconds without losing reversal strength. Use weights from 30 percent to 60 percent.

By sitting on a box up to eight seconds, Westsiders maintained the same concentric speed as normal box squatting that lasts roughly one second. Apparently, while on a box, some muscles are lengthening while others are becoming shorter, but never are all muscles held statically. This concept is very important and not to be overlooked

Eccentric Strength

Eccentric strength is the ability to lower a weight. Certain authorities proclaim that an individual can lower as much as 50 percent more than he can raise. True, but who cares? Not I. What good would it be for one of my 1,000-pound squatters to lower 1,500 pounds? None. We have to raise weight to completion. Jumping off a box and the proceeding landings build tremendous strength, and we know they work. Suppose a person is moving close to 9.8 meters per second (m/s) near Earth; which is the speed of acceleration of gravity. Why then would anyone lower a weight slowly? It produces muscle mass and causes muscle soreness due to damaged muscle fibers. Because there is a high risk of injury, a novice should never do slow eccentric movement due to massive delayed muscle soreness. When I see a coach using slow eccentric movement, I feel he lacks real experience.

Static Strength

Static strength or isometric strength is used when the exertion of a muscle increases but its length remains the same. I mention this because while an athlete is wrestling or two linemen are fighting for position, this is quasi isometric work. Merely staying at a motionless position requires static strength; for example, belt squatting in the skater's pose.

Speed Strength

Speed strength is the ability to exert maximal force during high speed movement. (Allerheiligen, 1994). It is developed with low resistance as these exercises must be very quick. For the development of sprinters, the weight should be 30 percent to 50 percent of a one rep max for starting strength. In regards to sports where resistance is great, the weights should range between 30 percent to 50 percent of a one rep max. This would include throwing events such as the shot and hammer throw or team sports such as wrestling or football; the barbell should move at least .8 m per second up to 1.2 m per second. Weights for reps in this intensity zones should be no less than two and no more than six. After six, the bar slows down, thus force development is decreased. The rest between sets is based around an individual's GPP level at that time. It is much better to do low reps and high sets. Why? A second rep is more explosive than a sixth rep; plus, low reps are easier to recover from. After all, explosive sports are of short play duration; for example, football is an average of 4.7 seconds a play. The throwing of an implement is a very short burst of strength. While speed strength is very important, an athlete's top absolute strength can be the determining factor. In Chapter 4-Periodization, there is a mathematical formula for raising speed strength concentrically with becoming absolutely stronger.

While jumping is very important to increasing speed strength to a great degree by adding resistance to the body, legs, or holding weights in the hands, a greater box height can be employed when the resistance is eliminated. As an individual implements the Westside weight program, top strength as well as speed go up. Consequently, this system uses speed work and strength work while simultaneously increasing muscle mass. When an individual is training and focusing on one type of strength for a period of three weeks, the other strength elements suffer. No one can lift a heavy weight slowly; therefore, an individual must accelerate through the complete range of motion. Depending on the amount of resistance, determines how fast the object moves. External resistance is the key element that dictates how quickly a person overcomes that resistance. This is due to the *force-velocity relation*. See *Science and Practice of Strength Training,* V.M. Zatsiorsky, pg. 29-31.

Reactive Strength

Reactive strength is the training ability used for jumping up and going from eccentric to concentric actions.

Starting Strength

Starting strength is measured by the maximal force an individual exerts at the beginning of a contraction.

Over speed eccentrics plus optimal eccentrics

We know drop jumps work, so why not lower weights as fast as possible under control? Implementing large amounts of band tension on the barbell increases the eccentric speed for added reversal strength. Through our experiments with 21 men who squat at least 1000 pounds, we found that using roughly 40 percent of an individual's eccentric strength capacities produces a much stronger concentric phase.

Strength Speed or Slow Strength

If strength did not matter, there would be no need for a strength coach and many people reading this book would be out of a job. A strong child is always better at running, jumping and throwing than a weak child. This formula should work throughout the sports career of all athletes. The max effort method is superior to all training methods, but seldom used in sports. This is ridiculous because the maximal effort method is superior to all methods for improving intramuscular and inter-muscular coordination. Sports science has proven that the CNS and muscles adapt only to the demands or loads placed upon them. Further information can be found in Zatsiorsky's *Science and Practice of Strength Training* (1995).

For Olympic lifting, the number of suggested lifts is at 90 percent plus four to 10 lifts with seven being optimal, according to Primplin in *Managing the Training of Weightlifters* (Laputin & Oleshko, 1982, p. 32).

The number for powerlifters should be no more than three lifts *(Westside Barbell Book of Methods, 2007)*. The loading for power lift calculations is based off the work of 90 Elite powerlifters, Olympic sprinters and football players. There is more than 32 years of research to support this. When intensity is up, the volume must be kept low in the barbell lifts, special or classical.

All strengths are important, but the amount of absolute strength is critical. By definition, absolute strength is muscular strength, not based on body weight. In sports, there are many different body-weights as well as weight classes, competing in the same sport. As men or women become more developed in combat sports, weight, or power lifts, the larger athletes are the strongest. However, this is not true in most football facilities. Many line backers and running backs are stronger than the lineman. This should not be the case because as an athlete becomes larger his relative strength decreases. To improve slow strength, I suggest the method of accommodating resistance, which can be accomplished with full range movements in the five classical lifts: squat, bench, deadlift, snatch, clean and jerk. Also included are all forms of deadlifting and pulls for the first and second movements of the Olympic lift. For all squats, front and back, a variety of specialty bars should be rotated. The first method is to attach chains to the barbell and add weights, teaching the lifter to accelerate the bar. Of course, this helps eliminate bar deceleration. If chains are implemented properly, it deloads a predetermined amount of weight by having the chains unload on the floor and reload as the concentric phase begins.

The general public cannot understand that this system builds a powerful start. Note that the chain weight can be as little as 40 pounds to 400 pounds or even 500 pounds. The body adapts quickly to the extreme overload at the top and tries to outrun the added resistance. Band tension works in the same manner, but the elasticity of the bands causes an over-speed-eccentrics phase, which increases kinetic energy for reversal strength. This is gravitational potential energy. The bands greatly increase velocity, which increases kinetic energy for reversal strength. If one triples velocity, kinetic energy would be nine times as great.

Eccentric Strength

Eccentric strength has been the focus of many studies, but there is little valuable feedback to increase the concentric phase. Eccentric strength can exceed concentric strength by 50 percent and isometric strength by 50 percent to 100 percent. However, I am concerned with raising a load, not lowering it. Many of the studies were done while lowering a load slowly, but if drop jumps work, and though dangerous, we know they do, the human body approaches 9.8 m/s, which is the force of gravity near earth. Why do coaches insist on lowering a weight slowly? Lowering a weight slowly accomplishes two things: it can make muscles larger, which is great for a body builder, but not for other types of athletes; it also causes the most muscular soreness. Both are two unnecessary occurrences for increasing athletic performance.

Research proves the hardest part of the squat is taking it out of the rack and standing still. Once the eccentric phase begins, this enormous amount of eccentric muscle strength takes over. Most injuries occur on the eccentric phase because of the lengthening of the muscle in an eccentric contraction. Also, the series elastic component (SEC) is exposed under concentric work (Siff, 2003). The muscular pain from eccentrics is due to the damage inflicted upon the myofibrils and connective tissue elements such as the Z bands, which is a part of the SEC. Friden (1983) and Siff (2003) found that extreme soreness disappeared and the ability to perform eccentric work increased by 375 percent by continuing eccentric work, lasting eight weeks with three workouts per week. Eccentric work causes more hypertrophy than concentric work because of greater tissue damage. The results are mixed on this subject. Look at the work of Hortobagyi (February 2000) *Journal of Physiology,* pp. 292-298.

What has been learned from all this research? Not a whole lot. However, the high speed, large acceleration smart movement along with aerobic and resistive training created by Lisa Ericson (1992) uses quick hand and arm movement eccentrically and concentrically with fast velocity. Her video is available from Sports Training Inc. The address is PO Box 46029, Escondido, CA 92046, U.S.A.

Because I was the first to employ chains with barbell weight for accommodating resistance, the Liberty University strength coach Dave Williams asked me to experiment with jump stretch bands. They were more or less used for stretching an athlete. I had never heard of such a band system, but I read that in L.P. Medvedev's *Fundamentals of Sports Training* (1981). He said an individual must use bands on rubber cords over the bar, so I had to try them. I knew the importance of increasing kinetic energy besides doing thousands of reps with light weight to thicken connective tissue, but how could I increase kinetic energy? Bands came to me. "What if I used a large amount on bands over the barbell to shoot the lifter into a faster eccentric phase or over-speed eccentrics?" If velocity is tripled, kinetic energy is squared. That's nine times as great (Komi, 1973; Siff, 2004). As velocity of contraction increases, so does maximum eccentric force because kinetic energy is stored in the tendons and the other series of elastic components in the lower extremity and spine. *Supertraining* (page 42-58 Siff, 2004; Garrett, 1986).

What would happen if I concentrated on kinetic energy? How? By using a large amount of band tension—sometimes 700 pounds of band tension alone   this would shoot the lifter down very quickly on the eccentric phase. I felt it could override the Golgi tendon response. Remember, Komi says as velocity of contraction increases, so does the maximum eccentric force increase. The Golgi tendon organ's main goal is to protect the contracting muscle if tension is too great. Conditioning the connective tissue through high repetitions such as sled walking and/or leg curls with light ankle weights using five pounds, 10 pounds and 20 pounds for 250 repetitions on an average per day is imperative. This is a must for the stress of over speed eccentrics as velocity is much greater with bands added to the bar, than just with barbell weight alone. This builds a greater stretch reflex for phenomenal reversal strength.

We know that superior athletes can produce higher forces than lesser athletes. In horse racing, the horses that come in last never get hurt; it is always the front runners or the top horses. Humans are the same with the body depending on two reflexes: the myotatic or stretch reflex that keeps the muscle close to a preset length, and the Golgi tendon reflex to prevent high and potential damaging muscle tension. Reversal strength depends on the amount of deformation energy built-up and then is used to enhance motor output in the important concentric phase of strength shortening cycle. For greater detail read Zatsiorsky's *Science and Practice of Strength Training* (1995, pp. 46-48).

We know the greatest athletes have the highest amount of stored energy where muscles stretch and contract. The Jump Stretch bands do the same, stretching as the muscles stretch on the eccentric phase and contracting on the concentric phase. With high band tension, it can force an individual down very compulsorily, causing a strong stretch reflex. How does this work? Remember deformation? Think of a basketball. Drop it and it falls at the speed of gravity near earth 9.8 m/s. When it recoils, the ball has some deformation as it contacts the floor, but if it is thrown downward with great velocity, it bounces up much higher. Why? Greater deformation acts much like the deformation of the tendon and muscle where the energy is stored. V.M. Zatsiorsky states that elasticity plays a large role in enhancing the motor output in sports movement. Rubber bands have elasticity, and the tendon and muscles have elasticity that is assisted or accelerated eccentric.

Note some of the findings I have made. A college setting cannot perform the experiments that I conduct because they don't have the athletes who can handle band tension plus weight that can approach 1,300 pounds at the top. This is supra-maximal efforts, and not recommended for just strong, but only the very strong. I have 21 men who are 1,000-pound squatters and four over 1,100 meet performance. Our training is on the box just below parallel. When squatting to a box, there is a collision, similar to two pool balls colliding. A virtual force effect is a force that is there, but not recognized. A part of the kinetic energy of the lifter is transferred to the box. Appearing motionless while sitting on the box, muscles are stretching and contracting much like pulling or pushing of a static bar (isometrics). The bar may be motionless, but the muscles are stretching and contracting like performing a box squat. See box squatting (page 115).

Static and dynamic are two forms of muscle work, which are similar to the timed relaxation of a runner's leg while not touching the track. One would think sitting on a box motionless would affect reversal strength. Wilson's *Supertraining* study found the stretch reflex lasts two to four seconds, but I have found sitting on a box for up to eight seconds does this. The separation off the box remained unchanged. The study was conducted at Westside Barbell with the top 10 world-ranked powerlifters.

I found some very interesting things. The eccentric phase was almost equal to the concentric phase. The faster the eccentric phase occurs, the faster the concentric phase, just like a bouncing ball. The quicker the acceleration going down, the faster the ball bounces upward. There are three training methods that have produced to date more than 21,000 squatters and four 60" box jumpers. These three methods include the following: accelerated eccentrics, optimal eccentrics and the virtual force effect, a force that exists, but is not recognized. All three elements of training are connected. See the articles below.

Eccentric Unloading

I have written about over-speed eccentrics citing why it is so important to lower the bar as quickly as possible to produce the most powerful stretch reflex as possible. If an athlete triples his velocity, the kinetic energy is nine times as great. Without bands, a lifter lowers the bar in roughly one second.

Using Jump-Stretch bands on the bar, the length of the eccentric phase can be cut in half to 0.5 second. For instance, 500 pounds in contact with the box causes a force of 750 pounds because of over-speed eccentrics. Another example occurs when sprinting. A 200-pound sprinter experiences a force per step of 200 pounds. However, while sprinting at top speed, he is able to produce five or six times bodyweight by over-speed eccentrics, which is caused by the speed of the foot colliding with the track. This is a virtual-force effect, a force that is present but not recognized. Although bands do accommodate resistance, which is obvious to the observer, they also produce added kinetic energy to produce a powerful stretch reflex.

I have written previously about optimal eccentric training. We all know that an individual can produce more muscle activation when lowering weight—up to 50 percent more. This is a good thing if he wants added muscle soreness. However, who wants that? Most hypertrophy occurs when lowering weights. An athlete can lower more weight than he can elevate. This is where the problem arises. Most tend to lower the barbell too slowly, destroying the stretch reflex. If lowering the barbell slowly is correct, then depth jumps and plyometrics are wrong, and we know that plyometric work, unquestionably. An experiment involving Matt Smith, when his best contest squat was 930, was conducted with the help of Dr. Akita, a calculus professor. Matt first squatted with 550 pounds of barbell weight to a parallel box. The eccentric and concentric phases were roughly 0.90 second. Bands were added to the bar, and the bar weight was reduced, so the total weight at the top of the lift was 750 and the weight on the box was 550. With the bands pulling down on the bar, an over-speed eccentric phase was caused; the eccentric phase was reduced to 0.57 second, and the concentric phase was 0.54 second. That's right, 0.3 second faster with 200 pounds more resistance at the top and the same 550 pounds on the box. How? Increasing velocity. If an individual triples his squat kinetic energy, the over-speed eccentrics cause a virtual-force effect when contacting the box. Why is this important? Muscle tension on the eccentric phase can be lessened to some extent, although the resistance is reduced somewhat by band shrinkage. The added bar speed increases kinetic energy when contacting the box, much like weight releasers. The brain thinks the weight or resistance is the same at the top as it is in the bottom. A benefit is that the band causes an accommodating resistance to the bar. For me, the hardest part of a squat is un-racking the bar from the monolift.

When the eccentric phase begins, eccentric muscle strength takes over. But how can optimal eccentrics be trained? One of the best methods is the lightened method. Here, two bands are connected to the top of the power rack. Depending on the band strength, a predetermined weight is reduced at the bottom of the lift. As the bar is lowered, some of the resistance is reduced as is muscle tension to some extent. A strong band at Westside lightens the load 155 pounds. If only 155 pounds is on the bar at the bottom of the lift, an individual can totally relax all muscle tension at that point, which means the lifter goes from relaxed to dynamic. This is one of the greatest ways to build explosive and absolute strength. Many fight the bar eccentrically until fully lowered, but with this method, if an individual lowers 310 pounds, it requires half the eccentric strength to lower the bar. In addition, he learns to lower the bar faster, causing a greater stretch reflex. This method can be used for all power lifts and Olympic lifts. There is a second method that can take enormous loads eccentrically by catching the bar or plates or even the lifter himself. It requires two foam blocks. The lifter takes the bar off bench racks and lowers it until the plates touch the blocks and sink into the foam. How far the plates sink into the foam depends on the bar weight. We have benched over 800 pounds using this method. Very heavy squats and Goodmornings can also be performed.

This method breaks up the eccentric/concentric phase, which is a must for power and strength. When box squatting, we place a seven-inch foam pad on the box. As the lifter sits on the foam, it sinks until he is sitting all the way on the box. The box itself represents a collision, producing kinetic energy for a strong stretch reflex. The foam causes a dampened effect. This promotes muscle work. If you have ever run in sand, you know how much it fatigues the muscles. The foam has the same affect. I watched a tape of a world class thrower doing plyometrics on a gym floor with hard-sole weightlifting shoes. In a different segment, he was wearing cross-training shoes, and the floor was covered with gym mats. This time his reaction time on the amortization phase was much slower. Why? He was using more muscle work on the mats and less connective tissue work. A top sprinter said that 80 percent of running comes from kinetic energy derived from the ligaments and tendons.

By doing both methods, the thrower is using all of his potential by jumping on both soft and hard surfaces. I thought why not squat and bench the same way? We now train mostly off a foam box, but we always do the circa-max phase or an all-time Personal Record (PR) off a hard box. We have used this method for two years with great success. Progress can be seen on our website and on our record boards at the gym. For deadlifting, stand on a thin foam pad, bringing the legs into the lift. Give this a try and see the results for yourself.

Assisted Eccentrics

There are a few who have read the exploits of a person who has been said to have made great progress doing eccentrics. But were there other factors involved in the training? I have read several articles by sports experts around the globe, yet none have conclusive evidence that eccentrics work. Mel Siff in *Supertraining* explains eccentrics as action in which the proximal and distal muscle attachments move away from one another. Eccentric work uses significantly less energy than concentric work. When doing slow eccentrics with large loads, there is no reason to associate these advantages with the possibility of developing the ability to move quickly and powerfully in concentric work. Lowering weights slowly builds larger muscles for bodybuilding, but will not assist concentric actions.

With depth jumps, an individual is accelerating close to 9.8 m/s when landing on the floor. Everyone knows these jumps work, so why would a person lower a weight at 0.1 or 0.2 m/s and destroy the stretch reflex? In the book *Science of Sports Training*, T. Kurz states some athletes can lower 10 percent to 60 percent more than they can overcome concentrically.

With all this said, slow eccentrics have no place in powerlifting or sports. To build larger muscles, yes. If an individual wants to become very sore, yes. What does it matter if someone can lower 60 percent more than he can raise? If I recall correctly, a lifter must raise the bar from the floor in a clean, snatch, and deadlift. In the bench press after the bar is lowered to the chest, after the pause, the lifter must raise the bar to completion, and the squat is similar. After lowering to parallel, an individual must, for a fraction of a second, hold the weight statically and then rise to completion. If an athlete loads the bar with 60 percent more than his best squat of, say, 1000 pounds, the total bar weight would be 1,600 pounds. Does this sound like a good idea? A weight that feels fine at the top becomes much too heavy in the bottom. How can a bar weight be perfect at the top and also at the bottom? It can't. That's precisely why we use a combination of bar weight and bands or chains to accommodate resistance, causing a reactive method. But that's another story.

The key to eccentric success is over-speed eccentrics. Hopefully, you already know that force equals mass times acceleration. The force, however, is almost always connected to concentric movements. What about eccentric work? Light weights can be lowered with greater acceleration than heavy weights, just as in concentric movements. It must be understood that the largest force may not always be associated with the heaviest loads. Jump-Stretch bands can produce much greater acceleration properties by pulling the bar down by means of great tension. This causes over-speed eccentrics, adding to kinetic energy. If a lifter could triple the bar speed on the eccentric phase, it would produce nine times the kinetic energy. In a simple action, such as a depth jump, a 200-pound man jumping off a platform of 10 feet produces many times his body weight.

Force decreases on concentric movements due to deceleration while force increases on eccentric movements due to acceleration. This leads us to a problem that many never consider: optimal eccentrics. How much muscle tension should someone use on eccentric movements? If it is true that an individual can lower 60 percent more than he can elevate, then applying 100 percent of his eccentric strength, he could hold the bar at any position. However, he would destroy the stretch reflex with heavy weights. Overcoming inertia is done implementing light weights with a fast eccentric stop to build reversal strength. This is ballistic training. The bar never touches the chest. One to three inches off the chest is recommended. If an individual drops a 10-pound rock and a one-pound rock from the same distance, both hit the ground at the same time. However, as he lowers a heavy weight, as the weight increases, the eccentric phase slows down. This is due to too much eccentric muscle action.

There are optimal bar speeds for velocity training, which is measured in concentric movements. The objective is fast movements with light loads, and for force training, the bar speed may be zero or very low to produce maximum force. Should there not be an optimal eccentric speed? Of course, it is just that no one has ever considered it until now. See the force-velocity relation in *Science and Practice of Strength Training*, V.M. Zatsiorsky, pg. 29-31.

How can a lifter learn to optimally lower heavy loads in the pressing, squatting, or Goodmorning exercises? A foam block for assisted eccentrics training can be employed. In my experiments with a Tendo unit, comparing the eccentric and concentric bar speed with speed strength benching and squatting, the difference was one-tenth of a meter per second (m/s). The same was true for a circa-max phase in the squat. A combination of band tension and weight was used. The bands cause an accommodating resistance effect on the concentric phase and an over-speed eccentric effect on the eccentric phase, increasing kinetic energy in the stretch reflex.

The eccentric/concentric phase on speed strength should be 0.7 m/s to 0.8 m/s. On near-max weights, this should be 0.5 m/s. Remember, this was done with adding bands to the bar. How does a lifter lower just weight in a quick manner? This is done by using roughly 40 percent of his eccentric potential. I have done ballistic benching with 200 pounds when my raw bench was 500. It should be noted that I dropped almost 40 percent of my best raw bench. I was lowering the bar at around 0.9 m/s.

While watching Elite benchers at Westside perform at similar eccentric speeds, I noticed that this has led to a faster concentric phase. How did we learn to lower heavier loads in the bench and squat? We use foam blocks to bench off of, lowering the plates onto the foam. We sit on the foam for box squatting.

Here are some of the methods we use. For floor pressing, lie on a seven-inch foam pad. The entire torso sinks into the foam, which causes an unstable effect. Floor presses can be done while lying on the floor and adding small—18" x 18"—foam pads only under the arms. This enables the arms to relax concentrically more than normal.

The king of all optimal eccentrics for benching is to lower the bar so the plates are lowered into the foam blocks, allowing the lifter to almost totally relax eccentrically. This contributes to a fast rate of reversal strength, adding to a powerful concentric phase. Undoubtedly, this helps not only raw benching, but also lowering weights in bench shirts.

For deadlifting, we stand on foam pads while doing pulls, building immediate leg drive in either the conventional or sumo style. For box squatting, we sit on a 24" x 28" foam block. It feels like a half box squat and half regular squat. We also stand on a foam pad while box squatting to get extra leg drive and for superior glute and hip development as well as lower back strength and flexibility. A standard box squatting method is to place a 7" x 24" pad on a hard box.

We have used these methods for seven years because they work. They also are great for rehabilitation of knees and ankles by walking in place without shoes. Proof positive is a high school senior jumping onto a 59-inch box. These methods work for explosive work as well as max effort work. If a lifter is smart, it will be pre-hab if he starts now.

Optimal eccentrics, a muscular and reflex phase of strength training, can bring about superior gains, just as Verkhoshansky found shock training produced after watching triple jumpers perform. A new idea, a new training method can revolutionize strength. Don't quit; rather consider Dylan Thomas's poem "Do Not Go Gentle into That Good Night." He writes, "Old age should burn and rage at close of day. Rage, rage against the dying of the light."

Optimal Eccentrics

What do we really know about eccentric (lowering) work? The eccentric phase causes most muscular soreness, which creates much of the burn that bodybuilders discuss. When performed slowly, the eccentric phase contributes greatly to muscle hypertrophy (growth). We also know that in an attempt to raise absolute strength, eccentric training alone fails miserably.

In the late 1970s, Mike Bridges experimented with eccentric bench pressing. He told me that the only result he got from eccentrics was a pectoral injury. This is confirmed by research that shows most injuries occur during the yielding or eccentric phase.

Vince Anello also experimented with eccentric work, doing eccentric deadlifts with as much as 880 pounds. When he returned to the conventional deadlift, his deadlift had decreased much to his dismay.

Vince told me that anything makes the deadlift go up—except eccentrics. What does this mean? Are eccentrics a waste? Well, yes and no. Eccentric training alone is a waste. However, a strength-shortening cycle, eccentric training followed by a concentric phase, can be very beneficial when done correctly, i.e., with optimal speed. When doing pure plyometrics—dropping from a prescribed height—the speed of descent is about 9.8 m/s, or the speed of gravity near earth. With depth jumps, there is an immediate rebound, causing a powerful stretch reflex produced from the kinetic energy of the dropping phase.

Plyometrics were developed by Verkhoshansky in 1958 after he watched a triple jumper train. He was astonished by the energetic rebounding following each landing in the triple jump. That energetic response was the basis of plyometrics. Plyometrics have proven vital in the training of explosive as well as absolute strength.

It is known that training with heavy weights adds strength potential to muscles, and light weights with a rapid concentric phase increases speed and explosive strength. It is obvious that without the lowering, or eccentric, phase there would be no sudden stretch preceding a voluntary effort. Kinetic energy is gathered in the eccentric phase. This causes a sudden release of elastic energy stored in the tendons and soft tissues of the body. Heavier weight does not add to the rebound phase as effectively as using an over speed eccentric phase. How can this be done? Using Jump-Stretch bands causes a forced over-speed eccentric phase, which is maximal power metrics. The combination of eccentric and concentric actions forms a natural type of muscle functioning called the stretch-shortening cycle (SSC) (Norman & Komi, 1979; Komi, 1984).

There is no eccentric phase in a depth jump. By definition, in an eccentric action the muscle must be active during the stretching phase, and the energy created by the body dropping is gravitational potential energy. When the body lands on a surface, the movement becomes kinetic energy, which is transferred in the body as a stretch reflex. In the calculation of kinetic energy, increasing velocity is much more important than increasing mass, because velocity is squared into the equation $KE = (1/2)\ mv$.

This is why the squat-under in Olympic lifting is so important. When the lifter falls under the bar, he is producing kinetic energy for reversing the direction of the bar. This dropping under the bar should not be confused with an eccentric phase. For an eccentric phase to occur, muscle tension must accompany the action. The squat-under has no such muscle tension.

We know that 40 percent to 50 percent more muscle can be used during the eccentric phase, which is where a real problem occurs. As the barbell grows heavier, a lifter tends to lower the bar slower and slower. However, this is counterproductive. When slowing down the eccentric motion, he is limiting the energy that can be stored in the muscles and tendons. The myotatic reflex occurs when a muscle is stretched by an external force. Yes, this causes a stretch reflex, but the faster the eccentric phase, the greater the stretch reflex. This, of course, can have a negative effect on the Golgi tendon reflex, which helps prevent extremely high and potentially dangerous loads to the tendon. With over-speed eccentrics, we try to override this phenomenon.

In *Science and Practice of Strength Training*, Zatsiorsky states that elite athletes develop very high forces of elastic energy in the tendons rather than the muscles. This should alert us to lower the barbell at an optimal speed as weights grow heavier. If the barbell slows down as the weight grows heavier, the length of the muscle is stretched and the muscle tension increases, which could lead to injury. Because this myotatic reflex is counterbalanced by the Golgi tendon reflex, an inhibition of muscle action occurs, causing a less than maximal concentric phase. Of course, this limits the potential to overcome heavier loads in training or at meet time.

The answer to this dilemma is to use only enough eccentric muscle tension to control the barbell in the correct path. If, in fact, an individual uses 40 percent to 50 percent more muscle tension to lower weights, does it not make sense to use only up to 50 percent of his eccentric strength when lowering a weight? This contributes to a stronger concentric phase, producing a higher result.

Using the Tendo unit, we found that when doing speed strength work in the bench press and squat, the eccentric phase moves at a rate of 0.7 m/s to 0.8 m/s. This is basically the same as the concentric phase, maximizing the stretch reflex. It can be stated, the faster down, the faster up. With near-maximal weight, the same trend was observed: the eccentric and concentric phases were both 0.45 m/s to 0.6 m/s. Band and bar weight were used to achieve these results. When all resistance was from barbell and plate weight, the lowering time was considerably longer. The eccentric phase was 0.4 m/s on speed squat and bench and 0.6 m/s for the concentric phase. With near maximal weight, the eccentric phase was 0.37 m/s and concentric phase was 0.40 m/s to 0.50 m/s. This means that bands can play a valuable role in increasing the eccentric phase of barbell lifts, teaching a lifter to use less eccentric muscle action. As weights grow heavier, the bar speed should find an optimal speed regardless of external resistance.

The above data was collected using eight 900+ squatters and eight 600+ benchers. The results were nearly equal for both phases; each 600+ lifter varying less than a tenth of a meter/second eccentrically or concentrically. With circa-max weights, I was the slowest by a small margin during both phases, and Dave Tate was the fastest. On speed work, the same results were obtained. J. L. Holdsworth was the fastest, and Chuck Vogelpohl was the slowest. Again, only one-tenth of a meter per second separated the eccentric and concentric phase of each lifter. The same results occurred in the bench press. In the above test, all bench subjects benched in T-shirts. All squatters wore standard groove briefs, no knee wraps, and squatted on a box. Each subject was at the same level of general physical preparedness.

The key to lifting larger weights is concentrating on the eccentric phase, especially with the over-speed eccentric method, i.e., using a large amount of tension. Learn to relax to reduce some muscle tension in the eccentric phase to prevent inhibiting the stretch reflex, and watch your total go crazy. Our results speak for themselves.

Verkhoshansky, known as the "Father of Plyometrics," observed a triple jumper and realized how energetic the preceding jumps were after landing. It was, of course, the stored elastic energy from the eccentric phase when landing, causing an energetic jump. Dr. Verkhoshansky preferred the name shock training when he formalized implosive training in *Supertraining* (Siff, 2003, p. 283). It mentions other shock methods such as: plyometrics, supramaximal methods, max-effort singles, contrast methods, maximal eccentrics, power rack work, forced repetitions, electrical stimulation. I have found all useful except the maximal eccentrics.

These methods may be rotated constantly to fit into the conjugate system. For upper body, I suggest ballistic benching with 40 percent to 60 percent of one rep max with some accommodating resistance bands chains, or weight releasers. Ballistic benching (eccentric phase) means moving the bar one inch to three inches off the chest as quickly and explosively as possible. This increases the kinetic energy on the reversible phase and teaches optimal eccentrics, which I believe is roughly using only 40 percent of one's true concentric strength level. A lifter must release muscle tension on the eccentric phase. There is a plyometric bench device that can be used such as the device on Page 219, Figure 4.6 in Mel Siff's *Supertraining*, 2003. A Plyo Swing also can be used as seen on Page 162, Figure 6.12 in V.M. Zatsiorsky's *Science and Practice of Strength Training*, 1995.

I have a United States patent on a similar swing; the difference is my Virtual Force Swing™ has band attachments to accelerate the swing speed, causing greater reversal strength. Large weight and strong band tension are used. Jumping rope is a very basic plyometric method. Young children can start jumping rope at an early age. High repetitions while jumping rope also thicken the ligaments and tendons that store kinetic energy. Be smart when it comes to eccentric training. Slow eccentric work is great for body building, but I don't see bodybuilders on a ball field. Study eccentric phase training carefully; much of what I have learned is from practical experiments over 43 years. For more information read Thomas Kurz's *Science of Sports Training*, 2001; V.M. Zatsiorsky's *Science and Practice of Strength Training*, 1995; and P.V. Komi's *Strength and Power in Sports*, 1996.

CHAPTER 2 - ENDURANCE
Endurance is the Ability to Counter Fatigue

CHAPTER 2 - ENDURANCE
Endurance is the Ability to Counter Fatigue

Much has been written about endurance. We know there is more than one type of endurance. A person who is good at endurance is very effective at doing very little. I believe sports provide anaerobic activity suitable for the sport an individual is participating. Endurance is only improved when someone is worked into a very fatigued state. Then, the work must stop and rest. Is there a better way to improve a marathon runner's work capacity? Is there a better way to improve a football player's endurance without running him to death? I think so.

Let's discuss some methods that have helped develop an UFC champ, Olympic sprinter gold medalists, and NFL ball players. Exercise specificity. What does that mean? Training for a particular sport. It does not help football players to run miles for a game that is measured in yards and inches. Yet, coaches do it over and over. Why? Because their coach did it this way. Look at the stats of a football game. They don't gain three miles a game, most of the time not even three hundred yards. Football is not a marathon, but several very short sprints. It is an interval sport with activity working from four to seven seconds with a 40-second rest. However long a football game lasts the offense or defense only plays half the time. While the offense is on the field, the defense is sitting down resting. Has a coach ever thought about this? Obviously not, or why else would he destroy his team physically? If you think running miles upon miles makes a player tough, then why not recruit marathoners? I think there is a better way.

Football teams are like a restaurant franchise. All trained the same with no improvements in the game. It's the physical powers of the players that make the success of a team. The better the recruiting, the better the team. Can great recruits be improved? Of course they can through physical training. For increasing endurance in a particular sport, an athlete must train specifically for his sport. In football the play time is very explosive with a 40-second rest; then, a player must train for the demands of football.

First, let's look at weight training. The best system for explosive sports is the dynamic method, which incorporates sub-maximal weights with maximal speed, $F=ma$. Briefly, a squat workout would look like this:

Squat on a Box

Week 1: 12 sets of two reps at 50 percent

Week 2: 12 sets of two reps at 55 percent

Week 3: 10 sets of two reps at 60 percent

The sets would represent 12 plays lasting roughly eight seconds. Using the interval method that is a 40-second rest between work sets followed by:

Week 1: 12 sets of one rep deadlift or power clean

Week 2: 12 sets of one rep deadlift or power clean

Week 3: 10 sets of one rep deadlift or power clean

Followed by benches:

Week 1- Nine sets of three 25 percent band tension

Week 2- Nine sets of three 25 percent band tension

Week 3- Nine sets of three 25 percent band tension

The deadlift is sumo style, and the power clean can be switched to a power snatch. Again, the rest interval is no more than 40-seconds and should last no more than 25 minutes. Do special exercises for hamstrings, lower back and glutes. The training must be dense, meaning the actual work completed during a training period. Consequently, serum testosterone drops after 45 minutes. An athlete can recover from two reps much faster than six reps, and he is much more productive for power recruitment. How? Drop a basketball and watch it bounce. Each time the ball bounces, it loses some of its re-bounding property. The second bounce is much higher than the sixth bounce. Case proven.

Bench training is the same: Eight to 10 sets of three reps with 40-seconds rest intervals between sets. After warm-ups, Westside lifters take no more than 20 minutes then add 20 minutes for special triceps, back and shoulder work. All weight training should be planned to be exercise specific. Perfect technique with weight is a forgotten art.

What does this have to do with endurance? I refer to it as explosive endurance, which is the ability to repeat explosive efforts without being fatigued. Why can't the last play of a game be as explosive as the first? It can be if the efficiency of the Central Nervous System (CNS) is raised, which happens when training is planned around a specific event. Push the Prowler for 10 seconds with 40 seconds or less rest. This can be done for a regimen of 10 to 20 pushes; to avoid accommodation, change the rest between sets, 20 to 40 seconds. Explosive endurance should have the rest intervals changing per workout and occasionally during a workout. It is best not to constantly stride for shorter and shorter rest, but rather to wave the rest intervals from slow to fast and back to slow. Progress comes, but be patient and plan to peak for the end of the season of camp.

More ways to avoid accommodation is to add ankle weights while pushing the prowler. This can range from five pounds to 20 pounds per leg. Wear a weight vest from 20 pounds to 100 pounds and combinations of both, and vary the weight of the prowler. Alternate prowler pushes with power walking using a weight sled. For football players, a measure of 60 yards for power walks is recommended by my experience with pro and college ball players. While running with the prowler is recommended, walking is a must for developing acceleration. Don't try to duplicate running style, but rather perfect sled walking. With each step, make as long a stride as possible, pulling through with the heel on each step. This makes each step even at the end of 60 yards, as powerful as the first step. It teaches a strong start as well as the importance of eliminating deceleration. Use resistance on legs along with weight vests and combinations of both while keeping rest under 40 seconds. There are many forms of sled pulling that are illustrated elsewhere in the book. I have talked about explosive endurance training; now, I will talk about general endurance.

General Endurance

General endurance is the ability to perform at low intensity or high intensity at any non-sport specific workouts for prolonged time.

Methods of endurance training include the following:

1. Continuous with variable intensity
2. Constant intensity
3. Circuit training
4. Interval training
5. Repetitive training.

Many rugby teams from Europe come to learn the Westside principles, and I have found some of their conditioning methods very simple, but very effective. The Rugby players are not as large as the average American football players, especially the linemen. Constantly practicing should be adequate for game conditioning, so what do the rugby players do? They walk. Yes, walk with a weight pack, or they cross country ski. They do not run; they do plenty of that on the field like American football players. The difference is American football coaches run the players to death, and we know that football is an explosive sport.

Explosive power requires explosive muscle fibers. Fast twitch muscle fibers contract very hard and expend oxygen very quickly, so then, the fast twitch muscles wear out rapidly. The football coach insists on running full gassers, and more gassers, and then on top of that half gassers or running stairs, and 100 meter (m) sprints. Why? Sometimes 400 m and 200 m with short rest is less than the rest between plays, but with three times the work in time. This is not exercise specificity. Why train at 6 a.m. when the game is at 12 p.m. or 4 p.m.? Overtraining occurs when a player loses six pounds to 10 pounds in one workout.

Wilmore and Costill (1999) concluded in their studies that maximal oxygen increases in mature athletes with hard endurance training for only eight to nine months; then, it plateaus even with increased training (Kurz, 1987). Yet year after year, the coach runs the player harder and harder with little or no improvement. After two minutes very few athletes can maintain maximal oxygen uptake while playing. If work is longer, his aerobic or anaerobic decreases even more. So, why run players until they are totally exhausted. What happens to the player is that he relies on endurance or slow twitch fibers for the majority of the workouts, and he becomes a slower, less explosive ball player. Why? He is forced to use slow or endurance muscle fibers.

I hope this makes sense because a sports scientist will probably complain my explanation is too vague, yet this may be over the heads of some football coaches. Remember, intensity of work is determined by how quickly one recovers. A faster recovery time could mean running plays every 25 seconds instead of 40. An athlete could simply run his opponent in the ground, forcing the opposition to interject second and third string players making them vulnerable. For increasing general conditioning, it is better to use methods of lower intensity, such as walking with or without added resistance as mentioned previously. Kettlebell swings and multiple jumps, jumping on and off even box heights, can be implemented for general explosive strength. Don't penalize the players with non-beneficial exercises, but rather schedule work that can contribute to a team's success, meaning train smarter, not harder.

A football team trains countless hours, which should be adequate for game fitness. Do you have a coach check the player's body fat on a regular basis? Are they getting leaner? How about faster? Can they jump higher? Are they stronger? In combat sports, weight or power lifts have weight classes. Why? The bigger the man, the stronger the competitor, right? Of course, but why then, are the biggest players not always the strongest? More times than not, it is the running back or linebackers. This is wrong and unacceptable. Remember, train specifically for a specific sport. If an individual trains in a power sport, then he should not train like a tri-athlete. All aspects of sports conditioning must be taken into account. Even a marathon runner sometimes sprints to the finish line. It takes many methods to fully develop a skill or ability for higher level sports, not just one. A fighter learns the ability to throw many complex combinations of punches to succeed.

A coach must learn the most complex training programs for special strength and restoration methods plus the correct volume and intensity zones to use and when to implement them throughout a multi-year plan. This is the revolving system commonly known as the conjugate system. Without revolving volume, training intensity exercises, and rest intervals, an individual suffers from accommodation, which leads to a speed barrier. The same training repeated over and over teaches the athlete to move at a certain speed and no faster. This occurs in weight lifting, reaching a plateau and not improving on a lifter's previous best. If an athlete ceases to jump higher or longer, he can rotate his training in some way or another, and he will never experience such a barrier. Many experts in the field such as Sozanski (1995) said to use verbal encouragement to run quicker and to learn the feel of going faster on special inclined tracks, using a lightened environment that reduces some of the athlete's weight.

I, too, believe in encouraging the runner or jumper to surpass his previous best, but on special means equipment like sleds, jump boxes, or adding resistance to slow the athlete down instead of having him speed up. I have a theory. If someone is slow, a method must be found to make him more explosive, and if he is quick, an approach needs to be used to slow him down by developing more force. Power walking and sled pulling are the Tai Chi of weight training or jumping with resistance to increase the difficulty of training. The theories of Sozanski PhD., Starzynski, Lasocki, and of course, YV Verkhoshansky were to increase quickness and explosive strength that lies between strength and speed. Explosive strength is the ability to rapidly enhance force (Tidow, 1990). More can be found in reference literature about the explosive power and jumping ability for all sports (Starzynski & Sozanski, 1995).

Neurologically speaking, I feel, an individual can only move his limbs so fast. He must exert more force each time the foot contacts the track. To do this, I make an individual stronger by using all types of resistance by implementing barbells or body resistance. Raising maximal strength improves the speed of movement if speed strength weights of 75 percent to 85 percent are utilized. I am one of very few who uses this approach. It seems to be in reverse of most theories, but I changed how people look at weight training all around world; I will do the same in running and jumping with your help.

Here is an example: A 200 m or 400 m or even an 800 m runner slows down or decelerates at the end of a race. A coach will almost always have the athlete run some distance further than the race length. This makes no sense. If the athlete is slowing down he or she is developing less force at the end of the race. Further running will produce even less force per step, which is counterproductive.

Let's look at science and the force velocity curve. A sprinter weighs just so much and produces just so much force with his or her strength potential. How is greater force produced while running? The answer is to add resistance to the athlete by means of a weight sled. For example: Pat Woods, a former decathlete power walked 60 minutes and 17 seconds with 135 pounds on a sled, but by adding weight to the sled to an optimal 250 pounds he covered the same 60 m using the same style in 11 seconds. How? We must increase force. Maximum Force (Fmm) is developed when velocity is small. V. M. Zatsiorsky and E.N. Matveev in 1964 explained the force-velocity relation. See *Science and Practice of Strength Training*, V.M. Zatsiorsky, (2006), as well as *Hill Equation of Muscle Contraction*, Mel Siff, Supertraining, (2004).

Explosive Muscular Endurance

Aerobic endurance is the amount of oxygen an individual can take in and utilize, if it is endurance that is sought after. Endurance has little use if muscular endurance or the ability to produce power for a certain time is insufficient. Muscular endurance is mostly tested with squatting or benching for high repetitions. The athletes with the highest absolute strength also should have the greatest muscular strength with sub-maximal weights just by the fact that 300 pounds may be 50 percent of his one rep max while it would be 75 percent for a person who could squat 600 pounds max. This is simple mathematics.

For lower body endurance, we never use squatting of any kind, except belt squatting. It's simply too dangerous because the back may fatigue before the legs, leading to injuries. Therefore, how do we work muscular endurance? By power walking with pulling sleds, striding out as long as possible and landing on the heel and pulling through simultaneously; the first step and the last step are actually a start. With doing this, one can develop a powerful start off the line of the initial step plus build the ability to accelerate and eliminate deceleration at the end of the race. This works for a 40-yard dash, indoor sprinting, 100 meter, 200 meter, 400 meter or any distance including the marathon.

This system was used on the third-ranked Olympic tri-athlete. I asked her what helped her running, and her response was the sled walking. I asked her how about the bike and the swim? Her reply was the sled. I used a similar system on George Nicholas, the Big Ten Indoor Sprint Championship while running the 100 m. His best 100 m time (1984) was 10.47. His track coach said he will never run any faster. I told him to come with me, and I would make him run faster. After working with me for nine weeks, he ran the 100 meter at 10.17 – three-tenths faster, and we never ran him.

I was given a 292-pound tight-end from an Olympic lifting college. Rudy Silla was his name. His 40-yard time was 5.1. His agent said if I could take a tenth off his time, he could make some big money. Johnny Parker was the strength coach for the San Francisco 49ers at that time and said Rudy could play both ways if he was a little faster. Johnny has visited Westside for 14 years. In two months at the same 292 pounds, Rudy ran a 4.77 and his best long jump increased from 8' 9" to a 9' 8". Again, we never ran him. His running was limited to football drills and 10- to 20- yard runs. I could go on and on, but last not least, Missouri called me about a young quarterback who was hurt, and the trainers would not let the strength coach train him with weights. They called me and followed my advice about no running, just power sled walking and box jumping. After two months with no running, they stretched him out, and he ran two 4.55 40-yard dashes. Oh, by the way, his previous best was 4.8 for 40 yards.

An individual powerwalks by keeping the feet close to the ground and making long strides, landing on the heels and pulling the pavement from out underneath the body. With football sled work, a player pulls a sled for 60 yards per trip for 15 trips with a rest interval of approximately 60 seconds. This is a 1:1 work-rest ratio, representing muscular endurance and conditioning at the same time. It makes best use of the player's time while increasing coordination and neuromuscular fitness. Our test is watching the player on each step. The sled must have a jerk to it on each step throughout the full distance. For football, baseball, or basketball, a distance of 60 yards a trip is perfect. Remember, the last step must be as forceful as the first step on the first trip, and the last step must be as powerful as the very first step at the end of 15 trips, showing an individual is much more powerful and has eliminated a lot of deceleration.

Sled pulling builds incredible strength in the calf, glutes, hamstrings, hip muscles and the lower back as well as muscular endurance. A weak lower back is precisely the problem with football players, which is why they pull hamstrings. Besides promoting stamina, anaerobic fitness, and a strong posterior chain, it improves connective tissue. I have never heard a weight coach address this, yet soft tissue injuries can stop careers.

What is a good exercise to follow? Leg curls with ankle weights. Diane Guthrie in her pre-Olympic regimens would do 250 leg curls with 10-pound ankle weights daily. When she reduced this extra work, she injured some leg muscles (Kurz, 1987). Reports by Toufexis (1992) noted Vasily Alexeyev would sometimes throw a 100-kg barbell over his head 100 times. After that he would spend up to 60 minutes in a pool lifting his legs one-thousand steps to strengthen his abdominals (Sklarenko, 1980 in *Science of Sports Training* by Thomas Kurz).

The sled provides hundreds of steps that are low impact with no weight on back, and ankle weight curls build the hamstrings directly and strengthen the connective tissue that is essential to strengthen the athlete. At the same time, working to avoid injuries, my 1,000 and 1,100-plus squatters do hundreds of these curls. To relax, a ½-mile to two-mile walk with or without ankle weight can be done four to six hours later for conditioning and restoration. For more on special sled pulling, look at sled pulls on Page 100.

Force production is very important while sprinting. Force production to stride frequency is more important than stride length though studies show that Elite runners have a faster stride rate than average runners of all distances. J. Daniels' running formula demonstrated in *Human Kinetics* (Page 80-82) shows an Elite runner will have at least 180 strides per minute. One must have good form to maintain 180 strides per minute for a significant time. This requires great strength and proper biomechanics. You must learn perfect form to avoid injuries and increase strength as well as, of course, speed.

I suggest reading books such as *The Pose Method of Running* by Nicholas Romanov, PhD. His views on running are simple explanations of a very complicated subject. Dr. Romanov demonstrates how to use gravity to help running instead of fighting gravity to use potential energy into kinetic energy, producing great force against the least resistance. Now we know the strongest runners with the best form run the fastest. That's why men outrun woman, out jump women, and produce more force. Work and power can be measured. Look at the definition of work in physics: work is defined as the product of the net force and the displacement through which that force is exerted or W=FD. The definition of power is defined as work done divided by the time used to do the work or P=W/T. The more powerful an athlete, the faster he can complete the work. In the case of running a prescribed distance with proper form, the more powerful an individual is, the quicker he can cover that distance or, as described in basic physics, work. We know that sprint fatigue leads up to a significant decrease in speed. Not only does force production drop, but also stride length in high-level athletics can decrease by three to five cm due to a decrease stride frequency by .25 to .30 strides per second. Because of this, it brings about an increase in flight time by 0.01 to 0.015 seconds.

There are two factors to address when excelling at running or sprinting: 1) force production and 2) deceleration due to muscular fatigue or lack of explosive strength endurance. Why does running speed drop? (Yakimovich, 1985, *Leg Kaya Atletika* 4:10). The great G.D.A. Coach H.D. Hill developed a style of running with a very powerful form using shortened strides and dominating the track scene in the 1970s. In 1972, M. Lettselter proved that the leading women sprinters were different from lesser sprinters, not by a greater stride length, but a greater stride frequency, 4.86 strides per second, and the shortest stride of 186 cm. (Tablhnik, 1987).

To make it simple, running is just falling forward with the help of gravity while placing one foot in front of the other to maintain balance. Motion is created by the destruction of balance. Leonardo Da-Vinci as well as men like V.M. Zatsiorsky, H.D. Hill and many others including N. Romanov, PhD., have found it a valuable tool to execute a free-fall motion much like how animals move for running distance. How do we use sled work for running? Not by running, but by power walking with different resistance. There are two methods. The first method is just what everyone has been told not to do. Land on the heel with a long stride and upon touching the surface very powerfully, pull the heel through. The sled should jerk when done correctly. Never run, but use as much force as possible and coordinate arm movement to synchronize with not only the legs but also the body. This accomplishes many things, which contributes to running faster. Use light weight—50 pounds for men and 25 pounds for women—for acceleration, done on grass.

The complete posterior chain, symmetrically from the bottom of the calf, the hamstring muscles, the glutes, hips, lower back and abs must be strong. The more resilient these muscles are the faster an athlete runs, providing he knows how to run. This style helps eliminate deceleration and is the key to winning most races when sprinting or completing the 40-yard dash. Sixty yards works well. The last step must be as powerful as the first step, and the last trip of power walking must be as powerful as the first trip. Objects with fast velocity produce small force. When power walking with a moderate to heavy sled, a slower velocity is used, but a higher force is produced. This is what sprinting is all about and is illustrated by Hill's equation for muscle contraction. The force velocity curve and the hyperbolic curve are based of Hill's work as well. If an individual can pull a heavy sled at full speed, even through it is at a slow speed, through 60 years, with no deceleration, imagine the force and acceleration at the end of a sprint without additional resistance, only body weight. This system is also unlike proper running form due to accessible forward lead. Remember, it is not perfecting running form, but building a more powerful body for running. Experiment with weight on a sled. One hundred thirty-five pounds may be too light to produce optimal force, but 225 pounds may be too heavy and 180 pounds could be the optimal resistance.

Second style

Just as Dr. Romanov administrates, *The Pose Method of Running* is more efficient through improved endurance and using gravity for an athlete's benefit. This style not only builds a more powerful set of running muscles, but also helps coordination. I refer to power sled work as the Tai Chi of weight training, encompassing very slow, deliberate motion with great concentration and impeccable form. This system can correct errors in leg and arm movement.

Many young runners rely on natural speed and reflexes, but these gifts can deteriorate through time. A solid base is what is lacking in many runners, but the sled work builds a solid base. Normally performed on a flat surface, remember that pulling uphill provides the shortest stride length, and downhill causes the longest stride. Although there are countless exercises that build calves, hamstrings, hips, legs and abs along with lower back flexibility and mobility, sled work can build all muscle groups simultaneously.

How can it perfect running form or technique? With a forward lean or free fall while staying on the ball of the foot to aid in kinetic energy (KE), merely lean forward with the sled attached to the waist using a weight belt. As the sled begins to move, the individual starts to fall forward to counteract the chaotic state. Lift a foot and place it on the walking surface, and as an individual continues to free fall forward, he simply and instantly places one foot in front of the other. This employs free energy or gravity to the individual's advantage while simultaneously building phenomenal power and muscular coordination. The amount of weight on the sled depends on each person's strength.

For football or short sprints up to 200 m, a 60-yard power walk works well. If an athlete recalls the definition of $W=FD$, then it is common sense to duplicate the time of his race while pulling a sled in either form, heel strike or on the ball of his foot. Example: 400 m walk for 50 seconds; 800 m 120 seconds; or a mile run up to four minutes with a light-weight sled. This works with a marathoner as well, but the amount of energy pulling a sled for a time of not more than 50 to 60 minutes.

For form power walking, ankle weights can be added. A weight vest with varying weight in the front compared to the back is used to perfect proper lean, which also increases general endurance. Form walking is done on the ball of the foot, aiding in the development of KE, which is the final effect of building a powerful down-force through foot velocity. The weight training must consist of low reps to develop force production ($F=ma$) and, of course, to increase velocity. If an individual could triple velocity, he will increase KE to nine times as great. The heel touching style is to build a foundation. For running, build an enormous amount of power in the muscles and soft tissue where KE is stored. There are many pictures to explain the methods described in this chapter.

Endurance must constantly be raised, but there is one factor many coaches fail to acknowledge when addressing increasing endurance. This factor is motivation or mental boredom. Studies about mental boredom were conducted by Kukushkin (1983). The type of training must be changed for athletes to avoid this syndrome. The conjugate system practiced by Westside rotates the exercises, volume, intensities and restoration. Individuals are never bored with the Westside system.

Endurance Summary

There are fundamental principles for training general endurance. The first principle is the length of the workouts, which depends on the sport or sport activities on which an athlete is concentrating. The second principle is the tempo of movement. The desired tempo must be maintained for a pre-determined time or work interval such as 100 meters or 10,000 meters. Close attention must be paid to the rest interval for adequate recovery, depending on the level of preparedness of the athlete. In turn, the athlete should be able to perform at least 60 reps per minute with 25 percent to 50 percent of a one rep max with light barbell exercises, belt squat walking or squatting with a lightened method.

Know the goal being achieved. If strength endurance is the goal, heavy training will be of no use if one tries to do several reps with 75 percent to 80 percent weights. The end result will be a gain in absolute strength. I prefer the low intensity approach with resistance. This builds general strength, general endurance, and thickens ligaments and tendons, containing kinetic energy to increase one's ability because that is where it is stored. Plus, soft tissue injuries are reduced greatly.

Low intensity workouts like walking with resistance and resistance sled work for pre-season training by reducing the load or the time of the actual work becomes a method of restoration.

The goals are to raise work capacity and learn the best rotation of special workouts for general endurance for not only a single sport activity, but more importantly, each and every athlete has his particular needs that must be recognized. A last note, do not use machines; they train only muscles not motion.

Emotional Stress

Westside is based on a weekly, sometimes daily, plan. If you don't know what you are doing, you can't stress about it, can you? Pain can also affect endurance. Most often, it is from doing the same exercises over and over, which is just another example of accommodation. By doing the same exercises repeatedly, some muscle groups are over worked while some are neglected, leading to injuries. Again, rotating exercises prevents this syndrome through the conjugate system. The conjugate system is also used to strengthen weak muscle groups and correct muscle group imbalances by strengthening a single muscle group.

What I have just described is general endurance training. It increases oxygen uptake, muscular endurance as well as strength endurance and prevents muscular and soft tissue injuries through prehab or the process of preventing injuries.

Low intensity work can be walking, although most experts say one should not use walking, even for speed walkers. They must not have used resistance walking by adding ankle weights; the most common weight is 10 pounds per leg, 5 pounds per leg for beginners, and up to 20 pounds per leg for elite athletes. By adding a weight vest for 20 pounds to 125 pounds, the intensity of work to the degree sought is raised. Use a brisk walking pace and sustain a heart rate at 155, and maintain a pace without laboring for ½ to two miles. This has a positive effect on cardiovascular and respiratory systems. Thigh cuffs also can be utilized, two pounds to four pounds is recommended, changing the weight combinations often. Example: Less ankle weights, heavier weight vest or vise-versa. If thigh weights are employed, no more than four pounds per thigh should be used. The weight vest makes it difficult on breathing, but when resistance is removed, the athlete's stamina is considerably higher.

It is common to see weight lifters and Rugby players use cross country skiing and cross country walking with back packs for their general endurance. Light sled pulling can be an alternative to the weight-resistance walking. After raising the heart rate to roughly 155 beats per minute (BPM), walk until fatigue affects stride.

Always do a cool down by walking without any resistance or alternately walk and jog. This is perfect for football players, especially the lineman. For other sports in the period of accumulation, this system of developing endurance is very beneficial when the sports activity is constantly running or sprinting. It is also advisable to do power walking on a non-motorized treadmill. For example, football players use short 5-, 10-, and 20-yard sprinting. Work on flexibility and mobility game skills, checking sprint times. As strength increases and endurance improves, speed and acceleration progression is very dependent on the development of box jumping. Don't neglect a sport's technical training. I trained an athlete in weight lifting in the mid 80s who had a 70' 10" shot put. While his strength training using weight improved, his throwing coach was not concerned with his throwing technique while at Westside. The throwing camps are focused on lots of throws, but little strength work. When strong, his throwing suffered, and when his techniques were good, his strength was down. His throws maxed out when his strength made 90 percent. There is a problem. Why can't strength and technique be equal?

CHAPTER 3 - CONJUGATE SYSTEM

CHAPTER 3 - CONJUGATE SYSTEM

The Westside system for fitness and special strength training is completely based on a revolving training system. The exercise for barbell training is switched each week for max effort work and some switching of exercises for speed or explosive strength training is on a weekly plan. Never exceed a three-week training plan or three weeks of doing the same exercise, same total volume, same intensity zone because progress will cease. This is due to the biological Law of Accommodation. Accommodation is the decrease in response in continuing the same stimulus. In training, the stimulus is physical exercise (Zatsiorsky, 1995). Westside avoids accommodation with the conjugate method.

We train 100 percent plus on max effort day. Science has taught us that after training with resistance over 90 percent on the same exercise, progress stops after three weeks. While training for speed, the same phenomenon occurs. An athlete does not become any faster due to accommodation. This is why the conjugate system is far superior to all others. For speed training, three-week pendulum wave is used. I have found the best periodization is to wave upward of 75 percent, 80 percent and 85 percent of the third week. This works best for speed strength development. In 1975 A.D. Ermakov and N.S., Atansov's data showed 51 percent of snatch and clean pulls fall into these percent range (Laputin & Oleshko, 1982). I have found the same holds true for the intensity zones for jumping with resistance. The exercises must be constantly changed, and the volume and training intensities must be altered. Most importantly, the rate of speed the barbells move must be altered constantly so accommodation does not occur. The box height, added resistance, or the length of sprinting must change frequently. To adapt to training is to never adapt to training noted Ben Tabachnik, PhD.

I look at resistance training not as heavy or light, but rather fast weights or slow weights. Supportive gear including shoes should be waved in and out of training. Meals and nutrition must be changed somewhat during the year, depending on the loading per iodization an individual is concentrating on at the time. An athlete needs to learn how important the conjugate system is in his weekly, monthly, yearly and multi-year planning. The Westside system is a complex of all principles of strength training. Inside of one week, an individual gets faster with the dynamic method, more muscular through a modified repetition method, and inhumanly strong through the max effort method as well as becoming more physically fit by doing small workouts for GPP. It makes the progressive overload system, also known as Western periodization or block training, totally outdated. It eliminates the detraining that occurs when leaving say a hypertrophy phase to a power phase.

Consequently, the conjugate system was first tested by a group of Soviet sports scientists in 1972. The Soviets had coaches, like Matveyev, who realized there was a much better method of planning. There has always been controversy over who came up with wave periodization. Dr. Yuri Verkhoshansky has been credited with the pendulum wave in 1964. The renowned Bulgarian coach Abadjieve even had a similar plan for waving volume and intensities.

The Dynamo Club had 70 highly qualified weight lifters do an experiment by rotating 25 to 45 special exercises, including the classical lifts. After the experiments were completed, one lifter was satisfied and the rest wanted more. It now had a name: the conjugate system. I was training alone and used lots of special exercises for all three lifts to reduce staleness. When the same routine is used over and over, there is a failure to make progress, which is known as accommodation. To avoid this, a rotation of small and large exercises must be cycled in and out of the plan. I followed this system without knowing it had a name for years, 13 to be exact.

In 1983 when I broke my lower back for the second time, I thought there had to be a better way. I started to buy books such as: the *Soviet Sports Review* translated by Dr. Yessis and the Soviet training manuals that Bud Charniga, Jr., had translated. Bud told me that these are textbooks. This is just what I was looking for because they opened my eyes. They are very math/physics oriented with a basis on Newton's laws of motion. I was hooked. During my first Elite United States Powerlifting Federation (USPF) event I achieved a total of 1655 in February 1973. I used no gear, not even wraps on my knees, elbows, or even wrists, just an Olympic weight belt, not a power belt.

If I wanted to continue to make progress, I had to get stronger, and I had to get smarter, much smarter. I started all over again. First, I used the pendulum wave in three-week cycles, going from training a heavy and a light day to a max effort day, working to a max single depending on my level of preparedness. A severe workout can be done every 72 hours, and the second day is devoted to the development of special strengths. It could be explosive strength, which is commonly known as the dynamic method.

The Westside conjugate system is the better of two advanced training systems: the Soviet system, where several special exercises are used to advance the training of superior lifters and athletes, and the Bulgarian system, where near-max lifts are performed every workout. The Westside system is a combination of the two.

Science has proven that training at a 90 percent or above for three weeks causes' physical and mental fatigue. With the Westside conjugate method, we switch a core barbell exercise each week to avoid accommodation, and the wide variety of special exercises perfect form. The similarities of the Westside conjugate system to the one devised by the Soviets at the Dynamo Club are obvious. The only difference is the exercises: one system for Olympic lifting and of course, the other for powerlifting. What I took from the Soviets was the sequence of wave loading. A. S. Prilepin was instrumental in regulating the number of repetitions and sets at a particular intensity zone. This truly enlightened me about the importance of calculating volume at each intensity zone and why it is a waste of time to do too many reps at a given intensity zone. Men such as Verkhoshansky, Bondarchuk, Matveyev, Vorobyev, and many more helped lead the way.

Westside pendulum wave cycles last three weeks for speed and explosive strength and two weeks for strength speed work, utilizing several special bars to establish different maxes. Because the reps and sets should remain the same at a given percent, the bar speed at this percent remains the same. The volume changes each week due to the difference between bar maxes. A front squat max is different from a safety squat bar max, and of course, both vary from a max squat. This is to avoid accommodation, which in this case is the constant overuse of the same loading patterns.

The Soviets and Westside count only all-time records, which amounts to roughly 600 lifts a year, similar to contest max lifts. The Bulgarian system mandated that the current training maxes were based on that particular day's strength, equaling about 4,000 lifts a year. They were not established on a certain percent. This was determined by Coach Abadieve's experiments. They used only six lifts: front squat, back squat, power clean, power snatch, clean and jerk, and snatch. One had to be well chosen for such a rigorous regiment of training.

Westside's system is to max out on this day according to an individual's level of preparedness. This means that a Westside max effort is the most a lifter is capable of that day. It may not be an all-time record, but it is the most a particular lifter is capable of on that day, week after week. This is just like the Bulgarian training with the exception of the number of lifts because they would follow this system six days a week. Six maximum lifts were done in the morning. After a 30-minute rest, six more maxes on pulling exercises plus six max squats, front or back were performed. This was repeated in the afternoon and evening.

Westside uses two max effort days a week, one for the squat and deadlift and one for benching. Seventy-two hours later a separate speed workout and max effort day for the same lift are executed. Three lifts at 90 percent and above are advised. This is more practical for powerlifting, on the basis of using this max effort system for the last 32 years.

A lot of hours and work have gone into perfecting the Westside system. It has more variety, volume, reps, and intensity zones as well as exercises that literally number in the hundreds. It has been a 40-year odyssey of pain, work, and experimentation. Look at our website and compare our lifts to those of other gyms: 89 Elites, 14 who squat over 1,000 and four over 1,100; 30 who bench more than 700 pounds and four over 800 pounds; 15 who deadlift over 800 pounds; six with a total more than 2,500 pounds; four with a total over 2,600; and one with a 2,700-pound total. In addition, I have made a USPF Elite total throughout the time period from February 1973 to December 2009, this last time at 62-years-old.

A Final Note

The Westside conjugate system is based on 20 percent barbell training of the classical lifts with 80 percent special exercises planned for an athlete's particular sport. It serves no purpose for the athlete to be strong in the wrong exercises. Westside has more than a 95 percent success rate on breaking records on max effort day.

I would like to relate a story told to me by Johnny Parker who was an NFL strength coach with four Super Bowl rings. While visiting Westside, Johnny was discussing a conversation he had with a former Soviet strength coach friend of his. He asked what he could do with the players after a game on Monday. The Soviet coach said to work their legs. Johnny wrote it down. "What about Tuesday?" he asked. The Soviet coach said to work their legs. Johnny wrote that down as well. "What about Wednesday?" and the Soviet coach said, "Work their legs." At this, Johnny said, "I am confused." The old Soviet coach said, "As long as you do something different each day, this is known as the conjugate system."

All training is connected. I suggest you do the same exercise for a few days so some adaption occurs, but not to master it. If an exercise or a specific load is repeated, then accommodation begins or the negative training effect. A weekly cycle could look like this:

Monday, Tuesday and Wednesday — Glute/ham raises

Thursday, Friday and Saturday—10-pound ankle weight leg curls 200 per day.

Sunday, Monday, Tuesday—Belt squats

Wednesday, Thursday, Friday—Sled pulls

Saturday, Sunday, Monday—Light sumo straight leg deadlift

Tuesday, Wednesday, Thursday—Box jumps

Friday, Saturday, Sunday—Walking with a weight vest plus ankle weights

This is a sample 18-day training plan for an elite athlete. The exercises must be switched just before accommodation begins to avoid a decreased training stimulus. The same must be done when concerning volume and intensity zones. The proper loading scheme must be paid close attention to so the training goal is accomplished.

Here is a sample of a 12-week training cycle to achieve explosive jumping ability through the dynamic method with barbell box squatting. Weights are not characterized as heavy or light, but in velocities.

500-Pound Max

Strength Speed .6 to .7 m/s

Week	Weight	Reps	Band Tension
1	250 lb.	5x2	250 lb.
2	275 lb.	5x2	250 lb.
3	300 lb.	3x2	250 lb.

Speed Strength .8 to .9 m/s

Week	Weight	Reps	Band Tension
4	250 lb.	12x2	125 lb.
5	275 lb.	12x2	125 lb.
6	300 lb.	10x2	125 lb.
7	260 lb.	12x2	125 lb.
8	280 lb.	12x2	125 lb.
9	320 lb.	10x2	125 lb.

Explosive Strength 1 to 1.2 m/s

Week	Weight	Reps	Band Tension
10	150 lb.	12x2	70 lb.
11	175 lb.	12x2	70 lb.
12	200 lb.	12x2	70 lb.

As illustrated in the tables, very heavy or slow work begins the cycle for the first three weeks for a strength speed wave at 50 percent to 60 percent for the development of speed strength. The last three-week wave or weeks 10 through 12 are for explosive strength. The 12-week pendulum wave cycle is to avoid accommodation by changing the type of special strength.

First, special strength is strength speed. This is where the barbell is moving slowly because of the external resistance. Next, volume is raised while the intensity is lowered and the barbell is now moving much faster. This is speed strength. The final three-week wave is devoted to increasing explosive strength. The barbell should be moving at least one m/s, and the load is reduced in volume and intensity. This system aids in developing some adaption or specificity without defying accommodation, a general law of biology.

The jumping exercises, flexibility, mobility, hand and eye training, prehab and rehab as well as restoration should be constantly rotated to bring about future development in a particular sport.

I hope this explains how the Westside conjugate system was created. I found the right way to train by observing the smart and resourceful lifters who succeeded compared to those who set their own plan and failed and withdrew from Westside.

There are many bar velocities that must be trained. Leave one out and you will certainly fail.

CHAPTER 4 - CONTRAST AND REACTIVE METHODS

CHAPTER 4 - CONTRAST AND REACTIVE METHODS

Medvedev said one must use bands or cords on the barbell, and he was right. Why? This helps eliminate bar deceleration. Dr. Fred Hatfield was experimenting on compensatory acceleration training (CAT). This was basically lifting concentrically with acceleration. It was a great concept, but with one small problem. The barbell decelerates in reality. Why? There is greater body leverage at the top of all lifts. Example: While lifting in a power rack, the higher the pin the greater the weight can be moved through better leverage or the force-posture relationship. I will explain it in simpler terms. The weight an individual can lift off the bottom pin would be too light to train with off the top pin, and max weight that can be lifted off the top pin would be too heavy to move off the bottom pin. What's the answer? It is Reactive methods.

Refer to Newton's second law F=ma. Remember the limitations of the power rack. How can a perfect weight be lifted from bottom to top? By using bands or chains on the barbell. Everyone has sticking points or mini max position. This is the human strength curve. There are three methods to increase force in the force-posture relationship.

1. Accommodating resistance
2. Accentuation
3. Peak-Contraction Principle.

Contrast methods can have great influence on eccentric muscle actions. Larger torque values than concentric and eccentric action were produced in studies like those of Westing (1988) featured in the *European Journal of Applied Science*. Most studies, such as those by Komi and Buskiak (1972) in *Ergonomics* 15, 417-434, however, have not shown much of a difference.

While I hold all studies by Komi and his associates in high regard, they never tested a group of men who could handle 700 pounds of band tension plus up to 600 pounds of bar weight. All of my studies were done with a recovery or concentric action after an eccentric action. Slowing down the eccentric phase is not advisable. This is what most studies performed with no contrast method. After all, we know drop jumps have a great effect on explosive and absolute strength. When performing such jumps, an athlete is accelerating at 9.8 m/s. If depth jumps work and we know they do, why would anyone lower a weight slowly? This is why the studies failed to produce any great value for sports performance.

Depth jumps at roughly 30 to 35 inches have a great influence for explosive strength due to a fast atomization phase. For absolute strength increases, much higher boxes must be used starting at 42 inches and upward to 60 inches for advanced athletes. The higher depth jumps have a much slower atomization phase contributing to maximum strength. This is true when lowering a bench or squat, as the weight grows heavier, the reversible phase becomes slower.

I have conducted studies with a Tendo unit, comprised of 20 men who had squatted at least 850 pounds, plus men that are 10 top ranked benchers and found that all participants were within 1/10th of an m/s when comparing their eccentric phase speed to their concentric phase. The faster down, the faster up.

A second study I performed was on only one lifter, Matt Smith, who at the time could squat 930 pounds. He later made an 1,160-pound squat. The study consisted of Matt box squatting 550 pounds with just weight. His eccentric and concentric phases were almost identical: just .nine-tenths of a second apart. We removed some bar weight and added band tension to the bar. At the top of the squat, it weighed 750 pounds, and while sitting on the box, it weighed 550 pounds due to the band shrinkage. His eccentric phase was .54 second, the second was .57 second. This was measured and timed by Dr. Ikita, a professor of calculus.

The two studies show a very positive effect of over-speed eccentrics caused by band tension using a contrast method. The eccentric phase was broken into two separate actions by sitting on a box. This made the two actions easy to compare. Box squatting represents an action known as contract (hold), relax against contract. This procedure of successive induction is introduced by the integrative action of the nervous system (Sherrington, 1906). As can be seen, training is not as simple as one might think. A combination of methods must be implemented to develop one maximum potential. Contrast methods, box squats, over-speed eccentrics together explore the upmost unit of human performance. I highly recommend using bands, chains, or weight releasers on multi-set training days. There must be an optimal weight in the bottom and top of a lift, which can only be possible when a contrast method is used. Plus, the concept of optimal eccentrics must be applied. This means using roughly 40 percent of one's eccentric strength potential for somewhat of a free-fall action.

There are several reactive methods for accommodating resistance. One method is the lighten method, which calls for placing jump stretch bands at the top of a power rack. Depending on the band strength, the barbell can be lightened in the bottom of the bench from 155 pounds to 65 pounds. Accelerate the barbell weight on the concentric phase. It's great for squatting and it teaches acceleration throughout the entire squat, bench, deadlift, power clean, or power snatch. When an individual reaches a near max, he will start to understand the concept of eliminating deceleration into acceleration. This is one form of compensatory acceleration training or CAT (Siff, 2003).

Chain Work

A second method that deloads eccentrically and reloads concentrically requires attaching chains to the barbell. By fastening chains on the bar while benching or squatting, the total weight in the bottom is reduced, making it more manageable to start quickly and accelerate through a mini max on to completion with little deceleration. Many studies have concluded that adding accommodating resistance to the barbell is not productive. I have found just the opposite. Why? Their studies were done with unskilled college students. At Westside I used no one who was not ranked in the top ten nationally, not a novice, but a well-trained lifter who has good form.

Below are samples of three-week waves with chains for a 400-, 600-, and 800-pound squat. Use a parallel box, and the weight on the bar is 50 percent to 60 percent over three weeks for speed strength.

400 Pounds Max

Percentage	Weight	Reps	Chains	Total Volume
50	200 lb.	12x2	80 lb.	4,800
55	220 lb.	12x2	80 lb.	4,800
60	240 lb.	10x2	80 lb.	4,800

600 Pounds Max

Percentage	Weight	Reps	Chains	Total Volume
50	300 lb.	12x2	120 lb.	7,200
55	330 lb.	12x2	120 lb.	7,200
60	360 lb.	10x2	120 lb.	7,200

800 Pounds Max

Percentage	Weight	Reps	Chains	Total Volume
50	400 lb.	12x2	160 lb.	9,600
55	440 lb.	12x2	160 lb.	9,600
60	480 lb.	10x2	160 lb.	9,600

Sample speed strength workouts for 200-, 300-, 400- and 500-pound raw bench. The bar weight remains the same week to week, rotating bands when becoming accustomed to chains.

200-Pound Bench Press Max

Implement 50 percent with 100 pounds for 9x3 reps with 40-pound chains. Use three different grips, and the index finger touches the smooth part of the bar for three sets. Move grip out two inches for three sets and have the little finger touching power ring. Rotate grips in any fashion.

300-Pound Bench Press Max

Employ 50 percent with 150 pounds for 9x3 reps with 80 pounds of chains. Change grips as mentioned above, moving bands when a decrease in the response to training is felt. This is accommodation.

400-Pound Bench Press Max

Use 50 percent with 200 pounds for 9x3 reps with 80 pounds of chains. Remember to change grips, accelerating the bar as quickly as possible.

500-Pound Bench Press Max

Apply 40 percent with 200 pounds for 9x3 sets of 120 pounds of chains. Here change the resistance by adding more chain weight. On all speed work, use a fast-eccentric phase, a quick-reversal phase and accelerate as rapidly as possible to lockout.

Look at weightlifting as fast or slow, not heavy or light. The athlete invariably becomes lazy with light weights. Chains work well for lower level lifters and athletes. There is not an eccentric action with chains unlike bands. By unloading on the eccentric phase and reloading on the concentric phase, chains truly provide accommodating resistance. The amount of accommodation can be altered through the amount of chains used and where the load distribution acts in the concentric phase.

Weight Releasers

Weight releasers were first used in the former Soviet Union. At first, they had a lifter lower into a squat, and two spotters or in this case strippers would remove a predetermined amount of weight before the lifter would rise to the top. This makes the load contrastingly different or in this case heavier in the eccentric phase compared to the concentric phase. Later, a device was invented by Bob Kowalski to automatically release some amount of weight by hitting the floor and kicking themselves off the bar. A lifter reacts to the original amount of weight used on the eccentric phase and blasts up explosively to the top with something less than he lowered.

This is caused by the contrast in stimulus triggered by the nervous system to produce a faster than normal concentric acceleration. The concentric phase is faster not only because of a lighter load, but a learned training effect due to the contrast style of training. To clarify, an individual will be able to move concentrically faster with or without weight releasers. One disadvantage is that only the first rep can be deloaded. The remaining reps will be a constant weight, or no contrast. I find this far more superior to stripping weights than going from one to two reps at 90 percent to three to five reps at 30 percent to 40 percent. Rest between sets is considerable dependent upon one's GPP. This method is commonly used in Europe for explosive power development.

Weight Releasers Workouts

For speed strength, apply 80 percent of a one rep max, including the load on the weight releasers. On the eccentric phase, use a controlled eccentric phase, but as quickly as possible, approaching overspeed eccentrics about seven-tenths to eight-tenths m/s. The weight releasers deload 20 percent of the original load and accelerate concentrically as rapidly as possible.

Maximal Eccentric

Through our experiments with no less than an 850-pound squatter, we found it best to choose a base weight at the bottom of the squat, preferably on a box.

Example: 600 pounds

Increase weight to the bar with weight releasers.

Example: Lower 600 pounds and release 100 pounds, following with the concentric phase. Add additional weight to weight releasers, not the barbell weight, and release it in the bottom, then concentrically raise it as fast as possible. Do not add weight on the bar for the concentric phase.

Some experts say a lifter can lower 150 percent eccentrically, but cannot elevate with the additional 50 percent. Do not lower slowly because this has never led to concentric strength gains. Slow eccentric work builds larger muscles, but not necessarily more explosive muscle actions concentrically. Eccentric muscle actions can cause the most muscle soreness. When doing drop jumps, the athlete approaches the 9.8 m/s, which is the speed of acceleration of gravity near earth. Everyone knows drop-jumps work, so why would anyone lower a weight slowly? Please don't read body building magazines, but rather the books mentioned in the text. Don't be confused. While lowering weight builds eccentric strength, drop jumps increase reversal strength.

Bands Over Bar Method

I feel it is superior to lower a weight, have it reduce the resistance by band shrinkage, and return concentrically while band tension is restored. By attaching rubber bands of different strengths, one lowers on to a box with a combination of barbell weight and band tension of a predetermined amount of total resistance, satisfying the needs of special strengths desired to be trained. One example: speed strength.

The barbell weight should be 50 percent to 60 percent of a one rep max. Plus, band tension that has a ratio of 25 percent at the top and 10 percent at the bottom. Lower as quickly as possible with the help of the bands' tension pulling downward, increasing kinetic energy before the lifter stops on the box and overcomes the load concentrically. This is over speed eccentrics (Simmons, 2007 Westside Barbell Book of Methods).

Below are examples of band workouts with 50%-60% weight and 25% band tension at top.

Speed Strength Workouts for the Squat

500 Max Percentage

Percentage	Weight	Reps	Band	Total Volume
50	250 lb.	12x2	125 lb.	6,600
55	275 lb.	12x2	125 lb.	6,600
60	300 lb.	10x2	125 lb.	6,600

600 Max Percentage

Percentage	Weight	Reps	Band	Total Volume
50	300 lb.	12x2	150 lb.	7,200
55	330 lb.	12x2	150 lb.	7,920
60	360 lb.	10x2	150 lb.	7,200

700 Max Percentage

Percentage	Weight	Reps	Band	Total Volume
50	350 lb.	12x2	175 lb.	8,400 lb.
55	385 lb.	12x2	175 lb.	9,240 lb.
60	420 lb.	10x2	175 lb.	8,400 lb.

Band Bench Workout for Speed Strength

300 Max Percentage

Percentage	Weight	Reps	Band	Total Volume
50	150 lb.	9x3	75 lb.	4,050 lb.
50	150 lb.	9x3	75 lb.	4,050 lb.
50	150 lb.	9x3	75 lb.	4,050 lb.

400 Max Percentage

Percentage	Weight	Reps	Band	Total Volume
50	200 lb.	9x3	100 lb.	5,400 lb.
50	200 lb.	9x3	100 lb.	5,400 lb.
50	200 lb.	9x3	100 lb.	5,400 lb.

450 Max Percentage

Percentage	Weight	Reps	Band	Total Volume
50	225 lb.	9x3	125 lb.	6,000 lb.
50	225 lb.	9x3	125 lb.	6,000 lb.
50	225 lb.	9x3	125 lb.	6,000 lb.

The bar weight stays the same week after week. Rotate band tension to chain weight to weight releasers every three-week wave to avoid accommodation.

Athletes and Olympic lifters need to slow down. Yes, I said to slow down. They both lack the ability to grind out a lift, especially if they are an Olympic lifter. Olympic lifting is a pure speed strength sport. When a lift gets hard, they fail because their absolute strength is low and so is their strength speed or slow strength. The athletes are the same. It is one thing to produce a fast rate of force development, but quite another to maintain it for any length of time. Example: Two linemen fighting each other at the line. How do they increase strength speed development? Band training at a certain combination of band tension and barbell weight. At least 50 percent band tension or higher must be used. This concept causes one to be slowed down. Remember no one can lift a heavy weight slowly. This is where time under tension will be longer to perform the same range of motion.

The band tension must be great in the bottom of the lift. If only bar weight is used, the barbell can be too heavy in the bottom or too light at the top. If a lifter employs only band tension, the bar will be too light in the bottom and too heavy at the top. There is a correct mixture of weight and band tension for special strength development. The coach can determine this through experimentation. Always use a box while squatting with the exception of belt squatting. The box supplies a virtual force effect. A force that is there, but is not recognized. A box also determines the desired depth of the squat over and over.

The reactive methods and contrast methods of training are invaluable for the development of power and explosive strength. This is accomplished by imposing special demands on the nervous system. Besides plyometrics, the methods in this chapter will rapidly increase an individual's sports explosive capabilities.

The use of band tension or chain weight can produce a perfect amount of weight or resistance in the bottom and top of the lift. This cannot be done with just bar weight, just band, or chain weight. This is known as accommodating resistance.

Bands over the barbell method have produced the greatest results in weights lifted and the training for jumpers. Of course, there are other methods of contrast training that are worth looking at. Before bands, chains, or weight releasers came to be, the Soviet coaches would incorporate a system referred to as complex method of power development.

One system of power development was to use heavy and light resistance together. They would perform three sets of two reps with 90 percent; then, reduce the weight to 30 percent for six to eight reps, which is certainly contrast training. Take a rest period between sets to fully recover. This method can be used in many exercises. The weight on the bar can be altered 70 percent to 80 percent. However, keep the reps in line with the studies of A.S. Prilepin's findings in 1974 in N.P. Laputin and V.G. Oleshko's *Managing the Training of Weightlifters*. After the barbell lifts, perform a jumping exercise, jump with Kettlebells, or dumbbells for six to ten reps for two or three sets. More can be found in *Soviet Training and Recovery Methods* by Rick Brunner and Ben Tabachnik, PhD.

Tabachnik was the inventor of the speed chute. Running with a speed chute that releases is a contrast method for speed development. Remember, a sprinter needs muscular endurance, and a long-distance runner sometimes has to sprint to the finish line. The speed chute can be used for long jumping and triple jumps. It can, of course, develop running endurance.

Band Resistance for Running

Band tension can be used for developing a rapid start. Wrestlers have used bands for take downs for years. It can be used for a sprinter's start as well or just general running resistance. The variety of contrast training is only limited to one's knowledge of the long range periodization of a specific sports activity.

More About Bands

Westside research has found that a particular percentage of band tension can greatly alter bar speed. For strength speed or slow strength to be developed, the band tension must be equal to or be more than the amount of bar weight on the barbell. For example: 225 pounds bar weight, 440 pounds band tension is for strength speed development, and 300 pounds bar weight plus 375 pounds band tension is strength speed. No one can lift a heavy weight slowly. The individual is either pushing or pulling as quickly as possible because of large amounts of external resistance. Hill's force-velocity equation in Mel Siff's *Supertraining* (2003) concludes that force decreases as velocity increases. This does not mean that lifting heavy weight makes a lifter slow, but on the contrary, it makes him fast once the maximum resistance is reduced to an intensity zone of 75 percent to 85 percent, standing to reason that as velocity is increased force is decreased. For those who are not strong, this may be hard to understand. Because for some, a light weight might be a 300-pound squat, but that same athlete could be capable of only a 400-pound max. The 300 pounds represents 75 percent of a one rep max. However, a strong athlete can squat 600 pounds; the same 300 pounds would represent 50 percent of a one rep max.

By training the Westside method, the stronger athlete would move the 300 pounds much faster. It is simple math. Therefore, if a player has to defend against a 300-pound lineman, wouldn't the athlete want to be as strong as possible? Let's look at a simple model of periodization. Max effort work should take place the day after a ball game or other sporting event. This eliminates the effect of delayed onset muscle soreness (DOMS) for the sporting event. Three days later a workout for explosive strength or speed must take place. The loading charts in the text explain the wave concept Westside uses to wave volume workout to workout. Remember extreme workouts can and should occur every 72 hours apart. When men and women run constantly, they feel fatigued. After weight training, however, they feel exuberated. Coaches should try asking the athlete for his or her input. Their responses may be surprising.

Static Overcome by Dynamic Method

The static overcome by dynamic method is used while box squatting and floor pressing. In this method some of the muscles are held static while other muscles are relaxed. By using this system, it builds the greatest explosive power as well as maximum strength, depending on the amount of what percentages of a one rep max with which a lifter is working (Siff, 2004).

This method exploits the fact that preliminary isometric tension using one or very few repetitions can increase the dynamic strength and explosive strength of a subsequent action. This method is implemented while box squatting, and so far it has produced 16 individuals with over 800-pound deadlifts, 16 individuals who are 1,000-pound squatters, and 31 individuals who are 700-pound benchers. This method is also responsible for box jumps of 57½", 63 ½", 63" and 60". It is recommended to push or pull against a static bar for one or two seconds; then, reduce load to 30 percent and overcome it, which is referred to as a static dynamic developer. This can be done while doing Judo throws. Simply try to throw your opponent while a third man holds him firmly on the ground. After a second or two, the assistant lets go, and the man is thrown. A single man is thrown by applying an effort that it takes to hurl two men.

Relaxed Overcome by Dynamic Effort

This method is also done on a box squat or floor press; the opposite happens at the same time. How? Concentrate on relaxing the muscles then violently contracting them. This is one method of shock training. A fighter throws a jab in this manner. His arm and body are very relaxed then forcefully extended by contracting the muscles that contribute to throwing a punch. Both methods—static overcome by dynamic and relaxed overcome by dynamic—have great benefits to power development and absolute strength. I highly recommend them for a large portion of an individual's training.

A Ratio of Bar Weight and Band Tension for Different Special Strength Development

Explosive Strength	30%-40% bar weight	150% band tension
Speed Strength	50%-60% bar weight	25% of band tension
Circa-max	47%-52% bar weight	40%-45% band tension
Strength Speed or Slow Strength	50% bar weight	50% band tension

These ratios of band tension and bar weight have been tested continuously for close to 20 years with many world records, NFL players, Olympic gold medal holders, and sprinters. The sets, reps, number of lifts, and days between max effort and speed development day must be 72 hours apart. Follow the recommendations laid out in the periodization and planning chapter for controlling volume and intensities.

Combinations of Resistance Methods

While Dr. Fred Hatfield was doing research in the early 1980s on Compensatory Acceleration Training (CAT), I was quite aware of Dr. Hatfield's work and completely agreed with his method. I wondered, however, if there was a more productive method that would almost completely eliminate the deceleration portion that occurs at the completion of the lift, especially with light or submaximal lifts. As early as the late 1980s Westside was using weight releasers for explosive power. An elder lifter asked me to explain weight releasers to him and how they worked. I explained it to him and he replied that it was similar to hanging chains from the bar. I thought about it and realized that they not only provided a deload similar to weight releasers, but an added dimension of providing a reloading process as well. This was truly accommodating resistance, making it possible to have a near perfect weight load at the bottom as well as the top of the lift.

Soon after, an 18-month experiment was conducted in our training of speed strength and acceleration training. Only after three major meets did I disclose the results and they were dramatic. Only the top 10 lifters were used. Dave Williams the strength coach at Liberty University asked if I would do an experiment with rubber bands. I had heard of them, but had never been exposed to them. Dick Hartzell was in Columbus with his Jump Stretch bands. I placed them over my shoulders and did a few squats and I was sold. I knew by placing the bands over a barbell with a certain amount of weight and a certain amount of band tension, I could provide an overspeed eccentrics as well as accommodating resistance. There was no overspeed eccentrics with just bar weight or even bar weight with chain weight. Through many experiments with bands on a bar and chains on a bar and many combinations of both types of resistance with our 75 personnel who squatted at least 800 pounds to 1,205 pounds, I was credited with the training system referred to as Combination of Resistance Methods found on page 409 in *Supertraining*. These methods have made it possible to increase jumping and running as well as lifting.

Virtual Force Effect

I am asked many times about band shrinkage and what happens when some of the band tension is lost in the bottom of the lift. This was a common question at Westside in the beginning of band plus weight training. We, of course, knew there was less tension in the bottom of the lift, yet we were extremely powerful going from eccentric to concentric. How? A Virtual Force Effect, defined as a force that is present, but not recognized.

If the goal is to increase kinetic energy (KE), it is better to increase velocity than mass. This is applied physics. If one could triple velocity, one would square kinetic energy or nine times as great. This is a form of potential energy. In the case of band tension it is referred to as Gravitational Potential Energy. This causes additional velocity on the eccentric phase that produces additional KE. Think about if you drop a marble six inches above a glass, compared to shooting a marble downward the same six inches with a slingshot. The added velocity developed by using the slingshot creates a higher force. Much like a 200-pound sprinter walks with 200 pounds of force with each step. But the same 200-pound sprinter running at top speed can produce up to four to five times the force due to overspeed eccentrics. We cannot move eccentrically at 9.8 meters per second with a barbell, this is the acceleration of gravity near earth. But we can increase the eccentric phase by using band tension.

Depth-jumps have a great effect on explosive strength over-shadowing other means of development. By dropping through space, you are developing explosive strengths due to activation of the muscles by the stretch reflex. Depth-jumps should be limited to three sets of eight for intermediate athletes and four sets of 10 for advanced. When using bands over a barbell use the correct percentage of band tension for a special strength (i.e. 25 percent for speed strength) as well as the correct amount of lifts during a weekly, monthly, and yearly plan.

CHAPTER 5 – PERIODIZATION – DIVISION INTO TRAINING PERIODS

CHAPTER 5 – PERIODIZATION – DIVISION INTO TRAINING PERIODS

I knew Western periodization was a dead end as early as 1973, which was the year I broke my back for the first time, but I knew no other way. In 1983 after breaking my L5 the second time, I had to find a better way. I would be strong in one lift, but not the other two. It would be a different lift that would go up while some other lifts were unmanageable. Ricky Crain, a great lifter, would call me with the same story. Dave Waddington, the first 1,000-pound squatter was in my living room and asked how to fix the same problem that Ricky and I had. I would tell him when he found the answer to call me.

So back to 1981. I was desperate. I made a call to Bud Charniga to buy some Soviet books on training. He said, "Lou, you know these are like text books written by their Sports scientists on very intricate matters on training." I told Bud that is exactly what I needed because Western gradual overload system led me down a dead-end road. It is more of a de-training system than anything else. Enough talking about the past.

I looked at the models of Matveyev, his wave system, and the wave-like concentration of loading for five to eight weeks at a time by Verkhoshansky. I then looked at a pendulum approach by Arosiev, which is used for alternating special strength preparation such as: speed strength, explosive strength, strength speed and even strength endurance. I also looked at Tudor O. Bompa, Ph.D., and his findings. It was interesting to me how effective the system was that made Naim Suleymanoglu the great Bulgarian weight lifter. I realized the system was for a model athlete or someone of perfect proportion for his sport. It was based on the hypothesis of Felix Meerson from *Plasticeskoe Obezpecenie Organizma* (1967) and Hiden's findings from 1960 to 1964.

Which one was the best, or was there a best? These were after all very intelligent men to say the least, but I found before that I did not like a long-term plan. I discovered in my training and my training plateaus that after going upward for three weeks, I would regress almost every time. I liked the wave system of training by Matveyev and Verkhoshansky, but Vorobyev's (1978) wave plan was a little less restrictive, somewhat like Ermakov's work in 1974.

Dr. Siff asked me how I came up with a three-week speed strength wave. I told him I became no stronger or faster after three weeks, and he was fascinated to hear that because V. Alekseev, the great Soviet SHW lifter, used the same three-week wave. On week four, he reevaluated the training and started a new three-week wave cycle. I think I won Mel Siff over at that time.

I implement some different approaches. I seldom do a regular squat or deadlift. The bench is done, but with very light percents, roughly 40 percent to 50 percent with the addition of accommodating resistance. As the meet approaches, we don't reduce special exercises, but push them to the limit to perfect form by concentrating on the weak muscle group. This is what the conjugate system does. There are three phases that are strength training: Maximal effort, dynamic method and repetition methods for hypertrophy, which are all trained simultaneously. There is built-in flexibility in a three-week pendulum wave.

The first graphs concerning volume and intensities zones also show the importance of waving the volume and percentage of a one rep max again to avoid accommodation. The speed-strength days show high volume and moderate to low intensity. On max effort days, the opposite will and must occur. The volume is 35 percent to 50 percent of the speed days, but as the intensities must be as high as possible, hopefully, a new all-time record will be set. Like the Bulgarian, the level of preparedness is the major factor for how much one can lift on max-effort day. The following graphs show volume and intensities

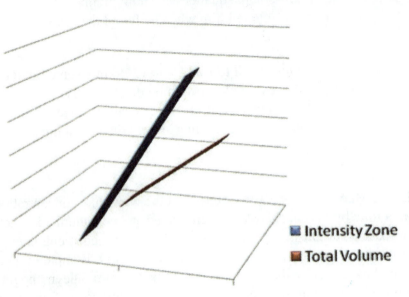

Figure 1.1 Low Volume training; highest intensity possible for 100 percent and above. Limit to three lifts of 90 percent and above to all-time max.

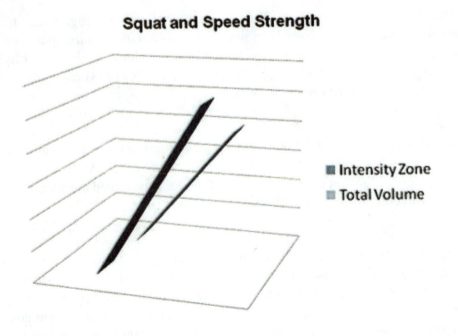

Figure 1.2 High volume training; Moderate intensity zones between 60 percent to 85 percent. Limit to 12 to 24 lifts per training session.

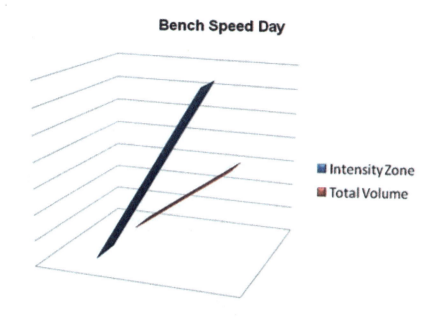

Figure 1.3 High Volume training; Low to moderate intensity between 50 percent to 60 percent. Limit 16 to 30 lifts per training session.

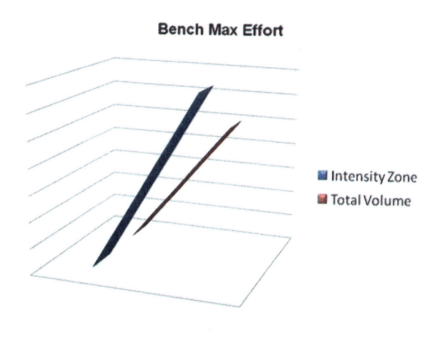

Figure 1.4 Low volume training; highest intensity possible. Limit to three lifts of 90 percent and above to all-time max.

There are four direct periods of periodization

1. Accumulation - high volume of training of all types to charge or build the body for speed or strength for a particular sport.
2. Intensification - now the athlete limits to some degree the exercises focusing on more specific speed work or strength movements that work best for him.
3. Transformation - now the value of the previous two cycles is tested while the athlete uses exercises that are most beneficial to the competition. For lifting, the top lifter uses a circa-max or near-max weight phase with limited special exercise that contributes to his highest achievements. A runner's work would be very limited to the very most important speed or speed endurance work.
4. Delayed Transformation - one reduces the high intensity work and relies on rest and restoration for two to four weeks leading to a competition.

It is imperative to know about these phases of training. Refer to the suggested reading for more information on periodization.

During the Westside system of using a three-week wave for speed-strength and explosive-speed training, the wave rotates from 75 percent to 85 percent in a three-week cycle, jumping five percent per week. By doing this, I can evaluate the progress of the athlete all the time. This makes more sense to observe the athlete to see if he has become stronger or faster as well as other physical qualities such as quickness or where muscle mass should be added. I don't have a crystal ball, so I have no idea where the athlete's progress will be in 12 weeks or 24 weeks. The three-week wave system allows for better observation on a continuous basis for speed strength and maximal effort work each week. The major barbell exercises are changed.

Soviet sports scientists found after three weeks of weight training at 90 percent or more, progress stopped. This is accommodation, but it is totally eliminated by revolving the barbell exercises each week. We can max out every week throughout the year, and extreme workouts can occur every 72 hours. Our weekly plan is to speed squat on Friday with high volume of 75 percent to 85 percent intensity zone for three reps per set. On Monday it is max effort work for squatting or pulling for max singles. The intensity is 100 percent plus all an individual can do on that particular day similar to the Bulgarian system. No more than three lifts from 90 percent up to a new max; of course, the volume is low much like the Rule of 60 Percent. Speed bench on Sunday. High volume and very low intensity zones range from 40 percent to 50 percent. Wednesday is max effort day, working up to a new personal record or as much as possible with single lifts not more than three lifts at 90 percent, approaching 100 percent; plus, in one week the speed work is 20 to 30 lifts while the max effort day is three lifts. It is almost a 10 to one ratio with speed lifts being 10, and max lifts being one.

The bulk of our system is special exercises. We do not have a system to form a model athlete, so it may take several combinations of special exercises to achieve success. Our entire training program is built around special exercises for weight lifting, powerlifting or running and jumping. I don't concentrate on what you have, but rather what you don't have.

An NFL agent brought in a lineman and asked me what I was going to do. I told him, and he said, "Why aren't you going to run him?" I asked him this question, "He ran for four years and this is how fast he is. Why do you think two more months of running with him will make a difference?" He replied, "Good point."

Let's look at pendulum waves with special bars. The graphs show a nine-week training cycle, consisting of three different three-week pendulum waves. The nine-week system employs three types of bars. They each have a maximum weight to calculate the percentages. All three maximums are different to avoid the mistake of accommodation or using the same volume repeatedly. The bar path will be somewhat different as well to ensure training all the leg and back muscles. The bar speed by percentage will be close, but the bar weight is quite different.

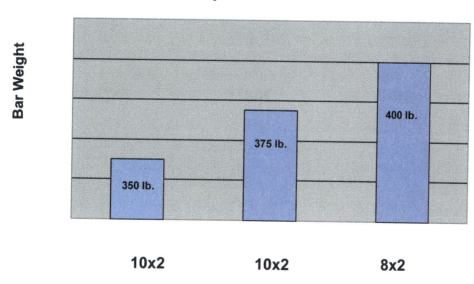

Figure 2.1: This graph shows bar weight for Weeks 1, 2 and 3

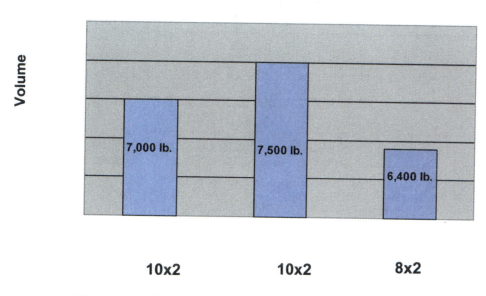

Figure 2.2: This graph shows volume for Weeks 1, 2 and 3

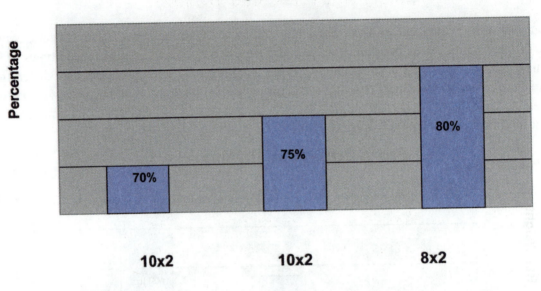

Figure 2.3: This graph shows percentages for Weeks 1, 2 and 3

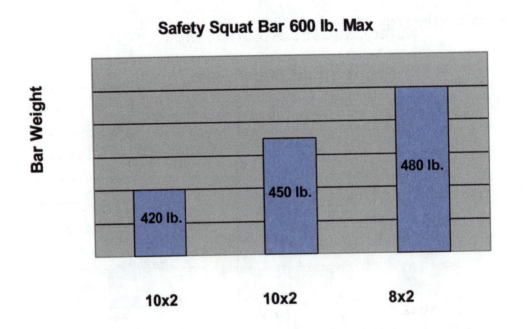

Figure 2.4: This graph shows bar weight for Weeks 4, 5 and 6.

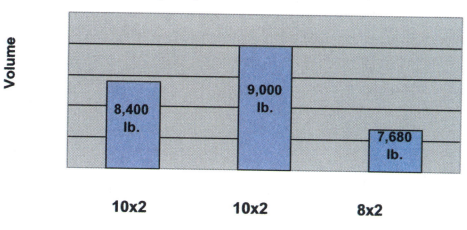

Figure 2.5: This graph shows volume for Weeks 4, 5 and 6.

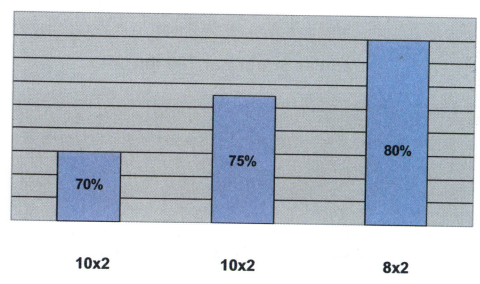

Figure 2.6: This graph shows percentages for Weeks 4, 5 and 6.

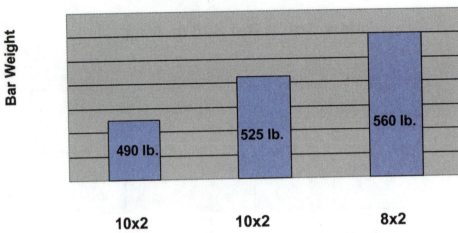

Figure 2.7: This graph shows bar weight for Weeks 7, 8 and 9.

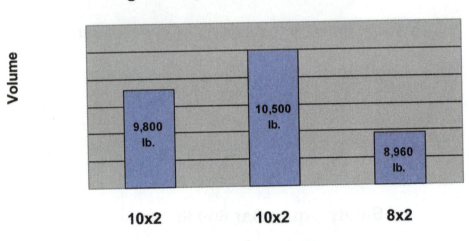

Figure 2.8: This graph shows the volume for Weeks 7, 8 and 9.

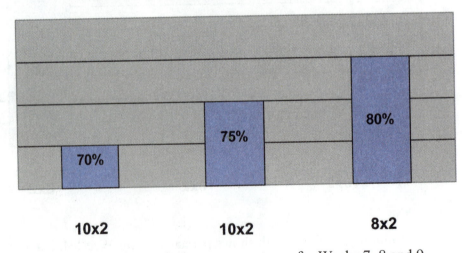

Figure 2.9: This graph shows percentages for Weeks 7, 8 and 9.

The wave cycles vary as bands, chains, or combinations of both are added to the barbell to accommodate resistance. When using weight releasers, the added weight on the first eccentric rep phase can be calculated. The variations of a wave are too numerous to list.

The speed strength waves for squatting and benching normally continue three weeks, and the strength speed waves last only two weeks due to their severity as well as the near max or circa-max wave phases. If the speed day waves are of ultra-high volume for squatting with speed pulls following, the squats are also of high-volume workout. A speed strength squat day is followed by a maximal effort day 72 hours later. Then, a high volume squat and deadlift follows 72 hours afterwards, then they de-load. Most can only sustain three max effort workouts in a row.

The next scheduled max effort is replaced by a repetition method workout to recover from the severity of such training. Then, embark on as heavy a workload for three or four more workouts. For the squat and deadlift, this approach works for the pressing days as well, such as: standing press or some form of bench pressing flat or angled. Remember, when you feel mentally or physically exhausted, replace the normal speed or max effort workouts with a repetition workout designed for working the less fatigued muscle groups. Repetition work meaning lots of extensions for the back, hips, arms and trunk.

Note to reader: Speed-strength cycles last two or three weeks progressively, going higher in percentage and somewhat higher in volume. On max effort days, the barbell exercise must change each week. For example, one week is a squat exercise, a deadlifting exercise the next, then a Goodmorning exercise and occasionally a repetition day thrown in for recovery for overtaxed muscles. These are in no particular order. Exercises must be chosen for individual goals. Again, repetition work must consist of single-joint exercises. Example exercises are back raises, glute/ham raises, tricep extensions, and the like.

Many athletes have a yearly or even a multi-year plan or the plan and methodology for an Olympic cycle that is planned with a timetable for developing certain systems. Their concept is to increase intensity while lowering volume, making a functional plan on how fast an individual will be, how high he can jump, or how much he can lift at a particular date during the year. Then and only then will progress be noted. Is the athlete ahead or behind schedule?

The Westside system of training can check speed strength every week. This is done with the three-week pendulum wave. Explosive strength can be monitored the same as jumping progress. Maximal strength for upper and lower body is monitored each week. Potential can be kept at more than 90 percent and sometimes even 95 percent year-long. Remember to note the four periods of training—accumulation, intensification, transformation and delayed transformation—are used only in the beginning of training. Then, all aspects are combined simultaneously through a yearly plan.

The Westside system prepares the athlete for the delayed transformation period or the circa-max phase Westside uses for power meets. It is a wave of the highest intensity. Hopefully, a new record of some type is set, depending on the sport. The critical delayed transformation phase, or the de-loading phase, trains from explosive to maximal strength, covering all elements of strength: coordination, fitness, flexibility, raising lactic acid, aerobic and anaerobic, and threshold barriers while increasing V02max. All components can and must be trained simultaneously. Delayed transformation was adapted from track and field as well as Olympic weightlifters from the former Soviet Union.

Periodization can be a weekly, monthly or yearly plan. This plan can lead to a four-year or an Olympic cycle. Speaking of Olympic cycles, a college athlete sports career can be four years for improving leg and back strength, and there must be a mathematical system to follow.

Westside has used the wave system of periodization for more than 30 years with great success. It is, of course, a math problem to be addressed that combines bar speed, total volume and precise intensity zones of a predetermined percent of a one rep max. This along with proper biomechanics and physics can spell certain success. One such plan follows.

A1: The Plan: From a 400-pound to a 1000-Pound Max Squat

400-Pound Max Squat

Percentage	Weight	Reps	Lifts	Band Tension	Volume
50%	200 lb.	12x2	24	25%	4,800 lb.
55%	220 lb.	12x2	24	25%	5,280 lb.
60%	240 lb.	10x2	20	25%	4,800 lb.
Bar Speed is 0.8 m/s avg.					

450-Pound Max Squat

Percentage	Weight	Reps	Lifts	Band Tension	Volume
50%	225 lb.	12x2	24	25%	5,400 lb.
55%	250 lb.	12x2	24	25%	6,000 lb.
60%	270 lb.	10x2	20	25%	5,400 lb.
Bar Speed is 0.8 m/s avg.					

500-Pound Max Squat

Percentage	Weight	Reps	Lifts	Band Tension	Volume
50%	250 lb.	12x2	24	25%	6,000 lb.
55%	275 lb.	12x2	24	25%	6,600 lb.
60%	300 lb.	10x2	20	25%	6,000 lb.
Bar Speed is 0.8 m/s avg.					

550-Pound Max Squat

Percentage	Weight	Reps	Lifts	Band Tension	Volume
50%	275 lb.	12x2	24	25%	6,600 lb.
55%	300 lb.	12x2	24	25%	7,200 lb.
60%	330 lb.	10x2	20	25%	6,600 lb.
Bar Speed is 0.8 m/s avg.					

600-Pound Max Squat

Percentage	Weight	Reps	Lifts	Band Tension	Volume
50%	300 lb.	12x2	24	25%	7,200 lb.
55%	330 lb.	12x2	24	25%	7,920 lb.
60%	360 lb.	10x2	20	25%	7,200 lb.
Bar Speed is 0.8 m/s avg.					

650-Pound Max Squat

Percentage	Weight	Reps	Lifts	Band Tension	Volume
50%	325 lb.	12x2	24	25%	7,800 lb.
55%	355 lb.	12x2	24	25%	8,520 lb.
60%	390 lb.	10x2	20	25%	7,800 lb.
Bar Speed is 0.8 m/s avg.					

700-Pound Max Squat

Percentage	Weight	Reps	Lifts	Band Tension	Volume
50%	350 lb.	12x2	24	25%	8,400 lb.
55%	385 lb.	12x2	24	25%	9,240 lb.
60%	420 lb.	10x2	20	25%	8,400 lb.
Bar Speed is 0.8 m/s avg.					

750-Pound Max Squat

Percentage	Weight	Reps	Lifts	Band Tension	Volume
50%	375 lb.	12x2	24	25%	9,000 lb.
55%	425 lb.	12x2	24	25%	10,200 lb.
60%	450 lb.	10x2	20	25%	9,000 lb.
Bar Speed is 0.8 m/s avg.					

800-Pound Max Squat

Percentage	Weight	Reps	Lifts	Band Tension	Volume
50%	400 lb.	12x2	24	25%	9,600 lb.
55%	440 lb.	12x2	24	25%	10,560 lb.
60%	480 lb.	10x2	20	25%	9,600 lb.
Bar Speed is 0.8 m/s avg.					

850-Pound Max Squat

Percentage	Weight	Reps	Lifts	Band Tension	Volume
50%	425 lb.	12x2	24	25%	10,200 lb.
55%	470 lb.	12x2	24	25%	11,280 lb.
60%	510 lb.	10x2	20	25%	10,200 lb.
Bar Speed is 0.8 m/s avg.					

900-Pound Max Squat

Percentage	Weight	Reps	Lifts	Band Tension	Volume
50%	450 lb.	12x2	24	25%	10,800 lb.
55%	495 lb.	12x2	24	25%	11,880 lb.
60%	540 lb.	10x2	20	25%	10,800 lb.
Bar Speed is 0.8 m/s avg.					

950-Pound Max Squat

Percentage	Weight	Reps	Lifts	Band Tension	Volume
50%	475 lb.	12x2	24	25%	11,400 lb.
55%	520 lb.	12x2	24	25%	12,480 lb.
60%	570 lb.	10x2	20	25%	11,400 lb.
Bar Speed is 0.8 m/s avg.					

1000-Pound Max Squat

Percentage	Weight	Reps	Lifts	Band Tension	Volume
50%	500 lb.	12x2	24	25%	12,000 lb.
55%	550 lb.	12x2	24	25%	13,200 lb.
60%	600 lb.	10x2	20	25%	12,000 lb.
Bar Speed is 0.8 m/s avg.					

Notice the bar speed is constant, roughly .8 m/s. Secondly, it requires a total of 600 pounds of volume to increase the squat 50 pounds, and the percent range is 50 percent to 60 percent. The rep range and total number of lifts remain the same. The amount of band tension or chains is also constant. The three-week waves for a period of time yields the 50-pound increase by building maximal strength on max effort day, 72 hours later plus special exercises.

By studying these graphs carefully, it can be seen how mathematics plays a large role in gaining strength and force production.

Let's look at the total volume for a 400-pound max squat. It is one-half of the total volume of an 800-pound max squat. A 400-pound max squat requires the person to maintain 4,800 pounds of volume; whereas, lifting 800 pounds involves 9,600 pounds of volume. This is twice as much as a 400-pound squat. A 500-pound squatter must maintain 6,000 pounds of volume. It takes 12,000 pounds to maintain a 1,000-pound squat, which is exactly twice the volume. While the goal as a coach may be to maintain a squat max of 400 pounds or 700 pounds for a lineman to be able to ensure the force development of the before-mentioned squat, the appropriate volume must be adhered to. This is a proven method of strength training, which is referred to as the dynamic method.

The primary goal is to develop a fast rate of force development in sports of all kinds. For those who use a Tendo unit, speed strength is the goal of 0.8 to 0.9 m/s average. Speed strength is trained at intermediate velocities. One must know at what velocity a particular special strength is trained or failure will ensue while attempting to improve a special strength. These speeds can be found on Page 150 in Mel Siff's *Supertraining* (2003).

To avoid accommodation in volume in a weekly plan, the special exercises will fluctuate to such an extent that accommodation is impossible. A second method is to change the total volume while training at a certain percent while using a three-week wave and a cycle is to use a special bar at the same percent. The workload can change. It is evident that a particular percent (this time of 50 percent) can greatly change the work load when doing a back squat compared to a front squat or an overhead squat. The example shows that a typical 500-back squatter would normally have a max front squat of 350-pounds and an overhead squat of an estimated 250 pounds. When looking at the first week wave at 50 percent in the three different squat styles, the total volume per set of two reps would be respectively 500 pounds, 350 pounds, and 250 pounds.

A2:

Max	Percent	Weight Pounds	Volume
500 lb. back squat	50%	250 lb.	500 lb. per set
350 lb. front squat	50%	175 lb.	350 lb. per set
250 lb. overhead squat	50%	125 lb.	250 lb. per set

This is the simplest way to change volume while maintaining bar speed at the predetermined bar speed at the fixed weekly percent. For more examples, the three graphs below show using chains for a 400-pound max squat; a 600-pound max squat; and an 800-pound max squat. For benching, the bar weight remains the same, but the accommodating resistance changes accordingly as maximum strength goes up

A3: Band Bench Workout for Speed Strength

300 Max Percentages

Percentage	Weight	Reps	Band Tension	Total volume
50%	150 lb.	9x3	75 lb.	4,050 lb.
50%	150 lb.	9x3	75 lb.	4,050 lb.
50%	150 lb.	9x3	75 lb.	4,050 lb.

400 Max Percentages

Percentage	Weight	Reps	Band Tension	Total volume
50%	200 lb.	9x3	100 lb.	5,400 lb.
50%	200 lb.	9x3	100 lb.	5,400 lb.
50%	200 lb.	9x3	100 lb.	5,400 lb.

450 Max Percentages

Percentage	Weight	Reps	Band Tension	Total volume
50%	225 lb.	9x3	125 lb.	6,000 lb.
50%	225 lb.	9x3	125 lb.	6,000 lb.
50%	225 lb.	9x3	125 lb.	6,000 lb.

These charts are guidelines for not only squatting and benching, but variations of the Olympic lifts or the deadlift. It should teach proper planning order to control volume and intensity zones and suitable bar speed.

Periodization by Percentages

Westside constantly talks about the value of controlling loading by a percentage of a one rep max. This solves the problem of overtraining or detraining. I found the importance of this after applying the advice of A.S. Prilepin's chart for loading at different percentages in *Managing the Training of Weightlifters*. He listed how many repetitions per set as well as how many lifts per workout. His findings show that if the number of lifts are vastly under or over, the training effect decreases. The subject can be thoroughly studied in *Managing the Training of Weightlifters* by N.P. Laputin and V.G. Oleshko. A sound conclusion was discussed in the book A.S. Medvedev's *A System of Multi-Year Training in Weightlifting*.

At the 1964 Olympics, Leonid Zhabotinsky had won the gold medal. Zhabotinsky's volume remained the same for the next two years although his intensity decreased. The result of this was no increase on his total. In 1967, the training intensity was raised and once again the totals started to rise once more. How does a sportsman increase his lift without overtraining or detraining while maintaining correct bar speed? The answer, a three-week pendulum wave for speed strength development because it controls volume and intensity for one's strength level. You don't fight without a mouth piece, you don't play football without a helmet, and you don't lift without some protective gear like a light suit with straps down or an average pair of squat briefs.

Below is an outline of a 50-pound jump to raise a squat from 400 pounds to 700 pounds. College sports are like an Olympic cycle—four years. If strength and speed have not increased by a great deal, the athlete and coach have failed.

400-Pound Max Squat

Percentage	Weight	Reps	Lifts	Band Tension	Volume
50%	200 lb.	12x2	24	25%	4,800 lb.
55%	220 lb.	12x2	24	25%	5,280 lb.
60%	240 lb.	10x2	20	25%	4,800 lb.
Bar Speed is 0.8 m/s avg.					

450-Pound Max Squat

Percentage	Weight	Reps	Lifts	Band Tension	Volume
50%	225 lb.	12x2	24	25%	5,400 lb.
55%	250 lb.	12x2	24	25%	6,000 lb.
60%	270 lb.	10x2	20	25%	5,400 lb.
Bar Speed is 0.8 m/s avg.					

500-Pound Max Squat

Percentage	Weight	Reps	Lifts	Band Tension	Volume
50%	250 lb.	12x2	24	25%	6,000 lb.
55%	275 lb.	12x2	24	25%	6,600 lb.
60%	300 lb.	10x2	20	25%	6,000 lb.
Bar Speed is 0.8 m/s avg.					

550-Pound Max Squat

Percentage	Weight	Reps	Lifts	Band Tension	Volume
50%	275 lb.	12x2	24	25%	6,600 lb.
55%	300 lb.	12x2	24	25%	7,200 lb.
60%	330 lb.	10x2	20	25%	6,600 lb.
Bar Speed is 0.8 m/s avg.					

600-Pound Max Squat

Percentage	Weight	Reps	Lifts	Band Tension	Volume
50%	300 lb.	12x2	24	25%	7,200 lb.
55%	330 lb.	12x2	24	25%	7,920 lb.
60%	360 lb.	10x2	20	25%	7,200 lb.
Bar Speed is 0.8 m/s avg.					

650-Pound Max Squat

Percentage	Weight	Reps	Lifts	Band Tension	Volume
50%	325 lb.	12x2	24	25%	7,800 lb.
55%	355 lb.	12x2	24	25%	8,520 lb.
60%	390 lb.	10x2	20	25%	7,800 lb.
Bar Speed is 0.8 m/s avg.					

700-Pound Max Squat

Percentage	Weight	Reps	Lifts	Band Tension	Volume
50%	350 lb.	12x2	24	25%	8,400 lb.
55%	385 lb.	12x2	24	25%	9,240 lb.
60%	420 lb.	10x2	20	25%	8,400 lb.
Bar Speed is 0.8 m/s avg.					

Look at the waves carefully. The bar speed remains the same during each wave regardless of the bar weight. Why is it important regardless whether it is 400-pound max as a freshman or a 700-pound max as a senior? Accommodating resistance with bands or chains must be implemented to promote accelerating strength. If strength does not increase, speed won't increase either. To become stronger, volume must increase at the same intensity zones. Each max has a correct amount of volume. Just like the great Olympic champion L. Zhabotinsky found, if volume stays the same, the results will stagnate. This multi-year system perfects skills as strength is increased, and one should be able to use perfect form while using moderate weights. Remember the equation $F=ma$. Three days or 72 hours later, a max effort day must occur. This builds absolute strength.

Experts like A.P. Bondarchuk believe in the theory that through perfecting skills an individual utilizes strength gains. My idea is that you increase muscular strength to perfect skills by increasing coordination. I am sure neither Bondarchuk nor I are totally correct, but this system blends both together. This system is simple mathematics.

Look at the raise in strength at 50-pound intervals and the volume climbs 600 pounds at the same intensities. Let's look at the bench press, although any style of pressing—overhead press, push jerk in front or behind head—can use this system. The bench waves stay at one constant percent with barbell weight. The change in resistance is made by changing the amount of bands, chains or weight releasers.

EXAMPLES OF A THREE WEEK WAVE

300 Max Percentages

Percentage	Weight	Reps	Lifts	Band Tension
50%	150 lb.	9x3	27	85 lb.
50%	150 lb.	9x3	27	85 lb.
50%	150 lb.	9x3	27	85 lb.

300 Max Percentages

Percentage	Weight	Reps	Lifts	Chain Weight
50%	150 lb.	9x3	27	80 lb.
50%	150 lb.	9x3	27	80 lb.
50%	150 lb.	9x3	27	80 lb.

300-pound Max Bench

Percentage	Weight	Reps	Lifts	Chain Weight & Band Tension
50%	150 lb.	9x3	27	80 lb. /25 lb. at top
50%	150 lb.	9x3	27	80 lb. /25 lb. at top
50%	150 lb.	9x3	27	80 lb. /25 lb. at top

300-pound Max Bench
Lightened Method

Percentage	Weight	Reps	Lifts	Unload Weight
80%	240 lb.	9x3	27	60 lb.
80%	240 lb.	9x3	27	60 lb.
80%	240 lb.	9x3	27	60 lb.

As you can see in the four examples, it is the method of accommodating resistance to develop maximal tension throughout the entire range of motion. Many times exercise machines use a special cam with variable lever arms to apply a larger force at the weakest point of the strength curve (V.M. Zatsiorsky). This is done with varying totals of band tension, chain weight or using the lightened method with different amounts of unloading in the bottom. Real weight must be employed. Machines build muscle, not motion. Always use three different grips, none being outside the power lines.

Westside Uses Three Types of Speed Pulls After Speed Squats.

1. **Speed Pulls on Floor with Bands**

The math is roughly 30 percent band tension at lockout plus 50 percent bar weight of a one rep max. A 700-pound deadlifter would use 345-pound bar weight plus 220 pounds at top of lift. A three-week wave would look like this:

Wide Sumo on Floor				
Week	Weight	Reps	Sets	Band Tension
1	345 lb.	3	10	220 lb.
2	345 lb.	3	8	220 lb.
3	345 lb.	3	6	220 lb.

Conventional Rack Pulls with Bands				
Week	Weight	Reps	Sets	Band Tension
4	345 lb.	2	10	250 lb.
5	345 lb.	2	8	250 lb.
6	345 lb.	2	6	250 lb.

Close Sumo on Floor				
Week	Weight	Reps	Sets	Band Tension
7	345 lb.	1	10	280 lb.
8	345 lb.	1	8	280 lb.
9	345 lb.	1	6	280 lb.

Conventional Rack Pulls				
Week	Weight	Reps	Sets	Band Tension
10	315 lb.	3	10	350 lb.
11	315 lb.	3	8	350 lb.
12	315 lb.	3	6	350 lb.

2. **Ultra Wide Sumo Deadlifts with Bar Weight**

Ultra Wide Sumo with Barbell weight			
Week	Weight	Reps	Sets
13	500 lb.	3	10
14	500 lb.	3	8
15	500 lb.	3	6

Notice how a three-week wave is constantly altered to avoid accommodation. The weight may vary or the stance may change from sumo to conventional to ultra-wide sumo to rack pulls.

3. Box Deadlifts

Discussed are box deadlifts. I suggest placing bar on mats to raise the elevation of the barbell. This maintains the feel of the mechanics of the bar. The band tension also changes each cycle or on the fourth week. The loading graphs are based on a 700-pound-max deadlift. All one needs is to reduce the amount of bar weight and band tension by 50 percent.

Wide Sumo on Floor 350-Pound Deadlift				
Week	Weight	Reps	Sets	Band Tension
1	175 lb.	3	10	110 lb.
2	175 lb.	3	8	110 lb.
3	175 lb.	3	6	110 lb.

Conventional Rack Pulls with Bands				
Week	Weight	Reps	Sets	Band Tension
4	175 lb.	2	10	125 lb.
5	175 lb.	2	8	125 lb.
6	175 lb.	2	6	125 lb.

Close Sumo on Floor				
Week	Weight	Reps	Sets	Band Tension
7	175 lb.	1	10	140 lb.
8	175 lb.	1	8	140 lb.
9	175 lb.	1	6	140 lb.

Conventional Rack Pulls				
Week	Weight	Reps	Sets	Band Tension
10	160 lb.	3	10	175 lb.
11	160 lb.	3	8	175 lb.
12	160 lb.	3	6	175 lb.

Ultra Wide Sumo with Barbell weight			
Week	Weight	Reps	Sets
13	250 lb.	3	10
14	250 lb.	3	8
15	250 lb.	3	6

Again, note that each three-week wave is somehow different. It may be the bar weight, it can be band tension, or it could be altered by a different stance or how far the bar is off the floor. By using a power rack or by placing plates on rubber mats, one can also stand on a two-inch or four-inch box. A 350-pound deadlift is half or 50 percent of the volume of a 700-pound deadlift. Mathematics is an essential part of weightlifting because a lifter must control the total volume of a training session. The intensity zones or what percent of a one rep max must also be considered. As graphs in this text show, the volume must be highest on speed strength day while the intensities are moderately low to moderate—50 percent to 80 percent. The max effort day would require the intensity zone to possibly be 100 percent plus, allowing the volume to be as low as 35 percent to 50 percent. The loading for power cleans and power snatches without bands or chains must also be regulated.

The training of top weight lifters must use a wide variety of exercises, not just power cleans and power snatch but the classical clean, jerk and snatch. More than 50 percent of all training must be comprised of special exercises such as: back raises, belt squats, inverse curls, box jumps, Reverse Hypers ™, Good mornings, a wide variety of pulls, squats, jerks and presses.

The Soviets were experts of calculating volume and intensities. Men like A.S. Prilepin, A.D. Ermakov and N.S. Atanasov provided studies in *Managing and Training of Weightlifters* that determined how many snatch and clean jerks were to be done in a single workout and how many reps and sets, and at what percent they should be monitored. Although my observations are very close to these, I find it is important to train optimally, not maximally or minimally. Plus, the percents for weightlifting are kept five percent lower than their recommendation. The data from 1975 by A.D. Ermakov and N.S. Atanasov in *Managing and Training of Weightlifters* found roughly 50 percent of the lifts fell between 75 percent and 85 percent. While it is fully recognized this is where speed strength is developed, many did not grow up doing weightlifting. I propose performing five percent less on each three-week wave.

Example:

300-Pound Power Clean				
Week	Percent	Reps	Sets	Lifts
1	70%	3	6	18
2	75%	3	6	18
3	80%	3	4	12

This workout can be done after Friday's speed squat workout. Rest between sets about 90 seconds. This requires good GPP. After all, you are an athlete, right?

250-Pound Power Snatch				
Week	Percent	Reps	Sets	Lifts
1	70%	3	6	18
2	75%	3	6	18
3	80%	3	4	12

This workout can follow a max effort workout on Monday. First, do a max exercise: low box squats, overhead squat, Goodmornings, box pulls, rack pulls, heavy sled pulls for 60 yards. Rest 90 seconds. After a heavy lift, a clean or snatch feels lighter and faster. Add variety like band tension of different amounts. I give credit to three great men: Ermakov, Atanasov and Prilepin's in *Managing and Training of Weightlifters*, and Verkhoshansky and Medvedev in *A System of Multi-Year Training in Weightlifting*, for not only guiding my career from 1982, but undoubtedly saving my lifting career. I have slightly modified the volume and intensity by using somewhat lighter lifts. One reason is due to a lesser background in GPP. and physical preparedness and second, we use a lot of powerlifting exercises.

A lifter must wave back down after a three-week wave, but also change something, at least slightly. Vary the amount of bar weight, band tension, chains, weight, box height, pin height, or bars to avoid accommodation. The speed-day volume will be the highest while intensity will be at a low 40 percent to moderate 80 percent. Seventy-two hours later on max effort day requires intensity to be a max of that particular day, hopefully meaning a near all-time max or an all-time max on some special exercise. It is gaining strength in the right special exercises that brings forth a next personal best in a clean or snatch or jerk.

If an individual fully understands the process or percents, he will never overtrain or undertrain. He needs to alternate weak muscle groups to prevent injuries and constantly make progress until he reaches his sport's potential. Use three, three-week-waves before trying a new max. In the beginning, progress is easy, but as an individual starts to lift weights close to his potential, as only a handful have, it becomes more difficult. It's lonely at the top.

For the weightlifter, it is most important to raise absolute strength to overcome larger loads, to become faster is secondary to strength. This is a common misconception of weightlifting coaches in the United States. After all, world record weights move slower than training weights. An athlete must use the optimal weight for his strength. The amount of work and rest must be monitored as well as movement tempo. Weightlifting requires a great deal of speed and strength. While speed is of course a major factor, speed strength is necessary to lift with speed for the development of quick strength.

As strength and speed at each percent increase, an individual achieves a new max to work from. This yields a larger training volume. Remember, the chart shows how a 400-max squat volume is 4,800 pounds, and how a 500-max squat requires 6,000 pounds of volume. For every 50 pounds gained in a max squat, a rise in volume of 600 pounds will be factored in at the same 50 percent to 60 percent. There is much to consider when perfecting form: GPP, recovery methods, relaxation, and above all, a selection of the correct special exercises for the individual. Mental, physical, and emotional maturity needs to be considered. Many require a plan. This is a plan for an individual's current strength level and how to raise it correctly. The amount of rest between sets must be a factor because this can be critical for recovery. The percent of a one rep max and the volume the training plan calls for is imperative. This is the interval method, much like track athletes use.

With small weights that football players use for speed development, the rest between sets of two reps represents the majority of football plays four to seven seconds. An individual should and must recover in 40 seconds for 12 sets of two reps, for explosive strength development, 24 sets of two reps can be performed with 40 second intervals, which builds explosive strength in a fatigue state and represents training at 70 percent to 85percent. The rest must be 60 seconds to 90 seconds between sets. Max effort work can require two to four minutes rest between singles, which is dependent of the athlete's level of physical preparedness.

A.S. Prilepin discovered and shared in *Managing and Training of Weightlifters* that too many reps per set can change a reduction in force development. It is best to perform high sets and low reps for recovery. The high rep sets should only include special exercise for individual muscles. While his recommendation was with weights at 70 percent to 90 percent, I have found my conclusion with 40 percent to 60 percent and the results were the same. If one watches a ball bounce with every preceding bounce, the rebound has less height. Why? It's due to the loss of kinetic energy.

The human body works in a similar fashion with the expenditure of kinetic energy in the soft tissue and muscle fatigue. Repetitions range for explosive strength or explosive power. Starting strength is inherited due to the amount or ratio of fast and slow twitch muscle fiber in the muscle. The same holds true for absolute strength where one lifts his maximum weight with no time limit. After years of following the guidelines set forth by A.S. Prilepin, A.D. Ermakov, N.S. Atanasov and many other sports experts from the former Soviet Union along with my own experience over 50 years, here are my suggestions for planning sets, reps per workout at a predetermined intensity zone for any athlete after a period of three years of general preparation.

If bar speed is reduced, the set must be stopped because of a power reduction. Pay close attention to the minimal and maximal total reps and amount of lifts per workout. For most, the optimal number of lifts is more beneficial.

Percent	Reps	Lifts
40%	4-8	36
50%	3-6	36
60%	3-6	30
70%	3-6	18
80%	2-4	15
90%	1-2	4-10

If you are greatly above or below the optimal number, the training affects are diminished. These are the recommendations of Louie Simmons, the author.

40% no less than 24 and no more than 48
50% no less than 24 and no more than 48
60% no less than 20 and no more than 40
70% no less than 12 and no more than 24
80% no less than 10 and no more than 20
90% no less than 4 and no more than 10

How to Change Volume at the Same Intensity Zone

Your three maxes for a front squat, safety squat bar, and of course, a regular squat bar max. Here is how:

500-Pound Max
Front Squat

Week	Percent	Weight	Reps	Lift	Volume
1	50%	250 lb.	12x2	24	6,000 lb.
2	55%	275 lb.	12x2	24	6,600 lb.
3	60%	300 lb.	10x2	20	6,000 lb.
Bar Speed is 0.8 m/s avg.					

600-Pound Max
Safety Squat Bar

Week	Percent	Weight	Reps	Lift	Volume
1	50%	300 lb.	12x2	24	7,200 lb.
2	55%	330 lb.	12x2	24	7,920 lb.
3	60%	360 lb.	10x2	20	7,200 lb.
Bar Speed is 0.8 m/s avg.					

700-Pound Max
Regular Squat Bar

Week	Percent	Weight	Reps	Lift	Volume
1	50%	350 lb.	12x2	24	8,400 lb.
2	55%	385 lb.	12x2	24	9,240 lb.
3	60%	420 lb.	10x2	20	8,400 lb.
Bar Speed is 0.8 m/s avg.					

Pay close attention to these graphs for continued progress in classical barbell lifts including the following: Olympic weightlifting lifts, powerlifting lifts, special squats, Goodmornings, pulls and pressing exercises. However, combining mathematics, physics, and biomechanics your true potential can be reached.

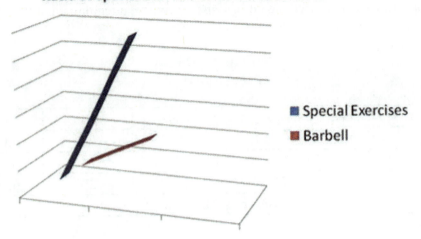

Ratio of Special Exercise to Barbell Exercises

Figure 3: As you can see by the chart in Figure 3, the ratio between barbell and classical lifts is 20 percent barbell exercises and 80 percent special exercises. This is proven by the research done at Westside Barbell by Joe Lasko on powerlifts and Olympic weightlifting as well as track and field. Because athletes are built differently biomechanically it can be dangerous to perform high repetition barbell lifts, as the weakest component of the human can become fatigued and sustain injuries. It is much safer to do special exercises directed to a particular muscle group that may be lacking.

Circa Max

Max Weight	Bar Weight	Weight Percent	Band Tension	Band Percent
800 lb.	500 lb.	62%	375 lb.	47%
850 lb.	550 lb.	61%	375 lb.	44%
900 lb.	600 lb.	66%	375 lb.	42%
950 lb.	650 lb.	68%	375 lb.	39%
1000 lb.	600 lb.	60%	440 lb.	44%
1050 lb.	650 lb.	62%	440 lb.	42%
1100 lb.	700 lb.	64%	440 lb.	40%
1150 lb.	750 lb.	65%	440 lb.	38%

Delayed Transformation Connecting Circa-Max Phase

The results at the contest are, of course, of greatest importance. It requires two proven methods of periodization. First, delayed transformation is a period of reducing the amount of volume and reducing the intensity zone somewhat to induce the highest level of sporting skill at contest time.

This knowledge was brought about through track and field and Olympic weightlifting from the former Soviet Union. For the squat training, it starts at 35 days out from contest date. Roughly 50 percent sets are done for the optimal amount of sets and lifts. The same is true for 28 days out of your contest.

Now it is interrupted at 21 days, but for Westside, it is a new or all-time record on a box squat. See the circa-max chart above and (circa-max meaning near max). A circa-max phase is performed with weights in the range of 90 percent to 97 percent if a one rep max. The number of lifts at those percentages are four minimal, seven optimal and 10 maximal. Westside uses the optimal method, utilizing seven lifts on the circa max day.

An 800-pound squatter after a warm up performs the following:

330 pounds bar weight x 2 reps + 375 pounds band tension

370 pounds bar weight x 2 reps + 375 pounds band tension

420 pounds bar weight x 1 rep + 375 pounds band tension

470 pounds bar weight x 1 rep + 375 pounds band tension

P.R. 510 pounds bar weight x 1 rep + 375 pounds band tension

If an athlete can perform this weight, he will break a new squat record and if the box height is correct (parallel and good form). During the second week of circa-max, the lifter will work up to approximately 370 pounds for a single.

This concludes the circa-max phase. It represents 21 days out and 14 days out. Now more recovery time is needed. Seven days out large men (275 pounds and up) will not squat, but instead do only special exercises. Two hundred forty-two pound men and lighter can squat light. For example, 330 pounds x 2 x 2 with no band tension or, if you prefer, 140 pounds of band tension.

As you see to assure all three lifts are at their max on contest day, Westside divides the delayed transformation phase in two parts: part one with extreme stimulus at 21 days out then part two back to the delayed transformation through 14 days out. Refer to chart 3.1 for an explanation of our combination method training by using bands on and bar weight.

This chart is the combined efforts of 75 men who have officially squatted 800 pounds up to 1,205 pounds. Look carefully at the bar weight percentage and the band tension percentage.

As a lifter progresses from 800 pounds to 950 pounds, the bar percentage goes from 62 percent up to 68 percent, causing the band tension to go from 47 percent to 39 percent. This means the bar percent goes up six percent while the band tension goes down eight percent.

As well let it be noted that at 1,000 pounds to 1,150 pounds, the bar percent goes up five percent while the band tension goes down six percent. I am asked about scientific studies; no one has such a study as Westside with world class strength athletes. This is like many of our conclusions. It a total work of more than twenty years of experiments more can be read about the **Delayed Transformation Phase pg. 30** in *Science and Practice of Strength Training* (Zatsiorsky **Circa Max Method 1995**; Verkhoshansky 2009 *Supertraining*).

CHAPTER 6 – GENERAL PHYSICAL PREPAREDNESS

CHAPTER 6 – GENERAL PHYSICAL PREPAREDNESS

General Physical Preparedness

A pyramid mathematically is only as tall as its base.

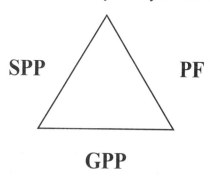

SPP = Special Physical Preparedness
PF = Physical Fitness
GPP = General Physical Preparedness

General physical preparedness is imperative to reach the top. An individual must recover from workout to workout. As the training becomes harder and more intense, better recovery methods must be employed. This can include flexibility, mobility, speed and endurance work. Sometimes perfecting form, receiving a massage, employing water therapy or electro stimulation, and using all rehabilitation procedures needs to be implemented. An individual should keep a record of his or her pulse and blood pressure to determine trainability at all times. If you don't have a plan, you plan to fail.

Speaking of the level of preparedness, general physical preparedness (GPP) must be a priority in training. But how?

The best GPP training I have found for both the upper body and lower body is sled work. Kettlebells are great for increasing GPP, but how much is too much and how much is not enough? When you do a lot, how do you taper the volume and how high should the intensity be? There are four training periods in the cycle:

1. Accumulation. A lifter must include as much work in his cycle as possible. High volume in training is effective. An intensity zone must be planned by the lifter or coach that is manageable, meaning loads that can be repeated fairly easy and that can be performed for some predetermined time. All muscle groups must be trained. Work on increasing bar speed for the powerlifter, and concentrate on technical weakness and, of course, raising GPP.
2. Intensification. Now, eliminate some exercises and concentrate on the main task.

    Example #1: Reduce belt squatting and raise the amount of box squatting per week and per month.

    Example #2: Cut back on slow deadlifts such as rack pulls and concentrate more on speed pulls. Eliminate some type of sled pulls by trips or weight.

Example #3: Do only the lat exercise that works best for you in volume and number of reps, concentrating more on full-range pulling.

3. Transformation. Now it's time to evaluate the two previous periodizations. The powerlifts, box squat, and deadlift are selected along with three or four special exercises that work best for you. Doing the wrong exercises will not work. Be sure in your selection that they will make you stronger on contest day. This prevents overtraining. While doing the heaviest training, or commonly circa-max phase, proper restoration methods play an important role during the last phase of training. Also, check your nutrition plan. It is important to pay attention to nutrition throughout the year, but during the transformation phase, it is very important.

4. Delayed transformation. This is a tapering-down phase that should last 14 to 21 days from a contest of high importance. The total volume and intensity zone are lowered considerably the previous training periods. You must be fully recovered on competition day. This is a guideline that Westside follows and so far has produced 11 2,500-pound totals and five 2,600-pound totals. By using the conjugate system, everything falls together. You are more muscular, faster and better conditioned and, most importantly, stronger. More information can be found in Thomas Kurz's *Science of Sports Training* (2001) and V.M. Zatsiorsky's *Science and Practice of Strength Training* (2006).

It is common to see Westside athletes pulling a light sled with one or two 45-pound plates for up to ¾ of a mile or using weight vests up to 100 pounds for a mile. Westsiders also walk with ankle weights from 10 pounds to 40 pounds for ½ mile or walk for a ½ mile with a Zercher harness with up to 135 pounds for ¼ mile at a time. A combination of any of the above can be implemented. Westside uses a non-motorized treadmill known as the tread sled. With this device, we attach bands around the waist or ankles. Vest and ankle weights also can be used.

GPP can be enhanced with bounding and jumping exercises. Long jump, triple long jump and box jumping should be done on a regular basis, adding ankle weights, weight vests, dumbbells or a combination of all three. Jumping while standing on foam also can be performed. Sitting on a lower box then jumping onto a predetermined box works well for standing long jumps as well. Remember, jumping is the most basic plyometrics (plyo) drill. Many of our powerlifters came from football backgrounds anywhere from high school to college. Jim Wendler comes to mind. Jim played at Arizona as a fullback. He was one of the most explosive lifters I have ever seen. He went on to squat a grand, and it was just as explosive. I surmise it was part genetics and a larger part GPP from his sports background.

The Soviets had a general plan for all athletes for the first three years known as the rule of three. This should occur in the early stages of training prior to specialization training for a particular sport. It is intended to develop jumping, coordination, endurance, flexibility and general strength abilities. If a youth is pushed into specialization, barriers can occur. The most common is the so called speed barrier. This means one learns to move at a certain speed but no faster. CNS automatically moves at a certain speed, developing frequency standards. Doing more of the same work does not help, but, in fact, compounds the problem. The answer is to use new stimulants to bring about new results in a way to make the lifter forget his physical and mental barriers.

Hypertrophy training is important. At Westside on all training days we, of course, try to increase muscle mass. After the classical lifts, we work on one or more muscle groups because we know strength increases when the CNS is stimulated and improved. Coordination is developed when muscular development is improved, providing the exercises are correct for the chosen sport.

It is common sense to train two to four smaller exercises after the barbell is retired for the day. On dynamic or ME day, the hamstrings, lower and upper back must be worked heavily and directly. The abs, calf and connective tissue must be strengthened through a wide range of repetitions up to 100 reps and higher for soft tissue development, which is important for storing the kinetic energy.

Performing 200 leg curls a day with 10-pound to 20-pound ankle weights is common at Westside. Also, doing 100 reps for a set or two with light dumbbells on the incline, decline, seated or flat bench on lower body day.

On dynamic day, it is common to do reverse hypers or glute/ham raises or both. For these two special exercises, a volume of 600 reps per month should be performed   that's 20 reps per day, a doable amount. As far as reverse hypers, 40 to 60 reps with heavy weight twice a week works best. That's 240 heavy reverse hypers a week and a total for reverse hyper work at 50 percent of the dynamic day and max effort day. Reverse Hypers ™ volume is about four times the speed squat volume.

Lat work is such a high volume; it's hard to estimate. Executed four days a week, it's more than 300 reps per week, repeated week after week.

Abdominal work is also completed using a very high volume. When using Kettlebells for overall body strength, the repetitions are astronomical. Sled work for upper and lower body, even for strength or strength endurance, can take up to two hours of training per week including restoration.

As can be noted, the above mentioned work can be implemented after the speed or ME workout. As an alternative to ME work, the Westside system allows one to alter the work from multi-joint training to isolating a muscle group as much as possible.

A hypertrophy workout for the lower back can be harder to recover from than from squatting and deadlifting because of such high volume: 80 percent special and 20 percent classical lifts.

All work is directed to one area. A good example is Reverse Hypers ™ done in a super-set fashion, which causes massive stimulation in the spinal erector and lumbar region.

Glute/ham raises completed as a super set along with ankle weighted leg curls in sets of 50 reps for curls and three to five reps for the glute ham raise will induce a massive amount of blood in the area.

This increases the number of myofibrils per muscle fiber and filamental area density by doing the cell size. The side benefit is increased size and strength of the soft tissue, including connective tissue, contributing to the ability to control and use a higher amount of kinetic energy. This is how imperative small workouts are because they can increase strength, especially explosive strength.

For the weight lifter or the powerlifter GPP should blend closely to special physical preparedness (SPP). Goodmonings in different styles to help a deadlifter who rounds over, hence bent over Goodmonings. A sumo puller or Olympic lifter could use the arched back style and, of course, a wide variety of pulls for the Olympic lifter or power. Sled pulling in slow motion sprinting. Cross country skiing or back packing are excellent non-stressful methods of GPP as well. Even short ballgames from soccer and football to tennis and table tennis for hand-eye coordination support GPP. Don't overdo it to where recovery is not happening. Just like training, GPP must be optimal to your level of physical preparedness. Always use a wave-style period action plan just like a weight program. My good friend Mark has his views on Kettlebells through his vast experience.

The Box Squat of Kettlebell Swings
By Mark Reifkind

Pavel Tsatsouline dubbed it the "Rif" swing (after my nickname). My wife Tracy, who uses it extensively in her swing classes, calls it "hike, swing, park" as this describes the mechanics best. I like to call them power swings as, just like in the box squat, more power is generated with its use compared to a squat or a swing that relies on the stretch reflex.

But whatever you call it, this version of the basic two-handed Kettlebell (KB) swings is a winner. I came up with it originally while teaching certification course as a corrective drill for a student who, while capable of reloading his hips after the first swing, did not do so. He would do the first rep correctly, then fall into 'mini' swings, never sitting back again and re loading his hips.

So I made him do just single rep swings; parking the bell on the floor and holding the hinge position, then hiking it back behind him strongly, then standing up as powerfully as he could. You pause in the bottom position between reps for at least one full second, in an arched back hinge position to ensure you've stopped most of the stretch reflex.

It worked very well for correcting the student's form, but, more importantly, I realized that this version of the simple KB swing was a seriously powerful one, and worthy of using as a special exercise in its own right.

The concept is the same as in the box squat—take the stretch reflex out of the movement so that all the force has to be generated by sheer muscle contraction each rep. Pavel estimates that it requires 35 percent more energy for each rep. More work in less time is a great way to increase intensity without increasing the mass of the KB.

With this drill you can also really concentrate on putting everything into each and every rep. It also works very well with a jump stretch band attached. This really requires huge starting strength, increasing the rate of force development, accommodating resistance AND creating a serious eccentric overload.

It also works as an excellent way to check your form as you have time in the bottom of each rep to arch the back. Retract the shoulders back into the socket and flex the lats and get ready to explode the next rep! One should never feel the lower back ache in the bottom hold position; the tension should be in the glutes, hips and upper thighs. It's a good check on one's correct hinge position.

This is an exercise that is good if one's back is tired or a bit touchy as you don't have to reverse the eccentric forces in the bottom of the swing and that is easier on the lower back.

Although it can be done strongly for up to ten rep sets without too much power loss, I recommend three to five rep sets. You can certainly limit the rest periods like you do in speed squat training off the box with these low rep sets to keep tension levels high. But it's not necessary either and one can use two to three minute rest periods to maximize force production on each rep and set making it more like a maximum effort exercise.

Medium weights work well for higher levels of RFD but the exercise also allows for heavy bells to be used as well. It can also be done with one arm swings, snatches and KB cleans for excellent effect and a very different training stimulus. Double bells also can be a good variation and are tough in their own unique way.

A most important thing is to NOT let the mid spine collapse as one hikes the bell(s) back. You must keep this area locked in and only use the lats to move the weight. Your bodyweight should be close to heels and you should shift back a bit prior to the start of each rep connecting the two centers of gravity involved (yours and the Kettlebell) into a combined center of mass. This will not only make the movement stronger, but safer.

I usually alternate this version of the two hand swing every other week with its ballistic brother. The first time I tried this it immediately brought to mind the box squat and all its unique attributes. I knew the KB version would be just as productive in its own way.

Swing Hard!

Mark Reifkind

MSFG

Mark Reifkind, Master SFG, has been training, competing and coaching since his gymnastics days in 1972. He has trained as a gymnast, endurance athlete, bodybuilder, powerlifting and KB athlete. He was the Head Coach for Team USA Women (IPF) in 1995 and coached Cathleen Kelii to her three top five IPF World finishes in the 56 kg class.

Reifkind is also the author of *Mastering the Hardstyle Kettlebell Swing* (2008) and *Lats, the Super Muscles* (2010), both available through his website http://Giryastrength.com.

More Workouts:

1. Lower back work with abs between lower back sets.

2. For the grip, arms, upper back and delts, implement Kettlebell cleans and snatches for 60 seconds of work and 30 seconds of rest between sets.

The workout must be dense, meaning to the actual work done in a time period not counting best. For example, perform heavy barbell rows for sets of six to 10 reps with Kettlebell work. An individual can't always super set when doing heavy isolated exercises because it depends on his level of preparedness.

Box Jumping

Jumping is a compilation of motor abilities. Timing, coordination and concentration play a large role. How strong an individual is depends on how much explosive strength and strength endurance he possesses. There has been a vast amount of literature on jumping and bounding plyometrics: lightened methods where some percent of the athlete's body weight is removed to perform a movement faster. Of course, if bodyweight is reduced, an individual should move faster. If there is a method that could make it possible to run and jump better, would you use it? Of course! It is called contrast method training.

My personal thought on jumping is to use mostly resistance jumping for sports although this falls into the General Preparatory Phase. The game performance requires one to not only jump in one direction, but in all directions. This is sport specific. The position coach should be aware of the sport's tasks that are required for his or her designated position. Jumping in the wrong direction is of no value regardless of how powerful the jump is. Consequently, knowing sports tasks are perfectly positioned, but with little explosive strength, is also of no or little value to a team's success.

Many of the greatest jumpers were Soviet weightlifters for two main reasons: they participated in a sport where the goal was speed strength and they were very strong. Dave Rigert, a Soviet weightlifter ran a reported 10.40, 100 meters at 198 pounds. He could outrun any Soviet sprinter for 40 meters. A 181-lifter Yuri Vardanyan could jump vertically 38 inches without specializing in jumping. Yuri also came close to a 12-foot standing long jump. Vasily Alekseyev, the 160 kg SHW Olympic lifting champ, ran an 11.50 100 - meter and had a 28-inch vertical (Yessis, 1987).

I mention his findings only because my powerlifters have exceeded these numbers except Yuri's long jump. They don't specialize in jumping either. However, how hard is it to jump with no weight after squatting 905 pounds at 181 bodyweight? It is a misconception that as a person becomes stronger, he gets slower, and it is true one must train correctly. One workout raises absolute strength; a second workout 72 hours later is used to develop acceleration, which is called the Dynamic Method. The method is also used to improve the rate of force development and explosive strength (Zatsiorsky, 1995).

Common sense is not that common, but if a lifter's max squat is 400 pounds, how fast can he move 200 pounds or 50 percent? It would make sense if he could squat 800 pounds, then, he could move 400 pounds as fast as the 400-pound squatter could move 200 pounds. They are both 50 percent of their max. Therefore, how fast could an 800-pound squatter move 200 pounds or the 50 percent of the 400-pound squatter when the 200 pounds is only 25 percent of his 800-pound squat? The answer is much faster. This is only understood by the well-trained, strong athletes who are few.

V.M. Zatsiorsky states that a shot putter who can max bench 440 will not throw farther if his bench goes to 551 pounds. M. Yessis, Ph.D., concurs with V.M Zatsiorsky (Yessis, 1987). Their assumption is that the 551 pounds would be slower than 440 pounds. This is not true if the Westside style wave periodization is implemented to develop a fast rate of force (F=MA), meaning the dynamic method.

Throwing sports are a speed-strength sport. With this being said, the coach or athlete should not measure a maximal lift to his throwing distance, but rather the bar speed with 75 percent to 85 percent weights for speed strength development.

At Westside a lifter with a max squat of 1,000 pounds is just as fast as a 700-pound, 800-pound, and 900-pound squat max of a different individual. How? The training is based on the percentages of a one rep max.

I have already discussed the training of a 400-pound max squat versus an 800-pound max squat while using 50 percent of their perspective max squat.

If five individuals train at, for example, 75 percent of their one rep max, regardless if it is 300 pounds or 700 pounds, after having the same background training for their event, the bar speed should be close to equal for all, at an equal percent of a one rep max tested by a Tendo unit.

Let's look at basic physics. Work is defined as the product of the net force and the displacement through which force is exerted or W=FD.

If the goal is to jump higher, it requires work. Then, how can one perform his task faster? He must become more powerful.

If two jumpers are to jump onto a predetermined box height, the more powerful one will do it faster. Why? Power is defined as work done divided by the time used to do the work. P=W/T

Remember the steeper the increase in strength, in time the greater the explosive strength (Tidow, 1990). It must make sense that raising speed is the key to success. The key is increasing speed strength; one must first pay attention to raising absolute strength speed work, or slow strength.

If increasing force is the goal, drop jumps can be performed, but the Soviets warned of their dangers. If jumping down from a surface for approximately one second, the body is moving at 9.8 meters a second (m/s). Falling for two seconds, a person is moving at 19.6 m/s, and after three seconds 29.4 m/s. Imagine the impact on the body after such a fall! It could end an athlete's sports career. This is acceleration in a downward direction.

It would make more sense to jump upward explosively and through deacceleration while landing softly on a box. One must build tremendous strength to jump higher and higher. The only way is to develop more power.

With Newton's first law, an object at rest tends to stay at rest, and an object in motion tends to stay in motion in a straight line at a constant speed.

When jumping, the equation F=MA comes to mind. It is developed by one of the most common methods of training, the Dynamic Effort method. This method indirectly builds maximal strength. Many books describe this method, but V.M. Zatsiorsky states in *The Science and Practice of Strength Training* (1995) that it is important to attain FMM in fast movements against intermediate resistance. Therefore, lifting a sub maximal weight with maximal speed improves the rate of force development and explosive strength. This is also the finding of Hill's equation of muscle contraction (Siff, 2003).

If I may, no one can lift a heavy weight slowly; Dr. Fred Hatfield said this, and he is absolutely right. A shot putter always works at gaining speed and raising strength, as much as possible in both cases, not trying to get a little faster or a little stronger, even though the shot weighs the same year in and year out. I will explain throughout this book how to build amazing strength and explosive power with proven Westside methods.

To increase jumping ability, an individual must increase his absolute strength and explosive strength. Because jumping is commonplace in sports, it is important to pursue a jumping program. Box jumping is the most superior method. First, overcome inhibitions to missing and hurting yourself. Although our aim is to increase the vertical jumping ability, it is in fact box jumping that will, in turn, increase the vertical jump. Just like weight training, three methods are used.

1. Max Effort Jumping

An individual must use a maximal amount of resistance in the following ways: weight vests, ankle weights, dumbbells, or Kettlebells. Any of these combinations will work. Achieve a record with some form of resistance on a predetermined box height, and vary box height each time jumping is done. Also, the resistance or combinations of resistance must be changed each time. Jump while standing on a foam pad or sitting on a box, duplicating a box squat and jump onto a second box. This is the conjugate system, which is a sequence system for jumping.

The max effort (ME) method is superior to all other methods for improving both intramuscular and intermuscular coordination. It is said that the central nervous system (CNS) and muscles adapt only to the loads placed upon them. The max effort method should be used to bring forth the greatest strength increments. If there is a CNS inhibition, it is reduced with this method because the most muscle units are activated (Zatsiorsky, 1995).

Many strength coaches say they know that the max effort method is the best system to become very strong, but they don't implement it. Instead, they may do weights in the 80 percent and 90 percent range. This is the method of heavy effort, not the max effort method. When doing weights in the 70 percent, 80 percent, or 90 percent ranges, only 70 percent, 80 percent, or 90 percent of an athlete's muscle potential is being used. That's simple math. A person's body only reacts to the demands placed upon it, which means it memorizes the changes in motor coordination to avoid high stress and high emotional states while training the max effort method. This should be reserved for competitions.

Of course, one must be highly motivated to lift heavy weight or to perform other extremely physical tasks such as hard jumping.

The coach must look for signs of overstressing, leading to overtraining and staleness. Signs of over working can be elevated blood pressure, general tiredness, anxiety, poor sleep patterns, and depression. This can be avoided by switching exercises regularly, as well as the volume and intensity zones. The conjugate system and periodization, especially wave cycling, do just this and prevent accommodation. By using several max effort lifts and a variety of jumping exercises, accommodation can be almost completely eliminated.

I feel the conjugate method is the best system for overcoming barriers and avoiding the biological Law of Accommodation. While doing maximal resistance jumping, strive for an all-time record.

2. Dynamic Method

Use sub-maximal resistance on the legs or body, or hand-held for multi-jumps. Calculate the box height by a percentage of one's all-time max-jump, lighter with resistance or zero resistance. Example: A box squat of 40 inches is 80 percent of an all-time box squat record of 50 inches. The calculation made by A.S. Prilepin's research in 1974 for the Olympic lifts works well for managing jumps per workout. After all, weight lifting is a speed-strength sport and speed strength is strength used in fast movement.

Many use the Olympic lifts for explosive power training. Thinking that by performing them, they will automatically make one more explosive. This is a fallacy. Any lift can be performed explosively. Squat, bench, and, yes, even a deadlift when using the correct percentage for explosive power.

Yuri Verkhoshansky is known as the father of plyometrics and explosive power training. Inside his book, there is, of course, lots of jumping, bounding, and depth jumps, but no Olympic lifts. If explosive power is the objective, then jumps must be performed. Why? The steeper the increase of strength in time, the greater is the explosive strength. This would require jumping with body weight. The only resistance would be air and gravity. Y.V. Verkhoshansky discovered the idea of plyometrics while watching a triple jumper perform in 1957. He noticed how after landing the preceding jump was so explosive. This was due to the muscle and tendon elasticity, which play a large role in increasing the motor output in sports and the explosive nature in track and field weightlifting and all ball sports.

A sprinter's foot contact is about one-tenth second and a high jumper is close to two-tenths second. So it is important that the amortization phase or shock-absorbing phase last no longer than .2 seconds. Wilson showed that the stretch reflex lasted two to four seconds (Siff, 2003). Studies by Louie Simmons have shown that when box squatting one can maintain the same concentric speed after sitting on a box for eight seconds. Slow eccentrics have never shown any benefits for strength. Studies have proved that there is greater muscle tension in eccentric actions, yet they have never proved that lowering a weight slowly contributes to raising a heavier weight. Some estimate you can lower 50 percent more than you can overcome concentrically. Who cares? I don't. I have to raise weight, not lower it.

3. Sub-Maximal Effort Method

The sub-maximal effort method is jumping with no or very light resistance to a predetermined box until near failure for a particular amount of sets. This method will stimulate muscle hypertrophy. Doing repetitions to near failure is superior in my experience. Total failure sets require a longer recovery time. By doing jump sets of a higher repetition range, a lifter not only increases muscle size, but also improves strength endurance. When muscle size increases so do ligaments, tendon size, and strength. Occasionally, it is important to do high reps to fatigue the muscles. The only way to bring forth more muscles is to exhaust the ones that contain the least amount of endurance. Fatigue first and then later performing reps will recruit more muscles that otherwise may not be used to perform the jump task. This method may involve 10 to 15 jumps per set.

Interval Method

Use the interval method for all jumping. This simply means choose a predetermined amount of jumps per set. The more demanding the jumps the longer rest between sets. I recommend never jumping down off boxes, but rather step down with any resistance. Drop jumps are used for stretch-shortening cycle. It is not advisable to add mass to a falling body due to the increased injury factors and knowing accommodation comes quickly. I prefer to sit on one box and jump onto a second box of a pre-set height. This system forces the jumper to overcome a dead stop in motion. Yet, the muscles of the lower body are yielding and overcoming while on the box. While one performs Isometric pulls or pushes while the bar is not moving, the muscles are. A similar action occurs while box squatting. More about this is in the box squat section (p.115).

Kneeling Jumps

Jumping with Barbells

To develop more absolute strength for jumping, kneeling jumps with barbells should be implemented into the jumping program. First, sit on the floor with feet out to the front and press Kettlebells or barbells overhead. This strengthens all muscles for jumping. Prepare for jumping by implementing five sets of eight reps. Second, while kneeling down with the glutes touching the heels, jump onto feet for five sets of 10 jumps. Place a light barbell across shoulders and jump onto feet. Do no less than five reps per set. Also, hold bar in front squat position and jump onto feet. Perform no less than five reps. Start adding weight until a goal is made. Example: 135 pounds while becoming proficient at this method start holding a bar on the thighs and jump into a power clean. Stay at five reps per set. Next, conduct a power snatch while kneeling. Finally, while holding a bar across thighs, execute a split-snatch, doing less than five reps per set. Vary two styles: one on knees while keeping body erect and the other with the glutes touching the heels while kneeling. Methods can be doubled by using Kettlebells. The more advanced can use ankle weights or thigh weights. Our record in the kneeling squat jump onto the knees is 265 pounds, which is by thrower John Harper.

Conjugate System of Jumping

The conjugate system is a constant rotation of the amount of work by intensity or volume, using explosive strength to maximal effort work and gaining hypertrophy in a weekly, monthly, yearly and multi-year system. The idea is to avoid accommodation, which is the decrease in response of a biological object to a continued stimulus (Zatsiorsky, 1995). In training, the stimulus is physical exercise. This tells us to make even small changes to avoid accommodation. Here are some sample programs for jumping to follow in any sequence you choose.

Jump on a 24" box with:

1. 5-lb ankle weights
2. 10-lb ankle weights
3. 15-lb ankle weights
4. 20-lb ankle weights
5. 20-lb weight vest
6. 40-lb weight vest
7. 60-lb weight vest
8. 4-kg kettle bells
9. 8-kg kettle bells
10. 12-kg kettle bells
11. 16-kg kettle bells
12. 24-kg kettle bells
13. 32-kg kettle bells

If a lifter employs a single type of resistance, he has 13 records. If he implements ankle weights and Kettlebells, he has 24 records. Adding ankle weights and a weight vest is 12 records. Kettlebells and a weight vest are 18 more records. Finally, a combination of all three resistances would equal 39 records. There is a possibility of 93 records off a 24-inch box. Just by adding a 30-inch box, the lifter has 186 possible records. Add a 36-inch box and a 42-inch box and there are 186 possible ways to break a record. If the same lifter jumps while standing on foam and jumps on all four boxes, he has 156 more. If he sits on a box and jumps onto all four boxes, there are 156 more variables to choose from. If the lifter sits on a box while standing on a foam pad or sits on a foam box while standing on a hard floor or foam, the possibilities are endless. Hopefully, we have eliminated accommodation, so I won't go into a 28-inch or a 32-inch, 34-inch, 38-inch, 40-inch or above 42-inch, but think about it and don't forget the goal, which is to increase the box jump with just bodyweight. This directly reflects on the vertical jump.

Posterior Development

Improve work capacity while eliminating deceleration, by maintaining sports conditioning and increasing posterior strength. The following special means are superior to all others.

Non-Motorized Treadmill

Walk, do not run, with heels striking first. This will resemble a partial glute/ham raise. Long strides are best to build the primary sprinting muscles. "Warning!" Do not duplicate your running form; the treadmill is to develop muscles. There are many variations to use. First, hook rubber bands around your ankles or thighs, keeping band attachment at the end of the treadmill. Walk as powerfully as possible. This builds the thighs, hips, abs and glutes. Interval training is the key.

For the 60-meter, walk for 10 seconds with 30-second rest intervals. The average sets are 15 to 25, depending on an individual's level of preparedness. For the most powerful athletes, add bands along with five- to 10-pound ankle weights. A strong band should always be attached to the waist through a weight belt. A weight vest can be employed as well. This combination builds general fitness power and dynamic endurance. For the 100-meter sprinter, do 15-second walks with 40-second rest intervals. The 400-meter sprinter power walks for 60 seconds with 90-second rest intervals, and the 800-meter sprinter power walks for two minutes and 30 seconds, trying two-minute, 30 second rest intervals. A 1,600-meter runner power walks five minutes with five-minute rest intervals. The number of work sets depends upon the athlete's level of preparedness. Rotate some type of resistance by including bands or weights. This eliminates the principle of diminishing returns, also known as accommodation, a general law of biology.

Power Sled Walking

For those in good climates, power walking can employ the use of a weight sled attached to a weight belt around the waist and long strides with heel touching first. This should feel much like walking on a non-motorized treadmill. Each step is a start; the sled should jerk with each step. Also, this almost eliminates deceleration. Sprinters competing up to 200 meters should powerwalk for 60 meters and use up to five 45-pound plates, keeping the power walking up to 25 seconds. Walks can be completed with 90 pounds, 135 pounds, 180 pounds and 225 pounds, keeping records of each weight. Also, ankle weights, a weight vest, or both can be added on some workouts. The heaviest sled walks should be done on Monday. For absolute strength, Wednesday drop 30 percent of weight and add trips for strength endurance. Use a lighter weight on Friday for a warm-up or restoration.

Pull a distance that last 60 seconds for the 400-meter. For the 800-meter, pull two minutes 45 seconds to start; a sled can be implemented. Use three plates to break records. Always walk on your heels with long strides. As the sled times are reduced so should your running times.

For the 1600-meter, powerwalk for five minutes and use at least three different weights as well as some ankle weights or weight vest at times. The number of work sets must be established by your fitness level. One third of all powerwalks should be on the balls of your feet.

Wheel Barrel Sprints

Interchange weights of the wheel barrel with at least three different weights. As with the other special means, keep records at each distance with each weight. You must sprint as fast as possible on the balls of your feet.

The wheel barrel works best for distances up to 800 meters. Pushing a wheel barrel for four minutes can be very taxing. Don't let an exercise drill take more out of you than you get out of the drill. A big advantage a wheel barrel can give to the athlete is balance and stability that comes from controlling the wheel barrel by holding the handles. This builds the entire body, especially the obliques that play a great role in all sports activities. Anytime you must grip an object tightly you bring forth many muscles, causing a greater and more intense workout.

Sumo Deadlift

A wide-stance deadlift while pushing your feet apart activates the hips and glutes to the fullest. High reps are in order. Note how many reps you can do in 30 seconds with 135 pounds or 225 pounds, or how many reps you can do in 60 seconds with 135 pounds or 225 pounds. You must always increase your one rep max. Use rack pulls with the plates three inches, six inches, and nine inches off the floor for max effort method. Again, when gripping a barbell, many more muscles are utilized. The deadlift sumo-style can be more effective than squatting. Always use a relaxed eccentric phase. This makes a relaxed, overcome by a dynamic, action very similar to sprinting.

Belt Squats

Westside uses two methods for belt squats. First, a belt squat to a soft box, i.e. foam on top of a hard box. Usa a fast, relaxed, eccentric phase while exploding concentrically for a predetermined time is used. Always go about 25 seconds longer than your 60-meter or 100-meter time and five seconds longer than your 200-meter and 800-meter. Exercise 10 seconds longer than your 1,600-meter time. Always count the reps and try to increase reps inside the pre-determined time period. Only add weight when you feel comfortable. For strength endurance, one rep per second for 60 seconds is recommended.

Belt Squat Walking

The belt squat walking method is to simply walk in the belt squat machine. Complete one minute up to five minutes and longer can be done, depending on your race time. Walk forward for glutes and backwards for quads. By pushing out to the sides, the hips are activated to the max. This is absolutely the fastest way to increase the entire legs and hips plus glutes.

Walking With Med Ball

Walking while holding a 20-pound to 100-pound medicine ball against the upper stomach using the arms will build the abs, but most importantly, will correct proper leg swing motion. No more knock knees, which causes numerous injuries that should never occur. By performing special exercises, large and small, sports performance will go up as injuries are eliminated.

Sled Work for Runners

Power Sled Walking

You can create a plan to prepare novice or highly qualified sprinters into long distance runners. A well-prepared program should be implemented to organize the connection between strength endurance, explosive power and restoration simultaneously to ensure the athlete constantly pushes closer to his or her ultimate goal.

Can one type of special training fulfill all of the combinations that link strength training and restorations? Yes. It is power walking with a weight sled while using a variety of resistance. Sled work can build the entire posterior chain, raise aerobic and anaerobic capacities while building explosive force, increasing strength endurance and working as a means of restoration. If a contest or meet is on the weekend, the heaviest sled pulling according to volume should be done on Monday. This provides an increase in an individual's top strength. On Wednesday a reduction in weight and additional trips provides a strength endurance workout. On Friday a lesser weight is utilized and a reduction of trips to the same amount as on Monday serves as restoration.

This style of training is cited in a fine book called *Adaption in Sports Training* by Atko Viru (1995). Constantly rotate a variety of sled pulls combined with box jumping with a different resistance on the legs, arms, or bodyweight vest, using the dynamic method for weight training with many combinations of accommodating resistance. This weight system employs sub-maximal weight with acceleration $F=MA$

The special physical training that provides raising maximum strength with weights, strength endurance with sled pulls and a fast rate of force development with bounding and jumping has been fulfilled. By changing training loads from high volume to moderate and small, with different training intensity zones the athlete will never suffer from accommodation. This simply means that if one uses the same training stimulus his response to training decreases. This is why workloads must fluctuate. Not only through weight training but jumping, sled pulling and even restoration, one must look at the ability of a muscle to gather the energy of elastic deformation through plyometric work. The best long distance runners use less energy to run more effectively during the eccentric and concentric phases.

While pulling a sled, change the surface. For example, pull through sand or water, or even a harder surface increases physical capacities for running. A non-motorized treadmill will greatly increase running speed with an assortment of body and limp resistance. Utilizing longer or shorter rest periods, and of course, one must increase the strength of the muscles that don't bear the burden of the runners work load, even using static work for the legs in the precise angles that the legs generate force. This can be done while belt squatting, or performing belt squats at a tempo of a rep per sec for 60 reps. Proceed to another set after a prescribed rest period. The rest cannot be too short that it interferes with coordination or not long enough to cause fatigue.

While the training is based on a yearly plan or multi-year plan, the Westside system can determine the athlete's state of preparedness every three weeks for endurance and a special strength. How? By checking his progress on box jumping. Coaches are responsible for maintaining the correct heart beats per minute (bpm). Of course, it differs in the type of training in which an athlete is specializing. Even a long distance runner must become stronger and may have to sprint to the finish line, and a short sprinter must recover during elimination runs. It is recommended to focus on many restoration methods, especially during all four periods of basic periodization. Most work by volume occurs early in the training. The phase referred to is accumulation where every type of work must be performed.

The jumping and sled work as well as resistance walking will be tapered somewhat during the second period of work known as intensification. The training goal is somewhat more sport specific. During longer rest periods, advanced athletes can maintain workloads higher than a novice. The third phase of training is the transformation phase. At this point, the athlete concentrates on his sport. Of course, non-directed work is reduced slowly, but not at the expense of the athlete's physical prowess. The fourth phase is called delayed transformation. Our work load in this phase looks like this for strength, and I suggest you follow a similar wave.

Delayed transformation for classical lifts.
Squat, bench, deadlift, snatch, clean-jerk.

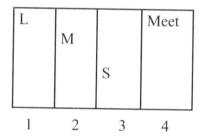

My experience with reducing your time is designed along this plan. It works well for any length of sprinting. *Supertraining* (Siff, 2004); *Science of Sports Training* (Kurz, 2001); *Complex Use of Training and Restorative Methods in the Preparation of Long-Distance Runners* (Praktike and Kultury, page 23, 1985); *A Strength Training Program for Long-Distance Runners* (Getmanets and Travin, 11:4-5, 1987); *Adapt the Method to the Athlete* (1987); *Powertraining for Sport* (Bompa, 1995); *Science and Practice of Strength Training* (Zatsiorsky, 1995); *Explosive Power and Jumping Ability for all Sports* (Starzynski and Sozanski, 1995); *Soviet Sports Review Volume 21 & 23*; (Yessis), and *Athletika* (Anormkivi, 12:14, 1987) are all important resources on this topic.

The Sled Workouts

Sled pulling is commonly used to warm-up, to raise one's aerobic capabilities, and to work our cardiovascular systems. Implement sled pulling with a strap hooked to a power belt and then walk forward and backwards for distances of 100 feet to one mile shortly pulling for maximal strength. Execute long pulls for restoration and general endurance. Pull with the straps backwards between the legs for the hamstrings, hip and knee extensions. Upper body sled pulling builds the muscles of the upper body. Walk with weight vests up to 150 pounds forward, backward and even sideways for ¼ of a mile to 1½ miles depends on the person. A warm-up for squatting or deadlifting or even benching would be ¼ to ½ mile. General conditioning and strength are done up to 1½ miles.

Mix workouts as needed. It can be one workout a day or two workouts, involving jumping and sled workouts. A common problem in sprinting is speed drops off at the end of the race. Why? Fatigue. Fatigue causes a loss of stride length and also an increase in flight time. It leads to an upward motion, not a forward motion. The force directed to the center of mass is changed to a less effected mechanical effort, which decreases muscle tension. While I am not a sprint expert, I recognize what does the work and how to maintain explosive strength endurance, which in turn, helps maintain maximum running speed, while fatigue hampers running skill. Many coaches add running at different distances at 90 percent to 95 percent of maximum or running up or down a hill at two to four degree changes. I feel coaches should encourage individual effort in power walking for a specified distance with the feedback coming from the athlete. Everyone has particular needs even when they were chosen for a particular sport because of their special attributes. There are many contrasting methods for increasing running speed.

1. The lighted method: This allows a certain amount of an athlete's body weight to be reduced with a special apparatus.
2. Other methods. Add weight on the thighs above the knee or attach bands to thighs above the knees. I have no trouble reducing an above-average runner, in one case a football lineman's time by at least .2 of a second in eight weeks without running the 40 yard dash once. Their only running was skill practice.

As far back as 1972, a sports scientist from GDA found the top sprinters for women had not a longer stride length, but a greater stride frequency over weaker sprinters. M. Lettsecter studied the work of coach H.D. Hill who trained most of GDR top women sprinters, and he found the very best women had the highest stride frequency. Although other coaches' techniques have worked well for their sprinters, a common denominator is a powerful group of muscles. A list of workouts below should be used to bring forth not only a more powerful stride, but perfecting running techniques by strengthening the running muscles of the calves, hamstrings, glutes, and hips, and of course, the quad along with the torso and upper back. Coach Hill referred to the top women as the "strong girls".

Sled Time Intervals

Always start with tension tight in regards to the strap. Straps must be attached at the waist of a lifting belt. Begin with a staggered start on preceding pulls, alternating the leading leg. For indoor sprinters, the length of a walk should be 10 to12 seconds per powerwalk. Rest intervals should be kept at a minimum. This depends on an athlete's level of preparedness. One must recover adequately to not have a decrease in force production. Remember the last step must be as powerful as the first step.

Let's look at the definition of power: $P=W/t$. Power is defined as work done divided by the time to do the work. If 100 meters is the work, the more powerful runner performs the work faster. The workout should not last longer than 45 minutes to ensure elevated blood testosterone levels. This workout can be done after a 30-minute break from a dynamic squat workout, incorporating weights ranging from 30 percent to 40 percent of a one rep max to 80 percent of a one rep max. The reps must be low-range —three to six reps— up to 70 percent and two to three reps at 80 percent. If the barbell exercises slow down at all, an individual is developing a lesser rate force. High sets, not reps, are in order along with short rest intervals of 60 to 90 seconds between sets. Speed deadlift pulls can be used after box squatting, using one to three reps with a pause between each rep. The combination of squatting and pulling can easily be done in 35 minutes. For example, 100-meter sprinters execute sled pulls ranging in length to 20 seconds per trip. The same guidelines should be followed for indoor sprinters. For 200-meter sprinters, the sled pulling time should increase to 20 seconds for top sprinters. However, the sled pulls must last longer than the sprinters best time. For 400-meter sprinters, the pull time is 50 seconds or longer, and the best time for an 800-meter runner's sled pull time is 2½ minutes or, of course, slightly longer than the athlete's best time.

Points of Importance

The heaviest sled pulls should be incorporated into the first workout after a race. Reduce the sled weight twice during training. This works as strength building, strength endurance, and restoration close to next race. To change intensity of pulls, implement thigh or ankle weights, a weight vest, or a combination of all three while changing surfaces from hard to soft or even sand. Look at different methods of styles to rotate, including upper body styles. Always change complex special exercise regularly.

For Longer Distance

Raise the heart rate to at least 150 beats per minute (bpm) with aerobic loading on a treadmill, motor or non-motorized. Then, start sled pulling for long distances. Monitor heart rate not to exceed 185 bpm. Also, avoid fatigue to the point of poor mechanics. The athlete must adapt to fatigue to increase endurance. For endurance training, 60 reps per minute can enhance endurance considerably. After 60 reps, let the heart rate return to 150 bpm and do additional sets of belt squatting or Kettlebell squatting. For 1500 meters pull continuously for six to eight minutes as long as power walking form is not disturbed or if extreme fatigue sets in. Don't neglect the technical aspects of running form. Likewise, power walking form must be carefully monitored as well as choosing and rotating the special methods.

Sled work can be divided into intervals of distance or time. It will be at the coaches' discretion to plan a general preparation period that leads to a special preparation stage to a competitive phase working toward a goal lasting eight to 10 weeks. Plan the training for the athlete. Top sprinters have 75 percent fast twitch to 25 percent slow twitch or endurance fibers; a sprinter must be trained with that in mind. For training middle distance runners or people who have close to equal fiber types (the average person has about 50 percent slow twitch and 50 percent fast twitch fibers in most of the muscles used for movement) use 75 percent explosive work and 25 percent general endurance training. This simply means that the training is an even mixture of fast twitch fiber work and close to an equal amount of endurance fiber work. To train a long distance runner, 80 percent of the training should be dominated by endurance work and 20 percent for speed development. Remember different runners have somewhat different mixtures of muscle fibers and may need a more sophisticated model to reach his or her potential. For more ideas, look at Legkoathleticheckie Metaniya 1:78-81, 1884 by A.P. Bondarchuk in *Soviet Sports Review*.

Sled Work for Football and Hockey

Football and hockey are more similar than people may think because they contain contact and lots of sprinting. Football has more contact while hockey has more sprinting. Rotate the sled work not only by reducing the weight on the sled as the week goes by, but also changing the weight on the ankles or adding a weight vest. My experience with Big Ten football players is that powerwalks of 60 yards work well. Hockey would be the same minus the amount of weight on the sled due to the different bodyweight of football players and hockey players. The coach must select the amount of sled work by selecting forwards, backwards, or side walking and the amount of each needed for a specific sport.

Jumping and sled pulling increase running speed and endurance by producing greater ground force while running. Neurologically speaking, an individual can only move so fast. Greater ground force increases running speed. Why? A study at Harvard University and explained in The Journal of Applied Physiology (2000) that it was not the minimum swing time, but a greater ground force that enables sprinters to increase top speed. This information can be found in Underground Secrets to Faster Running (Ross, 2005). These ideas fit my methodology in its entirety.

An individual must become stronger to run faster. Why? How? Why because the person must overcome gravity by using low reps to develop max force and speed. Through the dynamic method little muscle mass will be gained: $F=MA$. Remember the greater mass, the greater gravitational pull. The dynamic method, or using sub-maximal weight with maximum speed, will not produce a significant gain in muscle mass. Don't do high intensity training (HIT). HIT is merely bodybuilding in disguise. Larger men aren't always the stronger men, and HIT is really low intensity training. By definition it is high volume and low intensity.

When doing very high reps, the very last reps are totally responsible for success, which is the repetition method. This high rep system is fine for bodybuilding, but not for sprinters. I only point this out so someone does not make the mistake of thinking the only way to increase strength is to add muscle mass. The more mass the more gravitational pull.

There are three methods of training I have advised to be implemented: the dynamic method for speed strength, box jumps for explosive power, and power walking with a weight sled should replace roughly 30 percent of the running workout time for middle distance runners. With explosive weight training 32 percent of the running was replaced. A study published in 1999 by Leena Paavolainen titled *Explosive Strength Training* showed that Explosive Strength Training improves five km running time by improving running economy and muscle power (Ross, 2005). Our experiment came to the same conclusion. While it is optimal to increase force production, it can cause deterioration in running format. Be patient and timing will return. Running mechanics can be increased by developing strength in the weaker muscle groups. Power sled walking is the Tai-Chi of weight training. There are always top sprinters who have a particular yet effective style of running. The women under coach H.D. Hill of the former GDA dominated with a powerful shortened stride low seat, and Michael Johnson, the great 200- and 400-meter champion, used short, choppy steps and a backward leap. Both were quite successful.

I feel baseball players would benefit greatly from this style of training. Baseball is like powerlifting or weight lifting. An individual does nothing; then, he must be explosive at a given moment. A ball player rests, then must throw a fast ball, hit a home run, or run to first or steal second base. Just some words to think about.

Power Walking with Resistance

All kinds of resistance can be used for walking. Westside uses ankle weights, wrist weights, weight vest, Kettlebells, Indian clubs and wheel barrel, which are all common.

Ankle weights used could be five pounds per leg, which are worn around the gym or for a brisk walk. The top weight for each leg is 45 pounds and yes, this means 90 pounds for both legs. Besides building the legs and abs, they also remove traction from the knees, hips, and lower back. Hand weights, Kettlebells and Indian clubs can accompany any of the above. The hardest workout would be to pull a sled with a weight vest and ankle weights while carrying Kettlebells.

Wheelbarrow walking is great for hips, legs, and general conditioning. Again, the distance is calculated by how heavy or light the load is. Tread sled walking on a nonmotorized treadmill called the tread sled can be used with bands around the ankles or waist. Weight vests from 25 pounds to 150 pounds are implemented. Ankle weights of varying weights are added, and any combination of resistance can be and are used. High rep leg curls with ankle weights are performed on a regular basis. The hamstrings can be a troublesome area, and the high rep conditioning has proven to be a very effective method for avoiding hamstring pulls. Short walks and yes, there is even a mountain bike to ride at Westside.

It is common to see athletes who implement battling ropes and chains for all sports. It can build cardio as well as muscular endurance for athletes of any age or gender. It will build a better grip while conditioning the shoulder muscles, especially the rotators.

Indian Clubs

This system of conditioning was utilized by the greatest wrestlers in the world as far back as the 1700s, but it is still beneficial as ever today. Start with very light clubs—two pounds—and workout in weight when possible. Indian clubs are great for shoulders, wrists and hand grip.

Bike Riding

Bike riding is a simple, but most effective, method for training GPP. It is Non-impact even while adding ankle weights or a weight vest or both. GPP is a very important aspect of everyone's training. It is serious business, but can be made fun by alternating exercises throughout the year.

Do you lack GPP?

The question you need to ask is whether you or the athlete you are coaching can recover from a workout. If the answer is no, the athlete is over trained or detrained, or in other words, out of shape.

At Westside the system calls for one to establish a max lift and use a three-week pendulum wave to establish a high-volume moderate intensity workout. This workout would include 50 percent, 55 percent and 60 percent on the third week plus 25 percent band tension or chains at the top of the lift. A 20 percent to 80 percent ratio with barbell work being 20 percent, and 80 percent of the workout being special exercise. This means a 450-pound squatter's squat volume is 5,400 pounds. A special exercise volume is roughly 43,200 pounds. An 800-pound squatter's squat volume with the barbell is 9,600 pounds and the special exercises add up to 76,800 pounds. This represents a single squat workout. This accounts for all special exercises for the legs, back, hips, abs, and the like. Not to mention sled work, wheelbarrow and strongman yoke. As your squat volume is based on your top squats, it does not matter if you are male or female, drug-free or taking SPD's. This is simple mathematics. You should be able to recover. If not, you are out of shape.

It may take a period of time to adapt to this special exercise volume. A novice athlete should do one small workout on top of the regular four workouts a week—one for the upper body and one for the lower body. These are figured into the total exercise volume. Remember there are three methods for recovery. 1. Pharmaceutical, 2. Restoration, 3. Small workouts. I suggest using all three if at all possible. If you are in a sport at which I hope you excel, you must be a so called model athlete. If the rest of the team can perform the workouts, so should you. If not, it could be physical fatigue, mental fatigue or just plain laziness. Always analyze your training. How are your jumping ability, weight lifting and running times? Work on what you lack if you want to be a champion. Remember to increase endurance you must train through fatigue. And, of course, the only way to increase your work capacity is to train through tiredness or some muscular soreness.

Training of powerlifts

Powerlifts introduction

Lifting technique

When striving for proper technique, our intentions are to lift the most weight in contest situations. Proper technique isn't intended to produce a championship physique, but rather a world record performance.

Technique is a tool for a lifter to build the best leverages possible. With good form, a lifter can stress his strong points and eliminate weaknesses. To analyze and build technical skills, the lifts can be divided into smaller segments:

1. Setting up
2. Unracking the bar
3. Ascent
4. Reversing direction
5. Descent
6. Replacing the bar

For the deadlift, items 2 through 4 are unnecessary.

Squat

Most people think of the squat as a multi-joint movement. I see it as flexion of the spinal erectors and hip flexors with a slight extension of the knees. When watching a good squat technician, nothing moves but the hip joint. He bends only at the hips. His back doesn't move, and his knees don't go forward. Other muscles push gradually throughout the lift, just enough to accommodate the external force that is being applied.

The feet should point straight out and forward, forcing the hip muscles into play. It is hard to break parallel because the hip flexors and extensors are put into a very strong position for flexion. Turn the feet outward slightly if not flexible enough or if a thick waistline or thick upper thighs are possessed. If someone walks with his feet turned outward, he has weak hamstrings.

When squatting, think about pushing the feet out, not down. This ensures that the hip muscles are working correctly. Push the knees out the entire time, starting from the moment the bar is unracked. This should be felt in the hips. Next, start pushing the glutes to the rear as though searching for a chair that is too far behind to sit down. Arch the lower back hard, keep the chest and head up, and lean as much as possible, ensuring the bar stays as the center of gravity. To ensure correct bar placement, raise the chest and pull the shoulder blades together, which creates better leverages by placing the bar as far back as possible. However, if the bar is carried too low, it causes a lifter to bend forward while destroying leverages. The hands should be wide enough to avoid bicep tendonitis, and pull the elbows forward again by contracting the shoulder blades together.

Which stance should be implemented? Everyone should box squat with a wide stance. This builds important hip muscles. More than 30 years ago, the great Jim Williams said to train as wide as possible and for a lifter to pull his stance in so that he can break parallel in a meet. While descending, the lifter should always squat back, not down. When pushing the glutes back, the knees won't go forward. By forcing the knees apart, the lifter is significantly increasing his leverages. After breaking parallel, he must first push against the bar. After all, the bar is what we are trying to raise. Pushing with the feet first is a mistake. This causes the lifter to bend over and most likely the lift, too.

Breathing is important. First, take air into the abdominal section and chest. Hold the air until passing the hardest part of the lift, and exhale when nearing the top position.

Technical Tips:

George Crawford taught me a valuable lesson for squatting. How you take the weight out of the rack is how you will squat it. Meaning if you take it out wrong in the beginning, you will fail. If you take it out correctly like we suggest, your odds will go up dramatically. George was one of the greatest squatters in the 1970's and a former World Champion.

The original Culver City, California, Westside Barbell Club taught box squatting. Pat Casey was the first 800-pound squatter and he trained on the box squat. The top two squatters currently are 1,267 pounds and 1,265 pounds, both box squatters. Bill West and George Frenn wrote articles for *Muscle*

Power Builder and without knowing it, they were my only training partners. They led the foundation for my training from 1970 through 1982. I will forever be indebted to both of them.

Bench Press

For training the bench press, use three to four different grips. Alternate from the index finger just touching the smooth part of the bar to a grip that is two inches wider than the grip where the little finger is in contact with the power ring. A lifter should take the bar out of the rack by himself, pulling the shoulder blades together and gripping the bar as tightly as possible. Next, pull the bar out of the rack as if you were doing a pullover. This activates the lats properly. Pull the bar straight above the point on the chest where you want to lower it. Lower the bar quickly in a straight line.

Press the bar straight up and slightly toward the feet. This is the shortest distance to press and eliminates shoulder rotation. Rotating the bar back over the face can cause rotator and pec injuries.

Never intentionally push the bar over the face. Hold your breath for up to five reps because holding the breath defines heavy training. Take as much air in as possible before lifting the bar from the rack, and lower the bar as fast as possible. Stop the bar as quickly as possible and reverse to the concentric phase as fast as possible. When training, raise the head as the bar is lowered and keep the eyes on the bar throughout the movement. Use either a thumbless grip or a thumb grip.

Technique during competition should be the same as in training with one exception. Use a maximum wide grip with a thumb grip and use a lift-off. As the bar is lowered, raise the head first and then the shoulders as if you were doing a sit-up. This enables you to bring the bar lower on the body without rolling it out of the hands.

Once the press command is given, slam the head and shoulders back down on the bench for stability. Keep the feet out in front of the knees and press down on the heels to ensure that the butt stays on the bench. A longer torso is more advantageous for bench pressing. Therefore, avoid shortening the torso by arching the lower back. In addition, an extreme arch can cause an injury.

Technical Tips:

Larry Pacifico, the greatest powerlifter of the 1970's gave me two pieces of advice. 1. Start light. It's not what you start with, but rather what you finish with. Smart technical advice. 2. Work your triceps. Larry estimated that the triceps were 75 percent of your bench success and Westside agrees.

Bill Seno helped raise my raw bench from 340 pounds to 515 pounds. Bill was a pioneer in the weight game, winning six best chest awards while competing in body building up to the Mr. A. Bill also held early world records in the bench like other body builders of the 1970's. He told me that at my body structure of 5'6" and 170 pounds, I should use a very wide grip for sets of six reps. When doing extreme wide grip benching, I had to increase my tricep work and when rotating to a close grip I had to reduce the amount of tricep extensions, as to not over train them. Both men were living legends and will remain living legends in my mind.

Deadlift

When using the conventional style, center the bar over the joint of the big toe or a little closer. A good distance to start pulling is usually when the bar is three to four inches from the shins. If a lifter is too close to the bar, it may swing forward when pulling upward, which causes difficulties at the lockout. The shoulder joints must be behind or over the bar when starting the pull. Pull slightly toward the center of the body to keep the bar close to the legs and always push the feet out to the sides. For most lifters, pointing the feet out provides a stronger start because of the greater leg drive. This position enables a strong finish because of increased hip rotation. The back position can vary because of the wide variety of body structures. Most lifters arch their lower back while rounding the upper back at the same time. However, don't round the back too much because it will be difficult to lockout. A lifter may get stuck in the knees. It is an advantage as long as the bar stays close to the shins. The head position can vary anywhere from looking straight ahead to looking downward about six feet in front of the body.

The most common grip is the standard reverse grip. Some lifters use an overhand hook grip with the arms hanging in a straight line. As a lifter gets bigger, he may have to use a wider grip. When using sumo style in deadlifting, the width of the stance depends on flexibility. The longer a person's legs are, the wider his stance. Keep the hips as high as possible, provided the back is in the proper position, pulling himself slightly lower than his optimal starting position. Push the hips against the bar and rebound out of the bottom.

For breathing, keep the air out of the lungs—use abdominal breathing. This keeps the torso short for better leverages and builds stability.

Technical Tips:

Vince Anello was one of the greatest deadlifters of all time lifting 821 pounds at 198 bodyweight. Enough said.

I asked Vince what made his deadlift go up? He replied "Everything makes my deadlift go up." At first I didn't understand his answer. It seemed vague. I knew it made no sense to hold back secrets with his deadlift prowess. Then I got it. He was using a rotating exercise system just like Westside—just like the Soviet's Dynamo Club—it was the conjugate system. Vince knew by doing the same lift over and over the law of accommodation would interfere with further progress. Vince was smart. That's why he was a world champion and the king of the deadlift.

Tom Eiseman was a phenomenal deadlifter for many years with a 782–pound deadlift at a bodyweight of 181 pounds. Tom was doing his deadlift workout at Westside and doing both sumo and conventional style. After the workout I asked Tom several questions about his deadlift. He was ideally built to deadlift, so I asked where he feeds the effort physically when pulling a heavy pull. His reply was, "Everywhere, not one particular body part." I realized this was his success—no weakness any part of his body. This made perfect sense, even profound. No wonder he was so proficient. Tom used every ounce of his body to do the lift. This man and many more gave me incentive to perform the powerlifts: Ed Coan, Mike Bridges, Ernie Franz and the list can go on forever. My point is, don't be afraid to ask. The answer could change you from just a lifter to a super star like some that I have just mentioned.

Reasons for Failure

Squat

To start the squat you must push the glutes out to the rear. If this is impossible to do, you have weak glutes. You must do the following special exercises to ensure the glute and hip muscles are the strongest, which will cause them to contract first.

Exercises:
1. Belt Squat Walking
2. Reverse Hypers
3. Pulling Weight Sleds
4. Goodmonings
5. Glute/Ham Raise
6. Inverse Curls.

The chest must be held high. If not, your upper back and spinal erectors must be strong to maintain posture. To increase their strength do the following exercises.

Exercises:
1. Back Raises
2. Arched-Back Goodmonings
3. Static Hold Reverse Hypers
4. Shrugs
5. Upright Rows
6. Power Cleans.

The key to squatting is to push knees to the side from the time you take the bar out of the rack until you reach the bottom of the squat.

Exercises to force the knees outwards (Abduction Exercises)
1. Squat with bands around the knees
2. Powerwalk sideways
3. Band around the knees while seated
4. Abduction machine

To raise concentrically, you must push against the bar first so not to do a Goodmorning exercise. Also, it could be weak abs as mentioned above, or tight psoas. We know that the abs are responsible for the first 30 degrees to 45 degrees and then the hips take over for the last 45 degrees. When you increase IAP you reduce the load on the intervertebral discs.

Bench

The bar must be lowered and raised in an almost straight line. If this does not happen, you must increase your tricep work. The bar will travel toward the strongest muscle group. This means if the bar goes over the face, your delts are stronger than your triceps. This can cause injuries to the rotators or the pecs. How to correct this mistake is to increase tricep strength.

Exercises to strengthen the triceps
1. Dumbbell extensions
2. Bar extensions
3. Push downs
4. Close grip bench
5. Steep incline close grip
6. Pullover and press

Flatting out on bench.

Your upper back must be extremely strong to prevent this from happening.

Exercises to prevent flatting out on bench:
1. Shrugs
2. Dumbbell rows
3. Barbell rows
4. Pullovers
5. Lat pull-downs
6. Chin-ups
7. Chest supported rows
8. Bench shrugs

The bar rests opposite of the upper back, making it the foundation to lower the bar in the correct position. The lats are responsible for lowering the bar, not the arms. If the barbell plates shake, you are not using your lats correctly. Just because you have large lats does not mean you are using them correctly.

Bench Tips

You must not bend your wrist backward when benching. This causes the bar not to be centered directly over the forearm where it belongs. Stretch the bar to involve your triceps fully. Do high-rep dumbbell presses, with light weight for 100 reps per set as well as light band push-downs for 100 reps per set to build thicker connective tissues to prevent injuries.

Reasons Deadlifts Fail

If you fail at the start, you lack abdominal strength and knee flection from the hamstrings.

Exercises to correct this problem:

1. Leg curls (all types)
2. Inverse curls
3. Glute/ham raises
4. Ankle weights
5. Sled pulls with strap between the legs
6. Band in front of bar.

A major reason for failure at start is not being able to pull feet apart. This is usually due to weak abductors. If you fail at the knees, your lower back is weak. This is where the bar is the furthest away from the hip joint.

Exercises to correct this:
1. Bar raises
2. Pull throughs
3. Sled pulls
4. Belt squat walking.

Most commonly used for the traps:
1. Upright rows
2. Shrugs
3. Power cleans.

Your grip must be trained with:
1. A variety of exercises
2. Fat bar
3. Finger exercises
4. Static hold on chin up bar.

Remember to be a good technician you must be perfectly coordinated, perfecting the motor portion of your sport movement is known as kinematic chain, when multi joint movements are performed. You can learn more about the kinematic chain by reading *Supertraining* (Siff, 2003).

Box Squat

I first encountered box squatting when reading a magazine called *Muscle Power Builder*. The original Westside Barbell Club of Culver City, California, ran powerlifting articles for all types of routines and exercises. A box squat workout caught my eye.

My squat was 410 pounds at 14-years-old. When I was 19 my squat was the same at 410 pounds. I followed the program they advised, and after doing box squats for three months, I tried a regular squat and made 450 pounds. I could not believe it. Three more months later, I made 500 pounds, which was a dream come true. There was no supportive gear then. I progressed and in 1973, I made a 630-pound squat at 181 pounds, plus my deadlift rose from 525 pounds to 670 pounds at the same weight class of 181 pounds. I was sold. I could also power clean 320 pounds with a bar that did not resolve. I was sold all the way. I believe the box squat system came from European weightlifters and their track and field athletes.

Athletes have been doing some form of box squatting for years. Eskil Thompson of Sweden was visiting a Polish weight-lifting facility and saw box squatting demonstrated in a weightlifting manual dated back to the 1950s.

As I said before, Westside Barbell Club in Culver City, California, was using them in the final 1960s. They had the first 800-pound squat along with Pat Casey and many other world record holders at that time. I started doing them in 1968, and my regular squat jumped after no progress for five years. Donny Thompson has a 1,260-pound World record, and Vlad Alhazov has made a 1,250-pound record. Both were introduced to Westside Barbell, Columbus, Ohio. There is one way and only one way to perform a box squat.

Box Squat Technique

There is no difference between a close-stance and a wide-stance box squat. First, push the glutes to the rear and push out to the sides with the knees and feet. Keep the entire back fully arched, including raising the chin to help contract the traps. Don't think going down, but rather back until you are sitting fully on the box. The back remains tightly arched, the abs, of course, are pushed out into the belt, especially the obliques. Now, relax the hips for a second; then, reflex the hips. Push the feet out to the sides not down, I repeat, not down. Drive the traps into the bar. First, after all, the lifter is trying to raise the bar so he must push into the bar first or his glutes will rise prematurely and cause him to do a Goodmorning with the bar. This alone will help eliminates injuries.

Coaches don't squat, so they are unlikely to be able to teach someone to squat perfectly. There should be no excess stress on the spine and the abdominals properly prevent this. A box squat done properly is a leg curl; most don't recognize that fact. By sitting far back on a box, the shin is past straight up and down. The initial action is to pull the body upward with a leg curl action. There is no pressure on the patella tendon at all. A box squat is much easier on the knees than any other form of squatting. Always use a wide stance because this builds the largest muscle that not only enables squatting, but running and jumping. I hate the term "athlete squat." There is no squatting on any ball fields. If an individual is going to squat, do the most effective one, which is the box squat.

Box Squat Bonuses

When box squatting, a lifter always squats to the same depth. This does not happen when doing regular squats because as the weights get heavier, the athlete invariably squats higher and higher. Box squatting is a tool for flexibility. Start with a moderate stance and sit on a 17-inch box with light weight. After a rep or two, remove a one-inch mat and continue to do two reps. Remove the next one-inch mat and on and on until reaching a new depth record. Let's say you are using a 12-inch box, don't fall on to it, but lower the body onto it. Now, widen the stance and repeat procedure and add flexibility in the hip. This has a second bonus because it builds strength and flexibility at the same time. It is best to build strength through a great range of motion.

Boxes provide two methods of absolute and Explosive Strength Training: Relaxed overcome dynamically and static overcome by dynamic actions. These are two of the most important phases of strength training much like isometrics. The bar may not move, but the muscles are lengthening and shortening.

The Law of Conservation of Momentum allows us to compare a collision of two pool balls. As ball one hits the second ball, ball one stops and the second ball moves forward at the same speed of ball one. This is a perfect collision as their velocity is equal. When the athlete comes in contact with the box on the eccentric phase, part of the athlete's kinetic energy is transferred into the box. Resting momentarily makes it more difficult to overcome inertia. Remember an object at rest tends to stay at rest. This is Newton's first Law. Newton's Laws of Motion are constantly in force when lifting weights or running and jumping.

This sitting on a box is not a perfect collision. By using bands to pull the athlete eccentrically faster, the kinetic can be raised somewhat. This is a virtual force, a force that is present, but not recognized. It is more effective to increase velocity than mass.

Through Westside's studies with a Tendo unit, testing 20 men who each have more than an 850-pound squat, I found some men could sit on a box up to five seconds and sometimes eight seconds without losing acceleration on the concentric phase.

This happens with box squatting as well. By sitting on a box, there is a collision whereby some of the body's kinetic energy is transferred into the box. This makes box squatting harder than regular squatting, allowing an athlete to train with less and squat more. A lifter can sit on a box for a long time—up to 8 seconds—and explode up just as quickly.

This is great for long snap counts. The box squat can break the eccentric and concentric phase. When running, this happens. Sprinting has a relaxed explosive step. It's similar to separating off of the box. The regular squat demands the athlete use the same energy source to lower into a squat eccentrically, hold in the bottom statically and return concentrically. While box squatting, the body is lowered eccentrically when sitting on the box, and it uses greater energy to recover concentrically. While sitting on the box, the muscles are lengthening and shortening, not totally static.

With regular squatting, a static position holding all muscles at the same time reduces the stretch reflex. A trained box squatter is always more explosive than a regular squatter when regular squatting. Box squatting also builds a stronger pull, snatch, clean or deadlift because an athlete is moving from relaxed to overcoming a load through a dynamic action.

Box Squatting Summary

Box squatting allows a lifter to squat lower and wider on a box than when executing a regular squat. Box squatting also builds more explosive power than regular squats, and box squatters hold the stretch reflex longer than regular squatters. There are forms of PNF stretching, which are more therapeutic for knees.

As of 9/9/09, Westside had 15 lifters squatting over 1,000 pounds and four over 1,100 pounds. At that time, we had a 148-pound woman who squats 590 pounds, a woman who weighs 165 pounds and squats 740 pounds, and a 181 pounder who squats 770 pounds. Westside also has a teen who squatted 1,005 pounds at a 252 bodyweight. Sitting on a box and jumping onto a second higher box is a tremendous method for building explosive jumping.

If an individual's goal is to be a top strength coach, he must learn how to box squat, either on a hard box or on a foam box. The foam box causes the legs and lower back to work harder by forcing the smaller muscles to contract harder, producing a higher degree of stability.

Weight Training for Throwers

A shot putter must always strive to become stronger and faster. How does this happen? By the development of special strength and special means such as pulls, squats, inverse curls, reverse hypers, back raises as well as many forms of jumps. Special strengths are trained at a specified velocity. Explosive strength or power is trained at fast velocity through jumps and light barbell lifts at roughly 30 percent of a one rep max.

Speed strength is trained at intermediate velocity by doing weight in the 75 percent to 85 percent range with barbell exercises. Or you can train with a combination of weight at 50 percent, 55 percent and 60 percent of a one rep max, plus using 25 percent band tension at the top or lockout. This adds up to 75 percent, 80 percent and 85 percent in a three week pendulum wave that returns to 50 percent on the fourth week. The new wave should be done with a different bar or adjusting the amount of accommodating resistance a small amount.

Explosive Power

No matter how strong an athlete is, he must become more explosive simultaneously. Dr. Vladimir M. Zatsiorsky states in *Science and Practice of Strength Training* (1995) that if a shot putter throws 50 feet with a 440-pound bench, he may not increase his shot if his bench goes up 55 pounds. The barbell, of course, will slow down as it becomes heavier. If an athlete uses the methods described in this book, the shot will most certainly go up as well. Dr. Zatsiorsky assumes that an individual's maximal strength increase was due to the max effort method and by performing special exercises. If the athlete uses a second proven method to complement the increase of max strength—the dynamic method—his throw will indeed increase. With the dynamic effort the speed strength is developed at intermediate velocity 0.8 to 0.9 m/s.

The main theory of training by Yuri Verkhoshansky incorporates using very heavy weights 90 percent and above of a one rep max and jumping for explosive strength at a very fast velocity. Westside has discovered that all three velocities must be used in the same weekly, monthly and multi-year program.

Let's look at the difference between force and velocity. Motion velocity decreases as external resistance increases. Hence, maximum force (F_{mm}) is attained when velocity is small and, of course, according to Hill's equation, maximum velocity (V_{mm}) occurs when external resistance is close to 0.

Now that we have looked at both ends of the force velocity curve, what about the middle? Here is where intermediate velocity can contribute to success by developing acceleration while maintaining force by using accommodation resistance. This develops mechanical power (P_{mm}). Now you know why you must use all three types of velocity to produce a complete program.

Let's start with developing explosive power. It calls for movements in fast velocity. What is explosive power? It is the ability to rapidly increase force (Tedow, 1990). The steeper the increase of strength in the time, the greater the explosive strength. This means jumping, bounding and depth jumps. Throwers can increase absolute strength while increasing explosive strength through testing a shot putters release time. This time is close to 14 m/s and a javelin release time is about 30 m/s (Zatsiorsky, 1995).

Let's examine several types of jumps to rotate during your training in and out of the competitive season:
- Press bar over head while sitting or kneeling
- Kneeling jumps off knees to feet
- Kneeling power clean or snatch (remain on knees)
- Kneeling power clean on to feet
- Kneeling power snatch on to feet
- Kneeling split clean on to feet
- Kneeling split snatch on to feet
- Box jump with bodyweight
- Box jump with ankle weights
- Box jump with Bulgarian bag
- Box jump with Kettlebells
- Seated box jumps
- Jump with bar on back 30 percent to 40 percent of one rep max
- Consecutive jump with bar on back 30 percent to 40 percent of one rep max
- Depth jumps
- Kettlebell jumps

- Single leg jumps
- Consecutive jumps over hurdles (both legs)
- Consecutive jumps over hurdles (single leg)
- Vertical jumps with 50 percent to 60 percent
- Stadium jumps up and down
- Uphill bounding for a set distance
- Downhill bounding for a set distance
- Explosive isometric from a lower pin to a higher pin – use three or four starting points.

I have listed several types of jump. The coach or athlete should consider the most productive jumps and use them close to events—80 weighted jumps per week for most. The highest level thrower can work up to 120 jumps a week. Do 40 or 60 jumps and a speed strength or max effort workout. This causes a contrast effect. An athlete must at all costs increase all forms of jumping, from weight resistance to just bodyweight. The higher one can jump, the faster one can produce power and run faster.

Maximal Effort Method

The maximal effort method of training is far superior for improving intermuscular and intramuscular coordination. Because the central nervous system adapts only to the load placed on it, when lifting maximal weights, the max effort will deliver the greatest increases in strength and gains. The max effort method activates the maximal number of muscle units with optimal discharge frequency. When special exercises are used with a barbell, they must resemble the sports movement or closely resemble the classical lifts at least in part such as Goodmonings, second pull or a special squat.

We only use the max effort with singles in multi-joint exercises, squats, presses and pulls of all types. The reasoning behind this is to keep the barbell volume to a maximum, but with hope of attaining 100 percent plus in tension, meaning a new personal reload. Two or three rep max will build strength endurance. We have all coasted on the first and second rep. This is a waste for absolute strength and too much volume. The speed strength day of 72 hours has high volume and moderate intensity. One must go from high volume and moderate intensity to low volume and the highest rate of intensity possible to avoid accommodation. Little hypertrophy is developed on max effort day with the barbell. Special exercises play a great role in building hypertrophy. Remember 80 percent of the total volume is special exercises, only 20 percent with a barbell. Yes, you are maxing out, but with as little emotion as possible. This is a training max, not a contest max. When using an exercise at 90 percent or above for three weeks you will detrain. The Westside system rotates a different max effort exercise each world record to avoid this problem, which is commonly known as accommodation or the principle of diminishing returns. The Westside system is totally conjugated, meaning exercises small and large are rotated constantly and switched from high to low. Without becoming stronger, more explosive and being able to accelerate an object either a shot or a barbell, a max effort workout can be many things. I will discuss many barbell only, max effort workouts.

Listed below are several max effort workouts:

1. Safety squat bar on four separate boxes
2. Bow bar squat on four separate boxes
3. 14" cambered bar squats on four separate boxes

4. Front squat on four separate boxes
5. Zercher squat on rack pin or off the floor
6. Regular squat bar squats on four separate boxes
7. Regular squat, wide stance max
8. Regular squat, close stance max
9. Regular squat with squat briefs
10. Regular squat without squat briefs
11. Concentric squat off four pin heights
12. Belt squat with all bars.

Keep records on each style of squatting. Use just bar weight or band tension (at least three tensions). Example: 70 pounds, 140 pounds, and 250 pounds at top of lift; chain weight on the bar from 80 pounds to 300 pounds and combinations of both. I have just listed more than 50 combinations to max out on.

Deadlift Max Effort Workouts

Use sumo or conventional style:
1. Pull off the floor with 220 pounds or 250 pounds of band tension
2. Two-inch box deadlift with just bar weight
3. Four-inch box deadlift with just bar weight
4. 220 pounds or 280 pounds of band tension rack pulls (plates 3-inch, 6-inch, 9-inch off the floor)
5. Ultra-wide sumo pulls (any combination of bar weight or band tension)

Power Snatch and Power Clean

1. Snatch or clean with bar weight only
2. Snatch or clean with some amount of band tension
3. Snatch or clean with some amount of chain weight
4. Snatch with close grip
5. Clean with wide grip
6. Clean and snatch with close sumo stance
7. Clean and snatch off knees

Push-Jerk from Front and Behind Neck

1. Push-jerk just bar weight
2. Push-jerk with band tension
3. Push-jerk with chain weight

One-Arm Push Press Over Head

1. Push press with dumbbells
2. Push press with Kettlebells

   This also builds the obliques at the same time.

Goodmornings

While this is not to be used as a max effort, use three to five reps at 70 percent to 80 percent of your clean.

1. Wide or close stance
2. Come up on toes with feet parallel
3. Straddle leg Goodmonings
4. Use bands or chains for acceleration

Bench Press

1. Wide grip max
2. Close grip max
3. Max close or wide grip with 85 pounds, 125 pounds, and 200 pounds at the top
4. Max close or wide with chain weight 80 pounds to 200 pounds
5. Board presses to two, three, or four board
6. Rack press with weight above your best bench 10 percent to 20 percent more at lockout
7. Floor press
8. Standing press
9. Seated press
10. Incline press at three angles
11. Dumbbell press flat, incline, and standing

Specific Shot Exercises

Power clean at a tempo as gliding across the circle with feet. Pull, touch legs, touch chest, and push overhead. Think touch, touch, and release. With the barbell on shoulders, spin across the circle. Do this in both directions. With the barbell on your chest, step across the circle and press the bar upward with and without a release. To throw a great distance, one must possess powerful shoulders and upper body. Many believe that only lifts, cleans, and snatches play a great role in the success of all types of throwers. However, the important part is the development of the upper back and traps. This simply means one must select exercises that will increase those precise muscles as well as the arm muscles.

Here is a list of some exercises for all styles of throwers:

1. Deadlift
2. Clean
3. Snatch
4. Upright rows
5. Pull-downs
6. Low pull rows
7. Chest supported rows
8. Press behind head (close and wide grip)
9. Hammer curls
10. Bent over rows
11. Shrugs with a barbell
12. Shrugs with dumbbells
13. Goodmonings
14. Goodmonings with one leg in front
15. Kettlebell cleans
16. Kettlebell snatches
17. Pull-downs behind the head
18. Standing one arm press.

General Exercises

1. Push-ups
2. Pull-ups
3. Throwing and catch shot
4. Pull over on bench
5. Rotation work with shot
6. Rotation work with Kettlebells
7. Rotation work with bar on back
8. Laying leg raises

9. Hanging leg raises
10. Pull over and throw medicine ball
11. Throw Kettlebells between legs forward
12. Throw Kettlebells between legs backwards
13. From full squats, throw Kettlebells five to16kg with both hands while standing up
14. Throw shot three or four kg from behind head with both arms.

All Kettlebell throws are done 10 to 15 times.

Mobility

Straddle squats, jump over bar sideways doing splits exercise standing, laying and hanging. Continue to do shot exercises all year round, but not in absolute competitive style. Throw shot over a preset bar height, throw from the front of the circle.

One cannot just lift or just throw, but they must interact to fully develop strength as strength can also help develop form. This is what the conjugate system does. The Westside system is totally connected through the conjugate system by rotating velocities, volumes, intensities and exercises large and small as well as the restoration method.

Dynamic Method

It has been said that one cannot attain Fmm in fast movements against intermediate resistance. This leads to the conclusion that the dynamic method is not used for gaining maximal strength, but rather for improving the rate of force development and explosive strength. Although in conclusion, you must use all three methods; explosive, max effort and a combination on the third. You do this by adding accommodating resistance for the development of speed strength, and by using intermediate velocity to develop maximal mechanical power.

Maximum Mechanical Power

Maximum mechanical power is developed at an intermediate range of force and velocity. The bar speed should range from 0.7 to 0.9 m/s, which is close to 1/3 of maximal velocity (Power = Force x Velocity). This means that force and velocity are optimal when using rubber band tension at 25 percent of a one rep max at lockout of any lift and a bar weight of 50 percent to 60 percent or a one rep max.

It looks like this:

Band Weight	25%	25%	25%
Bar Weight	50%	55%	60%
Lockout	75%	80%	85%
Bottom	60%	65%	70%

The bottom equation is due to the band shrinkage. However, you must remember that due to over speed eccentrics, the eccentric muscle actions are much greater in the muscle and tendon elasticity for a greater stretch shortening cycle. This dynamic work occurs 72 hours later from a max effort training day and it is high volume and moderate intensity. Many think that as you become stronger you slow down. This does not have to be the case if you are following the Westside periodization in a three-week pendulum wave. A shot putter always tries to become stronger and faster. It can certainly happen by following the chart below. As you can see, a 400-pound max squatter trains at 50 percent to 60 percent or 200 to 240 pounds. A 600-pound squatter trains at 50 percent to 60 percent or 300 to 360 pounds, and an 800-pound max squatter trains at 50 percent to 60 percent or 400 to 480 pounds or twice the weight and twice the total volume of a 400-pound squatter with the same number of sets and reps and the same amount of lifts.

Squatting:

400-pound max train at 50 percent to 60 percent or 200 pounds to 240 pounds

600-pound max train at 50 percent to 60 percent or 300 pounds to 360 pounds

800-pound max train at 50 percent to 60 percent or 400 pounds to 480 pounds

However, the key is an 800-pound squatter moves his training weights at the same velocity of a 400-pound squatter. This means as his absolute strength increases, the bar velocity never slows down with the high volume training weights, which are between 0.7 to 0.9 m/s. An example is Westside lifter, David Hoff, who at 15-years-old weighing 200 pounds squatted 400-pound max and at 19-years-old squatted an official 1,005 pounds with a body weight of 252 pounds. This is true for all lifts (bench, deadlift, power clean or snatch) by following the path of A.S. Prilepin for sets and reps as well as total lifts per workout and the work of his countrymen, A.D. Ermakov and N.S. Atanasov whose data from 1975 can be found in *Managing the Training of Weightlifters* N.P. Laputin, V.G. Oleshko 1982 copyright and Bud Charniga, Jr.

Let's examine A.S. Prilepin's work in his 1974 research. No lifts under 70 percent or a one rep max are calculated. Why? They are too light to build speed or strength speed, but rather build explosive strength when jumping up on boxes, bounding, or depth jumps are utilized. The rep limit at 70 percent is six reps; the limit at 80 percent is four lifts; and the limit at 90 percent is two reps. The reason? The barbell speed will decelerate on further reps having a negative effect on strength gains. One should always follow the optimal number of lifts.

Optimal Lifts

Percentage	Lifts
70	18
80	15
90	7

There is also the fine work by A.D. Ermakov and N.S. Atanasov and their 1975 data. Fifty percent of the total lifts are at 75 percent to 85 percent of a one rep max.

The Westside system uses accommodating resistance, meaning rubber bands or chains correctly used on a barbell, 25 percent at lockout. Let's add the barbell weight and band tension for squatting.

Three-Week Wave

Bar weight	50%	55%	60%
Band tension	25%	25%	25%
Total – at top	75%	80%	85%

This is based on the work mentioned above. As you can see by the workout data, as Hoff's physical strength grew for maximal strength, total volume grew. Everything remained the same: sets, lifts, reps and most importantly, bar speed. This is important for a weightlifter or powerlifter, but much more important for a thrower, where the weight apparatus stays the same.

Here is the multi-year periodization plan Hoff used to raise his squat from 400 pounds at 15-years-old to 1,005 pounds at 19-years-old. At age 24, he squatted 1,200 pounds with a body weight of 279 pounds and squatted a world record 1,190 pounds weighing 275 pounds, allowing him to make the greatest male coefficient total of all times with 2,960-pound total at a body weight of 275 pounds.

400-Pound Max Squat

Percentage	Weight	Reps	Lifts	Band Tension	Volume
50%	200 lb.	12x2	24	25%	4,800 lb.
55%	220 lb.	12x2	24	25%	5,280 lb.
60%	240 lb.	10x2	20	25%	4,800 lb.
Bar Speed is 0.8 m/s avg.					

450-Pound Max Squat

Percentage	Weight	Reps	Lifts	Band Tension	Volume
50%	225 lb.	12x2	24	25%	5,400 lb.
55%	250 lb.	12x2	24	25%	6,000 lb.
60%	270 lb.	10x2	20	25%	5,400 lb.
Bar Speed is 0.8 m/s avg.					

500-Pound Max Squat

Percentage	Weight	Reps	Lifts	Band Tension	Volume
50%	250 lb.	12x2	24	25%	6,000 lb.
55%	275 lb.	12x2	24	25%	6,600 lb.
60%	300 lb.	10x2	20	25%	6,000 lb.
Bar Speed is 0.8 m/s avg.					

550-Pound Max Squat

Percentage	Weight	Reps	Lifts	Band Tension	Volume
50%	275 lb.	12x2	24	25%	6,600 lb.
55%	300 lb.	12x2	24	25%	7,200 lb.
60%	330 lb.	10x2	20	25%	6,600 lb.
Bar Speed is 0.8 m/s avg.					

600-Pound Max Squat

Percentage	Weight	Reps	Lifts	Band Tension	Volume
50%	300 lb.	12x2	24	25%	7,200 lb.
55%	330 lb.	12x2	24	25%	7,920 lb.
60%	360 lb.	10x2	20	25%	7,200 lb.
Bar Speed is 0.8 m/s avg.					

650-Pound Max Squat

Percentage	Weight	Reps	Lifts	Band Tension	Volume
50%	325 lb.	12x2	24	25%	7,800 lb.
55%	355 lb.	12x2	24	25%	8,520 lb.
60%	390 lb.	10x2	20	25%	7,800 lb.
Bar Speed is 0.8 m/s avg.					

700-Pound Max Squat

Percentage	Weight	Reps	Lifts	Band Tension	Volume
50%	350 lb.	12x2	24	25%	8,400 lb.
55%	385 lb.	12x2	24	25%	9,240 lb.
60%	420 lb.	10x2	20	25%	8,400 lb.
Bar Speed is 0.8 m/s avg.					

750-Pound Max Squat

Percentage	Weight	Reps	Lifts	Band Tension	Volume
50%	375 lb.	12x2	24	25%	9,000 lb.
55%	425 lb.	12x2	24	25%	10,200 lb.
60%	450 lb.	10x2	20	25%	9,000 lb.
Bar Speed is 0.8 m/s avg.					

800-Pound Max Squat

Percentage	Weight	Reps	Lifts	Band Tension	Volume
50%	400 lb.	12x2	24	25%	9,600 lb.
55%	440 lb.	12x2	24	25%	10,560 lb.
60%	480 lb.	10x2	20	25%	9,600 lb.
Bar Speed is 0.8 m/s avg.					

850-Pound Max Squat

Percentage	Weight	Reps	Lifts	Band Tension	Volume
50%	425 lb.	12x2	24	25%	10,200 lb.
55%	470 lb.	12x2	24	25%	11,280 lb.
60%	510 lb.	10x2	20	25%	10,200 lb.
Bar Speed is 0.8 m/s avg.					

900-Pound Max Squat

Percentage	Weight	Reps	Lifts	Band Tension	Volume
50%	450 lb.	12x2	24	25%	10,800 lb.
55%	495 lb.	12x2	24	25%	11,880 lb.
60%	540 lb.	10x2	20	25%	10,800 lb.
Bar Speed is 0.8 m/s avg.					

950-Pound Max Squat

Percentage	Weight	Reps	Lifts	Band Tension	Volume
50%	475 lb.	12x2	24	25%	11,400 lb.
55%	520 lb.	12x2	24	25%	12,480 lb.
60%	570 lb.	10x2	20	25%	11,400 lb.
Bar Speed is 0.8 m/s avg.					

1000-Pound Max Squat

Percentage	Weight	Reps	Lifts	Band Tension	Volume
50%	500 lb.	12x2	24	25%	12,000 lb.
55%	550 lb.	12x2	24	25%	13,200 lb.
60%	600 lb.	10x2	20	25%	12,000 lb.
Bar Speed is 0.8 m/s avg.					

Let's look at a separate plan for different special squat maxes.

500-Pound Max
Front Squat

Week	Percent	Weight	Reps	Lift	Volume
1	50%	250 lb.	12x2	24	6,000 lb.
2	55%	275 lb.	12x2	24	6,600 lb.
3	60%	300 lb.	10x2	20	6,000 lb.
Bar Speed is 0.8 m/s avg.					

600-Pound Max
Front Squat

Week	Percent	Weight	Reps	Lift	Volume
1	50%	300 lb.	12x2	24	7,200 lb.
2	55%	330 lb.	12x2	24	7,920 lb.
3	60%	360 lb.	10x2	20	7,200 lb.
Bar Speed is 0.8 m/s avg.					

700-Pound Max
Front Squat

Week	Percent	Weight	Reps	Lift	Volume
1	50%	350 lb.	12x2	24	8,400 lb.
2	55%	385 lb.	12x2	24	9,240 lb.
3	60%	420 lb.	10x2	20	8,400 lb.
Bar Speed is 0.8 m/s avg.					

You must calculate each bar weight max, as well as any special bar exercise for squats, benches, and pulls. Below are examples of some light benching for explosive strength. This can be done in ballistic style, meaning very fast, eccentric phase not touching the chest then followed by a fast concentric phase.

Few Examples of a Three-Week Wave

300 Max Percentages

Percentage	Weight	Reps	Lifts	Band Tension
50%	150 lb.	9x3	27	85 lb.
50%	150 lb.	9x3	27	85 lb.
50%	150 lb.	9x3	27	85 lb.

300 Max Percentages

Percentage	Weight	Reps	Lifts	Chain Weight
50%	150 lb.	9x3	27	80 lb.
50%	150 lb.	9x3	27	80 lb.
50%	150 lb.	9x3	27	80 lb.

300-Pound Max Floor Press

Percent	Weight (pounds)	Reps	Lift	Chain Weight and Band Tension
50%	150 lb.	9x3	27	80 lb., 25 lb. at top
50%	150 lb.	9x3	27	80 lb., 25 lb. at top
50%	150 lb.	9x3	27	80 lb., 25 lb. at top

300-Pound Max Bench (Lightened Method)

Percent	Weight (pounds)	Reps	Lift	Unload weight
80%	240 lb.	9x3	27	60 lb.
80%	240 lb.	9x3	27	60 lb.
80%	240 lb.	9x3	27	60 lb.

Here are two examples of a power snatch and power clean wave with only bar weight.

300-Pound Power Snatch

Percent	Weight (pounds)	Reps	Lift	Unload weight
70%	210 lb.	7x2	14	2,940 lb.
75%	225 lb.	7x2	14	3,150 lb.
80%	240 lb.	7x2	14	3,360 lb.

400-Pound Power Clean

Percent	Weight (pounds)	Reps	Lift	Unload weight
70%	280 lb.	7x2	14	3,920 lb.
75%	300 lb.	7x2	14	4,200 lb.
80%	320 lb.	7x2	14	4,480 lb.

When using some amount of band on bar, you must reduce some bar weight and add band tension to the top of the lift. Bands reduce deceleration and help the athlete in the squat under phase.

As you can see, there are three distinct velocities that must be trained to excel at sports of all types: Fast velocity for explosive power by utilizing jumping, bounding and depth jumps, intermediate velocity for speed strength and acceleration, plus slow velocity for strength speed.

All three velocities must be improved at all costs. Train the velocity that you lack. One must pick the special exercises that work for you. It does no good to be strong in the wrong exercises. Anatoliy P. Bondarchuk references this scenario as the *Transfer of Exercises*. Speaking of Bondarchuk, his thoughts on a reflex action must be accompanied by some amount of inhibition. Westside tries to override the process of inhibition by jumping up on boxes without fear and increasing weight on the bar that causes one to overcome the thought of failure.

When one makes a small jump, the brain has to process very little. But large jumps or extreme circumstances, such as a new personal record, will call great excitability of the CNN. With a three-week pendulum wave, the fourth week percent is adjusted back to the 50 percent range and inhabitation is restored to a more favorable level of activation. This is why you must use new max effort exercises each week. When doing an exercise for three weeks in a row, you will go into a detraining mode. The Westside system rotates a max effort lift each week and breaks any max effort exercise over 90 percent of the time by our statistician Joe Lasko.

Lastly, learn your sport. When reading or watching a DVD, pay attention and become your best coach. We all need a coach at some time, but you need good training partners all the time. They should be able to help you, and you them. By watching others, you will discover your own shortcoming in all physics of training.

CHAPTER 7 – OLYMPIC LIFTING

CHAPTER 7 – OLYMPIC LIFTING

While Olympic lifts are not for the improvement of sports, it is a great sport. Many think Olympic lifts will develop explosiveness, but they will not. There is no such thing as "explosive lifts" actually. The reference is to how a lift is performed. A squat, a bench, and even a deadlift can be done for explosive strength if performed in high velocity. The Soviet Union's experts on strength and speed development used bounding, jumping, and depth jumps to develop explosive strength. Y.V. Verkhoshansky is the so called "Father of Plyometrics," and his early thoughts on the matter came when watching a triple jumper in 1957. He was fascinated on how energetic the rebound was from the previous landing. Keep in mind, jumping rope is a basic plyometric execution.

Other experts like Tadeusz Starzynski and Henryk Sozanski, Ph.D., in their book *Explosive Power and Jumping Ability for all Sports* (1995) show no classical lifts, only individuals jumping off their knees with a barbell on their chest, on the back, or straight leg power clean or snatch. Dr. Verkhoshansky in one of his many publications titled *Fundamentals of Special Strength Training in Sport* (1997) talks about explosive strength development. The subject he discusses incorporates jumping, bounding and depth jumps. In Andrzej Lasocki's *World of Atlas of Exercises for Track and Field*, (2001) he shows drills for all sports for explosiveness, <u>except</u> the Olympic lifts, just to illustrate my point. If you are going to do Olympic lifts, you must learn how to improve them.

Volume and Intensity Zones

First, let's look at what volume and intensity zones an individual should use most often. The lifts need to be performed in the three-week pendulum wave. The percentages followed are 75 percent to 85 percent for the full clean power, clean full snatch, and power snatch. A.D. Ermakov and N.S. Atanasov's 1975 data shows that 50 percent of the lifts should be performed at 75 percent to 85 percent. I rely on a three-week pendulum wave.

Week 1   75 percent

Week 2   80 percent

Week 3   85 percent

Week 4   75 percent

Week 5   80 percent

Week 6   85 percent

Then, wave back to 75 percent and continue the waves.

This information can be found in *Managing the Training of the Weightlifters* (1982) by Nikolai Petrovich Laputin and Valentin Grigoryevich Oleshko. The great Olympic weightlifter V. Alekseev used this style of wave. I employ the recommendations of these men that were based on 780 highly qualified weight lifters. For loading and intensities of training, I use the work of A.S. Prilepin also shown in *Managing the Training of Weightlifters* (1982). Prilepin used 1,000 highly skilled track and field athletes as well as highly skilled weight lifters. This loading system made Westside Barbell the strongest powerlifting gym in the world.

The optimal number of lifts at 70 percent zone is 18 lifts, and 80 percent zone is 15 lifts. When doing the form of snatching or cleaning, a workout for speed technique should be nine sets of two reps at 75 percent zone, seven sets of two reps at 80 percent zone, and six sets of two reps at 85 percent zone. The rest interval between sets should be 90 seconds. After doing a snatch or clean speed workout, take the 10-minute active rest period to complete some easy jumping or walking then repeat the workout with the second lift. If the snatch is performed first, then 10 minutes later do the clean power, classic or the clean and jerk. A workout should be comprised of a classical lift along with two to four special exercises. Example of a few special exercises:

1. Belt Squat
2. Inverse Curl
3. Reverse Hyper™
4. Back Raise
5. Weight Jumps
6. Rowing.

A second workout variety is to only execute a clean or snatch in one workout; then, complete a speed strength workout in the squat for the optimal reps and sets mentioned before. After school, nap, or work, a second workout would be implemented with special exercises such as: power sled walking, lat work, abs work, reverse hypers, step-ups, etc. This work should last 45 minutes, concentrating on a particular weakness, which can perfect form in the classical lifts. Calculate volume only with 75 percent to 85 percent weight for speed day. A special exercise comprises close to 50 percent of the total volume on speed day by training with small exercises to bring a lagging muscle group up to par. A weightlifter should spend three years doing special exercises while learning proper technique. Employ the rule of three; then, concentrate on the squats, pulls, jerks, with less work on fitness.

Speed day can also mean strength speed work, which is used four weeks out from a meet. The lifts should range from four to seven at 90 percent to 97 percent with the key to Olympic lifting being raising the power clean, power snatch, and squat; save doing a classical lift with 100 percent effort on max effort day. Seventy-two hours later on speed day, the volume is highest and the intensity zone is moderate. The Bulgarian's used a faster first pull, and I suggest the same.

Max Effort Day

Here, the volume with a barbell is much lower with the intensities 100 percent on that day, depending on an individual's level of preparedness. This max effort system is based on the Bulgarian system with the exception of maxing without a barbell; special exercise such as a special pull, squat or Goodmorning should be implemented. On max effort day, the box squat is used to build the squat. Execute a wide stance on a parallel box or low box and a close stance on a very low box. Box squats must be done correctly to overcome resistance from a relaxed state. Push jerk or push press from the rack and use a close or wide grip. Pull from four different starting points or hold bar statically at a predetermined position. Apply different grips not used in competition. Do a wide variety of Goodmornings and Olympic deadlifts with shrug snatch and clean style for max singles. Three attempts are given on meet day, so train that way. One lift at 90 percent, a small new record or close to it, and one more small record and you are done. More is not better when it comes to near-max lifts. A new record is most important and possible most occasions. By now it must be understood to switch max effort exercises each week. Squat work should be completed, following a pulling exercises or a Goodmorning of some kind or a jerk or press exercise. While a powerlifter would use only one special barbell exercise, an Olympic lifter can do two because the time under tension factor is much less due to a faster bar velocity.

Olympic lifters squat three times per week, yet they are terrible squatters. This system builds strength endurance with moderate high weights, but it does nothing to raise their squat limit. I have outlined a fast weight day of F=MA. When a weight is too light, only a small force can be developed. This is why an athlete's training of 50 percent should be 75 percent to 85 percent. Weights under 70 percent are not beneficial. This can be explained by Hill's equation of muscular contraction and the limitations of high velocity movements. Remember light weights must be moved as fast as possible, which is known as the dynamic method. This method is not directly used for increasing maximal strength, but rather to improve the rate of force development of explosive strength.

The second main workout is the maximal effort method. This is the most superior method for improving intramuscular and intermuscular coordination that brings about the largest strength increments. Because most cannot do two max effort workouts a week, it is replaced with the dynamic workout. On speed day, two things can be accomplished on the same day. First, speed strength is improved and second, an improvement in technique mastery is achieved. This must be done with the 75 percent to 85 percent weights, causing one to learn to accelerate the barbell from the floor then below the knees, above the knees, and so forth. To help perfect form, special exercises for the legs and back muscles are implemented. As a coach or a lifter, an individual must decide when to rotate exercises special and classical during a weekly and monthly program. Pick exercises that work toward raising an overall total; do not just choose favorite exercises. Note that you are becoming faster, as well as stronger. Remember, a weekly plan turns into a monthly plan, which turns into a yearly then multi-year plan.

The conjugate system is always used throughout training. I can alter volume and intensity zones, and of course, small and large exercises are rotated as discussed earlier and well as changing the bar speed from very high velocity to zero velocity. Weight lifting in the United States is subpar for many reasons. One reason is that trainers and/or lifters repeat the classical exercises too often causing accommodation. When squatting three times a week, an individual is merely training strength endurance, but a weight lifter must increase the squat. Execute speed strength squatting on one day, then max effort work 72 hours later. This can encompass max out squats, including low box front and regular, close stance and very wide stance. Half squats help the recovery and aid in the jerk portion of the lift.

Isometric Work

Isometric work must be implemented at the four important positions: the floor, off the floor, below the knee, and above the knee. Lifting the barbell slowly should also be utilized from time to time. Hold a barbell for a time period; then, move the barbell slowly to a second position and hold again. Typically, this is completed during the preparatory and competition phases, our system calls for doing them throughout the year. When doing isometric work, the lifter or coach can examine form at precise angles. When done at full speed, it is difficult without slow motion film.

Isometrics makes it possible to do a large amount of work at important joint angles where doing dynamic work can only be displayed for a very short time. Don't overlook isometrics because they cause strength increases at 20 percent relative to the position worked. Special exercises should be done 50 percent of the time. A strong lower back is a must for the Olympic lifts. This means Hyperextensions, Reverse Hyper extensions and Goodmonings must be used to increase lower back strength. Because of possible overtaxing the back, the Goodmonings should average 50 percent of one's limit clean. Likewise, Hyperextensions should be 20 percent of one's percent clean. The Reverse Hypers can be 50 percent of a lifter's best squat due to an overtaxing effect as he becomes more suited to a yearly training. Goodmonings should be tapered while more emphasis is placed on Reverse Hypers and Hyperextensions. Keep Goodmonings to three to 10 reps per set. If leg strength is lacking, add belt squatting and step-ups into the workouts. Plyo swing jumps can be implemented to a second smaller workout. Do upper back exercises to strengthen the upper back with Kettlebells or hold a barbell overhead and shoulder shrug upward and to the rear for three to 10 reps, depending on weight that ranges from 10 percent to 25 percent of best clean-jerk. One must display force quickly during the clean portion, the jerk portion, and the snatch portion of the lift. Also, perform close-grip bench press flat or on an incline. Implement dips either seated or with weight. Jumps are important for the sprinters and just as important for weight lifters. The half squat, the jump squat, and jumps can be invaluable to success. There is no comparison to jumping without weight and the clean and jerk, but as the jumping section illustrates, jumps with resistance are very important for increasing jumping ability, and jumping with 50 percent of body weight has a correlation to the clean and jerk.

While strong legs and a strong squat are important, a lifter who jumps highest with 50 percent of body weight will possess the highest clean and jerk. Two of the greatest weight lifters of all time: Dave Rigert jumped 59 cm with 50 percent body weight 100kg and Yuri Vardanyan at 82.5 kg jumped 65 cm, or roughly 23" and 25", respectively. There are numerous special exercises to rotate for the clean and jerk. As anyone can see, it is more important to be stronger than faster when it comes to overcoming heavy resistance as in weightlifting. After all, a lifter's limit weights will move slower than his training weights.

Basic physics explains to us the terms: Power is defined as work done divided by the time used to do the work, or $P=W/T$. If two athletes are to do the same physical task, the more powerful athlete will do the task in less time. A.S. Medvedev stated in the 1970s that bands or rubber cords must be employed when lifting weights. This eliminates the deceleration of the barbell near the top of a pull or a squat.

Accommodating Resistance

What is accommodating resistance? Through the use of chains, bands, air or a cam with variable lever arms, the idea is to develop maximal tension throughout the full range of motion rather than at the weakest point. This method would be the peak contraction principle. For our training, we use bands or chains only. There cannot be a perfect weight at the top or bottom in a single repetition. The only realistic method to precisely find the correct resistance at different joint posture cures is to use accommodating resistance. The chain hanging on the barbell system provides an unloading and reloading system to the barbell. The bands over the barbell system allow not only an unloading and reloading system, but also causes an over speed eccentric effect. This system has devel- oped strong reversal strength action. I suggest using bands and chains in a designated squat workout. The lightened method is an excellent alternative to use for a different feel than bands or chains over the bar.

Special Pulls

Employ snatch and clean pulls for the start while using medium or high positions. With isometric pulls, bands can allow one to start the lift at any stage and hold at any position. Push jerk or push press jerk from behind the head also can be performed. Keep records while using different amounts of band tension and at least two tension strengths. This training makes everyone very strong. At first, a lifter may overpower light weights, causing his timing to be off by his new found ability to lift the same weight much faster than before.

Squat Under

A major part of success is the ability to get under the clean as fast as possible. Regardless of weight, the speed of gravity is constant, so how can someone become faster to get under the bar at a lower position? By using bands that force the barbell downward concentrically. Jerk by push presses and with bands; an athlete will easily jerk what he cleans.

Lightened Method

For a different contrast method, use the lightened method. The bands can be attached at the top of a power rack or special support so as they reduce the weight at the start.

Eccentric Work

I recommend doing slow eccentric movements. For the most part, they build size. This could, however, cause an individual to compete in a heavier weight division, which should not occur until he has exhausted his potential in his current weight class. Eccentric also causes most of an individual's muscular soreness, which he does not need more of.

Because the Olympic lifts are a speed-strength sport and with their abolishment of the press, they must be done sometimes at a slow phase train concentrically and eccentrically to build muscle tension expressly at precise angles of the lift. This will be outlined at the end of the chapter. You are training for a world or Olympic team, I hope. To do this, you need more than rubber plates, a Reverse Hyper, and a calf/ham/glute device. A set-up for contrast methods would include Kettlebells, weight vests, ankle weights, and an assortment of boxes to do jumping exercises. Also, needed are a soft surface to land on and to jump out of, a large arsenal of bars for squatting and Goodmonings, just to name a few. Don't train like you are competing at the county fair.

Things to Ponder

What are the most common reasons for failure to complete a snatch or clean and jerk?

For the Snatch:

Miss directing the trajectory of the barbell either forward or backward. The second is not completing the full extensions of the torso during the explosion. This is a technique problem, but why does it occur on the heaviest weights and not on the light weights?

It requires more strength to complete a heavier weight. To correct the problem, add more pulls at just above the knees and at mid thighs. You must start at these positions with plates sitting on pulling boxes. Train the snatch with 75 percent to 85 percent weights for the optimal amount of lifts. Do some with a closer grip then normal to force a longer pull. For the snatch pull, the weights should range from 90 percent to 105 percent of your best snatch. Do two or three lifts.

Do special exercises: belt squat combo pulls, arched back Goodmonings at 60 percent to 70 percent coming up on the toes very powerfully. Also do back raises, throwing the medicine ball over your head, inverse curls and static-hold Reverse Hypers plus abdominal work including oblique work.

If you can't recover from the squat, do a three-week wave cycle of front and overhead squats on a low box with a wider than shoulders width to raise hip and glute strength, as well as added flexibility. Always do box squats correctly. Much of this will work for the clean and jerk as well. Use bands for eliminating bar deceleration in the squat up, which helps in the all-important squat under.

For the Clean and Jerk:

Like the snatch, incorrect bar trajectory in the jerk is the main reason for failure. The second and third reasons for failure are that you are unable to recover from the clean and a lack of correctly working the legs in the drive off the chest for the jerk portion of the lift. Box squatting will improve the strength of the squat recovery when using a low box with a wider than normal squat stance.

For the jerk, a lifter will drop down eccentrically then reverse it concentrically for the quarter squat position. This reversible strength is built by box squats. Lower yourself on to a high box where your feet are mostly coming off the ground while sitting on the box, now explode upward with the bar and jerk overhead. By using band tension you will reduce greatly the barbell deceleration phase.

These reasons for failure can be found in *Managing the Training of the Weightlifters* by: N.P. Laputin V.G. Oleshko. Copyright Andrew Charniga Jr (1982).

Let's Analyze

The clean and jerk is two pulls: a front squat and, of course, a jerk. The weakest stage of the clean and jerk will determine the success of that lift. If an individual can clean 400 pounds, but he only front squats 370 pounds, he will only be able to recover with 370 pounds. If an athlete stands up with 400 pounds, but his jerk is only 380 pounds, then that is going to be the level of his success. The point is an individual must raise his weakness. There is no set weight to squat if one cleans 352 pounds, but can't stand up with it. An individual's squat must be raised. If someone fails in the jerk, he must increase special exercises for the jerk. If his squat is very strong, but he can't pull cleans high enough, he must work on his speed strength in the clean. Knowing the weakness is imperative. An athlete must also know when he needs to do more speed strength training with cleans or snatches or more strength speed development through special exercises, such as pulls, squats and back extensions of all types. Be conscious of when to utilize isometric work and at what positions. Know that the lighter weight class needs to be proportionally strong to concentrate for error in technique. The amount of GPP work with special work will change at times with the GPP, or the so called "classical lifts." What does it take to be a great Olympic lifter? A speed strength sport or a combination of things such as strength coordination in the actual lift, quickness or speed of movement. An individual must have the capability to be explosive; this takes good genetics. If a person is slow by nature, he will not reach the top.

Know why failure occurs in the snatch. The common error in the snatch is distortion in barbell trajectory. The bar falls forward or backward. This is from just pulling in the wrong barbell path, or if it happens only with heavy weight, it must be corrected with special exercises: back raises, Goodmornings, and special squats and pulls. The second error is an incomplete extension of the torso during the explosion. To correct this error, a lifter must increase back strength with back extensions, inverse curls, Reverse Hypers, and by building stronger abs. These are the most common, but there are additional reasons to fail, especially errors in the clean and jerk.

The most familiar error is distortion in the jerk trajectory because of poor technique or lack of concentration. Another error occurs during the clean and jerk, which entails a poor thrust phase during the jerk. This is timing or a lack of leg strength. Implement half squats with weight and bands or glute/ham raises, belt squats, or jumping with weight at 50 percent of body weight. The third most common reason to fail is the inability to recover from the squat because of a lack of back and leg strength. This can be corrected by special back work such as extensions of all types, box squats, Goodmonings, and jumps with weight of 50 percent of body weight. Looking at the jerk, one needs to do jerks and presses with bands over the barbell. Incline press with close grip and very wide grip, along with delt work like the Bradford lift. A Bradford lift is pressing a barbell overhead, just clearing the head, lowering the bar to base of the neck, and pressing just overhead and back down to the front of the shoulder for high reps.

A Multi-Year Plan

Why is the conjugate system best for the weight lifter? You must establish a base for the classical lifts that are quite strenuous on the body. Good technique must be developed in the beginning. For example, the legs are worked with belt squatting, belt squat power clean combos, lunges, jumping with a barbell, glute/ham raises in leg, and power sled walking. Just to name a few.

While the common idea is that by recovering from the snatch and clean, light to moderate squatting is sufficient, this is not true for all. In the US there are men and women who barely front squat more than their max clean. The odds of breaking a new front squat personal record and clean personal record at the same time, plus have a reserve for the jerk, is very low.

The information on Russian and Bulgarian weight lifters is on high-skilled weight lifters. They were not in the beginning world class lifters. However, in their early stages, much like you, they performed a wide variety of special exercises for the back such as back extensions, Goodmonings, Reverse hypers, rows, chin dips, pull ups, and the like.

The keys to weight lifting progress are the power clean, power snatch and front squat. Box squatting with a wider stance will build neglected muscles. Using bands for accommodating resistance and for eliminating bar deceleration is vital for the squat under and jerking power.

Strength is the main factor in weight lifting. If not there would be no need for weight classes. Of course, you must increase abdominal strength, improve shoulder flexibility with very close and wide-hand spacing. The average training plan would consist of 64 special exercises.

After about ten months you will understand what special exercises work for you and, more importantly, not to do the ones that don't work. The small special exercises will help perfect form, especially at the different phases of the lift. The large special exercises will build absolute strength like quarter and half squats, high pulls with different grips, clean and snatch grip deadlifts, and standing on a box to pull.

As the weight lifter becomes more proficient in technique, his special exercises will go up and the classic lifts will go down. Sixty-five percent to 70 percent of the training must be designed to make the weight lifter stronger. (Because your special physical preparedness, meaning they are a perfectionist at the classical lifts). The goal is to be more powerful and stronger. This calls for special squats and pulls, raising the amount one can squat, front squat especially and high pulls with different grips, and starting the pulls off the ground at three different positions. Increase the average weight of belt squats, back raises, Reverse Hypers and many small exercises.

It is of upmost importance that one concentrates on breaking special pulls, special squats and jerks as well as pushing small exercises for the back and legs while maintaining flexibility. These workouts should be as low volume with a barbell as possible while making a new personal record.

The power clean and power snatch should be trained at between 75 percent and 85 percent in a three-week pendulum wave. A max squat clean or squat snatch can be attempted on occasions. Test your limits 21 days from a contest and start your delayed transformation phase, leading into the contest.

Weight Lifting Programming

The author's thoughts: Let's look at the theory of the so-called Russian system compared to the Bulgarian system.

First, let's look at the Bulgarian's views of training. They chose very young men that could master lifting near max weights. Naim Suleymanoglu was the model weight lifter meaning someone that possesses genetic advantages others don't have. The Bulgarian's were using a limited amount of barbell exercises and carefully selected athletes from a smaller geographic area or in a way, ethnic selection. As mentioned in this chapter, their workout is the beginning of a large number of exercises that were employed to prevent and minimize any muscular imbalances. They were very fit and used the weight programs for their GPP. The workouts lasted 45 minutes to maintain high elevated blood testosterone levels. After a light snatch warm-up they would work up to heavy and heavier weights for six attempts. After a short 30-minute rest, the second part the same routine, but this time was the clean and jerk. Now, max front squats and this workout was done in 45 minutes. This called for much restoration and they used massages, steam baths and many others as well as nutritional supplementation. Sometimes they trained six to seven times a week, three to four times a day.

The special exercise were on the large nature after being introduced to the main training facility:

- Snatch
- Power Snatch
- Snatch Pull
- Snatch Deadlift
- Clean and Jerk
- Clean Deadlift
- Clean Pull
- Power Clean
- Front Squat
- Press
- Goodmonings
- Back Squat @ least 125 percent of clean.

Depending on the athlete's preparedness, he may have used singles at five, 10 or 15 kg under their max. Total volume must be raised at the optimal intensities; as the volume was raised the intensity must go up as well. Naim Suleymanoglu's volume was raised from 1982 systematically to his highest in 1988 then fell off in 1999 and 90 then rose again for the 1992 Olympics and again for 1996. The assistance exercise accounted for more than 50 percent of his training. Their training was based on not an all-time max, but a current day max. The mean average percent from the beginning to the end of a workout was 85 percent to 87 percent of an all-time max.

Let's summarize: they had a small group of lifters with a small selected group of exercises. With one training center and one main coach many more failed then succeeded, but that's true for all sports. It is to be noted that in one training session the volume was highest on the classical lifts and the next training session the volume was highest on special exercises. The Bulgarians added active rest such as soccer, table tennis and swimming, but as said before, their coaching philosophy was the weight training sessions that supplied the lifter with adequate GPP, or in fact SPP. As you see, almost all small special exercises were eliminated until a small number of special exercises for pulling and squatting came along with the classical lifts. I don't suggest you try the Bulgarian system, but if you do, be sure to research their training and find out what they really did. *Naim Suleymanoglu's The Pocket Hercules* by Yazam Enver Turkileri (2004) may give some insight to the truth, if they, in fact, told the truth about his training and success.

The Soviets had a different training cycle. (See the sample layout.) The workout's go from less than 100 percent weights to 100 percent or higher for max effort. They must rotate from fast to moderately fast and from moderately fast to slow weights of 100 percent plus. This happens on the special pulls and jerks as well as half squats or pin squats. Just as the barbell must go from fast to slow, the volume must go from low to high to prevent accommodation.

Comparing the Soviet System to the Bulgarian System

As you can see the Bulgarian's use fewer exercises, primarily the two snatches and the two cleans plus a jerk. The Soviets mean weight was around 80 percent. This is shown by the three-week waves going from 75 percent to 80 percent to 85 percent and, of course, a second workout leading to max effort.

The training of Naim Suleymanoglu shows this. You noticed the Soviets used a GPP day or what Westside describes as a deload, where no barbell work is used, but only small special exercises such as back raises, glute/ham raises, Reverse Hypers, inverse curls, shrugs, power walking, and the like. However, the Bulgarians had no such day, thinking that constant weight training gave them the ability to recover from workout to workout plus a wide variety of recovery means (water, massage, etc.).

Let's look at one of Naim's weekly programs concerning special exercises compared to classical exercises on a daily basis.

	Monday	Tuesday	Wednesday	Thursday	Friday	Saturday	Sunday
90% - 100% Classical Lifts	35	0	35	0	35	0	115
90% - 100% Special Lifts	23	26	23	26	23	26	151

At Other Periods of Training

	Monday	Tuesday	Wednesday	Thursday	Friday	Saturday	Sunday
90% - 100% Classical Lifts	50	14	50	14	50	14	192
90% - 100% Special Lifts	22	29	22	29	22	29	155

As you can see the ratio between classical and special lifts would rotate during the year. Naim, like all Bulgarian weight lifters, was almost perfectly proportioned for the squat. Recruiting was a must with most athletes coming from one area or ethnic background.

While the Soviets build weight lifters from the ground up, please read and see the comparison for yourself.

10 Consecutive Workouts:

Workout #1

1. P. Sn: 70 x 2 x 4
2. C + J: 70 + 1 + 1, 80 + 1 + 1 x 2, 90 + 1 + 1 x 3
3. Cl. Pu.: 80 x 3 x 2, 90 x 3, 100 x 1 x 3
4. Fr. Sq.: 55 x 4, 65 x 4, 85 x 4 x 4
5. Be. Pr.: 4 x 6

Workout #2

1. P. Sn: 60 x 2 x 4
2. Cl. Sn: 70 x 2 x 3
3. P. Cl. + J: 70 + 2 +1 x 3
4. B. Sq.: 50 x 3, 60 x 3 x 3

Workout #3

1. P. Sn: 70 x 3 x 4
2. C + J, Bel. Kn.: 70 + 1 + 1, 80 + 1 + 1 x 2, 90 + 1 + 1 x 2
3. Cl, Pu: 90 x 1 x 5, 100 x 1 x 3
4. B. Sq.: 50 x 4, 60 x 4, 70 x 5 x 4
5. Depth Jump: 4 x 10

Workout #4

1. P. Sn: 70 x 3, 80 x 2 x 3
2. Cl. Sn: Bel. Kn.: 70 x 3, 80 x 2 x 4
3. C + J: 70 + 1 + 1 x 3
4. Cl. Pu., Bel. Kn.: 70 x 3 x 5
5. B. Sq.: 50 x 3, 60 x 3, 70 x 3 x 2

Workout #5

1. P. Sn.., Bel. Kn.: 70 x 3, 80 x 1 x 3
2. Cl. Sn: 70 x 2 x, 80 x 2 x 2, 90 x 1 x 3
3. Sn. Pu.: 80 x 3, 90 x 3 x 2, 100 x 2 x 3
4. P. Cl.: 70 x 3, 80 x 2 x 3
5. Cl. Pu., Bel. Kn.: 80 x 3 x 5

Workout #6

1. P. Cl. + J: 70 + 2 + 1 x 5
2. Cl. Sn: 70 x 2 x 4
3. B. Sq.: 50 x 3, 60 x 3 x 3

Workout #7

1. P. Sn : 70 x 2 x 4
2. C + J: 70 + 1 + 2, 80 + 1 + 1 x 4
3. J. Fr. St.: 70 x 3, 80 x 2 x 2, 90 x 1 x 5
4. Cl. Pu. Slow + Fast 90 + 1 + 1 x 2, 100 + 1 + 1 x 4
5. Cl. Pu.: 80 x 3, 90 x 2 x 3
6. b. Sq.: 50 x 4, 60 x 4, 75 x 4 x 3

Workout #8

1. P. Sn: 60 x 3, 70 x 2 x 4
2. P. Cl.: 60 x 3 x 4
3. B. Sq.: 50 x 4 x 2

Workout #9

1. P. Sn. Stand on Blocks: 70 x 3, 80 x 2 x 5
2. Sn. Pu. Stand on Blocks: 80 x 5, 90 x 3 x 3,100 x 3 x 3
3. Lunge: 4 + 4 x 6

Workout #10

1. Cl. Pu., Stand on Blocks: 70 x 5 x 3, 80 x 4 x 4
2. Seat Press: 5 x 5
3. Lunge: 3 + 3 x 6

You have just reviewed programs of the greatest weight lifting dynasties of all time. The athletes were well chosen to be able to handle the dense training through a wide variation of drills and exercises. The same idea can be seen with the unbelievable Chinese weight lifters today (2013). Being a powerlifter for 48 years, I recall my first power meet, it was in 1966. I had lifted as a weightlifter for four years, from age 14 to 18. After just looking at the men lifting, I was amazed at the physical development of the powerlifters compared to the weightlifters. That was when I decided to do powerlifting from that point on. There were four men in that power meet that became world champs and world record holders. My weightlifting friends remained at their present level.

Now, it's 2013 at the Ohio State weightlifting championships. For me, it was Deja vu all over again. No one had a powerful build; no back, glutes, traps, hamstrings, no nothing. To my eye, it's simple. Young powerlifters do a vast array of exercises to build the powerlifts. The number is practically infinity. The weightlifter's do very little, if any. I call out the coaches for weight lifting to learn to build strength through small exercises. The greatest Olympic weight lifter, Vasily Alekseyev, had training that was much like Westside's. He found he must rely on many back and leg exercises to supplement the Olympic lifts even when the press was an Olympic lift or it was reduced to the snatch and C-J after 1972. Is this a mere coincidence? I think not. But it is an absolute necessity. In 1972 the Dynamo Club members in the Soviet Union were responsible for the conjugate system of training or using special exercises to increase the classical lifts. But, of course, to increase the lifts they must be closely related to the mechanics of the classical lifts that V. Alekseyev used: back raises and inverse curls to increase the Goodmonings and pulls that in turn raised the classical lifts.

Now to my point about weightlifting in the United States. The coaches in the United States can teach how to do the snatch and clean and jerk, but they have no idea how to increase strength in the vital areas of the lifter. In my opinion this is precisely why only a few can raise above state level and then a very few to the national level, but none to the model stage. The Westside methodology is based on the Soviet's methods and includes ideas from the Bulgarians' training of Olympic weightlifters. Westside has produced roughly 130 all-time world records. We hope to break the incredible record count of B. Alekseyev of 80 all-time world records. I have merely written my thoughts and views to hopefully make you think there is a better way. Albert Einstein said "I can win an argument with a smart man, but I will never win an argument with an ignorant man." Enough said.

Weight Room Programs

The world's top authorities on strength training have classified three methods of strength training to achieve maximal muscular tension.

1. Maximal Effort Method

This method is considered the best for raising both intramuscular and intermuscular coordination. The central nervous system (CNS) adapts only to the load placed upon it. This method brings forth the greatest strength gains. The maximal number of muscle units is activated with optimal discharge frequency and biomechanical parameters of movement and intermuscular coordination. Learn more by reading pages 100-101 in V.M. Zatsiorsky's *Science and Practice of Strength Training* (1995).

Max out each time on max effort day. Squatting and pulling exercises that day should occur the day after or the second after a game. This helps relieve delayed onset muscular soreness (DOMS). Our system calls for one to switch a max effort core lift each workout, meaning some kind of special squat pulls or Goodmonings. If an individual executes the same exercises for three weeks in a row, he could stall or even go backwards, which is the Law of Accommodation, a general law of Biology. For more read V.M. Zatsiorsky's *Science and Practice of Strength Training* (1995).

Pre-season training should resemble the following schedule for max effort workouts. Monday is for squatting, pulling, plus Goodmonings, working up to a new max or a max for that day. The Westside max effort system is much like the Bulgarian system, achieving the largest weight possible depending on an individual's level of preparedness. The total loading should be three heavy weights for singles; one around 90 percent, and one close to or slightly above current gym record.

Example: 600 Rack Pull

    1st 540=90%

    2nd 580=96%

    3rd 605= PR

Remember for the max effort workout, max out on a squat or Goodmorning, rotating exercises while choosing the ones that work best for you. The volume is low, but 100 percent intensity.

Max effort bench day is Wednesday. Just like max effort day for squatting or pulling, rotate a special barbell exercise to a max single. For example, look at a floor press with a current record of 405. After warming up, try for new records or the most possible on that particular day.

Example:

    365 x 1 rep

    390 x 1 rep

    410 x 1 new PR

During certain times of the year, an individual may or may not be able to break records, but he must try. As can be noted, the intensity is 100 percent plus. The volume is low, counting only weights at 70 percent and above to measure total volume.

After maxing out on a special squat, Goodmorning, deadlift, snatch or clean, the Westside system is almost all special exercises. The majority of the volume of exercises is for lower back, hamstrings, lats, abs, triceps, delts, etc. Good form is essential on all core lifts. On the smaller exercises, high reps are essential, working to a near failure not total failure, so many sets can be repeated to sufficiently work the muscle groups triggered for that workout.

2. The Repetition to Near-Failure Method

This method is never to be used on classical lifts. Football is a game where the average time of a play is four to seven seconds, so one, two and three reps per sets with 40-second rest intervals must be used. This is known as exercise specificity. Hockey uses a little longer spring time and less contact time, but the barbell system is the same. The repetition method to near failure is best for individual muscle groups. A small list of special exercises to follow a core exercise include the following: glute/ham raises four-eight reps for four-five sets; Reverse hyper 10 reps for four-10 sets; lat work of all types for eight-12 reps and for five-eight sets; tricep work five-six reps with barbells for six-eight sets; tricep work eight-12 reps for six-eight sets; and upper back eight-12 reps for six-eight sets. Other exercises like kettlebells can be performed for one-five minutes per set and belt squats for five-eight reps for five-10 sets can be completed.

A substitute on max effort day is doing a repetition workout of small exercises, such as: sled pulling, wheel barrow or prowler work. An individual should pick two to four exercises and rotate as often as he feels fit. Training must be dense, which means the amount of actual work done inside a workout. To review, the repetition to near failure method can sometimes replace a max effort day and be used after the four main workouts days. A max effort day and a dynamic effort day workout are separated by 72 hours, which is true for upper and lower body workouts a like.

3. The Dynamic Method

For those who could not handle two max effort workouts a week, the Dynamic Method was designed to replace a max effort day. This method is instrumental in developing a fast rate of force development, and it provides high volume with intensities of 60 percent, 70 percent, and 85 percent. If the bar weight is too light, it is impossible to attain Fmm against intermediate resistance. For this reason, bands and chains must be attached to the barbell to accommodate resistance, which helps eliminate bar deceleration. Because Westsiders use all three methods inside each week, we are more explosive, stronger and larger all at the same time.

The Westside system is an everlasting systematic method of achieving the highest results in speed, strength and endurance. Through 13 years of doing things incorrectly and implementing the secrets of Soviet Sports training for the past 27 years, we have eliminated what is wrong with training and concentrated on what's right and most beneficial. Although there are many types of sports, there is a best method of strength training, which is the Westside system.

Basic Training Methods-Explosive Strength

Explosive strength sometimes called explosive power is the ability to rapidly increase force (Tidow, 1990). The steeper the increase of strength in time the greater the explosive strength (Sozanski, 1995). An example is using a barbell combined with Jump Stretch bands and squatting on a box at or near parallel with a large amount of band tension.

Example:

Week 1	250 top tension on box	125 bottom tension	10x2 reps	
Week 2	320 top tension on box	160 bottom tension	10x2 reps	
Week 3	390 top tension on box	145 bottom tension	8x2 reps	
Week 4	2 bands (light and strong);	320 on top on box	160 bottom tension	10x2 reps
Week 5	2 bands (light and strong);	390 at top on box	195 bottom tension	10x2 reps
Week 6	2 bands (light and strong);	500 at top on box	250 bottom tension	8x2 reps

By using only band tension, there is a rapid eccentric phase because the bands force the athlete onto the box. The box ensures every squat is the same depth. It breaks the eccentric concentric phase when relaxing some muscles, causing a relaxed explosive phase.

Nine-Week Wave with Weight Releasers with a 500 Squat Max:

Week 1	70% with 350 lb. bar weight	70 lb. weight releasers	10x2 reps
Week 2	75% with 375 lb. bar weight	70 lb. weight releasers	10x2 reps
Week 3	80% with 400 lb. bar weight	70 lb. weight releasers	8x2 reps
Week 4	70% with 350 lb. bar weight	85 lb. weight releasers	10x2 reps
Week 5	75% with 375 lb. bar weight	85 lb. weight releasers	10x 2 reps
Week 6	80% with 400 lb. bar weight	85 lb. weight releasers	8x2 reps
Week 7	70% with 350 lb. bar weight	100 lb. weight releasers	10x2 reps
Week 8	75% with 375 lb. bar weight	100 lb. weight releasers	10x2 reps
Week 9	80% with 400 lb. bar weight	100 lb. weight releasers	8x2 reps

This nine-week wave concentrates on using slightly more contrast (weight releasers), beginning on every three-week wave, which is a reactive method for explosive strength.

Lightened Method

This method requires an athlete to suspend Jump Stretch Bands at the top of the Power Rack. A strong band takes 150 pounds out of the bottom of a squat or bench. A medium band takes 95 pounds out of the bottom, and a light band unloads 65 pounds out of the bottom. This system causes an individual to accelerate real barbell weight on the concentric phase after the weight is lightened on the eccentric phase.

Sample Workouts

Nine-Week Wave with 600 Max Squat:

Week 1	300 lb. bar weight	Lightened 150 lb.	10x2 reps
Week 2	330 lb. bar weight	Lightened 150 lb.	10x2 reps
Week 3	360 lb. bar weight	Lightened 150 lb.	8x2 reps
Week 4	300 lb. bar weight	Lightened 95 lb.	10x2 reps
Week 5	330 lb. bar weight	Lightened 95 lb.	10x 2 reps
Week 6	360 lb. bar weight	Lightened 95 lb.	8x2 reps
Week 7	300 lb. bar weight	Lightened 65 lb.	10x2 reps
Week 8	330 lb. bar weight	Lightened 65 lb.	10x2 reps
Week 9	360 lb. bar weight	Lightened 65 lb.	8x2 reps

To alter the contrast, start the nine-week cycle in reverse. Doing the lightened 65 pounds, the first three-week wave of 95 pounds remains the same in the second three-week wave and 150 out of the bottom on the last three-week cycle. These examples are for explosive strength, using more band tension on top of the bar or to lighten the weight in the bottom of the lift, and of course, by increasing weight to the releasers when employing them. Add weight to the releasers not the barbell, and always lower weight as far as possible. The concept of over speed eccentrics and combining optimal eccentric must be paid close attention, realizing the most potential for the stretch reflex.

Explosive Training for Bench Pressing

For speed benching, use weight roughly 50 percent of a one rep max. An example is a 405- pounds max with 185 pounds to 205 pounds for speed. Also, speed bench with mini bands over the bar. Forty percent at lockout works best, and there must be strong tension in the bottom or on the chest.

Example: 405 Max Bench Press

Week 1	8x3 reps	205 lb.	85 lb. band tension
Week 2	8x3 reps	205 lb.	85 lb. band tension
Week 3	8x3 reps	205 lb.	85 lb. band tension

More Speed Benching

Week 1	8x3 reps	205 lb.	80 lb. chains
Week 2	8x3 reps	205 lb.	80 lb. chains
Week 3	8x3 reps	205 lb.	80 lb. chains

Speed Bench with Weight Releasers

Week 1	8x3 reps	205 lb.	50 lb. weight releasers
Week 2	8x3 reps	205 lb.	50 lb. weight releasers
Week 3	8x3 reps	205 lb.	50 lb. weight releasers

After lowering roughly 60 percent of a 1 rep max, the weight releaser will unload 25 percent for a reactive method. One drawback is the first rep is the only rep affected by the weight releaser. Lower as quickly as possible under control. Also, try ballistic benching. After a fast eccentric phase, stop the bar one to three inches from chest and reverse as quickly as possible to lock out. If a lifter wants to be fast and explosive, he must train this way.

Lightened Method Benching

Example: 315-Pound Max Bench:

275x3 reps	Lightened 65 lb.	9x3 reps
275x3 reps	Lightened 65 lb.	9x3 reps
275x3 reps	Lightened 65 lb.	9x3 reps

The contrast method of benching for speed strength development refers to the fact that the weight is contrasting differently in the bottom compared to the top.

Speed Work for Pulling

Speed Deadlift 400-Pounds Max

Week 1	225 lb.	10x1 rep	220 lb. of band tension on top	100 lb. of band tension on bottom
Week 2	250 lb.	10x1 rep	220 lb. of band tension on top	100 lb. of band tension on bottom
Week 3	275 lb.	8x1 rep	220 lb. of band tension on top	100 lb. of band tension on bottom

I prefer deadlifting over power cleans or snatch by pulling a deadlift powerfully off the floor and then accelerating to the top. It is important to rotate three styles of deadlifts: conventional, wide sumo, and straight leg sumo. The deadlift is the missing link in speed development. Every team does Olympic lifts, yet they suffer from hamstring injuries. Why? Weak lower backs. The deadlift can dramatically change the team's performance in eight weeks. Everybody wants to do Olympic lifts. Why? It's the biggest bust in American sports, yet every team wants to do them for explosive power. Nowhere in the Soviet text does it call for Olympic lifting for explosive power training. They push jumps bounding, plyo's for their reactive training. Their best Olympic lifters did jumps for explosive training, not Olympic lifts.

I suggest straight leg clean and snatch. The Olympic lifts are just two exercises to help bring forth higher sports results, but they are not the only two and certainly not the best two. Here is a rotating system in three-week waves for the clean and snatch with straight legs.

Week 1	Power Clean 1 rep	Hang Clean 1 rep	12x2 reps	75%
Week 2	Power Clean 1 rep	Hang Clean 1 rep	10x2 reps	80%
Week 3	Power Clean 1 rep	Hang Clean 1 rep	10x 2 reps	85%
Week 4	Power Snatch 1 rep	Hang Clean 1 rep	10x 2 reps	75%
Week 5	Power Snatch 1 rep	Hang Clean 1 rep	10x 2 reps	80%
Week 6	Power Snatch 1 rep	Hang Clean 1 rep	12x2 reps	85%
Week 7	Power Clean 1 rep	Hang Clean 1 rep	12x2 reps	75%
Week 8	Power Clean 1 rep	Hang Clean 1 rep	10x 2 reps	80%
Week 9	Power Clean 1 rep	Hang Clean 1 rep	10x 2 reps	85%
Week 10	Power Snatch 1 rep	Hang Snatch 1 rep	10x 2 reps	75%
Week 11	Power Snatch 1 rep	Hang Snatch 1 rep	10x 2 reps	80%
Week 12	Power Snatch 1 rep	Hang Snatch 1 rep	10x 2 reps	85%

Olympic lifts are primarily a speed strength sport. They can be very complicated, but so can any sport. An individual needs to choose and focus on one sport to train toward.

Cycles can be rotated in a fashion per individual. For example, bands for three weeks, chains for three weeks, and weight releasers for three weeks. Lightened method for three weeks adds 5 percent per week or subtracts 5 percent each week. A combination of the examples mentioned can be employed. These workouts are intended to build explosive and speed strength through over-speed eccentrics, a fast reversal action and a fast as possible concentric phase. Like fine art, there must be contrast. After one of the sample workouts, an individual must choose two to four special exercises for the lagging muscle groups. I don't consider abs an exercise, but it is a necessary one. Squatting or pulling exercises the lower back and must have the highest priority. A strong man has a strong lower back, and a weak man has a weak lower back. This is where hamstrings' relative strength is measured.

I asked the New York Giants if they worked their hamstrings hard. They answered "Yes." I asked if they stretched the hamstrings regularly. Their answer was "Yes." I asked if they worked the lower backs hard. Their answer was "No." I asked if they pulled their hamstrings. Their answer was "Yes." If an athlete wants to eliminate hamstring pulls, he has to work the lower back. Consequently, many are afraid to hurt the athlete. The coach must have background in real weight training where goals are made. That means not a 300-pound bench press, but a 500-pound bench press. Not a 400-pound squat, but a 650-pound squat for lineman. And, finally, not a 42" box jump, but a 60" box jump. That explanation is for those who only have a degree and no practical experiments.

The Reverse hyper™, like pulling a weight sled in a slow, powerful pace, is full proof. Doing 250 leg curls with five pounds, 10 pounds, 15 pounds, 20 pounds or sometimes no weight is very effective for reducing injuries and making an athlete run much faster. Glute/ham raises must be done. I suggest 600 reps a month to just maintain. That's right, 600 a month, which adds up to 20 a day. Surely, an individual can make time for 20 a day. Along with some conventional back extensions, I suggest seated calf work and possibly some jumping or bounding at the end of the lower body workouts. For upper body workouts, the special exercises should start with tricep work because the arms are most important to pressing. The upper back and lats must be trained as much as possible, too. This builds a solid foundation and helps reduce shoulder injuries. Train abs at the end of a workout somewhat harder than the beginning.

Sample Week Waves for a 500-Pound Max

Week 1	70%	350 lb.	10x2 reps	80 lb. chains
Week 2	75%	375 lb.	10x2 reps	80 lb. chains
Week 3	80%	400 lb.	8x2 reps	80 lb. chains
Week 4	70%	350 lb.	10x2 reps	120 lb. chains
Week 5	75%	375 lb.	10x2 reps	120 lb. chains
Week 6	80%	400 lb.	10x2 reps	120 lb. chains

This is a six-week speed strength cycle, consisting of a two-to three-week wave. The second wave is 40 pounds heavier, using 40 pounds more chain, accommodating resistance to create the contrast method, which implements explosive strength in a three-week wave. Use a safety squat bar with weight releasers. The bar weight is 80 percent of a one rep max. Implement 400 pounds max with 20 percent released the first week, 25 percent the second week, and 30 percent the third week use a fast eccentric phase on the box

Week 1	320 lb.	10x2 reps	Release 80 lb.
Week 2	320 lb.	10x2 reps	Release 100 lb.
Week 3	320 lb.	8x2 reps	Release 120 lb.

600 Max

Utilize strength speed for a two-week wave followed by a three-week speed strength wave. Strength speed wave is 50 percent bar weight, and with 50 band weight a lifter should squat the total weight at top.

Week 1	300 lb.	8x2 reps	300 lb. band tension
Week 2	300 lb.	2x2 reps	300 lb. band tension
Week 3	320 lb.	1x2 reps	300 lb. band tension
Week 4	340 lb.	1x2 reps	300 lb. band tension

Second Wave Three-Week Speed Strength

Week 1	300 lb.	10x2 reps	250 lb. of band tension on top	100 lb. of band tension on bottom
Week 2	330 lb.	10x2 reps	250 lb. of band tension on top	100 lb. of band tension on bottom
Week 3	360 lb.	8x2 reps	250 lb. of band tension on top	100 lb. of band tension on bottom

Two-Week Circa-Max Wave—800-Pound Max for the Very Strong

Week 1	380 lb.	5x2 reps	375 lb. band tension
Week 2	400 lb.	5x2 reps	375 lb. band tension
Week 3	420 lb.	4x2 reps	375 lb. band tension
Week 4	400 lb.	5x2 reps	140 lb. band tension
Week 5	400 lb.	3x2 reps	140 lb. band tension
Week 6	Meet	Meet	Meet

Week 4 and 5 are a de-loading system commonly known as a delayed transformation. This period is for performance growth or a competition.

Speed Bench Three-Week Wave

For a 500 pound raw bench, use 40 percent to 45 percent of the one rep max for a period accumulation where volume can be high and intensity remains the same.

Week 1	205 lb.	10x5 reps	80 lb. of chains
Week 2	205 lb.	10x5 reps	80 lb. of chains
Week 3	205 lb.	10x5 reps	80 lb. of chains
Week 4	205 lb.	10x5 reps	85 lb. of chains
Week 5	205 lb.	10x5 reps	85 lb. of chains
Week 6	205 lb.	10x5 reps	85 lb. of chains
Week 7	205 lb.	10x5 reps	120 lb. of chains
Week 8	205 lb.	10x5 reps	120 lb. of chains
Week 9	205 lb.	10x5 reps	120 lb. of chains

The following three-week cycle is for intensification and less volume.

Week 10	205 lb.	8x3 reps	120 lb. of chains
Week 11	205 lb.	8x3 reps	120 lb. of chains
Week 12	205 lb.	8x3 reps	120 lb. of chains
Week 13	205 lb.	8x3 reps	80 lb. of chains
Week 14	205 lb.	8x3 reps	80 lb. of chains
Week 15	205 lb.	8x3 reps	80 lb. of chains

The next three-week cycle is the transformation cycle, which is the last three weeks of training before the contest.

Week 16	205 lb.	8x3 reps	80 lb. of chains
Week 17	205 lb.	8x3 reps	80 lb. of chains
Week 18	205 lb.	6x3 reps	80 lb. of chains

Here are several cycles of speed strength, strength speed, circa-max phase, and an explosive strength cycle for references.

Examples of Max Effort Day:

Each week the primary exercise is switched to avoid accommodation. Scientific studies have found that after three weeks of training at 90 percent on the same lift, progress ceases. This is precisely why a lifter must switch each week, going from a bending exercise to an arching exercise.

A 10-Week Wave Cycle

Week 1	Pin two rack pull to max singles
Week 2	Front squat to low box for max single
Week 3	Box deadlift on 2" box for max single
Week 4	Safety squat bar. Close stance on foam box max single
Week 5	Bend over Goodmonings max three reps
Week 6	Pull heavy sleds 10 to 12 sets for 60 trips
Week 7	14" cambered bar squat on low box max single
Week 8	Concentric Goodmonings max three reps
Week 9	Zercher squat for a max single on foam box for max single
Week 10	Belt squat max for 5 reps and 5 trips high sled

By changing the box height or the pin in the power rack or merely varying the type of bar or stance, an individual is able to max out each week and not suffer from the Law of Accommodation. After workouts, an individual should use two to four special exercises, strengthening the weaknesses and acting as some form of restoration.

Max Effort Workouts

The max effort method is superior to all other strength methods. It's best for improving intramuscular and intermuscular coordination. The muscles and CNS adapt only to the loads placed upon them. Avoid high emotional stress in training. Don't worry about injuries for athletes on max effort day; only a few can strain hard enough to hurt themselves. The max effort workouts are first and foremost for barbell exercises, such as: box squats, deadlifts of all kinds, bench flat, incline, decline, floor press, push press, push jerk etc. Small exercises follow; two to four are recommended for upper or lower body workouts. Not only rotate max effort core lifts each week, but also small exercises as often as seen fit.

Sample Workouts

1. Use a Safety squat bar for a max single after max. Four sets of glute/ham raises for four to six reps; four sets of Reverse Hypers for 10 to 12 reps; six sets of barbell rows for six to 10 reps; 100 to 200 leg curls with ankle weights ranging anywhere from five to 20 pounds per leg; abs; walk one mile with a weight vest.

2. Perform Goodmonings with a bow bar for a three-rep max; after doing five to six sets to a top set of three, complete eight sets of high sled pulls for 60 yards per set; light sets of Reverse Hypers for 10 to 12 reps; six sets of chest supported rows for eight to 12 reps; abs; for the second workout, integrate 200 ankle weight leg curls with 10 pounds plus box jumps for five sets of five at 85 percent.

3. Power clean push press for a max single; three sets of three reps of high pull clean grip. Five sets of 45 degree back raises for six to 10 reps; three sets of Reverse Hypers for 10 reps; power walk with sled for 10 trips for 60 yards; heavy abs.

4. Front squat to a max single on low box, do three reps per set on the first few sets; light bend over Goodmonings for sets of five reps as a secondary exercise; five sets of Reverse Hypers for 10 reps per set with heavy weight; push prowler for 10 sets of 10 second work for football with 40 seconds rest; abs.

5. Pull sled moderately high for 12 trips of 60 yards; six sets of glute/ham raises six to 10 sets; six sets of rowing barbell or dumbbell; abs work; walk one to two miles with a weight vest between 25 and 100 pounds with five to 10-pound ankle weights depending upon an individual's level of fitness.

6. Perform rack pulls 2", 4", or 6" off the floor with plates for 10 sets of three reps with band tension to fit an individual's strength level plus reps; Kettlebell power cleans for three one-minute sets with two Kettlebells at a time; five sets of Reverse Hypers of 10 reps per set; abs.

7. Complete Zercher squats off of the floor or rack pin to max three reps; 45 degree hypers for five sets of five dumbbells or barbell shrugs for six sets of 10 to 12 reps; heavy Reverse Hyper for four sets of 10 reps; heavy abs.

8. Deadlift sumo with bands over the bar to a max single; light front squat for five sets of six reps to low box; Reverse Hypers for five sets of 10 reps; abs.

9. Box deadlift on 2" or 4" box conventional stance to max single; light Prowler snatch for five

sets of five reps from hang position; chest supported rows for six sets of eight to 12 reps; four sets of Reverse Hypers for 15 reps with light weight; abs; 10 trips of 60 yards with light weight sled pulls.

10. Push Prowler for 15 trips for 10 seconds work and 40 second rest; walk one to two miles with light sled; one alternative clean for five minutes for two sets; three sets of Reverse Hypers light; abs.

11. Concentric Goodmonings. Work up to a three-rep max with a safety squat bar; low pulley rows for six sets of eight reps; glute/ham raise for six sets for six reps heavy; Reverse Hypers for four sets of 10 reps; abs.

12. Drag a sled while pulling off of the heels for lower body for 60 yards per set; pull 90 pounds, add 45 pounds per set until reaching fatigue; recovery must be under 120 seconds; six sets of glute/ham raises heavy; four sets of Reverse Hypers heavy; six sets of leg raises with weight.

You can choose from and rotate these twelve max effort workouts. By adding several amounts of chains or bands to the bar, the workouts become limitless. When squatting on a box, one max effort record can become five records if five different boxes are implemented. Rack pulls can have four pin records. By changing bands from mini to light, there is a possibility of 16 max effort records to be achieved. Box squatting can use several amounts of band tension on each box height. Rotate the small special exercises when lack of progress or boredom occurs.

If an athlete is going to perform Olympic lifts, then max effort workouts are essential. If the individual only executes snatch and clean movements, then accommodation happens. It is not productive to use the classical lifts or to stay with a standard training load over a period of 21 days. Implement dynamic day where speed strength is the goal with loads of 75 percent to 85 percent in a three-week pendulum wave, and 72 hours later perform max effort workouts, changing them each week. Listed below are speed strength workouts plus special exercises:

Week 1	Power Snatch	70%	10 sets; 2 reps
Week 1	Snatch Pulls	80%	6 sets; 2 reps
Week 1	Low Box Squat	75%	8 sets; 2 reps
Week 1	Glute/Ham Raise		6 sets; 6 reps
Week 1	Reverse Hypers		6 sets; 6 reps heavy
Week 2	Power Clean and Jerk	80%	10 sets; 1 rep
Week 2	Front Squat	80%	4 sets; 4 reps
Week 2	Goodmonings	70%	4 sets; 6 reps
Week 2	Reverse Hypers		6 sets; 10 reps heavy
Week 3	Power Snatch Close Grip	85%	6 sets; 2 reps
Week 3	Box Squat Bar on Back	90%	5 sets; 1 rep
Week 3	Back Raise Heavy		5 sets; 5 reps

Week 3	Glute/Ham Raise		6 sets; 4 reps heavy
Week 4	GPP Pull Sled Heavy		6 trips; 60 yards
Week 4	Walking Goodmonings		60 yards; 4 trips
Week 4	Belt Squat	80%	6 sets; 6 reps
Week 4	Glute/Ham Raise		6 sets; 10 reps light
Week 4	Leg Raise		5 sets; 6 reps
Week 5	Back Squat with Push Jerk	80%	10 sets; 2 reps
Week 5	Clean Pulls	90%	7 sets; 1 rep
Week 5	Inverse Curls	75%	6 sets; 6 reps
Week 5	Reverse Hypers		4 sets; 10 reps heavy
Week 6	Snatch and Overhead Squat	75%	10 sets; 2 reps
Week 6	Snatch Pulls	85%	6 sets; 1 rep
Week 6	Back Raises		6 sets; 6 reps light
Week 6	Reverse Hypers		4 sets; 10 reps light
Week 7	Power Clean with Wide Grip	80%	8 sets; 3 reps
Week 7	Front Squat to Box	85%	6 sets; 2 reps
Week 7	Push Jerk From Back	75%	10 sets; 1 rep
Week 7	Glute/Ham Raise		6 sets; 4 reps heavy
Week 7	Pull Sled Light		6 trips; 60 yards
Week 8	Straight Leg Power Clean	80%	6 sets; 2 reps
Week 8	Straight Leg Power Snatch	75%	6 sets; 2 reps
Week 8	Concentric Back Squat off Back Pin	70%	3 sets; 3 reps
Week 8	Inverse Curl		3 sets; 2 reps heavy
Week 8	Reverse Hypers		4 sets; 10 reps light

The eight speed strength workouts should be used one or two times per week, or one time a week plus max effort workouts per week, adding more GPP workouts if needed. A lifter must slowly raise his work capacity year after year. He can substitute seated Goodmonings or with lunges with a bar on back. An individual can perform snatch and cleans from a starting position above the knee from the hands. These exercises are most effective for speed strength and reactive ability. He can start from different starting positions to fully gain the best results for weightlifting. This concept was proven in two studies by Marchenko published in *Theory and Practice of Physical Culture* in 1993 and 1994.

While the weightlifting systems of A.S. Medvedev would constantly raise the number of classical lifts per year, it was for weightlifting. My system, however, is for the development of all special strengths. I advise one to do fewer classical lifts and more special exercises to fulfill our goals. Athletes come in all sizes and shapes, and many cannot do the classical lifts: clean jerk, snatch, squat, bench and deadlift. Remember the weakest muscle group will fail and can cause injuries, so an individual must complete special exercises to bring fourth the weak muscle group to ensure improvement. A clean jerk is four movements. The first movement is the pull, the second movement is a front squat, and finally, the jerk. Because most are not model weightlifters like the Bulgarians, who could make progress on six main exercises (the power clean, clean and jerk, power snatch, snatch, back and front squat) it's not feasible to duplicate the Bulgarian weightlifting system with people built to specialize in other sports.

The Father of Plyometrics (Y.V. Verkhoshansky) used jumping, bounding and drop jumps for explosive power, not Olympic lifts. The best method for reversal strength through Olympic lifting is from the hang. Why? Because of the eccentric phase. Why not squat? Handling a heavier weight raises muscle mass and is much more effective for increasing powerful leg strength. The following are examples of Olympic lifting max effort workouts:

Week	Exercise	Intensity	Sets/Reps
Week 1	High Pull Snatch Grip	90%	6 sets; 1 rep
Week 1	High Pull Clean Grip	90%	6 sets; 1 rep
Week 1	Wide Low Box Squat	80%	4 sets; 4 reps
Week 1	Reverse hypers		6 sets; 10 reps light
Week 2	Power Clean on 2" Box		Work up to 1 rep max
Week 2	Jerk Behind Head	80%; 85%; 90%	1 rep
Week 2	Belt Squat Regular Squat	75%	6 sets; 6 reps
Week 2	Glute/Ham Raise		6 sets; 3 reps heavy
Week 2	Reverse hypers		6 sets; 10 reps heavy
Week 3	Snatch Grip Deadlift		Max 1 rep
Week 3	Front Squat	80%	6 sets; 3 reps
Week 3	Kettlebells Clean; 2 Kettlebells		6 sets; 10 reps
Week 3	Kettlebells Clean; 1 Kettlebell		To max 5 reps
Week 3	Reverse hypers		4 sets; 10 reps light
Week 4	Front Squat Plus Push Jerk		Max 3 reps
Week 4	Overhead Squat	75%	4 sets; 3 reps
Week 4	Back Raise		6 sets; 5 reps heavy
Week 4	Lunge with Bar		4 trips of 60 yards
Week 4	Reverse hypers		4 sets; 10 reps heavy

Week 5	Clean Grip Deadlift	Max 3 reps
Week 5	Straight Leg Power Clean	Max 5 reps
Week 5	Glute/Ham Raise	6 sets; 5 reps heavy
Week 5	Reverse hypers	4 sets; 10 reps heavy

Week 6

Implement isometric pulls for positions at floor and mid shin; at knee and above knee. Never sit between sets, but relax muscles as much as possible, building tension gradually.

Week 6	Belt Squat		4 sets; 10 reps light
Week 6	Straight Leg Good Mornings		4 sets; 4 reps light
Week 6	Glute/Ham Raise		6 sets; 3 reps heavy
Week 6	Reverse hypers		4 sets; 10 reps heavy
Week 7	Dead Stop Clean Pull Below Knee		Max 1 rep
Week 7	Dead Stop Clean Pull Above Knee		Max 1 rep
Week 7	Overhead Squat	80%	4 sets; 4 reps
Week 7	Back Raise		4 sets; 6 reps heavy
Week 7	Reverse hypers		4 sets; 10 reps heavy
Week 8	Front Squat on Box		Max 3 reps
Week 8	Bend Leg Good Morning		Max 3 reps
Week 8	Inverse Curl		6 sets; 3 reps heavy
Week 8	Reverse hypers		4 sets; 10 reps heavy

All workouts should include abdominal work, and choice ranging from moderate jumps, sled pulls, or walking with some weight resistance. I recommend three rep sets to develop muscle tension. Olympic lifting became a speed strength sport after the press was abolished in 1972. Olympic lifting looks explosive because of the most advanced position during the second pull. In turn, Olympic lifts are too fast to develop Fmm, occurring at .4 tenth of a second. Unfortunately, strength and conditioning coaches have forgotten about real strength work, meaning absolute strength. Do not use machines because they build muscle not motion; strength should be measured in time, not heavy or light weight.

Bench max effort workouts

Week 1	Floor Press	Max 1 rep
Week 1	Dumbbell Press Flat	4 sets; 12 reps moderate
Week 1	Dumbbell Triceps	6 sets; 8 reps heavy
Week 1	Dumbbell Rows	6 sets; 10 reps heavy
Week 1	Dumbbell Power Clean	6 sets; 12 reps moderate

Week 2	Incline Press	Max 3 reps
Week 2	Push-ups	2 sets; high reps
Week 2	Barbell Triceps Extensions	6 sets; 6 reps heavy
Week 2	Front Plate Press	6 sets; 10 reps light
Week 2	Rear and Side Delt Work	6 sets; 6 reps heavy
Week 2	Chest Supported Row	6 sets; 6 reps heavy
Week 2	Hammer Curls	4 sets; 10 reps light

Week 3	Board Press- 3 and 2	Max 1 rep; 2 sets of high reps 15 or more Reps; 1 wide; 1 close 50% of 1 rep max
Week 3	Dumbbell Triceps Work	6 sets; 10 reps
Week 3	Front Raise Barbell	
Week 3	Low Pulley Rows	6 sets; 10 reps
Week 3	Hammer Curls	

Week 4	Rack Lockout	2 pins 2" and 6" off chest
Week 4	Dumbbell Incline Press	2 sets; 12 reps heavy
Week 4	JM Triceps Press	6 sets; 6 reps moderate
Week 4	Lat Pull Downs	6 sets; 12 reps light
Week 4	Hammer Curls	3 sets; 8 reps

Week 5	Heavy Dumbbell Press	3 sets to failure, example: 100 lb., 125 lb., 155 lb. rest 5 or 6 minutes between sets
Week 5	Barbell Rows	5 sets; 8 reps
Week 5	Front and Side Delt Raises	4 sets; 10 reps each
Week 5	Hammer Curls	6 sets; 8 reps heavy

Week 6	Mini Band Bench	Max 1 rep
Week 6	Push-ups	2 sets; high reps
Week 6	Triceps Pushdown	5 sets; 12 reps
Week 6	Chest Supported Row	5 sets; 10 reps
Week 6	Inverse Flies	4 sets; 10 reps
Week 6	Hammer Curls	3 sets; 8 reps

Week 7	Lightened Method-Strong Band Lighted 150 lb. work	Max 3 reps
Week 7	Drop to 75% of a 1 Rep Max and one Wide Grip Set for High Reps	
Week 7	Dumbbell Extensions	8 sets; 8 reps heavy
Week 7	Dumbbell Rows	8 sets; 8 reps heavy
Week 7	Front Plate Raise	4 sets; 8 reps light
Week 7	Hammer Curls	6 sets; 8 reps heavy

Week 8	Decline Press	Max 1 rep
Week 8	Dumbbell Press Incline	4 sets; 10 reps
Week 8	Chest Supported Rows	5 sets; 8 reps
Week 8	Dumbbell Power Clean	2 sets; 15 reps
Week 8	Hammer Curls	3 sets; 8 reps

This is just a few samples of max effort workouts. There are five strengths of bands to choose from to alter the workout. Chains also can be implemented to vary the exercises; one set 40 pounds or five sets 200 pounds can change an exercise completely. Each week change the max effort workout to avoid accommodation. Small exercises can and should be changed often to avert boredom and continue progress.

CHAPTER 8 – TRAINING FOR COMBATIVE SPORTS AND ARTS

CHAPTER 8 – TRAINING FOR COMBATIVE SPORTS AND ARTS

Introduction

When Louie Simmons asked me to write a chapter for this book I was both humbled and honored to be part of such a cutting-edge, innovative project. For the past 15 years the fighters and martial artists I have coached have used Louie's Westside Method of Training with outstanding results. These same methods will work for you if you do the work. In fact, The Westside Method of Training will give you great strength, explosive power and speed faster and more effectively than any other method. Not only will you gain greater muscular strength, speed, and endurance, you will also increase tendon and ligament strength to help protect you from the injuries that are so common in combative sports and arts.

You also will learn many special exercises to help you transform your general strength, speed, and explosive power into the specific physical qualities you need to succeed on the mat, in the ring, the cage, or in self-defense. Some of these exercises are relatively new — others have been around forever. The one thing they have in common is that they all work. With these exercises you will be able to strengthen weak links in your techniques that may be holding you back from top performance.

There are other things you'll need to know to reach the top, things like how to organize your training throughout the week, month, year, and longer. You will learn these things as well as how to use three-week waves and the conjugate method of training to help you make continual progress and reduce your chances of injury.

As Louie Simmons has often said, "To be a champion, do what others are unwilling to do." I am confident that if you discipline yourself to follow the training methods outlined in this book and practice your event diligently, you will achieve great success in your chosen combative sport or art. Now, it's up to you. Get started on this book and get to work! There are no limits to what you can accomplish.

John Saylor

This chapter is organized into three levels based on "The Building Blocks To Mastery"

- Level I consists of all-around **general** physical training. It is designed to lay the foundation for future training.

- Level II will introduce more **intense** and **specific** training into your program.

- Level III is the **peaking phase**, which you should use when fine-tuning for a major event.

Through an understanding of the three levels and what percentage of each is right for you, you will be able to structure your training to develop maximum fitness in the least amount of time.

Building Blocks to Mastery

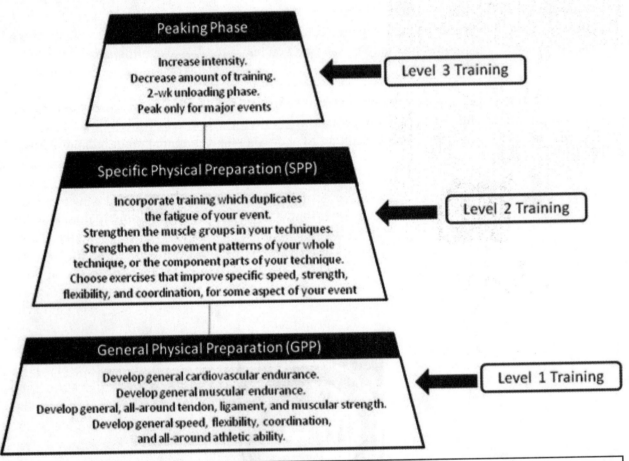

Keep Records

Get a small notebook or wire rim notecards and record your exercises, sets, and reps.
You should also record any other important information such as the date, your body weight, any illness or injury, or anything else that affects your training. This information will enable you to see your progress, to make any necessary adjustments in your training, and will help you determine when to rotate exercises in your routine. Your records will also let you know when you're not making progress. When you see that your progress has stalled, you'll know it's time to rotate exercises or make other changes.

LEVEL I: COMPONENTS OF GENERAL PHYSICAL PREPARATION

Cardiovascular Endurance

Cardiovascular endurance is the foundation of a fighter's preparation. Without a strong heart, lungs, and circulatory system, you won't get very far in any combative art. Nor will you be very healthy. Your heart is the pump that brings blood and oxygen to your muscles with each beat. It is vital, therefore, to train for cardiovascular fitness.

How to Train for Cardiovascular Endurance:

To develop cardiovascular endurance, choose an activity such as running, swimming, biking, grappling, or any other steady-paced moderate exercise that will keep your heart rate between approximately 130 to 150 beats per minute. When you're doing grappling for a cardiovascular workout, it's important to train with a partner who understands how to maintain a moderate pace. Too often it ends up being a contest with both fighters butting heads. There's a time for that, but not when you need to keep grappling for 30 minutes to one hour straight. Think of it as free-form drilling. If your partner achieves good position for a submission, give it to him. Just keep rolling. **A good rule of thumb, regardless of what type of cardiovascular work you're doing, is to train at a pace at which you can hold a conversation for the allotted time.** If you find yourself huffing, puffing, and gasping for breath, slow down your pace or pause until you can again carry on a conversation.

You could monitor your heart rate more precisely by figuring your maximum heart rate (220 minus your age), and then keeping your heart rate in a target zone of between 60 percent to 85 percent of your max. But you'll probably do just as well by observing our rule of thumb: **keep it at a pace at which you can hold a conversation.** Besides, it's really inconvenient to stop and take your heart rate throughout your workout. Train like this up to six times a week depending on your needs and goals.

Try to inject a variety of other exercises into your run, such as pushups, duck walks, solo takedown drills, and various kinds of jumps, pull-ups, punching and kicking and so on.

Photo: Sean Daugherty often uses the towing sled for a cardio workout.

Summary

- Figure maximum heart rate by subtracting your age from 220. Choose a steady-paced, moderate exercise that keeps you between 60 percent and 85 percent of your maximum heart rate.
- To avoid having to take your pulse continuously throughout your workout, **train at a pace at which you can hold a conversation.** If you exceed that pace, slow down or pause until you can again hold a conversation.
- Train at this pace for 20 to 60 minutes.
- Train like this up to six days per week depending on your needs and goals.

General Muscular Endurance

Another important attribute to develop during Level I training is muscular endurance. You can develop muscular endurance to some degree through martial art practice itself. But if you want to develop your full muscular endurance potential you should do high repetition body weight exercises outside of your regular martial art practice.

Your body will adapt to this kind of training by developing miles and miles of tiny blood vessels called *capillaries*. These capillaries serve as an oxygen transport system to your muscles. They also help to remove fatigue products like lactic and pyruvic acid. This enables them to work longer with less fatigue.

There are many good exercises to choose from, but for those of you who want to get going right now, the following exercises will give you a good start:

Basic Exercises for Muscular Endurance (The Shingitai "Six-Pack")

1. Neck Bridge

This is a great exercise for fighters of all kinds. It not only strengthens your neck, but also hits your hips, legs, back, and abs. The neck bridge will also make your spine more flexible.

To perform the neck bridge, lie down on the floor with a mat under the back of your head. Gradually bridge up and back until your nose is touching the mat. Don't worry if you can't touch your nose at first. Keep working at it and eventually you'll be able to do it. In the beginning you can use your hands to take some of the pressure off your neck. As your neck gets stronger you won't need to use your hands. <u>Hold the bridge between one and three minutes.</u>

Photo 1

Mike Mekoleske is shown demonstrating the neck bridge in excellent form. You should gradually work on your bridge until you can touch your nose to the mat. But don't push it—this takes time.

Before you move to the next exercise, let me digress for a moment and explain why it is so important to work your lower body.

Build The House From The Basement Up

The Hindu Squat was a standard of old-time Indian/Pakistani wrestlers like The Great Gama who is said to have performed as many as 4,000 reps per day. Gama included jumping squats and one-leg squats as well. Although some doubt the number (4,000 reps), it is clear that Gama devoted an incredible amount of time and energy to developing his lower body. So should you. High repetition Hindu squats will not only build a strong lower body, but also build incredible overall endurance.

Around 1977 I was training in the old weight room under Ohio State's football stadium. A world-class Austrian Shot Putter, whom I knew only as "Ernst," occasionally did full squats with 800-plus pounds. One day after a workout I asked, "Hey, Ernst, why do you concentrate on squats so much?"

"You build a house from the basement up," he replied, quoting an old training maxim.
"Think about it," he went on. "When I throw, it's a chain reaction. It starts from my lower body, goes through my torso, and then is released through my upper body."

"Yeah, that makes sense," I agreed. And it did. The same holds true for many judo and wrestling throws. On hip throws, for example, once you've turned in and dropped under your opponent, the first phase of the throw is started with the legs and hips, then is continued through the torso, and finished with the arms. This is exactly the kind of chain reaction Ernst was talking about.

The same is true for various pick-up throws where you secure the opponent around a leg or his waist, and then lift him up and slam him to the mat. Throws like Te-Guruma (Hand Wheel) or Sukui Nage (Scooping Throw), for example, are started with the hips and legs. Then, the back and abs come into it, and finally the throw is completed with the arms. As you can see, if your lower body is weak, you'll never be able to use these kinds of techniques with any success.

Photos 2

Pick-Up Throws and other throws and Takedowns require a strong lower body.

Photos by Steve Scott.

One of the fundamental exercises for developing the lower body is the Hindu Squat. Let's examine it more closely.

2. How to Perform Hindu Squats

Start with your feet approximately shoulder width and your hands hanging loosely at your sides. With your back straight and your hips underneath you, squat down as far as you can. As you come back up, curl your hands to your chest. There are different opinions on proper breathing as you perform the exercise. I believe that after a few workouts your body will establish a breathing pattern that is best for you, so don't worry too much about it.

Make sure your knees extend directly out in a straight line over your toes as you squat down. At first you may experience some soreness in your knees, but as your tendons and ligaments become stronger this should disappear.

Work up to as many as 500 reps in one set. This should take about 15 minutes. You can do Hindu Squats as many as five days per week, although you don't need to go to 500 reps each time. Allow for hard days and easy days.

Photo 3 and Photo 4:

Hindu Squats

Keep your back straight with your hips underneath you. Make sure your knees extend out in a straight line over your toes. Let your arms hang loosely at your sides and curl them up to your chest as you rise up out of the squat position.

Perform Hindu Squats at a steady pace and aim for 100 reps every three minutes.

Want To Lift Your Opponent?

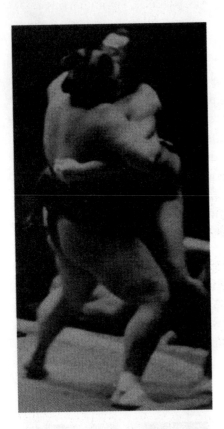

Whether it's Sumo or a street fight, the ability to lift up your opponent and slam him to the ground comes from strong hips and legs, low back, and abs. The arms merely secure the opponent to your body as you execute the technique. Sumo Wrestlers do up to 500 Shiko (Sumo Squats) per day. This develops tremendous lower body strength and flexibility. Occasionally they perform Shiko with one of the junior Sumo Wrestlers on their back for added resistance.

When you have more fully developed hips and legs you will have more weight centered in your lower body. This makes it much harder for your opponents to throw you with hip throws, and makes you more stable in general. So remember: your body is like a house. Build it from the basement up.

3. Glute-Ham Raises

This is an outstanding exercise for strengthening the hamstrings, glutes, and to a lesser extent, the calves. One of the main reasons people injure their knees is because they have far stronger quadriceps (muscles on the front of the thigh) than they do hamstrings (muscles on the back of the thigh). This exercise will strengthen the hamstrings to a high level and will help to eliminate muscle imbalances that can lead to injury. It will enable you to generate more force and speed, and it will help you lift an opponent up off the ground.

> **Benefits**:
> Glute-ham raises will strengthen your hamstrings and glutes like no other exercise. They will give you greater explosiveness and overall power in your lower body, and will also lessen your chances of knee injuries and hamstring pulls.

Below, Sean Daugherty is shown doing Glute-ham raises on a Glute-Ham Machine designed by Louie Simmons. This exercise was originally developed by Russian athletes who placed a gymnastics vaulting horse next to a set of wall bars that were very common in Russia. They rested their thighs on the vaulting horse and secured their heels under the wall bars. Then they performed the exercise as shown here.

Vasily Alekseev, the Russian Olympic and World Champion weight lifter, who first broke the 500-pound barrier on the clean and jerk, routinely did 60 reps to warm up. He also used 225 pounds for five reps, a phenomenal feat.

Photo 1

Curl yourself upright using your hamstrings and glutes. Notice that Sean's kneecaps are not contacting the pad. Also notice that the soles of his feet are in contact with the toe plate. At the up position your thighs should almost be vertical to the ground. Keep your back straight throughout the movement.

Photo 2

With your thighs resting on the pad and your heels secured …

Photo 3 and *Photo 4*

Sean adds a Bulgarian Bag.

> **Note:**
> Leg Curls really only strengthen the belly of the muscle, not the insertions that stabilize the joint. But once in awhile leg curls might be useful for the sake of measurement. Ad here to the following rule of thumb: If you can't Leg Curl at least 60 percent of what you can do for a Leg Extension, you are vulnerable to hamstring and knee injuries.

But don't despair. Glute-ham raises are a big part of the solution.

Or, if you can't afford a Glute-Ham Machine right now, try improvising with a sit-up board as we did for years before finally buying one (pictured below and demonstrated by John Marotta). Be sure to place lots of padding under your knees since there will be pressure on your knee caps. Take off just enough resistance with your hands to allow you to complete the rep, until over time you don't need your hands at all.

If the exercise is still too difficult, just concentrate on the lowering portion of the exercise. Push yourself up with your hands and lower yourself back down. Concentrate on resisting the downward movement with all you've got. Keep at it three or four days per week, and pretty soon you'll be knocking out some serious reps without the use of your hands.

Even if you don't own a sit-up board, you can perform this exercise on a mat while a partner holds your feet down. Again, be sure to use extra pad ding under your knees.

Photos by Melissa Stage

This is a hard exercise at first, so start with a few reps for several sets. Over time, build up until you can do 50 consecutive reps with your body weight. Do the exercise two or three times per week.

Glute-Ham Raises with Tubing

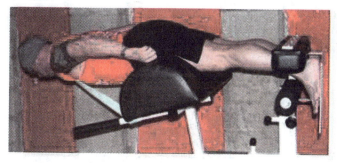

Many exercises can be made more difficult with the use of bands. Here, Sean Daugherty is shown doing glute-ham raises with a medium band. The bands will further develop your strength and speed.

Another method is to hold a weight to your chest or behind your neck as you perform the glute-ham raises. Advanced trainees who have worked on this exercise for a couple of years can try another variation by doing glute-ham raises one leg at a time.

4. Sit-Ups

> This is an old standard exercise for your abs that you're probably familiar with. Just make sure your knees are bent, and that you keep your hands from swinging by placing them at the side of your head or across your chest. You can sit up straight and touch both elbows to your knees simultaneously, or you can alternately twist to the left and right as you touch your elbow to the opposite knee. Do up to 200 reps depending on your fitness level and goals.

5. Push-Ups

> I'm sure you know how to do a standard push-up. Just make sure to keep your body straight and rigid throughout the movement. Depending on your fitness level and goals, work up to a total of 200 reps. This can be done in any set/rep scheme you like (e.g. 10 sets of 20 reps, four sets of 50 reps, etc.). Push-ups will strengthen your chest, frontal shoulders, and the tricep muscles of your arms. Later we will go over a number of push-up variations to work your muscles differently and to prevent boredom.

6. Pull-Ups (Overhand Grip)

The pull-up is an excellent exercise for the arms, lats, shoulders, and all the pulling muscles of the upper body. The pulling power you develop will be particularly useful in all grappling-based arts. Here, Sean Daugherty demonstrates flawless form for reverse-grip pull-ups.

Variations

To avoid going stale you should vary your pull-ups every week or two. Try some of the following variations:

1. Underhand grip (both hands facing you)
2. Parallel Grip (as can be found on monkey bars in most school-yards)
3. From overhead rings
4. With rock climbing grips (found at rock climbing supply shops)
5. Towel or GI pull-ups (drape a towel or your gi over the bar, grip it, and pull away).

*With any of the above variations you can execute three-second isometric holds at three or four positions throughout the range of motion.

*You can also vary the width of your grip, and attach weights or bands for added resistance.

How to Avoid Slumps in Your Training

The preceding six exercises ("The Shingitai 6-Pack") are the basic building blocks of your muscular endurance and strength program. If you're consistent in your training, they will give you good results. But even with the best of exercises, the time will come when your progress stalls. When this happens, you need to stimulate your central nervous system by injecting variety into your program.

Start by varying your grip, stance, or hand position on your exercises. This will work your muscles differently and get you back on the road to progress. But don't stop there:

- Vary your set and rep scheme
- Vary the speed of execution on your exercises
- Vary the type of resistance
- Vary the order of your exercises
- Vary the exercises themselves. Let's go into this last point in more detail:

Secret Training Methods of the World's Best Athletes

My friend Louie Simmons, coach of numerous national and world champions in Powerlifting, is fond of saying, "All the exercises work, but nothing works forever." The lifters at his world-famous Westside Barbell Club in Columbus, Ohio, constantly rotate their assistance exercises when one is no longer effective. Some even rotate them every week. Louie got this idea from coaches in the former Soviet Union who called it the Conjugate Method of Training. Louie's use of the Conjugate Method is one of the main reasons the Westside Barbell lifters keep setting new records year after year. By rotating their exercises on a regular basis they avoid going stale and they make continual progress.

Of course, you're not training for power lifting, but for jujitsu, self-defense, or some other grappling art. Your training needs to be specific to your martial art, but you can still use the Conjugate Method to help you avoid slumps and to make continual gains. The key is to rotate your exercises and drilling methods on a regular basis — at least every three weeks, and for advanced trainees, even more often. In fact, you should change something every single workout.

No two workouts should be exactly the same.

Read on for a list of suggested variations you might want to try.

Exercises to Substitute for Those in Your Basic Program

The basic "Shingitai 6-Pack" exercises are listed in the left-hand column. The middle and right-hand columns contain exercises that you can substitute for those in the basic program. Rotate these and other exercises for variety in your program.

Basic Exercises:	*Sample Alternative Exercises To Substitute For Basic Exercises:*		
1) Neck bridge	→ 1) Front bridge	→ 1) Four-way neck exercise w/ Bands	→ 1) Headstand neck exercises
2) Hindu squats	→ 2) One-leg squats (Pistols)	→ 2) Two-leg jumps-up squats	→ 2) Hindu jump squats
3) Glute-ham raises	→ 3) Leg curls with tubing	→ 3) Incline glute-ham raises (Feet elevated, w/Tubing)	→ 3) Lower body sled towing
4) Sit-ups	→ 4) Leg raises	→ 4) Side-to-Side Leg Raises	→ 4) V-sit-ups
5) Push-ups	→ 5) Hindu push-ups	→ 5) Push-ups w/feet elevated	→ 5) Triceps (triangle) push-ups
6) Pull-ups (overhand grip)	→ 6) Chin-ups (palms facing you)	→ 6) Horizontal pull-ups (feet supported in front of you)	→ 6) Rope climb

Note: Notice that the substitute exercises above, essentially work the same muscle groups, although somewhat differently.

These are just a few of the exercises you can substitute for those in your basic program. There are many more. When you learn new ones, write them down in a notebook and separate them by lower body, torso, upper body, and total body. Then draw from this arsenal when you need to rotate exercises.

Remember, no two workouts should be exactly the same.

Rotate something each and every workout. This is the secret to continual progress.

More Championship Strategies When Your Progress Stalls

When you first start out on your basic exercises, you'll make rapid progress for quite awhile. But no matter how hard you train, the time will come when your progress levels off or even declines. When you feel this coming on, it's important to inject some variety into your program. Later in this book I'll introduce you to more exercises that you can rotate in and out of your routine. But for now, you can add variety and greatly improve your overall physical condition by using the following five methods of exercising:

Five Methods of Exercising For Complete Development

The following systems of training can be done with most of the body weight exercises in your routine, and each will provide a different stimulus to your body:

1. **Do As Many Repetitions As You Can.**
2. **Do Your Reps As Explosively As You Can.**

Let's use **pull-ups** as an example: Stop at a dead hang. Then, as fast as you can, pull yourself up. Return to a hang, pause, and repeat for the allotted reps.

This same system works well for parallel bar dips, one-leg squats, and many of the more difficult body weight exercises.

Do 10 to 12 sets of three reps with a 30-second rest between sets. It's important to take the full 30-second rest so that you can explode on your next set. Remember, you are training primarily for *speed* with this method.

3. **Do The Exercise With Added Weights or Tubing (Bands)**

Simply add weight or use tubing to provide more resistance. Take pull-ups, for example. You can suspend weights from a rope tied around your waist, or buy a special belt for this purpose. Or you can attach tubes to immovable objects on the floor and loop the other ends through your belt. Then perform as many reps as you can. You can also use added weight or bands on exercises such as parallel bar dips, push-ups, Hindu squats, and many others.

But, if you are not yet able to do a pull-up, for example, loop two bands around the pull-up bar and rest your knees in the loops on the other end. This will lighten the resistance at the start of the pull-up, and should enable you to complete a rep or two. This is a form of what Louie Simmons calls, "The Lightened Method."

For variety, switch back and forth from tubing to weights, or use both simultaneously. Each works your muscles differently. By using various types of resistance you'll get more complete muscular development.

4. Do the Exercise with Isometric Holds Throughout the Movement

Take exercises like pull-ups, parallel bar dips, or any other body-weight exercise, and throughout each rep do three, three-second holds at three different angles. In other words, hold a position at the low position for three seconds. Move to the midway point and hold that for three seconds. Then hold a position slightly below the top for three more seconds. Repeat for the desired number of sets and reps.

5. Do The Exercise Slowly While Concentrating On Your Breathing

I first learned this method from former Russian "Spetsnaz" Special Forces operative, Vladimir Vasiliev. If you're doing a push-up, for example, inhale as you slowly lower yourself to the bottom position to the count of 10 or even 20, then slowly exhale as you push up to the starting position. Repeat for the desired number of reps. Then inhale, hold your breath, and knock out 10 or more fast reps. Vladimir Vasiliev has a number of variations of these breath control exercises, each of which affects the body somewhat differently.

__Warning: If you have high blood pressure, do not attempt to hold your breath.__

Each of the aforementioned methods emphasizes a different physical quality, as follows:

Method #1: Primarily develops *muscular endurance, and tendon and ligament* strength.

Method #2: Primarily *develops speed* strength.

Method #3: Primarily *develops absolute* strength.

Method #4: Primarily *develops isometric* strength.

Method #5: Primarily develops *muscular endurance and breath control*, as well as *tendon and ligament* strength.

> **Rotate the above methods. By doing so faithfully, you will:**
> - **Avoid staleness and injuries**
> - **Make continual progress**
> - **Develop all of the above physical attributes, not just one or two**
> - **Become a very well-prepared, dangerous fighter**

Okay, this sums up the basic exercises of the "Shingitai 6-Pack." They will help you to build a strong foundation. Later on, I'll introduce you to a number of other exercises and training methods to torture you into greatness. But do these exercises first. Remember, as Ernst said, "you build the house from the basement up."

Basic Exercises to Prevent Shoulder Injuries

Shoulder injuries are pretty common in grappling-based arts, but most can be prevented if you strengthen the shoulder girdle from a variety of angles. Do the following exercises twice a week to strengthen your entire shoulder girdle and reduce your chances of injury:

Shoulder Exercises with Tubing or Expanders

> 1. Alternate dumbbell (DB) overhead press (Eight to 12 reps. for one or two sets)
> 2. Alternate DB forward raises (Eight to 12 reps. for one or two sets)
> 3. DB side lateral raises (Eight to 12 reps. for one or two sets)
> 4. DB bent lateral raises (Eight to 12 reps for one or two sets)

For variety and a different stimulus on your muscles, try doing the above exercises with spring cable expanders, rubber tubing, or even doubled-up bungee cords. These will work your muscles in an entirely different way and make you much stronger.

After you've developed some strength in the aforementioned shoulder exercises, you may want to challenge yourself further by adding a couple new exercises and combining them all into one long, continuous killer set. Read on and I'll introduce you to what I call "The Russian Dumbbell Shoulder Routine."

The Russian Dumbbell Shoulder Routine

During the late '80s a couple of the guys from the U.S. National Judo Training Squad, which I was coaching at the Olympic Training Center, fought in The Tblisi Cup in the former Soviet Union. The Tblisi Cup was arguably the toughest judo tournament in the world, since any one of the top five Soviets in each weight class had a good chance to place or win in the World Championship or the Olympics. That year an American who spent a couple summers with us, Jason Morris, won the 189-Pound Division, the first time an American had won this prestigious tournament. Jason went on to win the silver medal in the 1992 Olympics in Barcelona.

While they were in Tblisi, a couple of our fighters picked up a great dumbbell routine from the Russian fighters for the entire shoulder girdle. Johnny Hobales, one of our top 156-pound fighters first showed it to me. It goes like this:

Russian DB Shoulder Routine

Pick up a pair of dumbbells with which you can do eight to 12 reps. (each arm) of the following exercises in one continuous set. In other words, don't put the dumbbells down between exercises, just go straight into the next exercise. Depending on your needs, do one to three complete sets. Okay, here it is:

1. Alternate Overhead DB Press (Photo #1)
2. Alternate DB Forward Raises (Photo #2)
3. DB Side Lateral Raises (Photo #3)
4. DB Bent Lateral Raises (Photo #4)
5. Alternate DB Cross-Body Curls (Photo #5)
6. DB Judo Swing and Pull (Photo #6)

Note: You've already been doing shoulder exercises 1 through 4. Now you're adding two more exercises, and you're doing them continuously without rest between exercises.

In addition to building strength and endurance throughout the entire shoulder girdle, this routine will also build tremendous endurance in your hands and forearms. Exercises like these, in which you work the shoulders from many different angles, are vitally important in grappling arts, since shoulders (and knees) are primary injury sites.

Photo 1

Alternate Overhead DB Presses

Alternately press the DB's overhead for the desired number of reps.

(Sean Daugherty)

Photo 2

Alternate DB Forward Raises

With a slight bend in the elbow, alternately raise the DB's straight forward to a point just above your head. This exercise strengthens the front delts.

Photo 3
DB Side Lateral Raises

Photo 4
DB Bent Lateral Raises

With a slight bend in your elbows and with both DB's held in front of your body, simultaneously raise the DB's to the point shown in the photo. This is a great exercise for the side delts.

Bend forward at the waist, and with both DB's held together at arm's length under your chest, simultaneously raise the DB's out away from your body in a reverse flying motion. This is a great exercise for the rear delts, an often-neglected muscle group.

Photos by Melissa Stage

Photo 5 & 6
Alternate DB Cross Body Curls

Swing the DB across your body up to your opposite side. This exercise primarily works the tie-in between the bicep and shoulder, as well as overall upper body muscular endurance.

Photo 7 & 8
DB Judo Swing and Pull

Take a step to one side as though you were taking the first step toward a forward throw. With the momentum this step creates, swing the DB's up towards your face just as if you were pulling an opponent in for a forward throw. This exercise works your arms and shoulders, as well as many of the stabilizers and rotational muscles of your torso.

Now, here's a dumbbell routine that's not quite as formal as the Russian DB Shoulder Routine, but it's every bit as tough. And since you're not just confining the work to leverage- type shoulder exercises, you can increase the weight of the dumbbells. I call it The Five-Minute Dumbbell Drill.

The 5-Minute Dumbbell Drill

Back in the late 1970's I started doing a 5-Minute DB Drill in which I took a pair of 50 to 60 pounders and did a variety of continuous exercises for two to three sets of five minutes. It was pretty informal. I did whatever exercises I felt like in whatever order I wanted. My objective was just to keep them moving and not put them down until the time was up. I had stolen the idea from Dan Gable's book, *Conditioning For Wrestling The Iowa Way* (1986), although I modified the time limits from 3x3 minute rounds, which coincided with a freestyle wrestling match at the time, to two or three five-minute rounds, the length of judo matches.

This was a highly intense upper body workout, and when I put the dumbbells down my hands and forearms were so cramped up I could barely release my grip off the handles. The feeling reminded me of a Biblical passage describing the exploits of one of King David's top three elite fighters:

> "…the men of Israel retreated, but he stood his ground and struck down the Philistines till his hand grew tired and froze to the sword." (2 Samuel 23:9-10 NIV).

Through the 5-Minute Dumbbell Drill I developed a new appreciation of what this warrior's hands were going through, and so will you. But the good news is that if you do this type of training along with circuits and body weight exercises on a regular basis, you will never get arm weary in a grappling-based match or fight. You have my guarantee: If you find that it's not true, that even after you've trained like this diligently for three months your arms are still getting worn out in practice or matches, then you have my permission to roll this book into a tightly compacted club and whack me over the head with it. And after my beating, I will refund your money. Now, obviously I'm pretty sure you'll get the results you're after. But first you must do the work.

Guidelines for The 5-Minute Dumbbell Drill

1. Choose a pair of dumbbells, the combined weight of which is one-third to one-half of your body weight.

2. Since the weight of your dumbbells is pretty heavy compared to The Russian DB Shoulder Routine, perform any leverage type exercises (e.g. forward raises, lateral raises, bent lateral raises) first while you're still fresh. After you've gotten them out of the way, perform exercises that work larger muscle groups. Some good exercises to include which work larger muscle groups are bent rows, alternate curls, bench presses, Judo swing and pull, etc. Use your imagination and see what you come up with. Just keep them moving and don't put them down.

3. Five minutes will probably be too long to start with. Start with what you can do, even if it's only one minute, and try to go a little longer each workout. Eventually you'll get to five minutes, maybe even for two or three sets.

4. If you stay on The 5-Minute DB Drill two times per week for more than three weeks, you'll start to go stale. When you feel this starting to happen, either switch to some of the other Shingitai Circuits for awhile, or take some time off any type of dumbbell drill or circuit, particularly if you don't have any contests close at hand. Instead, just concentrate on your body weight exercises, and on whatever weight exercises you need.

Note: Here are a couple more exercises to include in the 5-Minute DB Drill.

Photo 9 & 10

Alternately curl the dumbbells up to shoulder level. This exercise will strengthen your biceps and to a lesser extent your forearms.

Photo 11 & 12

Bend at waist and from arms length pull the dumbbell through a full range of motion up to your lats. The exercise will strengthen your lats, rear delts, and all pulling muscles of the upper back.

The Mother of All Sets

My judo friend, and a great coach from St. Petersburg, Florida, Jim Marshman, saw my fighters and me doing The 5-Minute DB Drill at the Olympic Training Center. He liked the idea and took it home to his fighters, but after awhile he decided it needed a little more structure. He found that when his athletes reached a certain level of fatigue they had trouble deciding what exercise to go to next. He was also concerned that they might not work opposing muscle groups enough, so he came up with the following DB routine that he lovingly named "The Mother of All Sets."

The Mother of All Sets is a continuous set of six exercises that consist of the following:

Choose a pair of dumbbells, the combined weight of which is between one-third to one-half of your bodyweight and have them nearby.

Warm up with 50 to 100 Hindu Squats, depending on your level of conditioning. Then, pick up the dumbbells, and without putting them down between exercises, perform the following in the order given: (See photos on the following page)

1. Overhead Press (Alternating or Together)
2. DB Tricep Kickbacks (Together)
3. Bicep Curls (Alternating or Together)
4. Judo Swing and Pull (Alternate Sides—Photos 6, 7, and 8)
5. DB Bent Rows (Together)
6. DB Shrugs (Together)

One set of the The Mother of All Sets consists of doing each of the above six exercises with 10 reps, then eight, six, and finally four **without stopping**. Put the weights down. Do 50 to 100 Hindu Squats. **That is one set of the** The Mother of All Sets.

Rest two to five minutes, or until your heart rate returns to around 120 beats per minute, before starting the next set. **If you're a serious competitor, ultimately work up to four to five complete sets.** Each set should take around five minutes.

Note: Although some of the above exercises are not specific in the movement, they are very specific in terms of the fatigue you will experience.

Below, Sean Daugherty is shown performing the first four exercises of **The Mother of All Sets** with a pair of 30-pound dumbbells. The last two exercises, DB Bent Rows and DB Shrugs, are not shown, but are fairly self-explanatory.

Photo 1 and Photo 2

Overhead Press

Photo 3 and Photo 4

DB Tricep Kickbacks

Photo 5, Photo 6, Photo 7, Photo 8
Judo Swing and Pull to the right and left

Whether you're doing The Russian DB Shoulder Routine, The 5-Minute DB Drill, or the more structured Mother of All Sets, you will develop tremendous muscular endurance and a good bit of strength as well. Again, I've never known anybody who's done these workouts for any length of time who's gotten arm-weary in a fight.

These workouts, along with the other Shingitai Circuits and the many body weight exercises, will cause your muscles to develop miles and miles of extra capillaries. These capillaries serve as an oxygen transport system, taking blood and oxygen into the working muscles and removing fatigue products like lactic and pyruvic acid.

When you train like this, you'll have a big advantage over more conventionally trained fighters. You'll be as tough in the last minute of a fight as you were in the first. This stuff is very hard, but it's much better to suffer in training than during a fight. Go to it.

The Value of Physical Work

Who would you bet on to win in an all-out scrap: a pumped-up, iron-pushing bodybuilder, or a guy who does hard physical labor day in and day out? My money would be on the laborer, the guy who works construction, lays bricks, picks, shovels, wheelbarrows, does cement or asphalt work — anything done by hand for long periods of time. Don't get me wrong; some forms of weight training have value, especially types described in The Westside Method. But the way most people train with weights has little to do with the ability to fight. You'd be better off doing some form of physical work around your house.

Even though some construction workers and other laborers I've observed tend to drink themselves into oblivion, smoke, and have other bad habits, they still develop a strong back, arms, grip, muscular endurance, and an overall toughness the average iron pushers miss. Physical labor works many stabilizer muscles that weight training misses, and is the type of conditioning that carries over to fighting.

On my farm we have an outdoor wood-burning furnace. Each fall and winter I go into the woods and chop or hand saw through tons of fallen trees. I usually cut them in four to eight foot pieces depending on the circumference and weight of the log. I then carry them to the trail, which, depending on where I am in the woods, could be up to fifty yards away. Next I loop a tow chain around the log, attach the other end to a strong loop through which I run a weight belt, and then tow the log behind me for several hundred yards over uneven terrain before finally getting back to the wood furnace. Talk about a workout!

John Saylor towing a log to the outdoor wood-burning furnace that heats the Barn of Truth Dojo. Hard labor builds physical toughness that's hard to duplicate in other ways.

Sometimes as I'm towing the log I turn around and pull it with my arms in a rowing motion. Needless to say, I get much stronger, and better conditioned, too.

You can do similar things even if you don't live out in the country. I'm sure you can find outdoor projects around your house that require picking, shoveling, wheel-barrowing, and the like. You could split wood with a sledgehammer and wedge. Or you could just make it a point to lift, carry, and throw awkward objects like rocks, logs, or even sand-filled duffle bags. You could even get an old tire, fill it with cement or rocks, and tow it through an open field or around the block. (Or, better yet, get a towing sled designed for that purpose. Contact us for information). Try doing sprints with it, too. You'll develop unbelievable strength in your hamstrings, glutes, and low-back, as well as cardiovascular endurance.

When doing awkward lifts and towing, there are many exercises to choose from. You're only limited by your imagination. Just be sure to use good lifting form and be careful where you drop heavy objects: your neighbors might not pass the sense of humor test if you drop a 150-pound rock on their cat.

How to Use Other Sports and Games to Develop General Speed, Coordination, Cardiovascular Endurance and All-Around Athletic Ability

Sports like soccer and basketball are outstanding methods of developing general speed, coordination, cardiovascular endurance and all-around athletic ability. And they're a lot more fun than running around a track.

When I was coach of the U.S. National Judo Training Squad at the Olympic Training Center, there were a few guys who always seemed to be injured when it was time to run and do conditioning on the track. They wouldn't run intervals on the track even if I threatened them with a cattle prod. But when we played soccer it was as though God had waved his hand over them and healed them all. Now, I believe in an all-powerful God capable of healing anything. But all of them *at once?!*

They sprinted, jumped, stopped on a dime, executed quick pivots, *and* they didn't want to stop after the hour was up! Truly miraculous. *Swifter, Higher, Stronger*: The Olympic Motto in action. So, guess what? I had them play a lot of soccer, and during the colder months, some basketball and volleyball. The end result was that they greatly improved their cardiovascular endurance, their general speed, coordination and athletic ability.

Sports and games are also great for recovery. The Soviets and other Eastern Bloc countries called this "active rest."

Restoration: Active Rest vs. Passive Rest

Some years ago sports scientists from the former Soviet Union found that "active rest" was better than "passive rest" for recuperation. Athletes who participated in other sports and physical activities (active rest) recuperated from heavy training loads faster than those who did nothing (passive rest). Soccer, basketball, cross country skiing, cycling, hiking in the forest, swimming and other sports that promoted increased breathing and circulation were found to have a restorative effect on the Central Nervous System and the body in general.

Other sports and games are enjoyable, develop athletic ability, and enhance recovery. So get out and play soccer, basketball, or tennis, or go biking, swimming, or hiking in the woods. Just make sure that you don't do so much that it becomes a big physical stress in itself. After all, you're doing these other activities for enjoyment and restoration, not to further wear yourself in the dirt.

Additional Means of Recovery

Sports scientists and top coaches from the former Soviet Union put almost as much emphasis on *restoration* from heavy training loads as they did on the training itself. They knew that if their athletes didn't fully recover from their heavy training loads, it would lead to illness or injury. Some of their methods were pretty high-tech: electronic muscle stimulation, ultra-sound, and acupuncture, to name just a few. Others like sauna, sports-massage, self-massage, stretching, various forms of hydrotherapy (e.g. hot and cold showers), and physical and psychological means of relaxation, are more accessible and are very beneficial to recovery.

To handle heavy training loads and to avoid illness and injury, be sure to include these and other means of restoration in your schedule.

Now, let's start putting the levels together

Before we get into the actual specifics of training let's get an overview of the different kinds of training and the purpose of each type. Please take a moment to read the following segments on **general, directed, and specific physical preparation**, and a few important concepts that will guide you through all phases of your training.

General Physical Preparation (GPP) or "Accumulation Phase"

This first phase of training is all about accumulating a solid base. This phase is vital to the success of the other two phases that build on this solid foundation. There are five primary objectives in the GPP phase. They are:

1) Develop general cardiovascular endurance.
2) Develop all-round muscular endurance.
3) Develop muscular strength (including ligament and tendon strength).
4) Develop general flexibility.
5) Develop agility, coordination and all-round athletic ability.

Directed Physical Preparation (DPP) or "Intensification Phase"

Directed exercises and training methods are those that are in some way specific to your technique or event, but are not specific in every way. Interval Training with running, for example, can be set up to use the same energy systems as those used in a competitive grappling or martial art contest. So in terms of energy systems it can be said to be a Directed Training Method. But interval training with running is not specific in other respects such as movement patterns, muscle groups, muscular endurance, and so on. It can, however, serve as a transition from the long slow distance running used to build up a base of general cardiovascular endurance, and the more intense anaerobic work required in high-level grappling, MMA, and martial arts practice and competition. In other words, during DPP you will be intensifying your training in preparation for the specific training to come.

In strength training, for example, a general exercise for the abdominal muscles might be a standard sit-up or leg raise. A directed exercise would be the Russian Twist, or Vertical Bar Twists done on The Grappler. The latter exercises mimic the twisting motions of all forward throws and of throws involving a twist to the rear. These directed exercises will help you develop a strong finish to your throw. Directed exercises allow you to strengthen some weakness in your technique or physical preparation. But a directed exercise is not the technique or event in its entirety. It doesn't exactly duplicate the entire movement, type of fatigue, speed, and the like, of your technique. In other words, a directed exercise is not completely specific. Rather, directed training is a transition from general exercises and training methods to the specific exercises and training methods you will be using at actual practice on the mat or in the ring.

Specific Physical Preparation (SPP) or "Transformation Phase"

This phase of training is very specific and is aimed at your unique needs as an athlete within the parameters of your particular sport or martial art. It is sometimes called the "transformation phase" because now you will transform the general and directed training of the previous two phases into your actual fighting ability.

The objectives of this phase are as follows:

1) **Develop muscle groups used in your techniques or event as a whole.** This is known as muscle group specificity. One example would be the need for great hip and leg strength for anyone whose favorite technique is some type of hip throw. A general requirement for any hip throw is to get your center of gravity lower than your opponents. While training in Japan I noticed that many westerners had stronger upper bodies than their Japanese counterparts. But the Japanese had greater lower body strength, which gave them explosive hip throws.

In 1979 while training at Tokai University in Japan, many mornings would start with a 20- to 25-minute run over paths dividing rice paddies, up parking garages, through streets, and ending up at the steps of an outdoor shrine. Tokai University was on the outskirts of Tokyo and some remnants of rural terrain remained, which we took full advantage of on the runs. Once at the shrine steps, though, the real work began. Often we would do various partner carries up the steps — piggy back, cradled in our arms like you would carry a baby, or sometimes loaded on our backs in a hip throw position. We did a number of trips up the stairs alternating carries with our training partner. But that was just the beginning. We then did various squat jumps up the stairs and finished with different push-up variations, sit-ups, leg raises, and other calisthenics before running back to the dormitories. The Japanese did much better than the westerners on the various jumping exercises, squat walks, and other lower body exercises. And this lower body strength helped contribute to their world-class technique.

Another example of muscle group specificity is the adductor strength needed for the "guard position" in grappling events. Without strong adductors you will always be vulnerable in the guard position.

Finally, let's not forget grip strength. When competing in any grappling event, with or without a gi jacket, you need tremendous grip strength. All the pulling power in the world won't do you much good if you can't keep your grip on the opponent.

Later in this chapter we will take a look at many of the exercises you can use to develop specific muscle groups for fighting sports.

2) **Develop metabolic conditioning.** In other words, incorporate training that duplicates, and occasionally exceeds, the fatigue and physical stress of your sport. If you are an MMA fighter, a jujitsu competitor, or compete in any other combative sport or art, you need to spar many rounds, not only to hone your skills against resisting opponents, but also to develop the specific endurance required for the event.

3) Incorporate the principle of **movement pattern specificity.** This simply refers to exercises and drills that duplicate the movement pattern of your technique or a component part of your technique. Many of these movement-specific drills and exercises are performed with a training partner, but there are numerous solo exercises you can do outside of your regular practice sessions to strengthen weaknesses in your techniques.Optimal Surplus: The Key to Reliable Performance

Throughout this chapter I will be using the words "**optimal surplus.**" I first came across this term in the book, *GYMNASTICS: How To Create Champions*, Arkaev and Suchilin (2004, Meyer and Meyer Sport Ltd.). This concept seemed the perfect way to describe what we're striving for in combative sports and arts. Simply put, "optimal surplus" means that you have more of certain psychological, technical, and physical qualities than you actually need for your event.

Optimal surplus for a martial artist or fighter does not require you to have the **strength** of a world-class powerlifter, or the general **endurance** of a Marathoner, only more strength and endurance than you actually need to attack with speed and power throughout your fight. As for **flexibility**, you don't need to be a contortionist; you just need more flexibility than you need to complete your techniques with complete freedom of movement. You also need an optimal surplus of **technique, mental toughness, and tactical preparation**, as well as **overall good health**. Although some of these factors are beyond the scope of this book, the optimal surplus of conditioning that you will build by following the methods described will definitely affect your skill, mental toughness, and health in a positive way.

Louie Simmons, The Great Guru Of Powerlifting

My friend, Louie Simmons, founder of the world-famous Westside Barbell Club in Columbus, Ohio, is one of the best strength and conditioning coaches in the world. He once wrote an article for *Powerlifting USA* in which he spoke of developing **an abundance of strength**. In this article he mentioned the Soviet Olympic Lifter and World and Olympic Champion, David Rigert. Rigert, when his feet were out of position in the bottom of the Snatch and with the weight held overhead, would squat walk into the correct position before driving up to a standing position to complete the lift, often setting a world record in the process. This was only possible, Louie wrote, because Rigert had developed an abundance of strength through special exercises, one of which was to squat walk across the floor with a barbell held overhead. **This abundance of strength compensated for small technical flaws or lapses and enabled him to win Olympic and World Gold Medals.**

Although Louie Simmons used the word "abundance" when speaking of Rigert, we are essentially saying the same thing when we speak of "optimal surplus." Again, you need to develop more of the required physical qualities than what you actually need to execute your skills or compete in your event. To paraphrase Arkaev and Suchilin, "Only through an optimal surplus of physical, technical, and psychological preparation can we achieve reliability of performance."

Optimal Surplus in Judo

How many times have you seen a top international-level judo man finish a forward throw even when his hip wasn't in a perfect textbook position? I'd venture to guess that if you follow World and Olympic Judo you've seen this happen often. Many times I've witnessed U.S Olympian and World Military

Games Champion, Leo White, finish his forward Soto Makikomi (Winding Throw) even when he didn't have his hip completely across in an ideal throwing position. And sometimes this was against a World or Olympic Champion as was the case in the 1984 Los Angeles Olympics when he threw 1980 Olympic Champion Robert Van de Walle of Belgium for a Waza Ari (half point) and then maintained his lead to win the match.

How did Leo White do this? Even though his hip position wasn't perfect — after all, his world-class opponents were defending strongly — the rotation of his torso was so strong that he completed the throw anyway! In other words, the overwhelming strength of his finish compensated for the small technical flaw of his hips not being in deep enough.

By doing the exercises and training programs in this book **you** will develop this kind of optimal surplus in your strength, endurance, and technique.

General Physical Preparation

General Physical Preparation (GPP) is the foundation of your career as a martial artist and fighter. It is the base from which you will build your body so that you can withstand the more intense and specific training of the future.

Think of your training as a pyramid. If the base of your pyramid is narrow, the peak cannot be very high. But if the base is strong and wide, you can build a tall pyramid with a high peak. The same holds true with your training. A wide base of GPP will ensure that you make more consistent progress, and with fewer injuries, as you advance to the directed and specific training to come. A high level of GPP will also ensure more stable results throughout your competitive career, and a much higher peak performance when you need it most.

No Weak Links in the Chain

GPP is designed to ensure that there are no weak links in your body. Your goal during GPP training is to develop all-around balanced muscular development, an efficient cardiovascular system, and good general flexibility, agility, balance, and speed. To accomplish this you will employ a wide variety of exercises and methods, many of which are not directly related to your event.

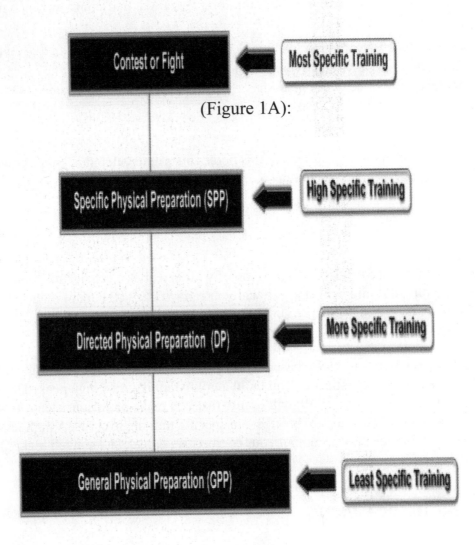

(Figure 1A):

Note: The base of the structure, GPP, is the foundation of your training. The training gradually becomes more specific as you go up the blocks.

If you are a more advanced martial artist or fighter you will still include GPP training in your schedule, although not as much, to maintain your base and to enhance recuperation from the more intense and specific training you've been doing.

Although the following figures are not meant to be used in an overly-strict manner, the percentages of GPP to SPP training would roughly look like this:

Beginning Fighter: **80% General, 20% Specific**
Intermediate Fighter: **50% General, 50% Specific**
Advanced Fighter: **25% General, 75% Specific**

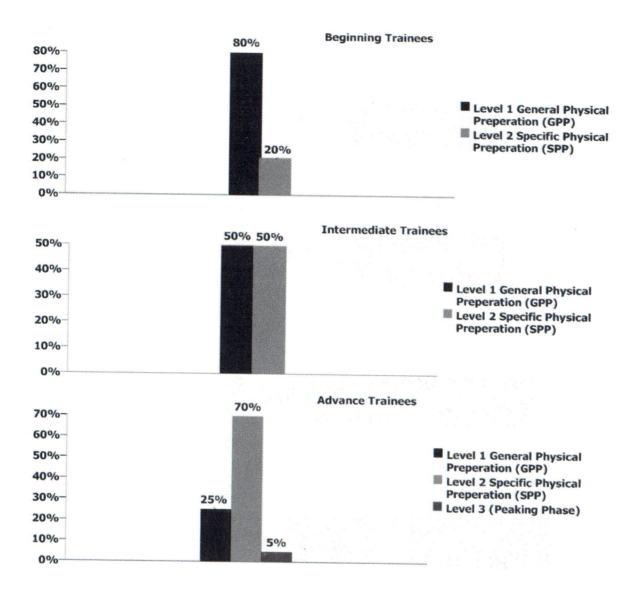

Note: You'll notice that we didn't include a graph for Directed Preparation. This is because Directed Preparation or Exercise is basically a transition between GPP and SPP training. Directed Exercises duplicate a similar movement pattern, energy system, or muscle group, but they are not exactly the same as your technique or event. But these directed exercises do allow you to concentrate on certain weaknesses in your technique, or event as a whole, and therefore will more fully prepare you to practice your event.

General Physical Preparation (GPP) in the Former Soviet Union vs. the U.S. Approach

In the United States children start sports at a very young age, often eight to 10 years old. Check out any neighborhood park and you will find dozens of kids playing soccer, football, baseball, or basketball, depending on the season. Rarely, though, is there any program to get them in shape for that sport prior to the season. Almost all their training is sport-specific. This approach produces fast results initially. But because these young athletes have no general foundation their progress stagnates within a few years. And unless they go back and do some serious work on GPP their progress will remain stunted. Since specific exercises and training methods are not designed to provide balanced all-around development, the young U.S. athletes are also much more vulnerable to injuries.

In contrast, promising young people in the former Soviet Union, at about age 12, were enrolled in sports schools. But unlike their U.S. counterparts, the Soviet youth were not allowed to play their sport yet. Rather, they were put through a well-organized, systematic program of GPP consisting of general strength, endurance, flexibility, agility, balance, and hand/eye coordination.

What the Experts Say Regarding GPP

Dr. Steve Fleck, world-famous sports researcher and head exercise physiologist at the Olympic Training Center in Colorado Springs:

> While I was the judo coach of the U.S. National Training Squad at the Olympic Training Center Dr. Fleck told me, "You just can't play your way into shape." Dr. Fleck wisely advised athletes to build a base through GPP before undertaking actual practice in their sport.

Louie Simmons, world-famous power lifter and strength and conditioning coach:

> In an article entitled "Teen Lifting," which appeared in Powerlifting USA, Louie Simmons listed GPP exercises that young Soviet Sports School athletes worked on. These were: pushups, pull-ups, rope climbing, medicine ball work, Kettlebell work, running and short sprints. Louie noted that through this program "they produced the model athlete for their sports system."

Ryzard Zenewa, former Polish National Judo Coach.

> From my talks with Ryzard Zenewa I learned that young athletes in the Eastern Bloc countries, in addition to the type of training Louie described, played other sports and games such as soccer, basketball, and various track and field events, to improve GPP.

Compare this to the typical U.S approach in which young athletes are started in a certain sport without any prior GPP. Although certain athletes who are genetically encoded for that sport may reach a level of success, the overwhelming majority won't get very far, or even worse, will suffer debilitating injuries. And what about those gifted few who do actually achieve a measure of success? Are they going to reach their full potential? Not likely.

In summary, by building and maintaining a solid base through GPP you will:

* Achieve more reliable results.
* Sustain fewer injuries.
* Make continual progress toward your ultimate goal.

Train like a Decathlete

When fighters ask for my help in designing training programs I always start by telling them to train like a decathlete. Think about the Decathlon for a moment. It is comprised of the following events:

1) The 100 Meter Run
2) The Long Jump
3) The Shot Put
4) The High Jump
5) The 400 Meter Run
6) The Hurdles
7) The Discuss
8) The Pole Vault
9) The Javelin
10) The 1500 Meter Run

Not only does the training for some of these individual events not benefit the other events, it often actually detracts from the results in the other Decathlon events. Take the Shot Put and the 1500 Meter Run, for example. These two events are diametrically opposed to each other! The trick then, for the decathlete, is to balance his training. In other words, the aspiring decathlete must devote just the right percentage of the training pie to each event. This is not only a science, but an art. When the decathlete sees his results in the 400 Meter or 1500 Meter Run going down because of too much max-effort strength work, for example, he must devote more training time to these events, even if it means reducing the volume of his strength work somewhat. Conversely, if his Shot Put and Discuss distances are noticeably below his best, the decathlete must add more strength and explosive speed work to his schedule. For the successful decathlete these kinds of adjustments need to be made all the time. The same holds true for all grappling, MMA, and self-defense athletes.

To Be a Champion You Need Balanced Development

Many observers believe Mixed Martial Arts (MMA) is one of the most demanding sports there is. To reach the top of the food chain in MMA you can no longer have a weak range of fighting. In the early days of MMA this wasn't necessarily true, and we often saw a grappler defeat a striker. Then the strikers started balancing their game by studying jujitsu and other grappling arts, thereby learning to defend the takedown. This cross-training enabled the strikers to stay on their feet longer and made them much more dangerous. Today MMA has evolved to a whole new level, and to be competitive you must be very well balanced in both your physical and technical training. To achieve balanced development from your physical training, train like a decathlete. That will give you the all-round development you need to make it to the top.

Now, let's look at other training methods you can use to develop the general physical qualities needed to lay down a solid foundation for your future success as a fighter.

Developing Specific Endurance with Circuit Training

Circuit Training is a great way to increase your muscular, and to some extent, your cardiovascular fitness for fighting. To construct a circuit-training program, select a number of simple exercises for your lower body, torso, and upper body. Then arrange them in a circle (circuit) so that you move from one exercise to the next with very little rest between exercises.

1.	Hindu squats	6. Glute-ham raises
2.	Push-ups	7. Horizontal pull-ups
3.	Sit-ups	8. DB overhead press
4.	Back raises	9. Technique drill
5.	Calf raises	10. Wrist roller

Note: The circuit doesn't necessarily have to be set up in a literal circle, but when you are dealing with multiple athletes at once, it's helpful.

It is best to train different areas of the body as you move from one exercise to the next. This way, as you're working one section of the body, the other areas are getting something of a rest.

Do a lower body exercise, for example, then a torso exercise, then an upper body exercise. As you progress through the next few stations, do a different lower body, torso, and upper body exercise, and so on.

Be sure to include exercises to work opposing muscle groups. If you started with Hindu jump squats, which primarily work the quads and hips, make sure to include an exercise like Glute-ham raises to work the hamstring muscle groups. If you do push-ups, for example, do horizontal pull-ups or some rowing motion to work the opposite pulling muscles. If you do an abdominal exercise, somewhere in the circuit do a lower back exercise, etc. This will help you avoid injuries caused by muscle imbalances.

Finally, be sure to include exercises for any injury-prone areas. Shoulders and knees are particularly vulnerable in grappling arts such as wrestling, judo, and jujitsu, so include exercises to strengthen these areas.

Research On Elite Judo Athletes at the U.S. Olympic Training Center

During my years as coach of the U.S. National Judo Training Squad at the Olympic Training Center, I frequently put my athletes through various physical tests, and occasionally through research projects. One of the most valuable of these was done with Dr. Steve Fleck, Head Exercise Physiologist at the time, and one of the most respected researchers in the world. I wanted to know which of our conditioning methods most closely approximated the fatigue our fighters experienced during their matches.

To help me find out, Dr. Fleck had his staff members prick the fingers of our fighters to draw drops of blood immediately after each of their matches at the U.S. Open. The U.S. Open was one of the largest international judo competitions in the western hemisphere, so the athletes had some tough fights. Dr. Fleck found that their blood lactate levels were very high. This was especially true of those who fought five or six matches to reach the finals. A few weeks after the U.S. Open we again measured blood lactate levels during our strength training sessions, interval running, regular judo practice sessions, and circuit training. The blood lactate levels during regular weight training were very low, not even close. Surprisingly, the interval running produced only moderate lactate readings. Some of the blood lactate levels were fairly high during randori (sparring), but nowhere close to those of contest. I suspect this was because the fighters weren't pushing as hard since they had just come off the U.S. Open a few weeks before.

Given that one flaw, the findings of the project demonstrated that the only method that produced blood lactate levels comparable to their matches at the U.S. Open was Circuit Training. The circuits I put the athletes through were real killers, lasting anywhere from ½ hour to 45 minutes of non-stop exercises. The only rest the fighters got was a few seconds as they moved to the next station. Of course, I started them off with only 2 rounds through the circuit to get them used to it. But as the weeks passed and their work capacity improved, they built up to as many as 6 rounds through circuits of between 12 to 15 exercises. Needless to say, the athletes who trained like this were able to pressure their opponents relentlessly throughout their fights. (In retrospect, however, the 45-minute time limit of some of the circuits may have been a little long.) Nevertheless, the lesson of the OTC Research Project is clear:

> If you want the specific muscular and cardiovascular endurance required in grappling arts like judo, wrestling, or jujitsu, be sure to include circuit training in your schedule.

Circuit Training will give you the muscular endurance needed for grappling arts such as judo, jujitsu, SOMBO, and various styles of wrestling.
Photos by Steve Scott.

Training Secrets Of South Korea's 1984 Olympic Judo Team

Kil Soon Park, a two-time judo world medalist in the 154-pound Class, (3rd in 1965, and 2nd in 1967), was hired to help prepare the South Korean Judo Team for the 1984 Los Angeles Olympics. Park worked with the South Korean team a total of eight weeks prior to the Olympics.

Park had been my coach for several years right after I graduated from high school. I learned from experience that he was a hands-on, and sometimes very brutal coach. Years later, during a visit to the Olympic Training Center, he told me about the training schedule he had put the South Korean team through. It went like this:

> 6 a.m.: Wake Up
>
> 6:15-6:30 a.m.: Warm Up
>
> 6:30-8 a.m.: Mountain running followed by Circuit Training
>
> 10 a.m.-12 noon: Technique Session:
> Uchikomis (Fit Ins), Drills, Throwing Practice, and Ground Fighting
>
> 3 p.m.-5 p.m.: Randori (Free Practice)
>
> 7-8:30 p.m.: Weight Training or Circuits

After a brief warm-up, the day started with running up a nearby mountain. When they got back down, the team did circuit training. The South Koreans had purchased a circuit of Hydra-Gym exercise machines for their sports complex. Hydra-Gym is a type of isokinetic machine utilizing hydraulic resistance. Normally, I don't advocate the use of machines, but these were great for circuits since there were no weights to change to slow down the pace. The machines were also unilateral. In other words, if an athlete was doing the Bench Press, he would have to reverse directions immediately and pull back in a rowing motion against resistance. If he was doing the Leg Extension, he immediately pulled his leg back in a Leg Curl. This double-direction exercise helped to ensure balanced muscular development and fewer injuries. Also, Park had them do bodyweight exercises like push-ups, pull-ups, jumps, and sit-ups in between the machines. This made for difficult circuits.

Park had the team do Circuit Training every day. The circuits were not long, drawn-out affairs, but were short and intense. After all, the judo practices themselves, coupled with daily mountain runs, were exhausting. Therefore, the circuits were usually completed in under 15 minutes.

Park also had them lift heavier weights two nights per week, concentrating on lifts like Power Cleans and Barbell Squats. But as I discovered when the South Koreans visited the Olympic Training Center for competitions and camps, they weren't overly impressive in terms of the poundage they could lift. But they were very strong on the judo mat. The remaining week nights were spent on additional circuit training.

This brutal regimen produced South Korea's best-conditioned and most successful Olympic team to that point. They won several medals in the lower-weight categories, and a gold medal in the 209 pounds and under in which Ha, the Korean, overwhelmed his Japanese opponent in the finals.

Two-time World Medalist, Kil-Soon-Park throwing me with flawless form around 1974. In attendance is the Korean Yudo (Judo) College Team.

What were the secrets of their success? For starters, their super-high work capacity played a huge part. Take a look at the amount of training: Four to six hours (or more), six days per week for about 10 years seems to be the norm for those who win World and Olympic medals. In addition to the judo workouts, mountain runs, and other conditioning, I believe the heavy emphasis on Circuit Training played a major role in the success of the 1984 South Korean Olympic Judo Team. It helped them physically dominate their opponents and it can help you, too.

Since you may not have a tough coach like Park making sure you do circuits, you'll have to take on that role yourself, assuming you are determined to become better. Let's take a look at some sample Circuit Training programs we use in Shingitai Jujitsu.

Shingitai Beginners Circuit

Warm Up: Easy stationary bike, jogging or jump rope (five minutes), neck bridge (one to three minutes)

1. Hindu squats (30 seconds)
2. Push-ups (30 seconds)
3. Sit-ups (30 seconds)
4. Back raises (30 seconds)
5. Calf raises (30 seconds)
    a) 1st set: Toes inward
    b) 2nd set: Toes straight ahead
    c) 3rd set: Toes outward
6. Glute-ham raises (30 seconds)
7. Horizontal pull-ups (30 seconds)
8. DB overhead press (30 seconds)
9. Osoto Gari (Major Outside Leg Sweep) (five right, five left, etc … 30 seconds)
10. Wrist roller (30 seconds)

Directions:

* Go through entire circuit one to three times depending on your goals and level of fitness.

* When you first start training, or after a layoff, rest as needed between exercises. After a few weeks, begin to reduce the rest in between exercises until eventually you can move from station to station without rest.

* Rest up to three minutes after completing a round through the entire circuit. As the weeks pass and you adapt to the training, reduce the rest period.

* Remember to rotate the individual exercises on a regular basis (The Conjugate Method).

* When you have completed your circuit, cool down by walking with deep breathing for several minutes. Follow this up with flexibility exercises.

* When this workout no longer seems challenging, proceed to the Shingitai Intermediate Circuit.

Shingitai Intermediate Circuit

Warm Up: Easy Stationary Bike, Jogging, or Jump Rope (5 min.), Neck Bridge (1 to 3 minutes)

1. Hindu push-ups (45 seconds)
2. Hindu squats (45 seconds)
3. V-sit-ups (45 seconds)
4. Pull-ups (overhand grip) (45 seconds) (Note: If you can't do pull-ups for 45 seconds, rest as needed, or jump up and lower yourself back down for the allotted time.)
5. Glute-ham raises (45 seconds)
6. Back raises w/twists (45 seconds) (alternate sides)
7. Forward throws w/tubing (45 seconds) (tie tube to post)
8. Punching w/tubing (45 seconds) (Drape tubing around your back. Loop your hands through the ends of the tubing and punch away.)
9. Two-arm rows w/tubing (45 seconds) (Tie tube to post and pull towards you with both hands.)
10. Lunges (w/body weight or while holding dumbbells) (45 seconds)
11. DB shoulders:
    a) Forward raises: 12 reps
    b) Side lateral raises: 12 reps.
    c) Bent lateral raises: 12 reps.
12. Jump rope (45 seconds)

Directions:

* Go through entire circuit two to three times.

* Rest one minute between circuits.

* Try to move from exercise to exercise as quickly as possible.

* Rotate new exercises into your circuits on a regular basis.

Congratulations! You've obviously worked hard. Now let's take the next step.

Shingitai Advanced Circuit

Warm Up: Easy Jogging, Stationary Bike, or Jump Rope. Neck Bridge (1 to 3 minutes)

1. Feet-Elevated Push Ups (1 minute)
2. Hindu Jump Squats (1 minute)
3. Incline Sit Ups (1 minute)
4. Parallel Grip Pull Ups (1 minute)
5. Glute Ham Raises (1 minute)
6. Headstand Press (or Barbell Press) (1 minute)
7. Mountain Climbers (1 minute)
8. Solo Uchimata (Inner Thigh Throw, alternating left and right) (1 minute)
9. Horizontal Pull Ups (Feet supported in front of you) (1 minute)
10. Side to Side Leg Raises (1 minute)
11. Back Raises w/ Twists (1 minute)
12. Shadow Boxing: Use punches, kicks, sweeps, takedowns, etc. (1 minute)

Directions:

* Go through entire circuit three to four times with a one-minute rest after each complete circuit. This will give you 36 to 48 minutes of actual work. High-level trainees can eliminate the one-minute rest after each completed circuit if they want to increase the difficulty even further. When peaking for a contest, shorten the circuit so that you can complete it in under 20 minutes.

* This circuit is made more difficult by the one-minute exercise duration, and by the introduction of more difficult exercises such as Hindu jump squats, headstand presses, feet-elevated push-ups, and mountain climbers.

* If you feel faint or nauseous during the circuit, stop at that point and try to do more the next workout.

* As in all Shingitai Circuits, rotate new exercises into your circuit on a regular basis. Don't be afraid to change your routine.

*As you near a major event, cut back on the number of rounds through the circuit. This will allow you to increase the intensity of your practices (see Level III Peaking Phase for more information).

Aerobic vs. Anaerobic Endurance

I have no desire to turn you into exercise physiologists. To tell you the truth, with a few exceptions, being locked up with a talkative exercise physiologist is one of the worst fates I could imagine, second only to being with an insurance salesman—my idea of Hell. So, I will try to make this as painless as possible and discuss only the absolute essentials. Aerobic and Anaerobic endurance are two terms you should understand. Let's take a brief look at each:

Aerobic Endurance

The word *aerobic* means "with oxygen." When training aerobically, your heart rate is somewhere between 60 percent to 85 percent of your max, and for our purposes is kept somewhere in that target zone for 15 to 60 minutes. The energy you expend comes from the oxidation of carbohydrate and fat. You should build most of your aerobic base during Level I training, and then do enough aerobic work during Levels II and III training to maintain that base.

Marathon running is the ultimate example of an aerobic activity. But marathon running will not give you the type of endurance you need for fighting. Yes, as a fighter you need to build an aerobic base so that you can recover quickly between intense bouts of exercise, but there is a point of diminishing returns at which more aerobic training detracts from your explosiveness and strength. I've worked with students who've run various road races and even marathons. They were shocked at how fast they ran out of gas during ground-fighting and randori rounds. That's because fighting, especially in contests of five minutes duration or less, is largely *anaerobic* in nature. The rounds are often comprised of a number of short bursts of attacks with periods of lesser activity in between. Let's examine anaerobic endurance further:

Anaerobic Endurance

Anaerobic means "without oxygen." When training anaerobically:

1. You'll build up an oxygen debt, and just like when you run up your credit card, it needs to be paid off.
2. A fatigue product called lactic acid will accumulate in your muscles, and if you don't ease up, your muscles will cramp up and shut down.

When training at high intensity anaerobically, your body can't get enough oxygen to your muscles and gets some of the energy for muscular work from carbohydrates that are stored as glycogen in the muscles. By including anaerobic training in your routine you do two things:

1. You train your body to recover to a lower heart rate more quickly between bouts of intense exercise, such as between intense flurries of attacks in a fight, or between matches.
2. Secondly, by training anaerobically, you train your muscles to tolerate lactic acid for longer periods of intense effort before shutting down. It also trains your muscles to drain off lactic

acid, and conditions your heart to bring in fresh oxygenated blood more efficiently.

Anaerobic training will enable you to make more strong attacks throughout the fight. And more strong attacks lead to more wins for you! Most of your anaerobic training will take place in Level II, and will be maintained during Level III.

One of the best ways to train for anaerobic endurance is called *Interval Training*. Let me show you how it works:

Interval Training

You can't sustain a near maximum heart rate for too long at a time. To do so would be dangerous, and lactic acid would eventually lock up your muscles. Instead, in order to keep the quality (intensity) of your work at a high level, you will do repeated high-intensity bouts of some activity that elevates your heart rate, followed by a *rest interval*. We will call this your *Work: Rest Ratio*. If, for example, you run a 110-yard sprint in 15 seconds and rest 45 seconds before running another sprint, you would have a 1:3 Work: Rest Ratio.

The idea of the rest interval is to allow your heart rate to return to about 120 beats per minute before doing another bout of exercise. This will allow you to put out repeated high-intensity efforts. As your anaerobic conditioning improves, you will probably be able to reduce your Work: Rest Ratio to 1:2, and eventually even to 1:1.

What Exercise Activity Should I Use When Doing Interval Training?

You could, of course, use running, cycling, or swimming, to enhance your GPP. But even better would be to use some element of your martial art. Since you're reading this chapter I assume you're a martial art student, fighter, teacher, or coach. That being the case, take some skill, say a throw, and drill it at high-intensity for a number of reps and sets. Follow this with a timed rest interval. Let's look at an example:

Interval Training Program Using a Throw

Using a forward or rear throw, execute as many uchikomis (fit-ins without completing the throw) as you can in the allotted time.

1. a) Do Forward Throw Uchikomis for 20 seconds.
   b) Have your partner attack for 20 seconds.
   c) Rest for 20 seconds before repeating.

* Repeat for three to 10 sets depending on your needs and level of conditioning. Then proceed to step 2 as follows:

2. a) Do Forward Throw Uchikomis (10 seconds)

   b) Have your partner do Uchikomis (10 seconds)

   c) Rest for 10 seconds before repeating.

* Repeat for three to 10 sets depending on your needs and level of conditioning.

This will give you a 1:2 Work: Rest Ratio. In other words, you'll rest twice as much as you work (sounds like a good deal to me). As you get in better shape, eliminate the rest period and just get your rest as your partner does his attacks. This will give you a 1:1 Work: Rest Ratio. When you get to this point, you'll be wearing your opponents into the dirt.

Alternative Interval Training Programs

For variety, you can do your uchikomis (fit-ins) while you and your opponent are moving about at random. This is more realistic since rarely will an opponent stand still in a fight, and this type of training will teach you to attack while moving. It will also get you into great shape. Make your work interval a little longer, since you won't be able to do as many attacks as you would with static uchikomis.

Pick a single throw, or attack with a variety of throws and combinations. Then, while moving about at random, execute your attacks for the following time periods:

Four One-Minute Rounds

Rest one minute between rounds, or let your partner attack you for one minute in between your rounds. Then move to the next set.

Ten 30-Second Rounds

Rest 30 seconds between rounds, or just rest as your partner attacks you for 30 seconds. You can stop here, or if you happen to be a competitor who's in great shape, do one more set, as follows:

Six 30-Second Rounds

Rest 30 seconds between rounds.

Not only will you develop world-class endurance, but also your throwing and takedown skills will improve rapidly.

Variations:

1. Do the rounds as listed above, only instead of doing uchikomis, do complete throws (Nage Komis) onto a crash pad. It helps to have three or four partners in a line so that after you throw one partner, another moves up for you to throw him, and so on.

2. Do your ground-fighting or randori (free practice) in interval style. Say your contest matches are five minutes long. Add an extra minute so that you build extra stamina and confidence. Then do a certain number of six-minute rounds. While I was coaching the U.S. National Judo Training Squad at the Olympic Training Center, I often had the fighters do 10 to 12 six-minute randori rounds with a one to two-minute rest interval in between each round. These randori rounds were usually done during our late afternoon practice.

Our morning practices usually emphasized ground-fighting and standing drills. Depending on the time of year and how close we were to major contests, we often did the same type of timed rounds for ground-fighting.

The general rule was that during the off-season, we did lots of lower intensity continuous work with only one or two short, higher intensity rounds thrown in so that we didn't forget how to turn up the heat. But as the major contest approached, we gradually increased our intensity and did randori, drills, and ground-fighting with timed rounds and rest periods. As you can see, this was a form of interval training.

Boxers and Kickboxers train in interval-style rounds much of the time. In boxing gyms, for example, you will hear a bell sounding the beginning of a round. Three minutes later it will signal the end of the round. Then, there is a one-minute rest followed by the bell and another three-minute round. This goes on throughout most of the practice.

During the three-minute rounds, the boxers are working on the various bags or the focus mitts, jumping rope, doing calisthenics, or actually sparring. A typical workout might look like this:

1. Jump rope (three minutes)
   One-minute rest

2. Heavy bag (three minutes)
   One-minute rest

3. Body weight exercises (Push-ups, Sit-ups, Medicine Ball work, etc.) (three min.)
   One-minute rest

4. Speed bag (three minutes)
   One-minute rest

5. Heavy bag (three minutes)
   One-minute rest

6. Focus mitts (three minutes)
   One-minute rest

7. Top and bottom end bag ("Crazy Bag") (three minutes)
   One-minute rest

8. Shadow boxing (three minutes)
   One-minute rest

* Stop or repeat this circuit as desired. Then go on to sparring.

Variations:

1. Mixed martial artists could add rounds of Thai Pad and Thai Bag work, as well as various grappling-based drills such as pummeling or hand fighting. Just be creative.

2. Sparring rounds are also done with three-minute rounds followed by one-minute rest intervals. As you can see, these time limits correspond to pro boxing rounds. The closer you get to duplicating the actual event you're entering, the better.

J.P. Pocock (right) on his way to a two-minute win in a professional mixed martial art fight in summer 2004. J.P. regularly incorporates boxing and kickboxing circuits into his training.

Photo by Karen Jacob

Specific Physical Preparation: Secrets of Developing Speed

Few things are more important to a martial artist than speed. Whether it's a kick, punch, or throw, speed enables you to execute a technique before your opponent can react against it. A fast, explosive technique is also a more powerful technique—it delivers more of an impact. Although speed is limited to some degree by heredity, anyone can become faster through proper training.

The Japanese word, *Shingitai*, embodies a useful philosophy that can serve as a guideline in your quest for speed. This word can be broken down into three separate words:

<u>*Shin*</u>-refers to mind or spirit

<u>*Gi*</u>- refers to skill or technique

<u>*Tai*</u>- refers to physical aspects, or the body

Mind and Spirit as a Factor in Speed

Shin: Notice that when combining the three words, Shin is always written first. This is significant, and, as it relates to the development of speed, means that you have to **think fast to be fast.** By mobilizing your will in order to explode on each repetition in your training exercises, you'll fully involve your central nervous system, which is a key to improving speed. In other words, will yourself to explode!

Also, you could see yourself in your mind's eye performing your techniques explosively and flawlessly. Or you could use visualization to enhance one of your training exercises.

Let's say you're doing jumps from the ground up onto a platform to develop explosive leg drive. Prior to each jump you could visualize your legs as heavy-duty, tightly compressed springs that explode into action when you release them. You can use this type of imagery with any number of your techniques and training exercises.

Skill as a Factor in Speed

Gi: The second factor, Gi, as it relates to speed, means that you need to learn the best possible technique. Once you've mastered the mechanics of a skill you need to refine it through thousands of repetitions. Not only will you acquire automatic, reflexive skills, but also **economy of motion**. You won't slow yourself down with unnecessary movements, like winding up to execute a punch, kick, or throw. Through constant repetition you'll eliminate all those little extra movements that detract from your speed.

Numerous repetitions also teach you to relax muscle groups that aren't directly involved in the skill. The ability to relax your muscles before exploding into an attack is an important attribute for you as a fighter.

When coaching on throwing, Yoshisada "Yone" Yonezuka, another of my former coaches, an All-Japan College Judo Champion and several time U.S. Olympic Coach, used to teach us to localize the tension in our forearms and our grip on the gi. The rest of your body, he told us, should be relaxed prior to an attack. When I had trouble relaxing my muscles during randori (sparring), Yone had me bob my legs up and down once or twice as a reminder to relax those muscles. This helped me to be more explosive on my throws. I realize this is much easier to talk about than actually to do, but if you work at it, over time you'll find yourself becoming much more explosive as well.

J.P. Pocock is shown executing an explosive Double Leg Takedown in a mixed martial arts fight.

Photo by Ken Jacob

Think about this: If I place a force plate measuring device on my opponent's chest, slowly place my chest on it, and then push forward with all my strength, it will register some force, but nothing to brag about. But, if I stand back at arm's length, then explode forward and strike the force plate with my chest, the device will record a tremendous surge of force—far greater than what I generated with maximum strength alone. This is the kind of specific explosive speed a fighter needs.

Remember, the type of speed you need for fighting or contest is not the same as speed in a 100-meter dash. If you're going to throw with Outside Leg Sweep (Osoto Gari), for example, you need to break through your opponent's grip and explode forward into his body. Basically, you're in a two to three-foot race to crash into your opponent at maximum velocity. This is where real power in throwing and takedowns comes from.

Physical Training to Improve Speed

Tai: Outside of the drilling you do in your practice sessions, what else can you do to increase your speed? Two of the best methods are jump training and speed-strength training with weights. Since there is still quite a controversy over weight training, I'll address that issue first.

To Weight Train, Or Not To Weight Train? That Is The Question.

Old-time coaches argued that weight training made an athlete slow and tight. Today, most coaches are on the weight-training bandwagon. I'm in the middle. If by weight training you're talking about what most Americans are doing in the weight room, I stand with the old-time coaches. Before you gather firewood and a stake, let me explain my reasons.

First of all, when you walk into a gym full of guys, what's the first question you usually hear? Ten to one it's, "How much do you Bench?" Most people, even athletes, spend way too much time and energy bench pressing. Over-emphasizing benching is largely a waste of time for fighters. Also, the average gym lifter is following some kind of hit-or-miss bodybuilding routine they picked up from one of the muscle magazines, or something from a friend. If that's the only kind of weight training you're doing, you're better off not doing it at all.

Secondly, the weight training of most athletes is producing dangerous muscle imbalances that will come back to haunt them with injuries. **You've got to work opposing muscle groups**. For example, an athlete who does squats regularly but does no hamstring work is asking for knee injuries and hamstring pulls. Always work the opposing muscle groups.

Finally, because they've been told explosive weight training is dangerous, most athletes aren't training fast on their lifts. How they come to believe that they can get fast by training slow is a mystery to me. **To be fast you must train fast.**

My friend Louie Simmons has produced too many national and World Champions in power-lifting to count. He has also worked with sprinters, a 70-foot shot putter, wrestlers and mixed martial artists, including a two-time UFC Champion. He's widely recognized as "The Great Guru of Powerlifting," but also as an expert in speed-strength development. The Shingitai fighters at our main dojo in Perrysville, Ohio, use Louie's methods for speed-strength training. Rather than try to explain his methods in detail, something I'm not qualified to do, in the next section I'm just going to briefly summarize how we use Louie's ideas with our fighters. But for those of you who are serious about weights, I suggest you pick up a copy of Louie's video, The Reactive Method, in which Louie shows how to train with weights with added bands and chains for maximum development of speed-strength. You can find information about The Reactive Method and Louie's other outstanding products by visiting our website at:

johnsaylor-sja.com

or by writing us at: SJA
P.O. Box 428
Perrysville, OH 44864

Our Shingitai fighters concentrate on box squats and various jumps for explosive starting strength. They also use a variety of other exercises, but when working for speed, they are done explosively. *Of course, you need to strengthen your tendons and ligaments prior to doing explosive training.* (See the Building Blocks to Mastery.)

Methods of Developing Speed Outside of Practice (Off the Mat):

Jump Training (sometimes called "plyometric" training)

Track and Field athletes, lifters, and other athletes from the former Soviet Union popularized this type of training, although former World and Olympic Weightlifting Champion and "World's Strongest Man," Paul Anderson, was doing this type of training even before the Soviets. He used to squat down and jump up onto a high table for repetitions, even though he weighed over 350 pounds at the time. Shortly after Paul Anderson returned from the 1956 Olympics where, prior to the competition, he had trained with these methods, the Soviets began to use similar methods with their athletes. Regardless of where the methods came from, one thing is certain: Various types of jump training can develop tremendous explosive speed.

Some of the most valuable jumping exercises for martial artists are as follows:

1. **Jumps Up Stairs**

    a) Jumps up stairs (both legs simultaneously)

    Start from a squat position and leap up, skipping as many stairs as you can in each jump. As soon as your feet hit, immediately rebound up, and again jump over as many steps as you can at a time. Repeat until you run out of steps. Do approximately three or four jumps per set for three to five sets.

    b) Jumps up stairs (both legs, one stair at a time)

    A variation of the above exercise is to squat down and jump up just one step at a time for about 10 steps. Do one or two sets.

    c) One-leg hops up the stairs (two variations)

    - Hop on one leg up one step at a time. Do about 10 hops on each leg for two to three sets.

- On one leg, leap upward over as many steps as you can. As soon as your foot lands, immediately rebound into the next jump. Do three to five of these jumps on each leg for two to three sets.

One-leg hops are great training for throws like Osoto Gari, Uchimata, and Ouchi Gari.

2. Box Jumps

From a standing position, quickly squat down about half-way. Without pausing, rebound up onto a strong box. Do three to five sets of five jumps per set. Gradually raise the height of the box as your explosive speed increases.

3. Various Hops and Jumps On a Flat Surface

a) One leg hops: three to five sets of 10 reps each leg

b) Standing long jumps (both legs simultaneously): four to five sets of five reps

4. Hindu Jump Squats

Jump forward about a foot, go into a squat, and with a scooping motion of your arms, jump back to the starting position. Do three to five sets of 20 reps.

5. Wide-Narrow Jump Squats

From a squatting position, leap as high as you can into the air. Touch down with your feet about shoulder width, and descend into a squat. Jump up and repeat, only this time, land with your feet wider apart. Alternate wide and narrow stances each time you land. Do three sets of 10 to 20 reps.

To reach the top in any sport or art involving takedowns and throws, you must develop explosive speed.

Note: Rotate the above exercises from week to week. Use only one or two jumping exercises during each workout. Speed exercises like the above jumps should be scheduled following a day off or after an easy day so that your body is fresh. This way you can generate more explosive efforts.

Photo

Throws, takedowns, kicks, punches, and other striking skills all require explosive speed. The exercises in this book will enable you to greatly increase your speed and power.

Photo by Steve Scott.

Summary and Guidelines For Speed Development

1. **Train Fast To Be Fast**

    When training for speed, you've got to explode in your movements. But first, make sure you've done adequate Level I (GPP) training to strengthen your tendons and ligaments to withstand the stresses of speed training.

2. **Will Yourself To Be Fast**

    This may sound funny, but don't underestimate the power of your volition in your quest to develop explosive speed. Will yourself to explode on each repetition.

3. **Flexibility Training**

    Flexibility reduces muscle tension that inhibits speed. It also increases your range of motion and reduces your chance of injury. For best results, do flexibility training after your muscles are completely warmed up.

4. **Learn to Relax Your Muscles**

    The ability to relax your muscles before exploding into an attack is an important attribute for you to have as a fighter. Explosive speed comes from relaxed, loose muscles.

5. **Schedule Your Speed Workouts For When Your Body Is Rested**

    Ideally, your speed workouts should be scheduled after an easy day or a day off, when your body is fresh.

6. **Perfect Your Techniques**

    A good technique requires almost no conscious thought. If you think too much, your breathing becomes sporadic, your muscles tighten up, and this detracts from your speed. When you perfect your technique, you'll also develop economy-of-motion. You'll eliminate extra movements that detract from speed.

    You'll also learn to relax muscles that aren't directly involved in the skill, and this will enhance your speed. Throw a lightweight partner for speed. Throw a heavy partner for strength. Also, inner-tube uchikomis are great for speed since you don't have to move an opponent's body weight or fight through his grip.

7. **Jump Training and Explosive Weight Training**

    Properly conducted jump training and explosive weight training can greatly improve your explosive speed. But be sure to condition your tendons, ligaments, and muscles prior to engaging in explosive speed training.

Weight Training For Maximum Strength And Speed

Our weight training for strength and speed is based on the philosophy of Louie Simmons, the world's foremost powerlifting and speed-strength coach. You won't find a bunch of isolation-type body building exercises like Triceps Pushdowns or Concentration Curls. And as I mentioned before, you won't find us emphasizing the bench press, which seems to be the big lift in most gyms nowadays. With all the various types of push-ups, dips, and pressing movements in our circuits, we just don't need to waste energy on body building exercises or bench presses that could better be used on more productive lifts. Instead, we focus our concentrated weight work on exercises that work the lower body, back, torso, and on chain reaction exercises that work the whole body in a coordinated fashion.

The purpose of our concentrated weight work is twofold:
1. To develop maximum strength.
2. To develop explosive speed.

We devote Monday to maximum strength, and Friday to the development of explosive speed. The rest of the week our extra workouts revolve around our conditioning workouts like body weight exercises for high reps, circuits, extra drilling, and so on. Now, let's take a look at our maximum strength day, and our explosive speed day separately.

Maximum Strength Day (Monday)

On maximum strength day we pick a major squatting movement for two weeks, say Zercher Squats, or partial squats off the power rack pins, or we do some form of Goodmonings. And then for the next two weeks, we do a pulling motion, such as clean pulls from the floor and from various hang positions, or dead lifts from various height pins. We usually alternate back and forth (two weeks with a squatting exercise, then two weeks with a pulling exercise, and so on).

Whatever our major exercise for that week, we try to work up to a personal record of some sort, either for a single, or double reps. We follow this by trying to set records, either for maximum weight or maximum reps, in several assistance exercises that are chosen to work specific weaknesses in our major lifts and in our fighting techniques.

We rotate our assistance exercises every one to two weeks. This is called "**The Conjugate Method**," and it is how we can train heavy all year long without going stale. The Conjugate Method is the secret to continual gains year after year. It also ensures more balanced all-round development, which translates into better performance and fewer injuries for our fighters.

Keep It Short And Sweet

Your Monday and Friday weight workouts should be short—preferably around 45 minutes, and certainly no longer than an hour. Remember, you're also going to be working your muscles with body-weight exercises, various types of circuits, and of course, in practice itself. When you get to the weight room, warm up quickly and get to it.

We'll take a look at some of our assistance exercises in a moment, but first let's look at Speed Day.

Speed Day (Friday)

The second concentrated weight workout of the week is our speed day, which we do on Friday. On speed day we use lighter weight, 50 percent to 60 percent of our maximum poundage for a single rep in that lift. We often choose some form of box squat for our major exercise. We then use a three-week wave, starting with 50 percent on week one for 12 sets of two reps. On week two we use 55 percent for 10 sets of two reps. On week three we use 60 percent for eight sets of two reps.

We rest only about 30 to 45 seconds between each set. After all, in a match or fight we are required to make strong, explosive attacks for the duration without the luxury of complete recovery between attacks. This is a form of "interval training" or "lactic acid tolerance training."

The lighter weights, 50 percent to 60 percent for only two reps per set, permit us to move the bar explosively. ***Always apply maximum speed and force on each rep even though you are using a lighter weight***. Louie Simmons calls this "compensatory acceleration," and it is one of the secrets of developing explosive speed. In any fighting sport or art, at least as far as fighting on your feet is concerned, you gain nothing by training slow. Always **train fast to be fast.**

Why Box Squats?

We use Box Squats because they build explosive strength and speed. This is important for all takedowns and throws, as well as for the ability to drive into an opponent with force. These skills are important to competitors, but also to students of self-defense. Street fights are usually over in less than 30 seconds, but because of the adrenaline rush that occurs, that 30 seconds is usually very intense and explosive. Box squats, as taught by Louie, will prepare you to win these short burst life-or-death encounters.

Also, because the shins are slightly past vertical when you sit back on the box (unlike regular barbell squats), there is no stress on the patella tendons. This is a big plus for us since with all the drilling, sparring, jumping, running, and other training we're doing, we need to be careful not to overstress our knee joints.

Accommodating Resistance

On both maximum strength day and speed day we often use "accommodating resistance," through the use of chains and bands. By attaching heavy chains to each end of the barbell, for example, the resistance on the bar is lessened as you lower the bar and is increased as you raise it. Take Box Squats, for example. As you lower down into the squat position, the chains pile up on the floor, which reduces the bar weight. At the bottom position you only have the weight of the barbell itself. This allows you to explode upward out of the bottom position. As you drive upward past the sticking point and reach what would otherwise be the easiest portion of the lift, more of the chain comes off the floor, which adds significant weight to the bar. In other words, the chains **accommodate** the weight to your weaker and stronger positions in the lift.

Bands do much the same thing, although they also pull you back down, something like a slingshot, creating an **over-speed eccentric**. This activates your stretch reflex and creates kinetic energy in your muscles, tendons, and ligaments, which adds to your speed and strength. Also, as you rise up out of a Box Squat, for example, the bands stretch out and add significant resistance to the lockout portion of the lift.

How To Choose Assistance Exercises

To further strengthen core lifts like the box squat, and our individual ground-fighting, throwing and takedown skills, we perform three to five assistance exercises. These are done after we've finished training our core lift on maximum strength day, as well as on speed day.

We choose exercises which strengthen our weaknesses. So, if one of our fighters lacks explosive speed coming off the box in a box squat, or in completing a hip throw, for example, it may be because he has weak hamstrings, or hips, or lower back muscles. *Once we've identified the weakness, we prescribe special assistance exercises to strengthen that area first.* If the hamstrings are weak, for example, he might do glute-ham raises, or seated leg curls with Tubing, or arched back Goodmonings.

Then we go on to work other important muscle groups like the abs, low back, glutes, lats, and shoulders. *We work our weakest area first,* and then go on to work our second weakest muscle group, and so on.

And of course, we're **always** looking for weaknesses in our techniques. If one of our fighters consistently fails to complete a rear throw, such as Osoto Gari (Major Outside Reaping Throw), for example, it may be because he lacks the leg drive needed to support that technique. To correct this weakness, we then have him drag the towing sled, push a car, perform various special uchikomis (fit ins), and other special exercises with a partner.

Or let's say one of our guys consistently fits into a good forward throwing position against his opponent, but more often than not fails to complete the throw. He probably needs to work on the rotational muscles of his torso, so we prescribe exercises such as the Russian twist, forward throw finishes with tubing, vertical bar twists with "The Grappler," Hypers with twists, and so on. In practice we also have him work with two partners on drills like three-man Uchikomis. In this way we help him get strong in the exact position he needs to be in to complete his technique.

Again, we use "The Conjugate Method" and rotate our exercises every one to three weeks. We arrange our training calendar so that our most effective exercise is scheduled a week or two prior to an important contest. This enables us to get our best results at contest time.

The following section is a sample of what a weekly training program might look like.

MONDAY
Maximum Strength Day: Lower Body and Torso

- Goodmonings: Work up to your best double.
- Russian twists: Two to three sets of 20 to 30 reps.
- Glute-ham raises: Two to three sets of 10 to 20 reps using added weight or band resistance.
- Short Five- to Six-Minute Circuit. (You may use the Repetition Method or Circuit Training right after your max effort work or speed work. Just keep it short in duration. In fact, try to finish the whole workout within 45 minutes.

* Goodmornings are a great exercise because of their applicability to wrestling and other grappling sports/

* Most of our exercises can be used with an accommodating resistance tool (bands or chains).

TUESDAY
Conditioning and Assistance Work

- Hindu squats: 500 reps. (Start with fewer reps and build up over time).
- Reverse Hypers: Three sets of 10 to 12 reps.
- Assistance Ab and hamstring work.
- Five-minute DB drill.

Fight Conditioning

- Circuit Training, 20 minutes

* When prepping for a fight, intense circuit training will replace the assistance work. Actually, many of the assistance exercises are incorporated in the circuits anyway.

WEDNESDAY
Maximum Strength Day: Upper Body

- Push-ups with medium to heavy bands: Five to six sets of five to eight reps.
- Bent rows with "The Grappler": Four to five sets of five to 15 reps.
- Triceps extensions with bands: Three to five sets of 10 reps. (No more than 30 seconds rest between sets).
- Five- to six-minute Circuit.

THURSDAY
Assistance Work

- Russian DB routine: Three to four sets through the sequence of exercises.

- Ab and low back exercises. Two to three sets of each.

FRIDAY
Maximum Speed Day

- Box squats (for explosive speed): Eight to 12 sets of two reps. 15 minutes (Rest: 30 to 45 seconds between sets).
- Russian twists: Two or three sets of 20 to 50 reps.
- Circuit Training: Six to 12 minutes (Include glute-ham raises in the circuit).

SATURDAY
Conditioning and Assistance Work

- Hindu squats: 500 reps, or whatever you are capable of in 15 minutes or less.
- Reverse Hypers: Three to five sets of 10 to 12 reps.
- Ab and hamstring assistance work: Two to three sets.

* The above workout can be replaced by an extremely challenging practice for fight prep. This is an excellent day for it because most competitions are on Saturday.

Sample Circuit for Fight Prep

1. Heavy bag (three-minute round)
2. Push-ups (25 reps)
3. Hindu squats (33 reps)
4. Sit-ups (25 reps)
5. Back raises (Hypers): (25 reps)
6. Dips (15 reps)
7. Pull-ups (15 reps)
8. Hindu squats (33 reps)
9. Glute-ham raises (10 reps)
10. Thai bag (three-minute round

SUNDAY
Active Rest

The following section is divided into Lower Body, Torso, and Upper Body exercises. This listing is by no means complete, but it represents some of our key exercises.

LOWER BODY EXERCISES

- As I mentioned earlier, box squats are one of our main exercises. Unlike the other assistance exercises, we keep some form of box squat in our program most of the time.

Box Squats (Variation 1)

Photo 1

After taking the bar off the rack, sit back on the box until your shins are just past vertical. Relax your hips and glutes while keeping the rest of your muscles tight. Push your knees out to the side.

Photo 2 and Photo 3

While pushing your abs out against your belt, explode upward with your glutes and legs.

Box Squats with Chains (Variation 2)

Chains provide accommodating resistance. As you squat back onto the box, for example, the weight of the chains is unloaded as they pile onto the floor. As you explode upward, weight is added to the bar as the chains come off the floor. In other words, the chains accommodate your strength curve, giving you less resistance at the bottom of the squat and more as you explode upward into your strongest portion of the lift. One of the biggest advantages of chains is that they allow you to come off the box quickly, thus developing tremendous starting and accelerating strength and speed. This is what you need for all throws and takedowns, as well as kicking techniques.

Note: Again, based on the advice of Louie Simmons, we switch to chains two or three weeks before a fight or match. Bands make us too sore because they speed up and overload the downward or eccentric portion of the lift even beyond what naturally occurs with gravity.

Throughout the year we generally go three weeks with bands, then three weeks with chains, and so on.

Photo 1

Loop a small chain around each side of the bar. Then drape heavier chains through the smaller chains.

Photo 2

Squat back onto the box until your shins are just past a vertical position. Explode off the box to an upright position.

Box Squats with Bands (Variation 3)

Normally bands or chains are attached to each end of the bar and then the other end is looped to the bottom of the power rack. In this case, though, the band is attached to your belt or the bar and then an end is looped under each foot. This method has an awkward feel to it at first, and it makes your legs feel wobbly. But it also works your muscles much differently, and it makes you very strong and explosive.

Photo 1

Attach a single band around your belt or the bar and loop the ends around each foot. Sit back onto the box until your shins are past vertical and.

Photo 2

Drive upwards just as though you were doing a regular box squat. Be sure to keep your back tight and push your abs out against your belt throughout the movement.

Belt Squats

Belt Squats are a great way to strengthen your thigh muscles without compressing your spine as can happen with other types of weighted squats. For this reason, we use belt squats when our backs are bothering us. In fact, belt squats actually act like traction, while simultaneously developing greater leg strength.

Sean Daugherty is shown doing belt squats on a Belt Squat Machine invented by Louie Simmons. If you don't have access to a Belt Squat Machine, you can attach weights from your belt and place your feet on two strong wooden boxes. Space the boxes apart so that as you squat down the weight goes between them. Repeat for the desired number of reps.

Do belt squats once a week for two to three weeks for a different stimulus to your muscles.

Photo 1

Squat down as far as you can. Keep your back straight and push your abs out against the belt.

Photo 2

Drive back up to a standing position as fast as you can. Repeat for the desired number of reps.

Note:

Since you're doing high reps on many of your body weight exercises, keep the reps low on your belt squats.

Example:

- Five sets of five reps
- Or six sets of three reps
- Or work up to a one or two repetition max

(Adjust your weights accordingly)

Zercher Squat

The Zercher Squat works the glutes, thighs and back, as well as your arms, which must hold the weight against your body throughout the movement. It is also a great exercise for strengthening various pick-up throws like Te-Guruma (Hand Wheel), and others in which you must secure your opponent with your arms and lift him up with your hips, legs, and torso.

Photo 1

Secure the bar in the crook of your elbows. While keeping your head up, and back tight and straight, squat down so that your elbows go between your knees.

Photo 2

Explode back up into the starting position.

Lifting throws like this Te-Guruma (Hand Wheel) require strong hips and legs, low back, and abs. Zercher Squats will help you develop strength for this and other pick-up throws.

Photo by Steve Scott

Leg Curls with Tubing

Hamstring strength is essential in increasing speed and reducing your chances of knee injuries; doing leg curls with tubing is another great way to develop it.

Photo 1

Loop the tubing around a secure post and place your ankles through the other end.

Photo 2

While sitting on a bench or chair, curl your legs back towards you. Repeat for the desired number of reps.

You'll notice that the tubing gives you more resistance towards the end of the movement. This is the opposite of most conventional exercises in which, after you get through the sticking point, inertia takes over and the exercise becomes easier. This is why tubing is so good. It strengthens the portion of the movement that other exercises miss.

Note: Exercises like this one and glute-ham raises are far superior to leg curl machines that don't work the muscles in a coordinated fashion as they are used in fighting or sports.

Torso Exercises (Low Back, Abs, and Sides)

Back Raises

This exercise is commonly known as the "*Hyperextension*," but to actually hyper-extend the back could cause injury, so we prefer to call them back raises. To perform the exercise, place your hands on the side of your head or across your chest and slowly go down to a hang position. Raise yourself back up only to the point where your body is in a straight line. You can do these without weight for as many reps as possible, or as you get stronger, you can hold a barbell behind your neck on your shoulders and do three to five sets of five repetitions.

This is a great exercise for strengthening the lower back, but like most exercises, only use it for two to three weeks before switching to another low back exercise.

Photo 1 and Photo 2

Sean Daugherty demonstrates the Back Raise.

Back Raise With Twist

With a barbell or pole resting across your shoulders, do a back raise, but when you reach the horizontal position, twist to one side so that your body forms a cross. Return to the face-down horizontal position, and lower yourself back to a hang. Raise yourself up to the horizontal position again, and twist to the opposite side, and so on.

These backward twisting motions are used in many throws and takedowns, as well as in certain kicks, and in many grappling situations. By strengthening these twisting muscles you will also reduce your chances of lower back injuries.

Goodmornings

The Goodmorning exercise strengthens the lower back, glutes, and hamstrings, all of which will help you lift an opponent up and slam him to the ground.

Photo 1

With feet slightly wider than shoulder width apart and knees slightly bent, push your abs out against your belt and keep your back flat. Then ...

Photo 2

bend forward at the waist until your body is at about a 90 degree angle. Return to the starting position and repeat for the desired number of reps. After a warm up of 10 reps, we usually work up to our max double or triple on Max Effort Day.

Goodmornings/Squat Variation

Photo 1 through Photo 7

Execute the first part of a Goodmorning, then drive your hips forward and under the bar as you complete a squat and return to the starting position. This is an excellent exercise for any grappling based art or sport because if the opponent is able to snap your head down he can execute a guillotine choke, front headlock, or in MMA or a street assault he could just knee you in the face. This exercise will give you the strength to drive your hips in and maintain an upright posture making it impossible for the opponent to catch you with those kinds of techniques. It will also give you the power to get under an opponent, pick him up and slam him to the mat.

Reverse Hypers

Photos by Melissa Stage on location at the Barn Of Truth Dojo.

The Reverse Hypers ™ is a great exercise for increasing strength in the lower back, glutes, and hamstrings, and for restoration. Louie Simmons used this exercise to come back from a debilitating back injury that had forced him out of Power Lifting. That was years ago. Today, many years later, thanks in part to Reverse Hypers ™, Louie's back is strong and he's setting lifetime records in his lifts. Reverse Hypers ™ were so important to Louie's return to lifting that he invented and patented "The **Reverse Hyper Machine**" (pictured below) so that others could benefit from this exercise.

If you don't have access to this machine, you can do the exercise by leaning over a strong, high table, attaching weights to your feet, and performing the exercise just as with a machine. Swing the weight up until your legs are in line with the rest of your body, then slow the weight down as it swings to a point just under your face. Repeat for the desired number of reps.

The part of the exercise where your legs swing under you is very beneficial to your spine and disks, since this motion elongates the spine, and even allows fluid to re-enter the disks. This is not true of most other conventional weight-lifting exercises in which the spine is compressed. This is why Reverse Hypers ™ are so important for restoration, and for developing a strong, healthy back.

Again, if you would like more information on "The **Reverse Hyper Machine**," or any of Louie's other products, visit Westside Barbell's website at: **http://www.westside-barbell.com**.

Do this exercise for three to five sets of 10 to 15 reps following your workout.

Photo 1 and Photo 2

Sean Daugherty is shown demonstrating the Reverse Hypers ™.

Photos by Melissa Stage

on location at the Barn Of Truth Dojo

Side Sit-Ups

The side sit-up is another great one to add to your arsenal of torso exercises. Side sit-ups strongly work the obliques (sides), which stabilize the spine and which are involved in all twisting and forward throwing motions. Also, your obliques are brought into play whenever you are struggling with your opponent, either from a standing position or on the ground.

Photo 1

Sean Daugherty demonstrates side sit-ups on a Glute/Ham Developer. With his feet secured under the pads he bends down sideways as far as possible.

Photo 2

Using the muscles of his oblique's he then curls himself upward as far as he can go.

Repeat for the desired number of repetitions, and be sure to work both sides equally.

> *Note:*
> If you do not have access to a Glute/Ham Developer, you can position yourself across a bench or a Swiss Ball and have your partner sit down and straddle your legs as you perform the exercise.

Russian Twists

The Russian Twist is a severe exercise for advanced trainees. It is difficult because, as you twist from side to side, not only are you working your obliques, but you must also isometrically contract your abs throughout the movement in order to keep your body horizontal to the floor. This makes breathing difficult, to say the least. But as tough as it is, the Russian Twist is an outstanding exercise for the rotational muscles of the torso which are vital to all forward throws of judo, wrestling, and other grappling arts. How many times have you seen a guy get into a good forward throwing position only to get stuck or countered? It happens a lot. The Russian Twist will help you develop a strong finish to your throws. It will also develop twisting muscles that are very useful in all types of ground grappling. These muscles also stabilize the spine, which helps prevent injuries.

Photo 1

Hold a barbell plate at arms length with a slight bend in the elbows. Twist to your right until your shoulders are vertical to the ground. Exhale forcefully and ...

Photo 2

grab a quick breath when the weight is in the upright (midway position). Without pausing ...

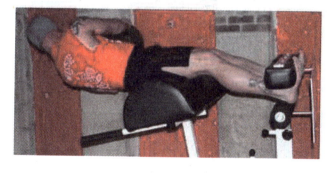

Photo 3

continue twisting to your left until your shoulders are again vertical to the ground. Repeat for the desired number of reps.

Note:

: If you are new to this exercise, start with a light weight (five or 10 pounds). If your form deteriorates and your back starts to bend backwards, stop the exercise. Build up gradually.

Side-To-Side Leg Raises

This is another good exercise for the rotational muscles of your torso, which are important in all aspects of fighting (The pattern flows from Photo 1 to Photo 2, then back to Photo 1. It then proceeds from Photo 1 to Photo 3, back to Photo 1, and so on. Don't worry; it's not nearly as complicated as it sounds.)

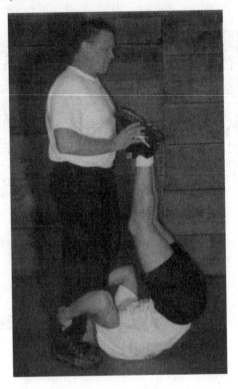

Photo 1

In the photo, I am preparing to push J.P.'s legs down the middle (not shown). Have your partner push your legs straight down the middle as well. Raise your feet back up, as shown here.

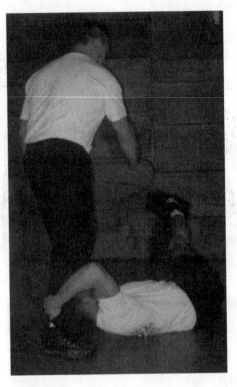

Photo 2

Your partner will then push your legs to the left. Return to the starting position shown in Photo 1. He will again push your legs down the middle. Return to the starting position again.

Photo 3

Your partner will then push your feet to the right. Raise your legs back to the starting position. Work to develop a rhythm, and repeat the entire procedure for the desired number of reps.

Vertical Bar Twists

Vertical Bar Twists are a great way to develop the twisting muscles of your torso needed for many different throws of judo, wrestling, and other grappling arts. It will also add to the power of Roundhouse Kicks, punches, and other striking techniques.

Photo 1

Place one end of a bar in a corner. Load the other end with weight and lift it up in front of you, as J.P. is demonstrating here.

Photo 2

With arms slightly bent, twist as far to your left as you can. Stay on the balls of your feet so that you can pivot them in the direction of the bar. This will prevent strain on your knee ligaments..

Photo 2

Bring the bar back and twist as far to your right as possible. Again, be sure to pivot your feet in the direction of the bar. Continue alternating from side to side for the desired number of reps..

Photos by Melissa Stage on location at the Barn Of Truth Dojo

> *Note:*
>
> Recently, Louie Simmons gave us a device he invented, called **"The Grappler."** We now do Vertical Bar Twists with **"The Grappler."** It has a much smoother action, and we can grab a bar in each hand, which makes the exercise even more effective. We also use **"The Grappler"** to perform many other exercises, including those that mimic the motions of our sport. To learn more about "The Grappler," visit **www.westside-barbell.com.**

Incline Sit-Ups

This is a basic exercise for your abs. Sit up and touch your right elbow to your left knee, then on the next rep touch your left elbow to the opposite knee on each rep. Repeat for as many reps as you can.

Variations:

While lying back, hold a heavy medicine ball over your head. Sit up and throw it to a partner. Have him throw the ball back to your chest. Catch it and repeat for as many reps as you can handle.

UPPER BODY EXERCISES

In the following short section are a few upper body exercise variations you may find helpful. This list is by no means complete, but it will give you an idea of how to modify exercises to make them more effective.

Hindu Push-Ups

This exercise was another favorite of the old-time Indian/Pakistani wrestlers like "The Great Gama." It not only builds great upper body strength and endurance, but flexibility as well.

> *Photo 1 and Photo 2*
>
> With your feet spread and your hips up in the air, dip down, arch your back and look up at the ceiling. Spring back up to the starting position and repeat for the desired number of reps.

Ring Muscle-Ups

Photo 1 thru Photo 4

Mike Mekoleske demonstrates a pull-up and press (Muscle Up) on the rings. On the far right Mike is attempting an Iron Cross. Exercises like these develop great upper body strength useful in all grappling arts and sports.

Photos by Melissa Stage on location at the Barn Of Truth Dojo.

Ring Push-Ups

Ring Push-ups are a great way to work all the muscles involved in a normal push-up, but the advantage with Ring Push-ups is that the rings move slightly as you exercise. This movement strengthens the stabilizer muscles in your chest, arms, shoulders, and throughout your torso. You can also accentuate the movements. For example, you could move your arms wide to the sides in a flying-type motion, or forward and back, or even in circles. All of these movements will work your muscles from different directions. This will make your upper body strong all over.

Once you master your body weight on this exercise, try doing it with a band across your back. Hold the loop on the ends of the band in each hand while you also hold the rings. As you push yourself up toward complete extension, the band will give you increased resistance.

Photo 1

Sean Daugherty is shown doing ring push-ups with feet elevated on a box.

Photo 2

Sean doing regular wide-ring push-ups.

Photo 3

Sean is performing various movements with the rings: forward and back with the hands, circles, etc.

> *Note*
>
> Sets and reps will depend on your level of fitness, and your needs.

Horizontal Pull Ups

Horizontal pull-ups develop the pulling muscles of your arms, rear delts, and upper back that are so important in grappling, whether standing or on the ground. Since in this program you're doing so many kinds of push-ups, pulling exercises like these will not only make you strong in the opposite direction, but will also help prevent injuries due to muscle imbalances. Remember: always work opposing muscle groups.

Photo 1
Grab a horizontal bar or rings and place your feet out in front of you so that you are in a prone position. From arms length …

Photo 2
Pull yourself completely up. Keep your body as rigid as you can throughout the movement. Repeat for as many reps as you can for several sets.

Variations:
Vary your grip from workout to workout. Also, try varying your body angle by raising your feet, or by lowering them to the ground. Another possible variation would be to secure a band over your chest and each end to the bottom of the rack. The added resistance of the band will make you very strong. Variations like this will make you strong from a number of different positions and angles, which is exactly what you need for fighting.

Rope Climbing

Rope Climbing is one of the best exercises for grappling and for developing all-around pulling power in the upper body. It is also a great way to develop a powerful grip.

Photo 1 and Photo 2

Sean Daugherty is shown climbing the ropes with his feet outstretched in front of him. In addition to working the pulling muscles, this variation also works the abs and hip flexors.

Photo 3 and Photo 4

This variation works the pulling muscles from an entirely different angle.

Photos by Melissa Stage on location at The Barn Of Truth Dojo

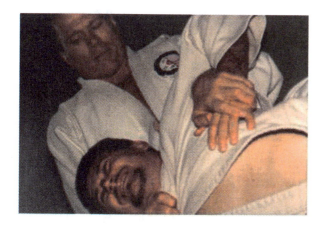

Rope Climbing and other pulling exercises are vitally important in grappling.

Here **three-time U.S. National Judo Champion and Coach of the U.S. National Training Squad at the Olympic Training Center,** John Saylor is shown strangling a student with a gi choke. Rope climbing will help you develop the grip and upper body strength necessary for these kinds of techniques.

Archive Photo provided from The Barn Of Truth Dojo.

Four-Way Neck Exercise with Band

A strong neck is essential for fighters of all kinds. Therefore, our fighters spend a lot of time doing neck bridges (both back and front), headstand neck work, and partner neck exercises. But the Four-Way Neck Exercise With Band is an excellent one to add to the other neck work. The band provides a different type of stimulus to your muscles. As you pull the band tighter you get more resistance, and you can work your neck in four directions. In fact, if you have developed your neck already with other exercises, you can move the tension from side to side, or change your head position in some other direction to work different muscles in your neck.

Photo 1, Photo 2, Photo 3 and Photo 4

Sean Daugherty works his neck from various angles.

Be sure to use a towel to prevent abrasions from the band.

Photos by Melissa Stage on location at The Barn Of Truth Dojo.

Hand and Forearm Exercises

Grip Training

It was early fall 1979, and I had spent the last month in South Africa with the United States Judo Association team. During the last day of our stay, Big John Tate, who at the time was the World Heavy Weight Boxing Champion, fought and defeated a South African fighter.

The next day we boarded our flight to New York City, and were surprised to find Tate and his entourage on the same flight. Once airborne, Tate made his way up and down the aisle, proudly displaying his championship belt and joking with friends. Angelo Dundee, trainer of such greats as Muhammad Ali, Willie Pep, Pinklon Thomas, Jimmy Ellis, Sugar Ray Leonard and many other world champions, was also on the plane. Angelo, who for all the world appeared more like an accountant on vacation than a trainer of world champion ass kickers, casually made his rounds around the plane talking with fighters and officials.

But the one who really caught my attention was Roberto "Hands of Stone" Duran himself. Duran had been lightweight world champion, and in the early 1980's his defeat of Sugar Ray Leonard gained him the middleweight title as well. Roberto, as you'll recall, wasn't the most sportsmanlike guy in boxing. I still remember him punching an opponent's corner man after winning what I recall was a 12-round unanimous decision in the late 1970's. After another victory, an interviewer reminded Duran that one of his recent opponents was still on life support systems and that he knew he would be concerned about his welfare. Roberto suddenly grabbed the microphone and yelled, "Next time, I keeel him!" A real class act. I still thank almighty God for Tommy Hearns, who utterly destroyed Duran in two rounds in 1984. But regardless, Roberto Duran was a great fighter.

Around this time, coaches and athletes alike were arguing over the merits of weight training, whether or not it slowed you down, and so on—an argument still going on today. Since I did a lot of weight training, calisthenics, and other conditioning, I was interested in getting Duran's take on it.

Our plane on this 18-hour flight was huge, with an entire row of seats in the middle and another seat on each side. I ambled back a few rows to the middle section where Duran was seated and plopped myself down in the vacant seat next to him. His sparse black beard and mustache were in stark contrast to the white ball cap he wore backwards hiding most of his dark hair. A tank top, faded jeans, and worn track shoes completed his totally relaxed look. After introducing myself and going through a little small talk in Spanish, we went on in English since it turned out his English was a little better than my Spanish.

I got right to the point:

"Do you train with weights?"

"No," he replied. "Weights make me tight and slow me down too much. I run, do bag work, push ups, sit ups, rope jumping, and stuff like that." Then he paused for several seconds and added,

"But I do this a lot, too."

With that he pretended to roll up an imaginary weight suspended by a rope from a thick stick or a dowel, an exercise known as the Wrist Roller. Then, as though doing a dumbbell reverse curl, he brought his arm up and flexed his forearm muscle. It looked like Popeye's.

"Go ahead, feel it," he said. It felt like a rock.

"Wow, that's really strong," I affirmed.

"When I connect with my punches," he went on, "I need strong wrists and forearms."

Then, for no apparent reason, Duran formed his hands like the so-called "Karate Chop."

"You guys can break things with these," he said as he moved his right hand in a downward chopping motion, "but I can break anything with these." With that he held up his left fist, then his right, and pointed to the knuckles of his famous "hands of stone." Each knuckle had what I would guess to be about one-half an inch of calcium deposits protruding from it. Somehow he must have gotten the idea that we were a Karate team. I resolved right then to start eating more and to train even harder, but laughingly just replied,

"Yeah, I'll bet you can."

Not wanting to overstay my welcome, I thanked him and went back to my seat. Roberto sauntered up a few rows where a classy looking woman in her early thirties, wearing lots of expensive jewelry, leaned against the window asleep. Roberto eased into the empty seat next to her, leaned to his left, and gently placed his head on her shoulder pretending to be asleep. The woman awoke with a start and recoiled backward against the window, terrified of this rough looking man next to her. His attempt at romance having been rejected, he got up chuckling and swaggered back to hang out with the other boxers.

Maybe he would have had more luck if he'd mentioned that he was a multi-millionaire who owned a sizeable portion of Panama.

I made a mental note never to use Duran's approach when seeking romance, but to follow his advice to the letter as far as the Wrist Roller was concerned. After all, if strong wrists and forearms were important to a world champion like Duran, how much more important would they be to a grappler? In judo, for example, the grip is vital—you're only as strong as what you can hang on to. In grappling events without the gi jacket, a strong grip enables you to tie up and secure holds on your opponent. And of course, in self-defense you need a powerful grip to crush and rip vulnerable parts of an attacker's anatomy.

Obviously the grip is important, but what is the best way to go about developing it? Well, the Wrist Roller is a great start, but there are a number of exercises to choose from.

Photo 1

Grip training will dramatically improve your choking techniques with a gi jacket.

Photo by Fritz Goss

> **Wrist Roller**
>
> Drill a hole through a wooden dowel and run a strong nylon rope through it. Tie the other end of the rope around a weight. Now you're set to go.

Want Super Hand & Forearms Strength? Try These ...

Exercises like these can be done at the end of a workout, or they can be done for 15 to 20 minutes a couple times a week as an extra workout in the evening. Most people don't do much grip training, and if you do it can give you an advantage over them.

To achieve mastery, "do what others are unwilling to do."

> **Wide Wrist Roller**
>
> For this one, use a wide piece of PVC pipe for your Wrist Roller. This makes it much harder to hold, and it will really strengthen your grip. Again, be sure to roll the weight up and down both ways.

Photo 1

Roll the weight up, then back down. On the first rep, roll your hands toward you. Then, after rolling it back down, roll the weight back up the other way. This will work both sides of your forearms. Don't be surprised if you feel a hellacious burn in your forearms and hands.

Photo 2

J.P. rolling up a 45 lb. Dumbell with the Wide Wrist Roller.

Other grip and forearm exercises could include Pinch Grips with the flat side of two barbell plates, a dumbbell or other objects, leverage lifts with a sledge hammer or similar object, grippers, and many others. These exercises can be done as short extra workouts in the evening or whenever. They don't fatigue your system or hamper your recovery, but they will greatly increase your grip strength which is an asset in any combat sport or art.

Total Body Exercises

Squat Thrust with Push-Ups And Pull-Ups Added

This is just like a standard squat thrust, only you will be adding a push-up and a pull-up on each rep. This exercise works your entire body and develops tremendous muscular endurance and strength. It's a real killer, so gradually build up your reps over time.

Photo 3

Thrust your feet backward until you're in a push up position.

Photo 1, Photo 2

Position yourself under a pull-up bar and squat down.

Note: This is a great exercise to use when you have limited time, but need to get in a good workout. It is as close to a total body exercise as any I know.

Medicine Ball Work

The Medicine Ball is an often overlooked workout tool that can be used to hit the hard-to-get twisting muscles of the torso, as well as many other muscle groups throughout the body. Boxers have used the Medicine Ball for years, generally eight, 12, and 16-pound sizes. We use 40-pound and 60-pound Medicine Balls since obviously they develop more strength. You can get heavy duty Medicine Balls from: **www. Westside-barbell.com.**

They're super durable and are made to be thrown onto asphalt, grass, or whatever. *You can do all kinds of motions with the ball.* Often times you can duplicate parts of a skill such as twisting movements of a throw.

Photo 1 and Photo 2

(J.P. Pocock)

From a half squat position spring up and push the ball out as far as you can. This is a good example of a chain reaction exercise. It starts with the legs, goes through the torso, and is released through the upper body.

Photo 3 and Photo 4

From a half squat position, reach down and grab the ball. Explode upward and with the power of your torso twist and throw the ball to your left. Walk over to the ball and repeat the motion to your right side. Continue alternating sides until you reach the desired number of reps.

> **Note**
>
> As far as reps are concerned, a good rule of thumb is as follows:
>
> When working for speed keep the reps under five, and do about five sets with 30 to 45 seconds between sets. When working for strength and overall endurance, work with the ball for as long as you can. Take a short rest, then switch exercises and again work as long as you can. Each week strive to do a little more. Keep increasing your work capacity. Again, the above exercises are just a few of many that you can do.

Barrel Lifts

The Barrel Lift is one of those awkward exercises that most people never do. As Brooks Kubik discusses in his book, *Dinosaur Training* (1996), barbells and dumbbells are made to be lifted. They have nice thin handles to grip and are perfectly balanced. In grappling with an opponent, though, we don't have such convenient handles, and he sure isn't going to stand there and balance himself perfectly so that you can pick him up nicely and slam him. This is where the value of lifting awkward objects comes in. Rocks, logs, barrels and the like don't have a bar to grip—you grip it however you can, and somehow hug it to yourself much like you might do with an opponent.

Take a look at the exercise photos below and then take a close look at the contest photo on the next page. Can you see any similarities?

Photo 1

Squat down, tilt the barrel slightly and hug it tightly to your chest.

Photo 2

With your back tight and straight, and with your hips underneath you …

Photo 3

drive upward to a standing position. From here you can do squats for a certain number of reps, or just take your barrel for a walk.

> **Note**
>
> The barrel in the photos is filled with water. You can use water, sand, gravel, or whatever. Just add more of whatever filler you use as you get stronger. If you use water add a touch of chlorine bleach to keep it clean..

Total Body "Chain Reaction" Exercises

Our Shingitai fighters often include exercises like clean pulls from the floor, clean pulls from various hang positions, power cleans from a hang position, and dumbell power cleans because they work the muscles of the body in a "chain reaction."

The strongest way to lift an opponent is by starting with your hips and legs, continuing with your low back and torso, and finally completing the throw with your upper body. The above mentioned exercises will help you develop the strength and coordinated chain reaction lifting technique for many pick-up throws.

Clean Pulls

Clean pulls will develop your hips and legs, lower and upper back, traps, and the pulling muscles of your arms. It's a total body exercise that teaches proper hip action for lifting, and it also develops that coordinated chain reaction between the various muscle groups of your body.

The clean pull should be done in various ways from workout to workout. You can start from what is known as hang position with the bar hanging from straight arms at a point just below your kneecaps. At another workout start from a hang position with the bar just above the knees. And at the next workout, start from the floor. You can also add bands at other workouts for a different stimulus to your muscles.

With his arms straight and his back perfectly flat, John Marotta starts the lift with his hips, legs, and back (Not pictured)

Photo 1

As his hips drive in he pulls explosively, starting with a shrugging motion of his traps and continuing with his arms. As he pulls, his elbows are out to the side. John comes up on his toes and pulls as high as possible. Notice that throughout the pull he keeps the bar close, within an inch or two of his body.

Photo by Dave FitzSimmons

Do clean pulls in sets of three reps when working for speed strength.

For example, do:

- 12 sets of three reps with 50 percent the first week.

- 10 sets of three reps with 55 percent the second week.
- Eight sets of three reps with 60 percent the third week.

Rest 30 seconds between each set.

Once a month or so work up to a maximum for one or two reps. Then when you start a new cycle, your 50 percent should be a little heavier than the beginning of the precious cycle since it is based upon a higher one-rep Max.

Dumbbell Power Cleans

DB Power Cleans are much harder than Power Cleans with a barbell because the dumbbells move independently of each other. This will help you develop greater coordination and athletic ability, and will strengthen your entire body.

Rotate (substitute) DB Power Cleans for Power Cleans with a barbell or Clean Pulls for two to three weeks.

Photo 1

(John Marotta)

From a hang position with a perfectly flat back and with the dumbbells at your sides just below the knees, begin the lift with your hips and legs. Continue pulling upward with your traps and arms.

Photo 2

When the dumbbells are just below chest level, drop under them with your legs as you turn the dumbbells over. Drive upward with your legs to a standing position. Repeat for the desired number of reps.

> **Note**
>
> The number of reps will depend on what physical quality you're trying to develop. If working for muscular endurance you could include this exercise in a circuit for 10 to 12 reps each time you get to that station.
>
> When working for speed strength keep your reps to three reps for 10 to 12 sets with a 30-second rest between sets.

Throwing and Takedown Exercises with Tubing

Photo 1

Photo 2

John Saylor demonstrates how to strengthen the finish of a forward throw. Grip the tubing and turn into a forward throw. Move forward until the tubing is taut. Then bend and rotate forward as though you were completing a forward throw. If you're doing a right-sided throw it may help you to think about touching your right ear to the mat (You won't make it, but this will help when you try to complete a throw).

John Marotta is shown doing an off-balancing exercise for forward throws. Loop your tubing around a post and imitate the initial pull of a forward throw. Do three or four sets of 10 reps. to each side.

Photo by Dave FitzSimmons

Variation:

You can also use the tubing to do uchikomis (fit-ins) of your favorite forward throws. Just grab the tubing as though it's your opponent's gi and execute uchikomis in sets of 20's or 10's for five to 10 sets.

Be sure to attack to both the right and left sides.

Photo 3

With one end of a heavy tube attached to a post and the other looped around his waist …

Photo 3

J.P. Pocock attacks his training partner with a low single leg takedown. Notice that J.P. moves forward until the tube is fairly tight before penetrating forward into the takedown.

Important:

Notice how his partner keeps a bend in his leg to avoid hyper-extending his knee. Be sure to do this to avoid injury..

Note:

These are just a few examples of how to strengthen specific fighting skills with tubing. There are many more. You can strengthen sweeping motions, punches, and many other skills as well. Just analyze your skills and look for ways to use tubing to strengthen those motions.

Climb Around Your Partner

This is a very hard drill that strongly works both partners. The man who is doing the climbing must not touch the ground with any part of his body as he circles completely around his partner. The support man must do whatever he can to maintain his balance as the other man does a complete revolution around his body. This will work all kinds of stabilizer muscles throughout the body that more conventional exercises often miss.

Photo 1

Brad Urwin adopts a strong stance as J.P. Pocock starts to climb.

Photo 2 and Photo 3

JJ.P. climbs around Brad in a clockwise direction and clings to whatever he can grab hold of to keep from touching the ground. Brad struggles to maintain his stance as J.P. climbs around him.

Photo 4

J.P. continues to climb around Brad.

Photo 5

J.P. returns to the starting position before setting his feet back on the ground. *At this point, the two reverse roles so that Brad is now the climber.

Note:

At some points throughout this sequence Brad is a little more bent than I would like to see, but this happens sometimes. Nonetheless, strive to maintain a strong upright stance throughout the drill.

Partner Carries

(Sorry, no photos are available for the following exercises, but they should be pretty self-explanatory)

Purpose: To develop overall strength and endurance, and to work stabilizer muscles of the body.

Variation 1: *Piggy Back Carry*

Have your partner climb on your back *piggy back style*. Run him the length of the mat (or a set distance) and put him down. Then climb on your partner's back as he carries you piggy back style back across the mat. He will put you down and climb on your back again. Run him back across the mat. Repeat the process for as many repetitions as your level of strength and conditioning permit.

Variation 2: *One Arm Shoulder Throw Carry*

The procedure for this drill is identical to drill #1 only now you will carry him in a One-arm Shoulder Throw (Ippon Seoi Nage) position. For variety you could also carry him with your arm wrapped around his waist or head, as in a Major Hip Throw (Ogoshi), or a Head Lock Throw (Koshi Guruma), or some other hip throw variation.

Variation 3: *Front Carry*

Pick your partner up in your arms as though you were carrying your bride over the threshold of her new home. Lovingly run your partner down the mat or field as in drill #1.

Variation 4: *Fireman's Carry*

Squat down and pick your partner up across your shoulders in a Fireman's Carry position. Run your partner and use the same procedure as in drill #1.

Note: For added difficulty and increased leg strength you could do all of the above partner carry drills up a series of stairs. This was something we often did with our Japanese hosts at Tokai University during early morning training in 1979. The stair workouts followed a run of about 20 minutes. What a killer workout. It soon became apparent that the Americans were usually at least as strong in the upper body, but that our Japanese hosts were much stronger in the lower body. These drills and the various jumps up the stairs which they did on a regular basis were, I'm sure, a large part of it.

> *Caution: Make sure you stop doing these drills at least a week to 10 days prior to a major fight or tournament. It takes time for your body to fully recover from the stress of such hard training and to transform it into fighting fitness.*

Exercises To Transform Your Off-Mat Conditioning Into Fighting Shape

This is a very important section. Many fighters are great in the weight room or on the track but can't seem to put it together when it comes to the fight. The following training methods and drills will ensure that you will transform your hard-earned conditioning off the mat into fighting shape.

Partner Assistance Exercises

The following exercises were developed by Wolfgang Hoffman, the 1964 Olympic Silver Medalist in the middleweight division and later a top coach in West Germany.

1. **Partner Jump Squats**

    Purpose: To develop anaerobic endurance and explosive leg strength for all hip throws.

    Directions: Face your partner, grab his belt and go into a squatting position. Perform jump squats for 30 to 45 seconds while your partner applies resistance with his hands on your shoulders (Photos 1 and 2).

    As soon as you've completed the jump squats, throw your partner five times with any two-leg throw (i.e. only do a throw in which both your legs remain on the ground) (Photos 3,4,5,6).

    Do three sets with a 1:1 or 1:2 work/rest ratio. A crash pad is recommended for this drill.

Photo 1 through Photo 6
(J.P. Pocock and Brad Urwin)

2. Partner Push-Ups/Grip Fighting (or Hand-Fighting)

Purpose: The idea of this drill is to pre-fatigue your arms and then force you to fight for grip if you're competing with a gi, or to pummel and do hand-fighting if you're competing without the gi. This is a great drill to prevent you from getting arm weary during tournaments or fights.

Directions: Have your partner provide resistance by pushing down on your upper back as you perform push-ups for 30 to 60 seconds, depending on your level of conditioning. Your partner should give you enough resistance to make it difficult, but not so much that you can't complete the reps. (Photos 1 and 2).

Photo 1 and Photo 2

When you've finished the pushups, stand up and grip fight or hand-fight with your partner. Push each other around as you try to break through his arm defense and throw him. If you can't break through within 10 to 15 seconds, your partner will let you through so that you can complete the throw. (Photos 3, 4 and 5)

Photo 3, 4, and Photo 5
J.P. Pocock and Brad Urwin pummeling and fighting for an upper body tie-up.

Once you secure your grip (with the gi) or upper body tie-up (without gi), execute your throw. For this drill confine your attacks to upper body throws.

* **Perform 2 to 3 sets of this drill with a 1:2 or a 1:3 Work/Rest Ratio.**

3. One Leg Hop and Drive/One Leg Throws

Purpose: This exercise will develop leg drive for such throws as Osoto Gari (Major Outside Leg Sweep), Uchimata (Inner Thigh Throw), and any other throw where you are driving off one leg.

Directions: With your driving leg on the ground, place your other foot on your partner's stomach (Photo 1). Push him down the length of the mat while he provides resistance. Again, your partner should provide enough resistance to make you work, but not so much that you can't move him. When your support leg is thoroughly fatigued, probably somewhere between 30 seconds to one minute, stop and throw your partner five times with any "one leg throw" such as Osoto Gari or Uchimata, driving off the same support leg that you just worked. Use a crash pad to save wear and tear on your partner.

Perform two to three sets on each leg with a 1:1 or a 1:2 Work/Rest Ratio.

Photo 1

Left, Brad Urwin (in black) drives J.P. Pocock across the mat. J.P. provides just enough resistance to allow Brad to keep moving, while forcing him to thoroughly work his driving leg.

Photo 2, Photo 3, and Photo 4

Brad Urwin throws J.P. Pocock with five Uchimatas (Inner Thigh Throw) after pre-fatiguing his support leg with the One-Leg Hop Drive.

4. Throw Your Partner and Drag Him Back Up (No Photos)

Purpose: To develop pulling power, a strong grip, and overall strength and endurance.

Directions: To perform this exercise your partner will need to wear a judo gi. Get a grip on your partner's gi jacket, throw your partner with a forward throw and drag him back up eight times. Repeat this procedure for two to three sets with a 1:1 or 1:2 Work/Rest Ratio depending on your level of conditioning. This drill is not a lot of fun, but it will make you tough all over.

Note: The preceding four partner assistance drills can be done as separate workouts two times per week for two or three weeks as a major competition approaches. Always drop these partner assistance drills at least a week to 10 days prior to contest to allow your body to fully recover.

How To Use Partner Assistance Exercises To Improve Weak Points In Your Technique

Partner exercises can also be used to strengthen some component part of your technique. Let's use a forward throw as an example, and let's assume that your pull is weak on the sleeve hand. By grabbing a belt, or a towel, and having your partner apply resistance, (Photo 1) you can strengthen that weak point in your technique. Notice how Brad Urwin pulls with his little finger upward, just as though he were pulling the opponent's sleeve hand.

After you execute a pull you will then provide resistance for your partner who will do the same pull on the way back. Go back and forth like this until you've thoroughly worked your muscles.

Then switch hands and repeat the same procedure to the other side.

Note: This is just one example of how to use partner resistance to overcome a weak point in your technique. I'm sure you can devise others. Just analyze your techniques and when you find a weakness try to create an exercise to strengthen that motion.

More Partner Pulling Exercises

The following partner resistance exercises will develop pulling power in your arms and back, which is so important for all grappling arts. To perform the exercise you and your partner will again grip opposite sides of a belt or towel. Give each other enough resistance to make the exercise difficult but not so much that your partner can't finish the movement. Use the following variations:

Photo 1

Partner high pulls.

Photo 2

Two arm tug-of-war. John Saylor and John Marotta are giving each other just enough resistance to make each other work hard, but not so much that they can't finish the movement.

Photo 3 and 4

Repeat the same procedure as for two-arm Tug-of-War only now you will be doing a set with your left arm vs. your partner's left arm, and then a set with right arm vs. right arm. Perform these exercises until you've thoroughly worked your muscles.

Photos by Dave FitzSimmons

Kettlebells

It's only been in the last decade or so that the average fitness buff in the United States has even heard of Kettlebells. Kettlebells have always been popular in Russia and have been used there by athletes of all types to develop strength and endurance.

While training at Tokai University in Japan in 1979, I noticed some judoists training with the old beat-up solid Kettlebells in their weight room. One of these was Yasuhiro Yamashita, three-time Heavy-Weight World Champion, 1984 Olympic Gold Medalist, and perhaps the greatest judoist in the history of the sport. In his book, *The Fighting Spirit of Judo* (date?), Yamashita is shown doing Alternate Overhead Presses with Kettlebells. Obviously the world-class judoists at Tokai thought Kettlebells had some value.

In the last few years Kettlebell training has really taken off in the West, largely due to the efforts of Pavel Tsatsuline and others who have produced some excellent videos and books on the subject. These are available through Dragon Door Publications. You can also purchase Kettlebells through them.

Kettlebells have several advantages:

1) They have wider handles which will strengthen your grip.

2) Kettlebells can be used in an infinite number of motions and exercises.

3) Kettlebells allow for a number of one-arm and rotational lifts that strengthen the stabilizer muscles of your sides and other areas, which are hard to reach in conventional lifting.

4) They can be used to develop great strength with heavier lifts or they can be used to develop muscular endurance by doing certain motions for timed rounds similar to *The 5-Minute DB Drill*.

5) Many of the Kettlebell exercises teach the muscles to work in a coordinated fashion as they are used in sports.

6) A Kettlebell or two is easy to load in the car whenever you travel.

Sometimes it's easy to get into a rut, and for some of us the hardest thing in the world is to change. We often dread going out of our comfort zone to try something new or unfamiliar. But that is not how we grow. Try new exercises and training methods from time to time. Like Louie often says, "You can't be afraid to change."

The following photos show Sean Daugherty doing a one-arm clean and press with a Kettlebell. This is a total-body chain-reaction type exercise that has a big carry over to combative sports. Throughout the year Sean rotates a number of Kettlebell exercises into his routine for a different training stimulus to his muscles and central nervous system. And if you have access to Kettlebells you can do the same.

Photo 1

Sean is shown doing Kettlebell Swings

> ***Note:***
>
> The following article appeared in a past Shingitai newsletter. The exercises described can be used at various times throughout Levels I, II, or even early in III to build or maintain GPP. We sometimes spend fifteen to twenty minutes working on these exercises in the evening. These little extra workouts may not seem to be much, but over a year's time they really add up.

Abnormal Training Methods For Abnormal Results

One Saturday afternoon back in the mid-1980's, during the time I was judo coach at the Olympic Training Center, I was browsing in Poor Richards, one of my favorite used bookstores in Colorado Springs. This particular day I was in luck. Almost hidden among a row of unpromising books on the shelf, I came across a real gem. I quickly paid the two dollars and walked out with a biography of Vasily Alexeev.

As you may recall, in Columbus, Ohio, in 1970, Alexeev became the first man ever to Clean and Jerk 500 pounds overhead. After I read his inspiring story, I lent this book to one of the Olympic lifters, who apparently felt he needed it more than I did and took it with him when he left the OTC. (You know who you are, you overstuffed milk-suck. Just send my book to the SJA address on page 210 and nobody will get hurt). This being the case, I can't quote him verbatim, but Alexeev said something like this:

> "Only with never-before-heard-of-training methods can
> you achieve never-before-heard-of results."

Alexeev often went beyond the confines of his conventional and somewhat authoritarian coaches, but they had to cut him some slack because, after all, he was smashing world records like a kid kicking down sand castles on the beach.

One of the photos in the book showed Alexeev, his head emerging out of the water, as he pulled a barbell upward from the river's floor. The water, you see, provided a resistance that couldn't be duplicated any other way, and it made him explosive and very strong. He also had many other unusual methods, which he combined with his more conventional exercises, and these permitted him to go beyond what any Olympic lifter had done before.

A man of similar philosophy is Louie Simmons. His Westside Barbell Club has produced so many national and world champions that Louie has lost count. Most guys would be ecstatic to sit back on this kind of coaching record. But Louie's never satisfied. He insists on proving his methods on himself first. Louie, at the time of this writing, is ranked 3rd in the world, and aims to be higher next year. On November 20, 1999 Louie did a 900-pound squat in competition (At the time of this publication he has done a 920 contest squat). A year later he celebrated his birthday by making a 600-pound bench press. Oh, and by the way, Louie is now 52 years old!

In my opinion, Louie knows more than anyone in the world about strength, speed, and conditioning—and not just for power lifting. He has worked with several pro football teams, world-class track and field athletes, wrestlers, and no-holds-barred fighters. Regardless of the sport, he knows how to "condition to win." Anyone with this kind of record in any field—whether it's martial arts, music, literature, checkers, or whatever, deserves to be listened to. There is something different about them—something in the way they think which sets them apart. Some other time I'll tell you about some of these people to illustrate my point. Meantime, back to Louie.

One evening in the parking lot in front of his gym, Louie and I spent about 10 minutes tossing a 60-pound medicine ball for distance. Once my humility lesson in this impromptu test of strength had been completed, we lounged around outside awhile. With strains of AC-DC and shouts of lifters spurring each other on to greater effort permeating the crisp fall air, Louie and I, as we often do, discussed his philosophy and training methods.

"You can't be normal," he remarked, "and do this. Normal people get normal results. To achieve abnormal results, you've got to be abnormal."

Louie was talking about a couple of things. First was attitude. "You can't worry about what the weight, or what your opponent, might do to you. That's what normal people do. You think like that, and you'll get hurt. You've gotta have an attitude."

Second was conditioning. "John," he said, "if I were training for what your fighters are doing, I'd be doing lots of super high-rep free squats, jump squats, push-ups, ab work, rope climbing, pull ups, neck bridging and other calisthenics like those Karl Gotch teaches. But," he continued, "I'd also do a lot of exercises to work my stabilizers and get strong at odd angles. For starters, I'd lift rocks or sand bags, and I'd do lots of towing." Pretty good advice.

I've incorporated lots of these odd exercises into my routine and have taught them to the handful of fighters I train. We've all gotten much stronger—-and it's the kind of strength that transfers over to fighting. I think these exercises will help you, too. Let me show you a few of them.

The first few exercises are done with a towing sled, which is simply a flat piece of steel with a pipe welded in the middle to hold weight plates, and some hooks with which to attach a tow chain. You will also need a strong weight lifting belt and a heavy-duty towing loop to connect the chain to your belt. These are just a few of many exercises that can be done with the sled.

Photo 1 and Photo 2

One Arm Pulls

As though you were starting a lawn mower, pull with one arm until your hand is at your side. Be sure to start with your arm fully extended, and alternate arms on each rep. This will greatly increase your pulling power, which is so necessary in grappling, both standing and on the ground.

Photo 3 and Photo 3

You can do a number of exercises with a Towing Sled. Here John Saylor is working the rotational muscles of the torso, which are so useful in throwing techniques and in all other phases of fighting.

Photo 5

Lower Body Towing: Take long strides forward and drag the weight for distance. Keep your elbows in close to your sides as you do so. This exercise will build up your hamstrings, glutes, and lower back, and will ensure that you don't get pushed around once you've clinched with your opponent. Also, if you do this exercise and those that follow for any length of time, say twenty minutes or more, it will greatly increase your endurance.

Photo 6 (above)

Sean Daugherty is shown walking backwards with the sled. This exercise works the quads in the front of the thighs.

Photos 7 and 8 (middle and right)

Sean is shown doing two arm high pulls. Notice in Photo 3 how his elbows are up and out to his sides. This is excellent for strengthening the initial off-balancing of all forward judo throws, and for developing general upper body pulling power.

Photos by Melissa Stage

Photo 9, Photo 10 and Photo 11

Sean is reaching between his legs and pulling the sled thru. This works the low back, hamstrings and glutes.

Photo 12

(John Marotta shoulders "the rock.")

You can do all sorts of movements with it. Use your imagination.

Note: Lifting awkward objects like rocks, logs, barrels, and sandbags, will work your stabilizers and grip, and make you very strong. Objects like this don't have nice handles to grip and they aren't perfectly balanced, so they are more like lifting a human body than conventional barbells or weight machines. Check out Brooks D. Kubik's book, *Dinosaur Training,* and Steve Justa's, *Rock, Iron, and Steel,* for a complete discussion of these and similar exercises.

Photo 13 (right)

A young Jeremiah Pocock is shown walking "the rock." This will develop strength throughout your entire body.

Photo 14

Gas prices got you down? Have your buddies over to push this little 4000 pound opponent around. This is a good exercise to substitute for Lower Body Towing (Photo 1) occasionally. It works you differently and involves the upper body as well. If you do this regularly, you won't get pushed around as you pummel for upper body tie-ups and positions. As you can see, you don't need fancy equipment or a gym membership to get strong, just some imagination and the discipline to work hard and persist over time.

Photos by Dave FitzSimmons

How's This For An Abnormal Training Method?

My judo friend, Bill Montgomery, spent several months training with Anton Geesink in Holland. Geesink, as you'll recall, was the 1964 Heavyweight Olympic Gold Medalist and 1965 World Judo Champion. He was the first non-Japanese to win an Olympic or World Gold Medal in Judo.

Although he didn't weight train much, he told Bill that **he often did Power Cleans with 100 Kg. (220 lbs) for 20 minutes straight!** This will give you an idea of the strength and conditioning of the world's best fighters. And even though Geesink didn't do much other formal weight training, I'll never forget his book, *My Championship Judo* (date?), which contains a photo of him pausing from his run up a mountain trail in the South of France with two long logs resting on his shoulders (pg. 34). Also, etched in my memory are the times as a kid at Camp Olympus in the mountains of West Virginia when Anton effortlessly tossed me around in randori.

Photo

Anton Geesink using abnormal training methods to achieve abnormal results.

Level III
Peaking Phase: A Tricky Business

In the Shingitai Method of Training, Level III is a peaking phase. You should use it very sparingly, when you have a contest or event of major importance, and only if you have prepared by going through Levels I and II. I'll discuss the reasons for this shortly, but for now *the general rule in peaking is to gradually reduce your total amount of training as you increase the intensity.*

Four to six weeks away from major event:

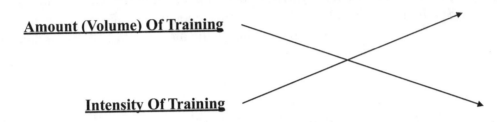

Gradually decrease the total volume of training and increase the intensity about four weeks away from your major contest or event. By gradually dropping back on the amount of training you will gain extra energy to allow you to increase the intensity.

The final two-week phase prior to your major contest or event is very important and can make the difference between a peak performance and a mediocre one. The trouble is, sometimes the more dedicated you are, the more danger you are in of training too much right before a major contest.

I had to learn this the hard way. The closer a contest approached, the more anxiety I felt. The more anxiety I felt, the more randori rounds I fought, the more extra conditioning I did … and the more beat up and worn out I got. I had mistakenly thought I was out of shape and kept trying to increase <u>both</u> the amount <u>and</u> the intensity of my training. This vicious circle continued until by contest time I often had a bad cold, was all dinged up, or both. Once, in 1977, I even spent 14 days in the hospital with cellulitus from a bruise that became infected. As a result of my misguided thinking, I left some of my best fights back in the dojo. Make sure you don't do likewise.

Peaking is a tricky business. You must use it very sparingly, and only for very important events. Most of the year I don't think it's possible to do too much work—-especially lower intensity work. But as you get close to the most important contests, you must cut back. Keep the following in mind when you set out to reach a peak:

1. To reach a high peak you must have a huge base of Level I and Level II training (GPP and SPP) behind you.

2. You must allow your body to fully mobilize its resources by gradually reducing the total amount of training while simultaneously increasing the intensity. Start this process four to six weeks away from a major contest.

3. Use the two-week "Unloading Phase" described in this chapter.

Super compensation

The Russian sports scientists first noticed that as a result of the unloading period, the athletes' physical abilities climbed far above their previous capacity. In other words, they reached a new peak. The Russians called this phenomenon "super compensation." But in order to achieve "super compensation," you must guard against the natural tendency to do too much at the last minute. Provided that you've done a lot of training in Levels I and II, the unloading period will bring you to a high peak when you need it.

A Word Of Caution

Some fighters try to achieve a Level III major peak for every contest or event they enter. **Big Mistake!** First of all, it's not possible to be at 100 percent every contest. The idea is to work so hard that your 80 percent will be better than everyone else's 100 percent.

Secondly, if you keep cutting down on the amount of training in order to peak for every event, you'll lose much of your physical base. And remember, you need a physical base to give you consistency and to support a peak performance.

If you're not a competitor, but are more interested in the self-defense aspects of martial arts, you should forget about Level III training altogether. After all, how could you possibly time a major peak for when you're attacked on the street!

If you're a self-defense student, a possible exception as far as peaking is concerned, might be a belt rank promotion test. Maybe achieving your black belt is an important goal for you and you need to be at a peak for the test. In such a case you may want to use the Level III peaking phase. But again, just don't use it very often.

Photo

My good friend Steve Scott is shown doing a perfect hip throw in contest. Today Steve is one of the best judo, jujitsu, and SOMBO coaches in the country. Steve has always managed to bring his fighters to the big contests in peak condition. If you follow the advice in this chapter you too will be able to bring out your best performance when it counts.

Two-Week Unloading Period

Many fighters leave their best performances back in the gym. Often this is the result of their anxiety over the upcoming event. As they get more nervous, they try to cram in more training at the last minute. This is self-defeating, as I learned the hard way in my early days of competition. *The time for lots of training is in the Level I and II phases.*

If your goal is to reach a peak at the most important contest, the Two-Week Unloading Period is vital. "Unloading" simply refers to dropping back on your training load. You should still do a few high intensity workouts, but they should be short and sweet. At your jujitsu practices, for example, the first week of unloading should include at least two high intensity workouts in the 90 percent to 100 percent range. Just cut back on the repetitions in drills and on the number of ground-fighting and sparring rounds. Concentrate on speed and precision, and on putting the final polish on your techniques.

As far as your conditioning sessions are concerned, do them at a high intensity but keep them short. Circuit Training, for example, is a great way to get in a short, high intensity workout. Since you'll be going from one exercise to another with almost no rest, you'll get a lot of work done in a short period of time. After a warm up, your circuit should take no more than 20 minutes.

If you don't have to run to make weight, don't do much running the last two weeks. You want your legs to be explosive, and too much running will take the spring out of them.

During the second week of the unloading phase you can still have one or two fairly high intensity jujitsu workouts in the 80 percent to 90 percent range, but keep them short, say 30 to 40 minutes. If, for example, your contest is on Saturday, you can have a short, high intensity (approximately 90 percent) practice on Monday, including a few ground-fighting and sparring rounds. On Tuesday, you could do a short drill training session including some tactical situation drills, but leave the sparring alone. *You want to avoid injury at all costs.*

Stay off the mat the rest of the week. You can still do some conditioning workouts, but keep them very short, about 20 to 30 minutes. And don't forget to keep doing some flexibility training. Basically, you want to do just enough work to stay sharp. Remember, by allowing your body to fully recover, you'll be able to mobilize all your mental and physical forces for a supreme effort when you need it most—*at the big event!*

A Few Closing Remarks

Since you've read this far you are probably one of the few highly motivated people who will actually do the work required to be great. I wish you all the luck in the world. I am confident that if you apply the methods in this book and diligently practice your sport, you will achieve any goals you set for yourself.

There are many other things I'd like to share with you, but the confines of a single chapter prevent me from doing so. If you would like to learn more about how the best athletes in the world train you can find many helpful resources at **www. westside-barbell.com.** You might also be interested in becoming certified to teach **The Westside Method of Training.** This course will prepare you to teach and coach at the highest levels and I would encourage you to look into this.

If you have any questions on the material presented in this chapter I'd be happy to try and help you. You can contact me at **www. johnsaylorsja.com.**

Good Luck in Your Training!
John Saylor

CHAPTER 9 – SPORTS NUTRITION AND HYDRATION

By Shane Sweatt

CHAPTER 9 – SPORTS NUTRITION AND HYDRATION
By Shane Sweatt

My athletic background is very diverse as I am an experienced tri-athlete. I have sixteen years of martial arts experience, and I have also competed in cycling road races, time trials, and point races in the USCF. I have had the pleasure of working with many world-record-holding power lifters — male and female — and a Tae Kwon Do Olympic "Athlete of the Year." I have worked with top-ranked boxers and MMA fighters in the UFC and other highly ranked MMA leagues the world over. My athletes have been featured in such magazines as: *Powerlifting USA, FLEX, Triathlete, Power*, and on several cable channels, such as: Spike TV and HD Net.

For competitive athletes getting ready for a competition, I look at everything as an advantage or disadvantage. If it is not an advantage, it is a disadvantage. I have all my athletes write out a checklist. The list includes everything that pertains to their sport. For example with a MMA fighter I would consider such things as reach, condition, strength, speed, skill sets standing and on the ground, nutrition, hydration, recovery, quality of sparring partners and coaches. These are just a few of the many things I would consider.

In that check list, I would never as an athlete or a coach give up an advantage that is controllable. For example, I cannot change if my opponent has an advantage in reach. But I can change other factors and you can, too. Throughout this book, you are learning how to gain the advantage in strength, conditioning, speed, recovery, and in this chapter nutrition and hydration. We want to turn our disadvantages into advantages, or at least minimize the advantage our opponent has in that area. Eventually, over time the goal is to evolve the athlete to the point that all controllable advantages are his or hers. I have always felt if an individual doesn't evolve, he dies.

In training the Westside system one is set up for constant evolution, and one's diet should be as well. Food should be organic and free range, never processed. Use stainless or bamboo utensils for cooking to stay away from products that contain and can leak BPA. Also, individuals should always eat foods that are in season in their area. This ensures ingesting the highest available nutrients. In life everything is in waves from the light to which vegetables and fruits we eat and grow to the body's central nervous system and even the cells in the body. By eating this way, it helps one to follow the natural waves in life and to eat more optimally.

Protein

Protein is the building blocks of the human body. It always bothers me how many athletes choose to slack on their protein intake because protein is essential for gaining or maintaining muscle mass. It is impossible to recover from training or an injury optimally without adequate amounts of protein. The next time you are feeling over trained or your body is aching and you don't feel like you are recovering optimally, take an honest look at your protein intake. When I was a young athlete, I did not understand the importance of protein intake. Unfortunately, I did not take enough in, but I trained and competed intensely. From the lack of protein, I suffered injuries that slowed down my progress and ultimately led to injuries that I have had to deal with ever since. This is what led me to study everything I could about nutrition and to run experiments on myself and my athletes. I wanted to help others avoid the problems I had incurred because of lack of knowledge in this area. Coaches make sure athletes understand the importance of protein intake, and athletes understand it is their responsibility to follow nutrition plans.

Protein molecules have multiple functions in the body, including the building of muscle mass. They make up certain enzymes and hormones and serve as important regulators in the body. The body uses protein for building and repairing bones, blood, teeth, skin, hair, nails, and internal organs. Proteins help regulate blood pressure, blood sugar level, and metabolism. Looking at all the benefits, it is obvious why optimal protein intake is essential. The building blocks of proteins are amino acids, and adequate amounts must be available in an athlete's rest periods after training for optimal recovery.

Essential amino acids (EAAs) cannot be produced by the body and must be provided by food or supplementation. This is one place an athlete can gain an advantage. Since the body does not produce it, an athlete must take it in through diet. Because some athletes will not follow their diet perfectly, this is where someone can gain an advantage in recovery that will help boost training and performance on competition day. Non-essential amino acids are produced by our body and are not as much of a priority to have in our diet. The body does not perceive a difference between mental and physical stress; therefore, training and eating optimally is imperative, so the production of non-essential amino acids proceeds efficiently for recovery.

Complete proteins are foods that contain all nine of the essential amino acids. All dietary proteins are converted into amino acids by enzymatic actions in the digestive track. The chemical structure of protein is carbon, oxygen, hydrogen and nitrogen atoms. Strip the nitrogen atom from protein, and one has the atomic formula for a carbohydrate, which can readily be used for energy. Proteins are our major source of nitrogen. Nitrogen is not found in carbohydrates and fats. Proteins can be used as an energy source: one gram of protein yields four calories of energy.

Essential	**Non-essential**
IsoIeucine	Alanine
Leucine	Arganine*
Lysine	Aspartate
Methionine	Cysteine*
Phenylalanine	Glutamate
Threonine	Glutamine*
Tryptophan	Glycine*
Valine	Proline*
Histidine	Serine*
Tyrosine*	Asparagine*
Selenocysteine**	Pyrrolysine**

(*) Essential only in certain cases

(**) Truly unclassified. Added to sustain the 22 numbers of Essential Amino Acids.

Anabolism and Catabolism

Proper nitrogen retention is necessary for anabolism. Taking in frequent meals with the proper amount of protein is optimal for proper nitrogen retention. Nitrogen balance occurs when the dietary nitrogen intake is equal to the amount of nitrogen excreted. An athlete looking to maintain bodyweight wants to keep nitrogen coming in at the same speed it is being excreted. Athletes who are looking to gain muscle mass, however, need to maintain a positive nitrogen balance. Lack of protein produces a negative nitrogen balance and leads to a catabolic state. This information can be found in *Specialist in Performance Nutrition* (Gastelu & Hatfield, 2000).

Catabolism is controlled by glucocorticoid hormones: cortisol, cortisone corticosterone, and deoxycorticosterone (cortisol is the prime hormone in this group). These hormones send signals to release stored proteins. This process is catabolism, which is the breaking down of muscle tissue. The amino acid glutamine mitigates the catabolic effects of cortisol. When cortisol is allowed to remain elevated after exercise, protein breakdown continues.

Optimal muscle growth and repair is achieved when the body stays anabolic. With optimal training and nutrition, more time will elapse being anabolic than catabolic. This is one reason some athletes implement anabolic steroids. Anabolic steroids raise androgen levels, meaning fewer cells will get the message to release protein. In turn, the body is in an anabolic state more often even if diet is not optimal. Therefore, it is important for athletes or coaches to fully understand what their bodies need in terms of nutrition before any start of hormone supplementation. After an anabolic steroids regimen is started, I recommend tracking all changes in nutrition and performance, ensuring optimal gains if an individual chooses to take anabolic steroids. If one's diet is off slightly, performance gains can still be achieved while on anabolic steroids, but they are not optimal. Think about working a body part hard. That body part is going to need amino acids for repair, and if a sufficient amount of protein is not ingested, the body will pull amino acids from stores in healthy body parts, which is counterproductive.

We want our athletes to be anabolic as much as possible because this is when your body recovers and builds. If an individual is not anabolic, then he is catabolic, which means his body is breaking down muscle for energy. During this time, he cannot recover from workouts or repair any injuries. It is no coincidence that my athletes who have the most aches, pains and injuries are the same ones who struggle with following their diet. The body becomes catabolic from either lack of food or training. We have our athletes use protein and Branched Chain Amino Acids (BCAAs) to achieve a positive nitrogen balance and increase muscle mass. A steady intake of quality carbohydrates and all of the amino acids required for protein anabolism must be in the blood during recovery periods. Doing this prevents protein catabolism during prolonged exercise. It promotes muscle glycogen synthesis following exercise, and helps prevent sports anemia by promoting an increased synthesis of hemoglobin, myoglobin, oxidative enzymes, and mitochondria during aerobic training. This keeps our athletes recovering optimally and making continuous performance gains.

Amount of Protein an Athlete Should Consume

When I am training athletes, I ask them how much protein they eat in a day. Many times they give me an answer that would be a sufficient amount of protein to meet their needs. However, if I look at their progress and see that they are not making the gains they should, then I know they are not eating enough protein. I ask them if they keep a log and track their nutritional intake every day. Inevitably they say no. I then tell them they are not getting enough protein and to keep track of their food intake for the next three days and report back. Without fail they never take in enough protein. Most consume half as much as they thought they did. I tell all my athletes to log their food intake if they don't know if they are taking in enough. Our body requires energy first before it does anything else.

Also, make sure to fuel the body with the proper amount of carbohydrates and fats to lessen the chance of using protein for energy. The more carbs used as energy the less carbs stored as fat. If athletes do this, they won't have to eat higher amounts of protein to compensate. This provides you proper ratios of nutrients, making it easier to control fat intake. Many protein sources are high in fat including saturated fat. If the body is not optimally fueled, it hunts the stored reserves of nutrients, causing it to rob other muscle-tissue of glutamine and other amino acids. On paper it seems like an individual is getting enough protein. Without the proper amounts of fats and carbohydrates to supply the amount of energy burned, an athlete will not repair optimally or have a proper nitrogen balance. Athletes use protein for energy instead of repair.

Be careful looking at studies done in the United States: half of them say an individual needs more protein while the other half tells him he doesn't. The studies are often performed on amateur lifters. We do all of our studies on high-level athletes, world champions and world record holders. To give an example, the American College of Sports Medicine, American Dietetic Association, and Dietitians of Canada in their recent joint position stand on nutrition and athletic performance (2000), concluded that protein requirements are higher in very active individuals and suggested that resistance athletes need 1.6 g to 1.7 g protein/kg body weight, while endurance athletes need approximately 1.2 g to 1.4 g protein/kg values that are about 150 percent to 200 percent of the current United States Recommended Dietary Allowances (USRDA). National Academy of Sciences (NAS) determined that in view of the lack of compelling evidence to the contrary, no additional dietary protein is suggested for healthy adults undertaking resistance or endurance exercise. In contrast, studies in the Soviet Union showed that a minimum of 2 grams per kg (.907 grams per pound) of bodyweight and up to 3 grams per kg (1.36 per pound of body weight) were needed for athletes in their studies. These requirements were not for protein levels but selected amino acid levels. More about this can be read in the *Science and Practice of Strength Training* (Zatsiorsky, 2006).

Leucine, for example, (commonly found in BCCA supplements) is depleted at a high rate for energy in muscles during workouts. This is why supplementing during workouts with BCAA's is effective. If leucine is depleted, it restricts protein formation. This applies to any essential amino acids since the body can't manufacture them. BCAA's typically contain the amino acids most used during training. Remember, in the Soviet Union these studies were performed on elite athletes by the government for the sole purpose of increased performance for national pride. Unlike here where many times companies run studies just to back the results they want. No two people are identical, and different sports deplete the body in different ways, so this has always made sense to me. Strength athletes believe more protein is important to build muscle. More is not better. What we need is optimal. Strength athletes actually require a high carbohydrate intake and adequate glycogen stores to fuel their workouts. A strength training program dictates how much muscle mass and strength is gained because all high intensity, powerful muscle contractions, like one sees in powerlifting, are fueled with carbohydrates. Many athletes are not just concerned about the amounts of protein they take in, but also how to get it into the muscle. Anabolic hormones do not increase the transport of amino acids into tissue. That is why some athletes use insulin, a hormone that increases the transportation of nutrients into cells. Also, aging athletes require more protein for recovery. When increasing protein intake, make sure to increase water intake as well; this keeps the kidneys healthy. Many people are concerned that too much protein hurts the kidneys. It won't unless not enough water is consumed. I have trained many athletes over the years in various sports, and I have never come across anyone who has had kidney problems due to a high intake of protein. I also like my athletes to use multiple protein sources in each meal when they can, giving them a broader spectrum of amino acids.

Quality of Protein

The Biological Value (BV) of a protein is a value that measures how well the body can absorb and utilize a protein. The higher the BV of the protein used, the more nitrogen the body can absorb, use, and retain. As a result, proteins with the highest BV promote the most lean muscle gains. Egg protein has the highest BV value for a natural protein with a rating of 100, with milk proteins being a close third with a rating of 91. Beef rates at 80 with soy proteins a distant 74. Bean proteins, due to the fact that they are plant-based proteins, only rate a 49. I feel Dan Gastelu and Dr. Frederick C Hatfield explained it best in their book *Specialist in Performance Nutrition*. When talking about BV, a score greater than 100 is possible. However, bear in mind since eggs are approximately 95 percent useable protein (based on essential amino acid configuration), whatever differences there may be in the comparison of BV measurements for eggs with designer whey products must fit into the remaining 5 percent (because the rating exceeds 100, the body cannot retain more than 100 percent) In other words, a score of 157 in comparison to eggs' 100, actually represents only a 5 percent difference in its usability in synthesizing protein. They give a great example on how science has been bent to meet marketing requirements, something I touched on earlier in this chapter. There are other methods like Protein Efficiency Ratio (PER) or Net Protein Utilization (NPU) for determining protein quality, but they both have their positives and negatives. Net Protein Utilization (NPU) is the ratio of amino acid converted to proteins to the ratio of amino acids supplied. This value can be determined by determining dietary protein intake and then measuring nitrogen excretion. One formula for NPU is: $NPU = ((0.16 \times (24 \text{ hour protein intake in grams})) - ((24 \text{ hour urinary urea nitrogen}) + 2) - (0.1 \times (\text{ideal body weight in kilograms}))) / (0.16 \times (24 \text{ hour protein intake in grams}))$

It should be noted that the quality of the protein consumed is very important. We should only use the highest quality we can get our hands on. Remember all food is fuel for an athlete. Would you put low-quality fuel in a race car that is expected to perform to its full potential?

Protein Sources

The bulk of an athlete's protein intake should come from food. A supplement is just that, a supplement. In food sources proteins are found in animals and plants. Meat sources and protein from nuts also contain fat. Supplemented protein does play an important role: supplemented protein is digested faster and is easier to prepare and consume. It is also an optimal choice for post workout due to its faster absorption rate. I recommend a mixture of organic meat proteins every day. AJ Roberts, a power lifter who holds the total world record at 308, did this getting ready for his first world record total and swears by it. An example of a good place to start follows.

I recommend organic and free range for your protein selection.

Beef: Beef tenderloin, Filet Mignon, Sirloin, Flank Steak, Round Steak, Top Round, Roast Beef, Ground Round, Ground Sirloin, Ground Beef (93% Fat Free or Leaner).

Poultry: Chicken breasts (no skin), canned Chicken Breast, Turkey Breast, Turkey Breast Cutlets, Ground Turkey Breast (95% Fat Free or Leaner), Canned Turkey Breast.

Fish: Just about all kinds, the best are: Tuna (canned in water or fresh), Cod, Flounder, Halibut, Haddock, Orange Roughy, Salmon (canned in water or fish, but limit to twice weekly), Red Snapper, Scallops, Shrimp, Whitefish, and Swordfish.

Other Meats: Buffalo, Ostrich, duck, horse and venison. Worldwide there are many varieties of meat that are great choices of protein.

Dairy: Eggs, Milk, Cottage Cheese, Yogurt

Most animal proteins, such as meat, poultry, fish, eggs, cheese, and milk, contain all of the essential amino acids and are therefore called complete proteins.

A quick point of interest on eggs: always cook eggs or use carton egg whites that have been pasteurized. Eggs contain a substance called avidin, which blocks uptake of vitamin B6 and vitamin H, causing a vitamin deficiency. It also binds with biotin and iron, making them unavailable; once this bond is formed, the body cannot break it, allowing the body to only absorb up to 50 percent of the protein. By cooking eggs (or egg whites), it will denature the protein avidin, enabling the body to absorb 98 percent. If you eat raw eggs, you can develop a partial to full Biotin deficiency syndrome.

Proteins found in vegetables are usually lacking one or more of the essential amino acids, which is why they are called incomplete proteins. Combine two incomplete vegetable proteins to make a high quality complete protein. Some common vegetable proteins are grains, legumes, nuts and seeds. The following examples can be combined to make a complete protein using vegetables: grains and legumes, meat and vegetables, nuts or seeds with legumes or grains. I have always liked combining brown rice and black beans it gives me a complete protein and a high quality carbohydrate all in one easy to eat meal.

Protein Supplementation

The following are popular sources of protein used to supplement protein intake.

Egg protein: Egg white (egg albumin) contains a number of different types of protein: Ovalbumin, Ovotransferrin, Ovomucoid, Globulins, Lysozyme, Ovomucin, Avidin and some others. This diverse protein makeup enables the body to easily digest and absorb this protein. It contains all the essential amino acids required for optimal recovery after intense anaerobic workouts. Today athletes are taking egg white protein supplements to build lean body mass. Egg protein is also called a 'perfect protein' because it contains all the building blocks of life, such as: proteins, minerals, vitamins and good cholesterol. It is also a rich source of BCAAs and arginine. Egg protein is a good choice for post workout. Fortunately, there are egg white protein products available, and of course, separate the yolks and cook the whites. It is the most affordable and complete protein available, making it one of the best choices for building or repairing muscle.

Whey protein: It comes from milk. During the process of turning milk into cheese, whey protein is separated out. Whey has the highest amount of leucine of all protein powders, which helps stimulate protein synthesis. Whey protein has the highest value in providing BCAAs: Whey Protein Isolate: Max BV of 157 is the highest yield of protein currently available. Its short chains and peptides make it available for absorption as quickly as ten minutes after ingestion. Do not exceed 30 grams of whey at one time. Because of its quick digestion rate, the body will not utilize all of it. Whey is more readily used as an alternate source of energy (That's the reason you have to use enough carbs when supplementing with whey for bulking.). When on low carb diets, whey can be used as an alternate source of energy, sparing muscle protein and glutamine stores within the body. This makes it a great choice of protein when trying to lean up. Drinking milk with whey, the casein slows the absorption of whey.

Casein: This is the other protein that is isolated from milk. The benefit is that the protein synthesized from casein is used more directly in muscle-building than that synthesized from whey. Casein is the perfect complement to whey so combining the two is a great choice for athletes: The whey protein gets in a person's system quickly, while the casein is long acting, so there is a quick and continuous influx of amino acids and both stimulate protein synthesis in the muscle. Casein is extremely slow digesting and continues to feed the muscles long after other protein supplements have been digested. This makes it ideal for the last meal before bed, or if it is going to be a while before one's next meal.

Soy protein: This protein is derived from soy beans. Soy protein can be used by athletes who are lactose intolerant, and it is utilized as a meat substitute for vegetarians. Soy protein can also be used for cooking instead of flour, producing high protein foods that are low in fat. Soy also helps lower your low-density lipoprotein (bad cholesterol) levels.

Hemp protein: Hemp protein is a good choice for a vegan; it is basically just a milled hemp seed. Hemp protein is not an isolate, so it is hard to get a high amount of protein in a shake because of the high amounts of fat and fiber in that shake. Not ideal for an athlete with a high protein requirement. However, it does make a good additive to shakes because of the healthy fats and fiber.

Timing

When ingesting protein, always consider timing. The effects of quality and quantity will be diminished if timing is not optimal. In the morning there should be a combination of fast and slow digesting protein; the fast digesting helps to quickly get an individual into a positive nitrogen balance after fasting while sleeping. The slower digesting protein helps keep a positive nitrogen balance until one's next meal. During the day, a combination of slower digesting protein is best.

Consume EAAs or fast digesting protein prior to and immediately following exercise. This helps prevent a catabolic state and keeps one in an anabolic state. Post workouts I always want fast acting protein or a combination. This helps ensure there is a quick uptake of amino acids when the body needs it the most. Attention to nutrition must continue well past post-exercise period. Four hours after intense strength training, protein synthesis will be increased by 50 percent. After 24 hours, it is elevated by 109 percent, not returning to baseline until 36 to 48 hours later with proper nutrition. Without proper timing of protein, athletic gains will be limited. Even through post workouts, growth hormone and testosterone levels are raised while protein synthesis is still degraded at this time, so all the essential amino acids must be present in the muscle in order for proteins to be made.

During the day, a combination of slower digesting protein is best. For the last meal, I want slow digesting protein like casein. Protein comes from a Greek word meaning "of primary importance," and once an individual understands protein, it becomes clear. When training is complete for the day, an athlete should realize what he did before and after for nutrition dictates how well he competes and how well he makes gains in performance.

Carbohydrates

Growing up as an athlete, it was common practice for our coaches to have us carbohydrate load the night before a competition. While this was a start, we did not go about this optimally. This caused us to give up a possible advantage to the other competitors or team that did not need to be given. Anyone who knows me knows that one thing that irritates me is giving up a controllable advantage. This section on carbohydrates illustrates how to gain the advantage.

When carbohydrates are ingested, they are broken down into glucose and stored in the muscles and liver as glycogen. Glucose circulates in the blood, also known as blood sugar. Carbohydrates are an athlete's main energy source; one gram of carbohydrates is four calories. Carbohydrates are not necessary for energy. The body can obtain all its energy from protein and fats, but it is essential for training and competing and is the preferred fuel. They provide energy more rapidly to working muscles than protein or fat. Carbohydrates can provide up to five times as much energy as fats during anaerobic training.

Unlike fat and protein, carbohydrates can be broken down very quickly without oxygen to provide large amounts of extra adenosine triphosphate (ATP) via a process known as glycolysis during (anaerobic) training. ATP is formed a lot faster from carbohydrates compared to fat. The average person contains only 250 grams (8.8 oz.) of ATP, and turns over his own bodyweight in ATP each day. This additional energy route is important for maximal performance. The higher the intensity the more carbohydrates are used for energy. This makes carbohydrates extremely important for strength athletes and anaerobic training.

Carbohydrates are responsible for fueling the central nervous system (CNS) and brain. The brain uses 70 percent of the available blood glucose. Earlier in the book, the importance of the CNS was discussed, so don't just employ the training methods to keep CNS peaked, implement the nutrition methods as well. The brain and neurons generally cannot burn fat or protein for energy. This is why bodybuilders who are going through carbohydrate depletion phases during contest prep have a hard time making decisions and concentrating. Their thought processes are impaired. If brain cells are deprived of glucose, an athlete will not have the mental edge needed to compete. Performance will suffer because muscles are controlled by the brain. If glucose levels are depleted enough, this will leave one feeling weak and shaky. If the nervous system does not have optimal levels of glucose, it can leave an athlete with impaired reaction time and leave him lethargic, which affects an athlete's motor skills and ability to recover. Athletes need their CNS optimally fueled or an athlete cannot perform optimally, another reason athletes should not be on low carbohydrate diets.

Carbohydrates and Muscle Contractions

I use carbohydrates with my athletes to peak their energy levels and to get optimal muscle contractions. Glycogen is necessary for muscle contraction. Think about that. If an athlete has depleted his glycogen his muscles will not contract, and he will not be able to perform. It is necessary for athletic performance. If enough carbohydrates are not ingested or enough rest is not obtained, the level of glycogen steadily declines, leaving the athlete fatigued and unable to perform optimally.

Over the years, I have found carbohydrates to be a better choice than fats for maintaining intensity during exercise and competition. A study done by Jacobs et al. (1984) found that glycogen depletion in both fast- and slow-fiber types was associated with impaired maximal muscular strength produced during a single dynamic contraction, as well as with increased muscle-fatigue patterns. Strength athletes are usually worried the most about protein intake to build muscle mass. What they actually need is a high carbohydrate intake fuel for their workouts. Their workout program is where they will get faster and stronger or acquire more muscle. Remember carbohydrates are needed for high intensity training, and powerful muscle contractions.

I tried an experiment with Laura Phelps-Sweatt. We dropped her carbohydrate levels and raised her fat levels in her diet while keeping her calorie and proteins count the same. Laura had a dramatic drop in strength in a very short period of time. We kept the study going for a month, and her strength continued to drop. We switched back to carbohydrates, and she immediately started gaining strength again. We always follow the Westside system of training, so the training wasn't varied.

Carbohydrate and Intensity

With increasing exercise intensity, the active muscle mass becomes progressively more dependent on carbohydrates as a source of energy. However, the oxidation of exogenous carbohydrates seems to remain constant at intensities of 50 percent to 60 percent VO2max or greater (Pirnay et al., 1982).

There are many studies that show female strength athletes do not deplete glycogen as fast and synthesize less glycogen than male strength athletes during resistance training. In these studies high carbohydrate diets are not considered optimal for the performance of female strength athletes. Not all athletes are the same. Laura Phelps-Sweatt has always required more carbohydrates in comparison to the other female strength athletes with whom I work, which includes multiple world-record holders. As a coach, pay attention to individual needs of athletes. Sometimes you will have to go outside of what is normal for them, making sure they log their food intake and performance. If you don't, it could be costly for your athletes. Eventually, an athlete should be his own best coach—it is his body. He knows exactly how he feels, so for strength-athletes, carbohydrates are necessary. Strength athletes in general just don't need as many carbohydrates as endurance athletes.

High glycemic carbohydrates (sugars) commonly found in sports drinks and fruit cause the body to stimulate an insulin response from the pancreas, releasing insulin. Insulin counteracts cortisol and minimizes protein breakdown. This is why athletes use high glycemic carbs with their post-workout protein shakes. The combination of insulin and carbohydrate also increases glycogen storage in the muscle, which improves intensity and performance during training or competing. That's why when an individual wakes, he wants to take in carbohydrates and fast digesting protein. The carbs help the body uptake the protein faster. A good example would be to eat a banana and oatmeal, so he has faster and slower acting carbs; this gives the insulin release for a fast protein uptake and sustained energy. If the body does not have any use for the glucose, it is converted into glycogen and stored in the liver and muscles as an energy reserve. The body can store about half a day's supply of glycogen, and if the body has more glucose than it can use as energy or converts to glycogen for storage, the excess is converted to fat.

Types of Carbohydrates

Simple carbohydrates are made up of a single basic sugar. Table sugar or corn sugars are all types of simple sugars. On consumption, these sugars are directly absorbed in the blood as glucose. Glucose enters the bloodstream at a rate of roughly 30 calories per minute. Glucose provides instant energy as it reaches different parts of the body via blood. Cells absorb glucose and convert it into energy to drive the cell. A set of chemical reactions on glucose creates adenosine triphosphate (ATP), and creatine phosphate bond in ATP (ATP-CP). This is what powers the first eight to 15 seconds of activity. These are the fast acting carbohydrates found high on the glycemic index.

Simple sugars are in fruits, vegetables, milk and milk products. In addition to these, honey, molasses brown sugar, corn syrup and maple syrup are rich sources of simple sugars. There are some fruits like blackberries, blueberries and raspberries that are low on the glycemic index. A sweet taste is not always an indicator of how fast a carbohydrate enters one's system.

Types of Simple Sugars:

Monosaccharides

- Fructose: This is a monosaccharide found in fruit.
- Glucose: This is a monosaccharide found in fruit, vegetables and grains
- Galactose: This is a monosaccharide found in milk and milk products.

Disaccharides

- Sucrose: This is a disaccharide (fructose and glucose) found in sugar cane and table sugar.
- Lactose: This is a disaccharide (glucose and galactose) found in dairy products.
- Maltose, dextrose: This is a disaccharide (glucose and glucose) found in commercial foods and germinating seeds.
- Malodextrin: This is dextrin (glucose polymer)

Complex carbohydrates, also known as polysaccharides, are digested slower than simple carbohydrates, so glucose enters the bloodstream at a rate of roughly only two calories per minute, depending on exactly what complex carbohydrate one is ingesting. Examples of complex carbohydrates are breads, rice and pasta. Starch and fiber are also considered complex carbohydrates, but fiber cannot be digested or used for energy.

There are two kinds of fiber: soluble and insoluble. Soluble fiber lowers cholesterol and has many other health benefits. Insoluble fiber helps remove carcinogens and absorbs water as it moves through the digestive system, easing defecation. Woman should take in 20 to 30 grams of fiber and men should take in 30 to 40 grams of fiber per day.

Starch is a very important energy source in an athlete's diet because it is broken down and stored as glycogen. Foods high in starch include whole grain breads, cereals, pasta, and grains. How the starch is processed before we eat it makes a difference in how fast we absorb it. The more processed it is, the faster it is absorbed. Processing is essentially doing some of the work of our digestive system. These foods are turned into sugar within minutes of being in our bodies. Flour (including whole grain flour) and most breakfast cereals are the most rapidly digested starches. If grains or legumes, such as beans, brown rice or whole barley, are not processed, the starch is broken down into sugars much more slowly. Some will never be turned into sugar and will reach the large intestine intact. These are called resistant starches.

How to Choose Type of Carbohydrate

Many people believe that all complex carbohydrates are digested slowly, and simple carbohydrates are digested quickly. This is simply not true. I choose my carbohydrate source by where it ranks on the glycemic index and by the type of muscle fibers I am trying to fuel. *Glycemic index* is a measure of how quickly food glucose is absorbed; whereas, *glycemic load* is a measure of the total absorbable glucose in foods. How fast carbohydrates get in your athlete's system depends on the other nutrients consumed with the carbohydrate, how the food is prepared, individual differences in metabolism, and by where the carb ranks on the glycemic index. Understanding where a food ranks on the glycemic index helps with carbohydrate selection. I choose low glycemic carbohydrates for most of my meals and I use high glycemic carbohydrates for right after workouts or when I need to get nutrients in quickly.

The types of muscle fiber to be fueled also makes a difference in which carbs are needed as stated in *Nutrition for Serious Athletes* by Dan Benardot (2000). Fast twitch or type llB fibers have a high capacity to store glycogen, but a low capacity to store triglycerides. *Fast twitch fibers* are what we are trying to fuel in athletes in strength sports and explosive sports like the 100 meters. They have a high capacity to store and burn glycogen (stored carbohydrates) and a low capacity to store triglycerides (stored fats). *The intermediate fast-twitch muscle fibers* (type llA fast to intermediate muscle fiber) also produce a tremendous amount of power. These muscle fibers can be trained to behave more like the Type 1 slow-twitch fibers that are a characteristic of endurance athletes, but they can quickly revert back to their baseline, which is more like Type llB. Then, there is slow-twitch Type 1, which is ideal for endurance athletes. These fibers have a great capacity to store and burn fats. The type of training an athlete does will change his macro nutrient profile.

Carbohydrate Oxidation and Intake

Endurance athletes need to keep in mind when setting up a nutrition plan that exogenous carbohydrate oxidation rates do not exceed 1.0 to 1.1 g/min (Jeukendrup & Jentjens, 2000). (The metabolism of carbohydrates, proteins and fats into energy is referred to as oxidation.) Highest rates of exogenous glucose oxidation and the greatest endogenous carbohydrate sparing were observed when carbohydrate was ingested at moderate rates (60 g/h) during exercise (Wallis et al., 2007). This knowledge implies that athletes who ingest a single type of carbohydrate should consume about 60 g/h to 70 g/h for optimal carbohydrate delivery. A carbohydrate intake from a single source any greater than this does not increase carbohydrate oxidation rates any further, rather the carbohydrates accumulate in the intestine, causing gastrointestinal discomfort. When multiple carbohydrates are ingested at high rates, greater maximal rates of exogenous carbohydrate oxidation can be achieved.

In studies involving multiple carbohydrate sources (Jentjens et al., 2004abc, 2005ab, 2006; Wallis et al., 2007) very high oxidation rates were observed with combinations of glucose plus fructose, with maltodextrins plus fructose, and with glucose plus sucrose plus fructose. The highest rates were observed with a mixture of glucose and fructose ingested at a rate of 144 g/h. With this feeding regimen, exogenous carbohydrate oxidation peaked at 105 g/h. This is 75 percent greater than what was previously thought to be the absolute maximum.

To fuel an endurance athlete during competition, we want to ingest carbohydrates from multiple sources. Some people have concern over health issues from ingesting high amounts of carbohydrates, but endurance athletes taking in the proper amount of low glycemic carbohydrates do not need to worry about this. Complex carbohydrates are low on the glycemic index, and they include grains and vegetables. Even though both simple and complex carbs provide needed glucose, the complex carbohydrates provide several nutritional advantages, such as additional vitamins, minerals, and fiber needed for good health and performance. Athletes should never consume refined carbohydrates. Athletes who are in great condition are insulin sensitive. This is exactly what we want. A steady intake of carbohydrates and protein and being insulin sensitive will optimize protein uptake. An athlete training hard and following a proper nutrition plan does not have to worry about becoming insulin resistant. Consuming two grams to five grams of carbohydrate per pound of bodyweight covers the needs of most athletes. (The amount varies due to individual metabolisms and type of training and work load.)

Carbohydrate Digestion

The final products of carb digestion are all monosaccharaides (even complex carbohydrates); water soluble, and absorbed immediately into the portal blood. Therefore, they are transported to the liver. In the liver the galactose and fructose are rapidly converted into glucose. Ninety-five percent of all the monosaccharaides that circulate in the blood are the final product—glucose.

Glucose is transported into cells via facilitated diffusion. The presence of insulin increases the rate of facilitated diffusion by 10 times or more (except for liver and brain). Once in cells, glucose undergoes almost immediate phosphorylation into glucose-6-phosphate, thus trapping the glucose in the cells. This does not occur in the liver, kidney and intestine. After entering a cell, glucose can be used immediately for energy or stored as glycogen, which is just a large polymer of glucose and actually precipitates into granules, protecting the osmotic pressure of intracellular fluid. All cells can store some glucose as glycogen, but the liver can store five percent to eight percent of its weight as glycogen and muscles can store one percent to three percent of their weight as glycogen. Maximize glycogen storage by eating smaller and more frequent carbohydrate meals. This aids in muscle recovery after exercise.

Carbohydrate Super Compensation

For super compensation or "carbohydrate loading," we use a modified version of the Sherman/Costill method. This method has been proven the safest and most effective for glycogen storage. The majority of endurance athletes should consume between 55 percent and 65 percent of their calorie intake from carbohydrates. Using this method during the week leading up to a competition, an athlete wants to up his carb intake to 60 percent to 70 percent carbohydrate in preparation. Remember, it takes 24 to 48 hours of taking in optimal levels of carbohydrates and water to recover spent glycogen stores fully. It is necessary to follow a delayed transformation phase not only for the central nervous system, but also for optimal glycogen stores.

We modify it just slightly because we use the Westside method of delayed transformation phase for our taper-down in training. This method of tapering has been used time and time again with amazing results, contributing to countless world records. We have our athletes use glucose polymers, maltodextrins and starches as they are the most effective for storing glycogen. Carbohydrate loading is ideal for any endurance event lasting more than 90 minutes. It is not recommended for short duration events that require a high degree of skill. This is because when an athlete carbohydrate loads, for every gram of glycogen the muscle retains, it also retains three grams of water (water follows glucose) and can cause some muscle stiffness.

Too Many Carbohydrates?

Some people have concerns over health issues from ingesting high amounts of carbohydrates. Regular body composition checks and logging workout performance and work load help individuals choose the right amount of carbohydrate intake. A person always wants to have plenty of energy and a drive to work out. If either of these is low, it is possible he is not taking in enough carbohydrates. Consuming one and one-half to five grams of carbohydrate per pound of bodyweight will cover the needs of most athletes. Also, 23 percent of the calories from carbohydrate get burned up being converted into energy.

Glycogen Depletion

Competing in a century (a 100-mile road race), I "bonked"—a term used by endurance athletes. I was glycogen depleted. I finished the race just out of sheer will; the last 10 miles I was swerving all over the road. I could hardly stay on my bike, and I was in the easiest gear my bike had on a flat road. I could barely turn my pedals over, and I had a hard time keeping my head up to see the road. Concentrating was difficult, and I was hallucinating. When I passed the line, I just fell over; I couldn't contract my muscles hard enough to even put my feet down. This is glycogen depletion. I was drinking water the whole race, but I did not carry any carbohydrates with me. Bonking is a defense mechanism the body has to stop an athlete from exercising to use all remaining glucose to maintain necessary body functions. Anyone who has ever experienced this will say it is miserable, and he would do everything to prevent it.

Depletion takes between 30 to 90 minutes or more depending on the length and intensity of exercise. It was imperative for me to ingest carbohydrates while riding. Endurance athletes will be constantly depleting it if the intensity and duration is long enough. Therefore, carbohydrate loading and an intake of carbs during competition help postpone depletion and improve performance.

Our maximal carbohydrate storage is approximately 15 grams per kilogram of body weight [15 grams per 2.2 pounds]. A 175-pound athlete could store up to 1200 grams of carbohydrate [4,800 calories]. It takes less than 24 hours of fasting to completely drain the liver's glycogen stores. If enough carbohydrates are not ingested, the body will use up its glycogen stores, forcing the body to switch to less efficient fuel sources. Utilizing fat and amino acids for energy is not only less efficient, but takes away amino acids needed for muscle growth and repair. This lowers one's recovery ability and raises injury rates, causing unneeded stresses to the kidneys, due to the extra work they have to do to eliminate the byproducts of protein breakdown.

Carbohydrates are necessary to compete at an optimal level in any sport, and there will be negative effects if enough are not consumed. Remember for the brain to process thoughts optimally and for the muscles to have the ability to contract, an individual has to ingest carbohydrates. They are not an option but a necessity. A race car with no fuel goes nowhere!

Fats

There are many views on nutrition out there. Some promote high fat and low carb diets while others endorse high carb low fat. I view nutrition the same way I perceive training: every component is necessary. Choosing the proper ratios is imperative for optimal nutrition. Using the Westside system of training, we execute maximal effort, dynamic effort, repetition method and recuperation methods every week. All components are important. It's the same with food. Athletes need the proper ratios of everything: proteins, carbohydrates, fats, vitamins and minerals. Remember, Westside does not train minimally, and they do not train maximally. They train optimally! We follow the same principal with our nutrition. Ingesting too much or not enough of any particular macro nutrient just leads to poor performance.

Fat is essential for the optimal functioning of the body and brain. Fats provide essential fatty acids, which are not made by the body and must be obtained from food. Because of this, it is necessary to have an optimal fat intake. Fats are also important for controlling inflammation, blood clotting, and for building cells, cell membranes and nerves. All athletes need to keep inflammation under control; fats can provide a way to help with that. Healthy fats play an important role in keeping an individual on top of his mental game, and they help fight fatigue. As athletes, we want to be mentally peaked for training and competition. This is a controllable advantage we do not want to give up. Fats are calorie dense: they provide nine calories per gram, more than twice the number provided by carbohydrates or protein. One pound of stored fat provides approximately 3,600 calories of energy. All the energy from stored carbohydrates would supply, at most, the energy for a 19.8 mile run, but the fat an average person has stored would provide energy for about an 800 mile run (McArdle, Katch & Katch, 1991). Keep in mind that an athlete's aerobic system depends on fat for fuel.

The more energy a person derives from fat, the more energy available. The less fat stored helps stabilize a person's blood sugar levels (Maffetone 1990). When carbs are not used for energy, fats become the primary source. Animal and human studies have consistently demonstrated that low carbohydrate, high fat diets consumed for more than seven days decrease muscle glycogen content and carbohydrate oxidation, which is compensated for with markedly increased rates of fat oxidation, even in well-trained endurance athletes. Endurance athletes might not notice a loss in performance, but strength athletes will. They will not get the intense muscle contractions needed for their sport.

Comparing athletes with untrained persons exercising at the same intensity, athletes with extensive endurance training have greater fat oxidation during exercise without increased lipolysis. The breakdown of lipids is known as lipolysis. It involves the hydrolysis of triglycerides into free fatty acids followed by further degradation into acetyl units by beta oxidation. The process produces Ketones, which are found in large quantities in ketosis, a metabolic state that occurs when the liver converts fat into fatty acids, and ketone bodies, which can be used by the body for energy. Lipolysis during stress occurs in the fat cells, increasing cholesterol during chronic stress. It also promotes water loss and curbs appetite, which may be good for a bodybuilder getting ready for a show, but not for an endurance athlete. For every gram of glycogen the body stores, the body will store up to three grams of water. This is how depleting glycogen stores and going into ketosis can cause dehydration. Ketosis also causes dizziness, light-headedness, and fainting, which will not help performance and can be very dangerous. The following hormones induce lipolysis: epinephrine, norepinephrine, glucagon, growth hormone, testosterone, and cortisol. Lipolysis testing strips such as Ketostix are used to recognize ketosis along with bad breath being used as an indicator for those who are familiar with it.

Endurance athletes need a steady intake of fat because they will run out of carbohydrates for energy. If carbohydrate intake is decreased, fat intake must be increased. Because carbohydrates are critical to athletic performance, the athlete should be aware that decreased carbohydrate intake will result in decreased intensity and performance. I have witnessed this first hand many times. Omega 3 fats make you feel full longer. This helps while dieting or if hungry between meals, but if fat intake is too high, it will make it harder to consume enough protein and carbohydrates.

Fats help the body absorb and move vitamins A, D, E, and K through the bloodstream. If you live in an area that lacks an optimal amount of sunlight like I do (Ohio), fats are the only other way to get vitamin D. Over 80 percent of people are vitamin D deficient in Ohio. If you live in an area like this and do not take in the optimal amount of fats, you may develop bone density deficiency and other health issues.

Triglycerides are hydrolyzed to glycerol and fatty acids. They are transported to tissues where they are oxidized to provide energy. Almost all cells (not brain tissue) can use fatty acids and glucose interchangeably for energy. Oxidized in the mitochondria, fat serves as the storage substance for the body's extra calories. It fills the fat cells (adipose tissue) that help insulate the body. (If an athlete consumes only 10 percent or less of their dietary requirement of fat they will not perform optimally and they will develop health problems.) Keeping fat intake this low can put an individual at risk of becoming deficient in essential fatty acids and fat soluble vitamins. This could affect fat mobilization and oxidation, important in energy production. It also lowers the circulating levels of hormones, most notably for athlete's insulin and testosterone, extremely important hormones if an athlete wants to train and compete optimally.

Essential Fatty Acids

Essential fatty acids (EFAs) are where an athlete will get his biggest gain in performance and health when it comes to fats. Essential fatty acids must be taken in by diet. Omega-3 and omega-6 fatty acids are polyunsaturated fatty acids. Alpha-linolenic acid (ALA), an omega-3 fatty acid, and linoleic acid (LA), an omega-6 fatty acid, are considered essential fatty acids because they cannot be synthesized by humans, and they are essential to be healthy. Nutrition plans should include omega-3 fats every day. Over the years of training and competing in different sports, I have found EFAs necessary to keep my inflammation down, so I can keep training. There are three essential fatty acids: Linoleic, Linolenic, and arachidonic acid. They are very important for cholesterol transport, blood clotting, and serum cholesterol and membrane structure. Omega-3 fatty acids are highly concentrated in the brain.

There are Several Different Types of Omega-3 Fatty Acids:

- EPA and DHA—Eicosapentaenoic acid (EPA) and docosahexaenoic acid (DHA): have a vast amount of research to back up their health and performance benefits. EPA and DHA are found in cold-water fatty fish.

- ALA—Alpha-linolenic acid (ALA) comes from plants. The performance and health gains are less pronounced from this form of omega-3 than EPA and DHA. The best vegetarian sources include flaxseed, walnuts, and canola oil. The best meat sources are fatty fish such as: salmon, herring, mackerel, anchovies, or sardines, or high-quality cold-water fish oil supplements.

- Omega-3 fatty acids benefit the brain in the following ways:
    - Prevent and reduce the symptoms of depression
    - Protect against memory loss and dementia
    - Improved cognitive function (memory, problem-solving abilities, etc.)
    - For the treatment of mental health issues and helps elevate and stabilize mood

Optimal omega-3 fatty acid intake can help you fight fatigue and can be helpful in the treatment of depression, attention deficit/hyperactivity disorder (ADHD), and bipolar disorder. Omega-3 fatty acids have also been shown to have the following benefits on the body.

- Reduced risk of heart disease, stroke, and cancer
- Reduced joint pain, and inflammation
- Supports a healthy pregnancy

When supplementing with omega 3 fish oil, it is the total amount of EPA and DHA on the label that is most important to look for. Some bottles will say 1,000 milligrams of fish oil, but the EPA and DHA might only total 200 mg. I prefer using fish oil in liquid form. It is usually cheaper for the amount of EPA and DHA you get, and it keeps an individual from burping it up such as with capsules. I have all my athletes take fish oil supplements. The proper omega 3 fatty acid intake is not a choice; it is mandatory for performance and longevity in sport. Choose fish oil that is mercury-free, pharmaceutical grade, molecularly distilled, and contains both DHA and EPA. Higher concentrations of EPA are better. I also like using cod liver oil due to the high vitamin D intake along with high levels of EPA and DHA. For athletes I recommend three to five grams of EPA and DHA when healthy, but if injured I have my athletes go up to five to seven grams per day because of the anti-inflammatory properties.

I increased the amount with one of my professional MMA fighters who was having a hard time passing an eye pressure test due to an injury as a kid. After a few months of seven grams a day he passed the test with ease. This proved to me how well it works. More importantly, it let him continue his professional fighting career. Understand as a coach that finding that one thing might mean the difference between early retirements and having an amazing career in the sport you love. It is our duty as coaches to never stop searching for ways to keep our athletes healthy and competing at the highest level they possibly can. This constant search keeps our athletes and programs evolving so future generations can improve their performances and lower injury rates while increasing longevity.

Good Fats

Monounsaturated fats and polyunsaturated fats are unsaturated fats known as "good fats" because they are good for the heart, cholesterol, and overall health. Be aware because just like with fats, there are good and bad types of cholesterol. HDL cholesterol is the "good" kind of cholesterol found in blood. LDL cholesterol is the "bad" kind. Ideally, keep HDL levels high and LDL levels low. High levels of HDL cholesterol help protect against heart disease and stroke while high levels of LDL cholesterol can clog arteries, increasing the risk of heart disease. This is important for everyone, but especially if an individual chooses to take anabolic steroids for performance enhancement. In turn, minimize the risk by eating optimally. If not disciplined enough to do this, then don't take performance enhancing drugs. Polyunsaturated fats lower triglycerides and fight inflammation, but unsaturated fats have a lot of calories, so they need to be limited.

Most, but not all, liquid vegetable oils are unsaturated. (The exceptions include coconut, palm, and palm kernel oils.) There are two types of unsaturated fats:

- Monounsaturated fats: Examples include the following: avocados, almonds, peanuts, macadamia nuts, hazelnuts, pecans, cashews olive and canola oils.
- Polyunsaturated fats: Examples include fish, safflower, sunflower, corn, and soybean oils.

Unhealthy Fats

Saturated fats are the biggest dietary cause of high LDL ("bad cholesterol") levels. The biggest influence on the total and LDL cholesterol is the type of fats eaten — not dietary cholesterol. Focus on replacing saturated fats with unsaturated fats. Saturated fats have no place in an athlete's diet. We train our whole lives to be able to do things few to no other people can. Why not set yourself apart when it comes to the diet, especially with the performance and health gains you get out of it. Saturated fats are found in animal products such as: butter, cheese, whole milk, ice cream, cream, and high-fat cuts of meat such as beef, lamb, pork, and chicken with the skin. They are also found in some vegetable oils --- palm, and palm kernel oils. These are all foods an athlete has no business eating.

Trans fatty acids (trans fats) are the least healthy of all fats; since they not only raise bad LDL cholesterol, but also lower the good HDL cholesterol. Trans fatty acids are found in fried foods, commercial baked goods (donuts, cookies, crackers), processed foods, and margarines, packaged snack foods (microwave popcorn, chips), and candy bars.

Fat Intake

A dietary fat intake of between 20 and 25 percent in men is optimal while 20 to 30 percent in women is what we have found to be optimal, depending on the type of training, the type of competition, and the athlete's individual physiological make up. Fat is slow digesting and can be converted into a usable form of energy, but may take up to six hours depending on the type of fat ingested. I do not recommend consuming fat immediately before or during intense exercise. Fats have a high oxygen requirement. This is one of the reasons why they are best for slow pace aerobic activity. While these calories are less accessible to athletes performing quick, intense efforts like sprinting or weight lifting, fat is essential for longer, slower, lower intensity and endurance exercise such as easy cycling and distance running. Fat provides the main fuel source for long duration, low to moderate intensity exercise (endurance sports such as marathons, and ultra-marathons). Even during high intensity exercise, where carbohydrate is the main fuel source, fat is needed to help access the stored carbohydrate (glycogen). It is in this way that protein, carbohydrates and fat are all necessary in the proper ratio for optimal performance.

Hydration

Growing up as a lifter in southern Michigan, I saw many extreme season changes. Every summer I would hear other lifters complaining about their body weight and strength dropping. They never asked why this was happening, but it was important for me to know the reason. Looking back now, I know that lack of proper hydration was one of the key reasons. Many athletes love to train hard and put everything on the line come competition day. There are few athletes willing to go the extra mile when it comes to hydration. I attribute this to their lack of understanding of how other factors   temperature, humidity, altitude and individual physiology—affect how much water you need during exercise. Remember, the body uses water to transport oxygen and nutrients to your cells and waste products away from them. Losing as little as two percent bodyweight through dehydration can lower performance levels by 10 to 15 percent, reducing the speed, endurance and power available to train or compete at high levels.

McGregor et al. (1999) tested the effect of water deficiency on soccer performance. They examined the impact of fluid replacement on the athletes' ability to complete a 90-minute variable-intensity shuttle-run with timed-embedded 20 meter all-out sprints, followed by a soccer dribbling test. The semiprofessional soccer players were dehydrated by 2.5 percent of their initial body mass when fluids were restricted. Fluid restriction was accompanied by greater perception of effort late in the shuttle run protocol as well as degraded ability to sprint late in the shuttle run. The time to complete the soccer dribbling task was reduced five percent when no fluid was consumed, but maintained when fluids were consumed. This shows coaches that not only does dehydration affect strength and speed performance, but it affects skill level as well.

Hydrating Optimally

I want my athletes to train, eat, and hydrate optimally. Understanding the basic physiological processes the body goes through is necessary to know how to hydrate an athlete. A properly formulated carbohydrate drink will absorb from the stomach to small intestine faster than water alone because physiologically water follows glucose in the body, but if the carbohydrate concentration is too high, it slows down absorption. An athlete should have a steady intake of fluids all day. An hour before training, we want our athletes to consume an excess amount of water. They consume up to half of the weight they will lose from the upcoming work. This is a form of super compensation.

Sweating rates can vary from less than 0.5 to more than 2.5 liter per hour, depending upon exercise intensity, fitness level, and heat acclimation state (Sawka 1992; Sawka et al 2007). The rate of sweating is determined largely by the intensity of exercise as well as the environmental conditions in which the athlete is performing. Athletes can calculate their rates of fluid loss by simply weighing themselves pre and post workouts. I tell my athletes to keep a log of their weight before and after exercise and the environmental conditions they were exposed to that day. They can plot trends of their fluid loss and hydration status with the data they collect. This information can then be used during competition to determine how much fluid needs to be replaced. Also, consider the color of urine as this can give insight on hydration levels. Clear to lemonade color means hydration. The darker the color, the more dehydrated an individual is. There are urine color charts than can be purchased to help with this. Coaches can also use urine test strips; they are very easy to use and measure specific gravity. Urinalysis has been shown to be the most valid and reliable method for determining moderate changes in fluid balance.

Here is a method of analyzing urine specific gravity using a refractometer:

- Purpose: Urine specific gravity is a scientific measure of hydration by measuring the density (concentration) of a urine sample.

- Equipment required: A refractometer, urine specimen containers for urine collection, cleaning cloth / disposable tissues, fridge or ice cooler for urine storage, gloves.

- Collecting the urine: Collect a urine sample first thing in the morning, or after a 12-hour fast. Some coaches will take a urine sample right before practice. It is not ideal, but convenient for coaches and athletes. Even though not ideal, it does give the coaches insight on pre-practice hydration status.

- Results: The measurement may be done immediately after collection, or the specimen can be stored in refrigeration for later analysis. The specific gravity results will range from 1.000 (which is equivalent to water) up to 1.035 (very dehydrated). There are several levels that are used in the literature to indicate dehydration, such as a value of 1.15 or greater.

- Comments: The sample is usually collected first thing in the morning. It also may be of interest to collect samples prior to or post exercise, though there may be a time delay for the effect of dehydration to show in the specific gravity measure.

- Precautions: Certain medicines, vitamins or the presence of glucose may cause the urine specific gravity to change and give incorrect readings of dehydration. If any of these situations occur, then the test is unreliable.

- The refractometer should be calibrated before you begin testing and then again after every ten samples or so to ensure that the calibration remains accurate.

- Advantages: The hand held refractometer is very easy to operate.

- Disadvantages: This test requires the collection of urine and the purchase of a refractometer for measurement.
- Comments: There is a minimal difference in the accuracy of the related measures of urine specific gravity, urine osmolality, and urine color (Armstrong et al. 1998). How much water or other fluid you need before, during and after exercise largely depends upon the intensity and duration of the exercise. The impact of temperature, humidity, altitude and individual physiology, however, cannot be discounted.

Hydration Facts

- Most endurance athletes are chronically dehydrated.
- Everyday living can have a dehydrating effect. Athletes need to consume plenty of fluids regardless of training volume or intensity.
- The human body is 40 percent to 70 percent water depending on sex and the proportion of adipose tissue (body fat percentage). The leaner and more muscular someone is, the higher their percentage of total body water. More than half of that is in the blood and muscle tissue.
- It is estimated that the average person, weighing in at 170 pounds and undergoing moderate non-athletic activity, requires about 80 ounces of water each day to match water loss.
- During exercise replacing 80 percent to 100 percent of the fluid lost is optimal.
- As an individual dehydrates, blood volume drops, causing heart rate to climb at the same level of exertion.
- Dehydration decreases the flow of blood to muscles. This reduces the amount of metabolic byproducts including lactic acid and CO_2 that are removed from the tissue and also reduces the amount of O_2 and nutrients that are delivered to the tissue.

If training regularly, you will probably need between one half and one whole ounce of water (or other fluids) for each pound of body weight per day.

To determine your baseline range for water requirement, use the following formula:

- Low end of range = Body weight (lbs.) x 0.5 = (ounces of fluid/day)
- High end of range = Body weight (lbs.) x 1 = (ounces of fluid/day)
- For example, if an individual weighs 150 pounds, his approximate water requirement will be between 75 and 150 ounces each day.

When to Hydrate with Water and When to use Sports Drinks

To keep optimally hydrated, create healthy habits like always carrying a water bottle throughout the day. After exercise, the athlete should replace 150 percent of the weight lost due to dehydration. Water or an electrolyte drink (without carbohydrates) is best suited for training or competitions that take no longer than an hour to complete. Many believe there is no need for carbohydrates in competitions or training that last less than an hour in the belief the body should have enough energy from following proper nutrition to complete the task. While this is true, I still like a low level of carbohydrate, like a 3 percent carbohydrate solution in my athlete's drinks for optimal muscle contractions.

Relying on thirst as an indicator of when to drink more is unreliable as there is a time lag between being dehydrated and then feeling thirsty. The rule of thumb in endurance sports is if an individual is thirsty, he is already too late. He has already suffered a loss of performance. Drinking too fast or just drinking plain water increases the osmosis effect and could lead to extra urination. An intake of; 500 ml every 30 minutes is adequate. Make sure if using the color of urine as a guide that it is not observed right after a large intake of water. Fluids cannot be moved through the stomach any faster than 25 ml per minute or .9 oz. per minute.

The ideal electrolyte drink for an athlete who has not been tested for an individualized hydration plan is 20 mEq/L of Na and 3 mEq/L potassium or 460 mg sodium and 117 mg potassium per liter of fluid. Electrolyte replacement drinks and carbohydrate replacement drinks are beneficial when training and competitions exceed an hour in duration. We use three percent to seven percent carbohydrate solution (30-70 grams) with 460 mg sodium and 117 mg potassium per liter of fluid per hour so that it is absorbed as fast as possible. If training for more than an hour and doing multiple training sessions, look to have some sodium, sugars and protein in your recovery drink or food.

Some believe by having a mixture of sugars—glucose, sucrose, maltodextrin, and fructose—a variety of transport mechanisms into muscle cells are opened. I would like to see more research on this.

From the research that is out there as well as my own, it seems more important to have a drink with the proper concentration of sodium, potassium and carbohydrates to maintain optimal electrolyte and cellular glycogen levels. This way, energy enters cells and they don't get dehydrated. This also helps maintain the proper intravascular volume. As Chris Carmichael wrote in his book *Food for Fitness* (2004), a sports drink should accomplish the following:

- Stimulate the drive to drink (increases the odds you are more likely to hydrate optimally)
- Accelerate fluid absorption (Dehydration = decreased flow of blood to the muscle)
- Improve performance by providing carbohydrate (energy and transportation for water into cells)
- Maintain blood volume (it is one of the main reasons to consume fluids while training)
- Quickly restore normal hydration levels

Carmichael is Lance Armstrong's coach and has worked with USA cycling to get athletes ready for the Olympics. I recommend his books and articles to anyone in endurance sports. To fight dehydration the Soviets have their athletes take 400 ml to 500 ml (14 to 17 ounces) of fluids about a half hour before competition or before the start of the race. During the event, the ideal fluid consumption levels are about 100 ml to 200 ml (3.5 to 7 oz.) of liquid four to six times.

The temperature of the replacement fluid should also be considered. Athletes competing in hot weather benefit more when they consume drinks that are at 4°C than at 19°C. This is because lower temperatures have been shown to decrease the effects of heat stress and increase the amount of time it takes an athlete to reach exercise limiting core temperature. Athletes should not drink fluids in excess of their sweat rate as they can over-hydrate and risk developing exercise-associated hypernatremia (EAH). Hyponatremia happens when the body's stores of sodium are too low. It can lead to agitation, confusion, lethargy, seizures, and death. The symptoms can often imitate symptoms of dehydration such as disorientation, nausea, or muscle cramps. If the athlete has hypernatremia and consumes more water at this point, they can make the situation worse.

Electrolytes

Elite level athletes can have their actual sodium and sweat concentrations and losses calculated. Then they can replace their deficit with an individually formulated drink. As fitness levels increase athletes are able to work harder. They generate more power, maintain a faster pace and increase their endurance. This translates into sustaining a higher work output for a longer period of time. The ability to produce more power and to compete at a higher pace for longer periods of time comes at the price of generating heat faster and for a longer period.

The body attempts to keep core temperature stable under these added demands by the following physiological changes:

- Sweating will begin sooner: The body's sweat response gets quicker as fitness levels increase. The better the fitness level, the sooner an athlete will start sweating. This occurs when warming up. The body starts ramping up the cooling process more quickly to stay ahead of the rise in core temperature.

- The volume of sweat increases: The body becomes better at creating sweat. The more one sweats the more skin is covered with sweat. This increases one's odds of keeping core temperature down.

- Fewer electrolytes are lost per unit volume: As the body is adapting to sweating more and sweating sooner, it also changes the composition of sweat so that more electrolytes are retained. Replenish electrolytes during exercise, but this adaptation helps to keep the electrolyte requirement manageable.

Elite level athletes sweat more because they need to. They generate more heat and for longer periods of time. They have to produce more sweat in order to maximize their evaporative cooling capacity. Core body temperature increases also, causing blood to be shunted to the skin to cool the body, also decreasing blood flow to muscles. Heart rate increases to compensate until it is maxed out.

By testing endurance runners we have found that each individual runner posted their best times with the smallest amount of body weight loss. By using a refracotometer to test urine specific gravity, it was shown that the lower the weight loss the less dehydrated the runner was. The runners with the lowest weight loss had faster finishing times, lower body core temperatures, enhanced recovery, a lower heart rate for the first 20 minutes post-race, a decreased feeling of exertion at a higher pace, and a better psychological state. Lowering core body temperature .5 degree C decreases metabolic rate up to seven percent. That means elite athletes have to consume more fluid so they have more to contribute to sweat.

The average athlete can estimate they lose a little less than a gram of sodium for every liter of sweat. During periods of intense sweating, the athlete should replace the sodium as well as fluid. Potassium is also lost through intense sweating. A replacement drink that contains electrolytes should replace water during these periods of intense sweating.

Sweat collection is a way to test sodium loss. Sweat patches can be used to determine the composition of sweat.

- Purpose: Apply sweat patches to the skin to collect a sample of sweat for analysis.
- Equipment required: Sweat patches, alcohol wipes, centrifuge, razor, sweat analyzer (or external laboratory).
- Procedure: There are many possible skin sites to use for sweat collection. The site used may depend on the purposes of testing. Commonly used are the upper back, chest, forearm, thigh and forehead. If standard sites are used, they need to be measured and marked for correct placement. Prepare the skin by shaving any hair and clean with alcohol wipes, then allow the area to dry. Another method is to wash the area with deionized water. Place the small absorbent sweat patches on the skin. At the conclusion of the exercise protocol, the patches are removed and placed in a centrifuge where they are analyzed for electrolyte content. If the analysis equipment is not available some laboratories are equipped to handle the analysis for athletes.
- Analysis: Most commonly tested is the electrolyte content including sodium (Na), potassium (K), and magnesium (Mg^{+2}). This is important, as depletion of sodium, the primary electrolyte in sweat, can lead to muscle cramping.
- Results: The results can be used to give feedback to the athlete to improve their hydration practices. Some people may be found to be 'salty sweaters,' meaning they have high concentration of Na in their sweat. These individuals may benefit from appropriate modification to their fluid and food intake for optimal electrolyte replacement. Research can also be performed to determine if sodium losses change throughout an endurance event as well as under different conditions and exercise intensities.
- Reliability: If the subject is to be retested or athletes are being compared, accurate placement of the patches is very important for reliability. It is also important to standardize the testing conditions so that the exercise intensity, duration, clothing, and environment are the same.

The cost and requirement to send the sweat off for laboratory analysis makes this testing method more suitable for research purposes. Sweat patches are also used to test the levels of sweat chloride as a test for cystic fibrosis.

Dehydration affects strength athletes as well. Experienced lifters know that after a water cut, lack of proper rehydration can drastically affect performance. For example, if a power lifter with a 2,500-pound total loses just five percent of strength from dehydration that equates to a 75-pound loss on their total. This is not taking into account that water is a natural lubrication for muscles. An athlete will have a much higher risk of muscle strains and tears when dehydrated. Hydration is just as important as nutrition and training. If any of those three are not optimal, the door is opened to injury and defeat.

Water Cutting

Athletes use water cutting to gain an advantage. Water cut properly can be a great advantage; do it wrong, and it can cost a win, a world record or even one's health. We use a standard of five percent for woman and five to seven percent body weight loss maximum for men. Anything more than that, and there is a risk of loss in performance. Some athletes can cut a little more; some a little less. As one's body evolves through training, age and competitive experiences, the amount of weight you can cut through water manipulation can change. Seasoned athletes tend to be able to mentally be able to handle water cuts better.

Consider an athlete's body composition: obese peoples' water content can be as low as 40 percent, while a very lean athlete can be as high as 70 percent. Keep this in mind when figuring out how much to cut a young athlete. It is common to see fighters who have cut weight many times with great success have to lower their percentage of weight loss from water manipulation as they get older. Their bodies change and they cannot cut as much effectively. We also do not recommend diuretics for fighters as it can pull water weight from around the brain, making it easier for the fighter to get knocked out.

When we have a new athlete, I will do a mock water cut. This lets us know how they will feel and how they perform and it lets me know how their body handles a water cut. As an example of a typical water cut, let's look at Laura Phelps-Sweatt, pound for pound and by formula the strongest female powerlifter in the world. Laura would eat six meals a day of six ounces of chicken, and four ounces of sweet potato for the first three meals the week of her competition. We used to cut carbs, but found this gave us no additional weight loss, only a loss in energy. The amount of carbs we use for this athlete is less than normal because she is going through her delayed transformation phase of training. She is resting at this point and doesn't have high energy requirements. Along with the chicken and sweet potatoes, she would have one cup of broccoli five times a day. For bigger athletes, I go up to two cups. Then, I double the average daily water intake. Laura typically drinks 1.5 gallons a day. She would take in three gallons a day for Sunday, Monday and Tuesday. She would also add ¼ tsp. of sodium five times a day.

Water loading with salt is necessary to prevent hyponatremia and brain swelling, and causes the body to ramp up and begin diuresis. While adding sodium and water, an individual is also carb depleting. Remember, water will always follow glucose. As one depletes the cells of glucose, water leaves the cell and is excreted by the kidneys.

On Wednesday of that week, Laura would eliminate the salt from meals three, four and five. I would also cut the water in half to 1.5 gallons and add potassium to meals three, four and five. Supplementing with potassium pulls sodium out of cells via one's sodium potassium pump. On Thursday, there would be no added sodium and no more than one liter of water to be finished by 3 pm. On this day, she would only eat three meals with protein and absolutely no carbohydrates. Even as an individual cuts salt, the body continues to rid itself of excess water. And adding in potassium in each of the meals on Thursday will further dry the cells out (if this is done properly-no corners cut). At this point, there is no more food or water ingested until after the athlete weighs in. The exception to this is the athlete who is ahead of schedule for making weight and would benefit from either an intake of a little water or food. That would be if the water cut started below the five percent level. When the weigh-in is set for 9 a.m., I always have my athletes weigh in as soon as possible. This provides them with as much time as possible to rehydrate.

Diuretics

Many athletes use diuretics to cut water weight. This can be an effective and safe way to cut water. However, more often than not the athletes and their coaches do not have proper knowledge of how to time and properly dose the diuretics. Many people time them wrong and continue to lose water weight after weigh-in. This makes it harder to get back to desired weight. During this time, they should be retaining fluids.

Diuretics increase urine output by decreasing sodium and water reabsorption by the kidneys. They are classified by the way they work. Loop diuretics such as: Lasix, Bumex and Demadex cause the body to lose potassium, calcium and magnesium as well as sodium and water. Losing too much potassium or calcium can cause heart arrhythmias, so care must be taken in using these drugs. All drugs should be taken under the supervision and care of a physician. Most athletes are taking potassium supplements as part of their water cut and this should be adequate to cover any loss incurred by proper dosing of Lasix. Twenty milligrams is the typical dose to give. A 20 mg tablet will cause onset of diuresis within one hour and will peak in one to two hours with a total duration of effect about six hours. If the drug is given IV or IM, (again 20 mg) the onset is five minutes. It will have a peak effect in 30 minutes and total duration of effect will be two hours.

Potassium sparing diuretics and carbonic anhydrase inhibitors are weak and generally not used for a water cut. Thiazide and thiazide-like diuretics are used mostly to treat high blood pressure. They are only available orally. Hydrochlorothiazide (HCTZ), chlorthalidone, metolazone and indapamide are examples. These diuretics also cause a loss of potassium and magnesium, but in contrast loop diuretics calcium is reabsorbed. HTCZ, chlorothiazide and chlorthalidone all cause diuresis to begin about two hours after ingestion. HTCZ peaks in three to six hours and with a duration of six to 12 hours. Chlorthalidone peaks in two hours with a duration of 49 to 72 hours. That is way too long to even be considered for a water cut. Chlorothiazide peaks in four hours with a duration of six to 12 hours. HCTZ and Chlorothalidone are available in 25 mg, 50 mg and 100 mg tablets. Chlorthizide is available in 250 mg and 500 mg tablets. The minimum amount of each drug to reach the desired effect is optimal. The non-diuretic water-cut method mentioned above that Laura Phelps-Sweatt uses is safest and easiest to dial in and repeat. For athletes it is very important to be able to reproduce optimal water cut at every competition.

Saunas and Whirlpools/Jacuzzi

The morning of weigh-in, if there is any excess water to lose, or if it is a big weight cut the night before, we may use a sauna or whirlpool. Always record how much weight is lost by morning if cutting weight the night before. Record weight loss, the room temperature slept in, and total bodyweight percentage of the cut. If using a sauna or a whirlpool the night before, an athlete doesn't have to cut to competition weight because he will lose some overnight and that could be too much and affect performance. The heat in saunas vary, meaning some are hotter than others, so time spent in them will vary. We start with 10 minutes to 14 minutes in the sauna for the first round. Then, two minutes out of the sauna. Following that, seven minutes in, two out for the rest of the rounds until the desired weight is reached. Have your doctor check your pulse on every two-minute break to make sure you are not too dehydrated. If your heart rate goes way up or your stomach starts cramping, it can become very dangerous, so always make sure you are monitored by your team doctor. Some people like saunas better; some like whirlpools/Jacuzzi's better. When doing Laura Phelps-Sweatt's water cut, if she needed to cut more weight, she preferred using the whirlpools. She felt, as many athletes I have worked with that it was more comfortable and weight came off easier. Our protocol for a sauna was 20 minutes in and two minutes out for the first round, then 15 minutes in two minutes out for the rest of the rounds till desired weight is reached. Again, like with the sauna, always make sure you are being monitored by a doctor.

Post Water Cut Rehydration

I always have my athletes carry water with a glucose concentration of three percent to seven percent post water-cut. As one carbohydrate loads, the glucose goes back into the cells, pulling the last remaining excess water into the cells with it. If the glucose level in a rehydration drink is too high, it will slow down water absorption into cells. Until the glucose is metabolized into the cells, water will stay in the intracellular space. This is what happens to bodybuilders on stage who spill over their water. They ingested too many carbohydrates. The carbohydrates will stay in their blood stream and pull water from their cells leading to a "soft" or even bloated look. For an athlete, this means that the water is not entering the cells, where we need it to compete at a high level.

A tip given by Shawn Frankl, 198- and 220-total world-record holder and biggest total by formula, is to do a very light, low-intensity workout after he weighs in and gets some water and carbohydrates in him. This makes sense. Remember what I said earlier; glucose follows water. By doing a light workout, your muscles will take up the glucose you have provided through carbohydrate loading and the water from rehydration will follow the glucose into your cells. During exercise, glucose utilization by muscle is increased, which is largely independent of insulin. Muscle will take up glucose even without insulin present during exercise, and water follows the glucose into the cells by osmosis. The rehydration will give a noticeable muscle pump. The light workout helps ensure that your muscle cells are as fully rehydrated as possible and the glucose intake will provide maximal energy for the muscle cells during competition.

Carbohydrates and fats are more important than protein post-water-cut. As soon as the athlete steps off of the scale, he starts to consume our drink with three percent to seven percent glucose. Depending on the athlete and the sport that he competes in, I will adjust the concentration between three percent and eight percent. We keep logs of trial runs and what we do in competition to pick up trends to decide the exact amount. We choose carbs that are low on the glycemic index, like sweet potatoes, brown rice, oatmeal and the like. To a lesser degree we include some healthy fats like almonds, avocados, fish oil, and so forth. We do eat protein with our meal, but not as much as we normally do so we can have more room for energy (carbohydrates and fats). Remember our goal is to rehydrate and refuel, so we have maximum energy and output for competition day.

Rehydration

The best way to rehydrate, providing the resources are available, is to "bag up" as some call it, or to use IV bags if there is access to the equipment and medical professionals. We use one of two types: bags either normal saline solution (nss) or lactated ringers. IV bags offer instant hydration on a cellular level. We "bag up" immediately after we weigh in. Sometimes we will put the port in the arm before the water to make it easier, because it is harder to find a vein after the athlete is dehydrated.

- Normal Saline Solution—nss has the same concentration of sodium and potassium as your blood. Using large quantities of nss can lead to hyperchloremic metabolic syndrome, so don't overdo it.
- Lactated ringers—My preferred IV solution, lactate is metabolized by the liver in to bicarbonate and glucose, and it also contains potassium and a small amount of calcium. This is the ideal solution because of its electrolyte concentration.

Alternatives for Water Retention

For powerlifting some lifters use phenylbutazone (Bute), which is an analgesic (relieves pain), and anti-inflammatory medication. They use this to help retain water, but we have found it seems to work well for benchers as their hands swell up a little from water retention. This makes the weight feel light in the hands. However, we have noticed a negative effect for dead lifters, especially those with smaller hands. The swelling makes it harder to grip the bar, and lifters tend to lose their grip during the lift. We like to use ibuprofen. It helps the lifter retain water and makes his joints feel better, making the weight feel lighter, but without the swelling in the hands.

High glutamine concentrations exert an osmotic effect, pulling water into the cell. Hydration is a powerful anabolic signal, and using two to four grams of glutamine in a post-workout recovery drink helps the athlete rehydrate and recover faster. For endurance athletes, there is an alternative to help the body retain water or super hydrate by using glycerol. Adding glycerol to water helps athletes store more water and can be easily metabolized for energy, giving them an advantage in endurance events in hot and humid environments. In Dan Benardot's book *Nutrition for Serious Athletes* (2000), he gives a word of caution on this practice and provides the following formula, which we have found to work very well. Many endurance athletes feel sluggish and stiff while their body is holding the excess water, but also feel that having the extra water at the end of the race, when it counts the most, is beneficial because while others are overheating and dehydrated, they feel fresher. Many endurance athletes do this, but there has never been an adequate test done for safety, and we do not know how much additional stress there is on the cardiovascular system when additional water is stored. The following is a formula for adding glycerol to water for super hydration.

- Use one gram glycerol and 21.4 milliliters of water per kilogram of bodyweight
- Drink the entire glycerol-added fluid portion, except 16 ounces, using typical fluid consumption protocol within two hours before exercise.
- Reserve 16 ounces of the glycerol-added fluid to drink about 30 minutes before exercise
- Drink additional pure water or a sports beverage as necessary to make urine clear prior to race.
- Continue to drink sports beverage at every opportunity during the race. Usual intake should approach three to six ounces every 10 minutes.

Remember to always try anything new during training, not the day of competition.

Putting it All Together

Knowing the importance of macronutrients, you will now learn the best way and timing to take them in. Food should be organic and free-range. Ingest foods that are not, or minimally, processed with no preservatives or artificial ingredients. Also always eat foods that are in season in your area. This ensures you ingest the highest available nutrients. To make sure to get in a broad spectrum of nutrients, everyday take in vegetables from all color groups; white or light brown, blue or purple, green, red and yellow or orange. An athlete's food is fuel: Never miss a meal! Missing a meal takes away many things: optimal recovery, optimal training, and peak performance on competition day. When taking into consideration that progress stops when the required amino acids and other nutrients are not delivered on time (usually every two to three hours) in optimal amounts, you can see as an athlete how you would lose an advantage that didn't have to be given up.

For increased athletic performance, raw or minimally cooked is best due to minimizing the loss of nutrients during preparation. As an athlete, it is also important to prepare your own food instead of eating out. This lowers the chance of catching a virus that could slow down progress in training or ruin your chances to win the day of a competition. This also sets up a healthy schedule and routine, which will make it less likely for you to miss a meal. Also, use stainless or bamboo utensils for cooking to stay away from products that contain and can leak bisphenol A (BPA). BPA is found in some plastics and is often used as a resin found in the liners in many canned goods. Use glass, porcelain, stainless steel, or BPA-free plastic containers for hot foods and liquids.

Using Macro Nutrients Properly

When putting a nutrition plan together, make sure to utilize macro nutrients properly. For example, many athletes take in too much protein, believing that if their muscles don't need it for repair it can be used as energy. While it is true it can be used as energy, this is not optimal. When protein is used as energy, the body goes through a process called deamination. This is where the body removes nitrogen from amino acid chains. When increasing the excretion of nitrogenous waste, water loss is also raised through urine, increasing the risk for dehydration. Tissue repair would not be optimized nor would the building of enzymes or hormones be maximized. To properly fuel the body, everything eaten must be recorded along with workouts and at what intensities they were executed. The more anaerobic the exercise, the more carbohydrates are used compared to fats.

I would also include notes of stressful days. As an individual evolves as an athlete, his training and nutrition must evolve. Remember the longer an athlete trains the more neurologically efficient he becomes and the higher work capacity he achieves. This was the case with AJ Roberts; AJ broke the all-time world-record total for the 308 class on March 6, 2011. One of the major alterations he made before that amazing feat of strength was changing his nutrition. He said with the changes in his nutrition, it gave him more energy, allowing him to increase his work load, leading to improved leverages and strength. AJ's numbers have continued to climb since that meet and his workouts have continued to evolve. The higher an athlete's output the more fuel he will require. Keeping a journal will make it is easier to track trends, so that proper adjustments can be made as soon as possible. This helps if you ever get a special case like Michael Phelps, who during training season, takes in 12,000 calories per day at a body weight of 185 pounds, which has obviously worked for him.

Waving Food Intake

Just like in training, food should be waved as well. We wave foods by only eating foods when they are naturally in season and by where we are in our training. The different phases of the wave are off- season, pre-season, in-season preparatory phase and a competition preparatory phase, which begins once an individual starts his delayed transformation phase. For example, during off-season; our food intake should reflect the desired changes we want to take place during this time period. If our goals are to recover from our season and put added muscle mass on, we increase our food intake to the point where we may put on a little body fat, making sure we are getting in plenty of nutrients to meet our goals, thus allowing a mental break from a strict on-season. Then comes the pre-season preparatory phase where bodyweight should be closer to our competition weight. Here we start to scale back our calories and get down to the body weight that is optimal for training for competition. Then our in-season phase places us at the bodyweight we will compete at, so if an individual cuts weight, this puts him at the weight that he wants to be on competition day, not what he has to weigh in at. There is also a contest preparatory phase where our nutrition is adjusted for the change in work volume dropping during the delayed transformation phase. You must properly fuel for the competition that week and execute super-compensation, if needed, depending on the sport.

Endurance Athletes

Endurance athletes have an optimal weight they need to maintain for their sport. This is important as is the fact that they carry less muscle mass than strength athletes. They require much lower levels of protein. Therefore, we use the remainder of the calories in their diet to fuel them. In the off-season phase for most endurance athletes, we cut their calories back since their work load is backed down. During the in-season phase, we increase their calories to give the athlete optimal recovery and energy levels while getting their bodyweight to their desired level. The contest preparatory phase happens during the delayed transformation phase in training. We back down the protein intake and go into a carbohydrate loading phase explained earlier in the chapter. During this phase, work load is drastically reduced and the need for protein for recovery is greatly reduced. We concentrate on optimally fueling the athlete instead.

The following meal plan is a guideline for the macro nutrients that work for the majority. It is designed for a 150-pound cyclist using .9 grams of protein per pound of bodyweight. This meal plan utilizes a ratio of 65 percent carbohydrate, 15 percent protein, and 20 percent fat. This is an example of a pre-season diet. As the intensity increases, when switching from pre-season to in-season, I will lower the fat percentage and raise the carbohydrate percentage.

Meal 1

- 1 cup orange juice, ½ cup oatmeal, banana, 1 muffin with 3 teaspoons (tsp.) honey, 5 egg egg-white omelet with yellow orange and green bell peppers, sea salt, and 4 tsp. fish oil.
    - o   Cal: 820.1
    - o   Carb: 135
    - o   Pro: 32.4
    - o   Fat: 18.7
- Morning pre ride nutrition: Start drinking one bottle of water with one scoop of carbohydrate sports drink mix 30 to 45 min before and continue during ride. During the ride ingest two 750 ml water bottles with 1.5 scoops of carbohydrate sports drink per bottle. This is good for an hour and half ride. We always use three percent to eight percent carbohydrate solution (30-80 grams) with 460 mg sodium and 117 mg potassium per liter of fluid per hour. If additional fuel is needed I have riders carry things like fig bars, honey, organic stinger waffles, power bar gel, and Cliff shot blocks.
    - o   Cal: 352
    - o   Carb: 88

Meal 2
- One scoop whey and casein blend protein powder. Add one banana, 3 tsp. raw honey, and two scoops carbohydrate mix like Cytosport Cytomax and 2 tablespoons (tbsp) safflower oil.
    - Cal: 844
    - Carb: 125
    - Pro: 23
    - Fat: 28

Meal 3
- Mix one cup quinoa with 2 ounces (oz.) pinto beans and 2 oz. red pepper.
    - Cal: 483
    - Carb: 100
    - Pro: 14
    - Fat: 3

Meal 4
- Mix 3 oz. venison with 1/2 cup brown rice and 2 tbsp. tomato paste with five diced cherry tomatoes. Add chili powder to taste. Eat with one slice whole wheat bread and dip in 2 tbsp olive oil. With a 4 oz. bowl of cranberries and 1 tsp. fish oil
    - Cal: 491.7
    - Carb: 55
    - Pro: 23.6
    - Fat: 19.7

Meal 5
- An example of a bulk meal to use for the week, six servings: 12 oz. whole-wheat bow-tie pasta; 2 tbsp. toasted pine nuts; 1 tbsp. extra-virgin olive oil; 12 oz. boneless, skinless chicken breasts, trimmed and thinly sliced; sea salt and freshly ground pepper to taste; two small, red bell peppers, thinly sliced; two shallots, minced; two cloves garlic, minced; one cup reduced-sodium chicken broth; 1/4 cup balsamic vinegar; 2 tsp. chopped fresh rosemary or 1 tsp. dried; 9-oz. artichoke hearts. This makes six servings. Each serving is:
    - Cal: 388
    - Carb: 51
    - Pro: 28
    - Fat: 8

Meal 6
- One-half cup cottage cheese, 4 oz. pineapple and 4 oz. blueberries

- o Cal: 213
- o Carb: 32
- o Pro: 14.5
- o Fat: 3

Totals
- o Cal: 3600
- o Carb: 586
- o Pro: 133

Strength Athletes

Look at individual sports and the athletes themselves. For example, football players in general do not do much work in the off-season compared to athletes in many other sports. During the off-season phase of the nutrition plan, I often cut back their calorie intake, so they don't gain too much body fat, making pre-season harder on them. If needed, I allow for more cheat meals, so they mentally get a break from strict dieting. Then, during the pre-season preparatory phase, their calorie intake increases to handle the additional work load. During the season, it is common for most football players to lose weight and strength. Throughout this book, it has been explained how not to lose strength during a season with correct training methods. Another big portion of why football players lose strength and size during season is because they do not take in an adequate amount of calories. As a coach, this has never made sense to me as to why this has not been addressed aggressively until the problem has been solved. It does not make any sense to go into the most important games of the season at one's weakest and smallest. Therefore, during the in-season preparatory phase for football players, the majority should increase in calories. This is because of the increased demands physically and emotionally. Remember the body does not perceive physical or mental stress any different. During the season, there is the added stress of trying to make play-offs or to win a championship or to keep a position on the team from being taken from another teammate.

Consideration also should be given to where an athlete is in his career. For many mixed martial artists, they are going to stay near fight shape, so they can be ready for a last-minute call to step up to a bigger league. They would need to stay in an in-season preparatory phase until a date is set for a fight. Here is an example of a 6,800 calorie diet for a 250-pound football player with a protein level of three kg per pound of body weight. This athlete's diet is a 55 percent carbohydrate, 20 percent protein, and 25 percent fat ratio. This breaks down to 935 grams of carbohydrate, 340 grams of protein, and 189 grams of fat. If I feel the athlete needs to keep his protein intake that high, but feel the calorie intake is not enough, I can change it to a 65 percent carbohydrate, 15 percent protein, and 25 percent fat nutrition plan. This would raise the calories from 6,800 to 9,100, but keep protein intake the same.

Example of an in-season football player:

Meal 1

- Shake consisting of ½ cup oatmeal, 1 cup pineapple, two bananas, 4 tsp. raw honey, 7 tsp. fish oil, and two scoops of protein powder.
    - o Cal: 1245

- - - Carb: 180
    - Pro: 52.5
    - Fat: 35
- Snack: Pre workout drink, 45 minutes to one hour before workout, consisting of three scoops, 66 grams of carbohydrates, and 270 calories. For example, accelerade, Cytomax, and endurox.
    - Cal: 264
    - Carb: 66
- Workout: During your workout, drink water mixed with a BCAA powder.

Meal 2

- Post workout: Shake within 15 minutes of workout, consisting of one banana, one cup strawberries, 3 tsp. raw honey, 8 oz. of almond milk, 2 tbsp. peanut butter, 2 tbsp. safflower oil, and two scoops of protein powder.
    - Cal: 1154
    - Carb: 113
    - Pro: 54
    - Fat: 54

Meal 3

- 1.5 cups Quinoa, 2 oz. almonds, and 4 oz. of buffalo steak.
    - Cal: 985.5
    - Carb: 129
    - Pro: 51
    - Fat: 29.5
- Snack: 4 oz. raw sweet potatoes, cut and eat like carrot sticks, with 10 oz. raw orange juice.
    - Cal: 224
    - Carb: 54
    - Pro: 2

Meal 4

- Salad consisting of two cups of baby spinach leaves, one cup red leaf lettuce, 3 oz. raw sweet potato, 3 oz. tomato, 2 oz. cranberry, 2 oz. yellow pepper, 2 oz. pear, 3 oz. hardboiled egg whites, 3 tbsp. cold pressed olive oil, and as much balsamic vinegar as you like for the dressing. One cup black beans and rice, 10 oz. of cantaloupe, 4 oz. of turkey breast.
    - Cal: 930
    - Carb: 143.5
    - Pro: 54
    - Fat: 15.5
- Snack: two apples = 50 grams of carbohydrate and 200 calories

Meal 5
- One cup brown rice, three figs, 6 oz. avocado, and 7 oz. salmon
    - Cal: 823
    - Carb: 63
    - Pro: 46
    - Fat: 43

Meal 6
- 10 oz. sweet potato, 1 tsp. fish oil, sandwich with two slices of whole wheat bread, mustard and 5 oz. of chicken.
    - Cal: 718
    - Carb: 121
    - Pro: 44
    - Fat: 6.5

Meal 7
- 1.5 cups cottage cheese with 1 cup blueberries and 2 cups of broccoli.
    - Cal: 277.5
    - Carb: 16
    - Pro: 41
    - Fat: 5.5

- Totals
    - Cal: 6821
    - Carb: 935.5
    - Pro: 344.5
    - Fat: 189

As can be noted, it takes a lot of food to fuel a big athlete. I put more carbohydrates and fats earlier in the day when the majority of work will be done. By cutting the carbohydrates and fats down later in the evening, I can keep body fat levels in check. Coaches should make sure to do a body composition analysis often on their athletes.

Example of a Permissible Clean Food List

Protein:

Beef: Beef tenderloin, Filet Mignon, Sirloin, Flank Steak, Round Steak, Top Round, Roast Beef, Ground Round, Ground Sirloin, Ground Beef (93% Fat Free or Leaner).

Poultry: Chicken breast (no skin), Canned Chicken Breast, Turkey Breast, Turkey Breast Cutlets, Ground Turkey Breast (95% Fat Free or Leaner), Canned Turkey Breast.

Fish: Just about all kinds, the best include the following: Tuna (canned in water or fresh), Cod, Flounder, Halibut, Haddock, Orange Roughy, Salmon (canned in water or fish, but limit to twice weekly), Red Snapper, Scallops, Shrimp, Whitefish, and Swordfish.

Other Meats: Buffalo, Ostrich, and Venison.

Complex Starchy Carbohydrate:

Oatmeal, Cream of Rice, Cooked Rice (brown), Quinoa, Potatoes, Sweet Potatoes, Red Potatoes, Beans (white, pinto, kidney, or black).

Fibrous Vegetables:

Asparagus, Broccoli, Brussels Sprouts, Cabbage, Carrots, Cauliflower, Celery, Cucumbers, Green Beans, Kale, Lettuce, Mushrooms, Spinach, Tomato, Water Chestnuts, Zucchini.

Fruit:

Apple, Blackberries, Blueberries, Cantaloupe, Grapefruit, Kiwi, Nectarine, Orange, Peach, Raspberries, Strawberries

In the permissible food list above, there are just a few examples of the many foods an individual should eat for proper nutrition and recovery. Realize that most people who feel they are over trained are not. They are either under prepared or under recovered. There are many components to recovery and proper preparedness for training and competition. Nutrition and hydration is a very important part of that. Without fuel a race car goes nowhere. It is the same for an athlete. Without proper nutrition, desired bodyweight cannot be maintained for a particular sport nor can an athlete fuel workouts or competition, rendering training useless. To be the best in the world takes sacrifice. Eating the right food for fuel and not the wrong food for enjoyment is one of those sacrifices. For optimal nutrition, an athlete should never miss a meal. When we consider the fact that progress (repair and recovery) effectively stops when there is a lack in adequate nutrient intake, realize that missing a meal is not an option. Preparing meals ahead of time and becoming well-organized is essential for an athlete.

CHAPTER 10 – RESTORATION AND RECOVERY METHODS

CHAPTER 10 – RESTORATION AND RECOVERY METHODS

As Americans we are forever trying to duplicate the Russian and Bulgarian training systems without a single thought about restoration. I am amazed at our Olympic lifting coaches and how they try to follow the Bulgarian system over and over with no real results. The Bulgarians had not only model lifters, but among other things a required height and weight for each weight class.

Sports and recovery must be linked for success. There are times in dense training when a non-recovery time period must be maintained while attempting to increase the size of the muscle cells (Siff's *Hyperplasia*, p.65). One must look into electric stimulation trigger points or pressure point therapy for recovery purposes. Another avenue for restoration and recovery is targeting specific muscle groups using Proprioceptive Neuromuscular Facilitation (PNF) or even acupuncture by qualified persons.

Restoration includes many things, like the right amount of sleep. No stone can go unturned as far as recovery goes. There are many methods of restoration that I have not discussed, but I hope, I have made you think about making progress when not in the weight room.

What are the most common recovery methods?

1. Anabolic Steroids

The reason there are tests for steroids is because athletes are taking them. Of course, they work to make one stronger but they play a large role in recovery. If an individual is going to reach the very top in his sport, he will most likely take some form of anabolic steroids to reach his goals. Though anabolic steroids are against most rules, they are available through a prescription from a doctor legally. There are those taking steroids, passing drug tests because the steroids are not detectable. If someone can break a world record without taking them, why test? The fact remains they help recovery.

Anabolic steroids have been with us since the 1940s. They were used for recovery from injuries and in attempting to treat malnourished prisoners of war. What role do anabolic steroids play? They trigger a buildup of tissue or anabolism, which generally refers to an increase in tissue of particular muscles. They also help in the process in which energy is used to build organic compounds, leg enzymes, and nucleic acids that are necessary for lift functions. In summary, anabolic steroids stimulate protein synthesis and muscle growth. I personally know more people who take them than don't take them. Yes, I have known abusers, but not one person became sick nor showed a fictional side effect known as "roid" rage, and I have never seen anyone show signs of depression. The depression symptoms show up in those who stop taking them, or those who were depressed before. There are aging clinics for men and yes, women to turn to who show signs of a lack of testosterone as they age.

Not much was talked about concerning anabolics for years in the United States or the former Soviet Union. By 1960 anabolic steroids were being used heavily in the wide world of sports. The Soviet sport's system felt they were safe with supervision. It was not until 1972 that there was an investigation into their potential for increasing sports performance. The investigation was conducted by a group of Soviet researchers and sent to top coaches who discussed the effects men and woman had while using them while winning most if not all the medals. In 1988, the international Olympic committee started testing not only at events, but randomly. I personally think testing is ridiculous. I worked with an Olympic caliber athlete who could send in a sample to find how long he could take performance enhancing drugs and still pass the IOC test.

The DDR had total management over drug use for their athletes and never had one test positive. Much of this information came from *Soviet Training and Recovery* Methods by Rick Rubber and Ben Tabachnik, Ph.D.

As for a restoration tool, pharmacological agents will always be connected to sports performance. Even if an athlete takes steroids in the early stages of training, such as in the accumulation and intensification phases of training and stops usage, the athlete will still receive the prolonged benefits of their effects through advanced restoration methods. If an individual chooses to use performance enhancing drugs, he should consult a doctor, but not just any doctor. It needs to be a physician who has possibly set up the drug cycles for several top athletes. I highly suggest reading all you can from a medical standpoint and learn from athletes who have used them for long periods of time. Do not consult a doctor who has no experience or is clueless in the matter. Because of their ability and work ethic, the most admired and able athletes in the world should be monitored closely to help the health and performance of the average man and woman. I am in no way recommending anyone to take any drugs that are illegal or otherwise.

2. Therapeutic

Common therapeutic restoration methods:

- Ice bath—applying ice to an over stressed muscle group
- Hot tub—alternating ice or cold baths
- Dry sauna
- Wet heat
- Ultra sound cold laser ultra violet
- Electric stimulation
- Hand sport massage
- Rolfing the deep tissue
- Working on flexibility to aid in range of motion
- Active Release Techniques (ART)
- Chiropractic
- Self-Massage

Massage and other related methods of recovery are essential; a deep tissue massage is vital to recovery. The Russians knew that massage was a large part of recovery. It can be as simple as a self-massage for five to 10 minutes. When an individual is given a massage by a trained massage practitioner, it normally lasts 45 to 60 minutes. For a lifter, the hamstrings, glutes, lower and upper back should receive the most attention; however, a runner's massage should focus on the calves, thighs, ankles and feet. While the weight lifter would receive a lot of massage on the trunk including the abdominals, the runner would not.

Dr. Rolf, Ph.D., was the innovator of deep tissue massage, which was and is very effective. Dr. Rolf held a degree in biological chemistry, and she studied mathematics and atomic physics. Her system is well thought out as she studied yoga, chiropractic medicine, osteopathy, and both the Alexander technique and Korzybski's work on states of consciousness by working with the disabled. This work was later known as structural integration. Dr. Rolf advanced all massage techniques, and thanks to her tireless work, I highly recommend this procedure, especially to serious athletes.

In the United States there are cookie cutter tactics, but there is a special approach like Active Release Therapy (ART), which was created by Dr. P. Michael Leahy. The therapy stretches a limb while vigorous massage is used in correlation with a precisely directed tension with specific patient movement; Muscle Activated Therapy (MAT) is a similar process. It combines compression, extension movement and breath.

3. **Mental Recovery**

Learning to relax not only between workouts, but during the lifts as a part of a workout is critical. Hypnosis with assistance or self-induced can be of great help. Meditation must play a role in recovery; it is as old as sports themselves. Many skilled coaches can administer these procedures for the athletes. Correct music for the athlete's state of mind can be very motivational or relaxing depending on the situation. I feel the athlete should do as much as possible for himself.

The Russians separated recovery in three categories:

a. **Psychology**—These techniques were more relaxing for the athletes, such as vacillation and relaxation music. They also encouraged time to learn techniques by watching replays of the athlete and others.

b. **Coaching**—The coach must devise a plan to accommodate work, rest, and recovery. A balance between GPP and SPP is essential. More can be read from Verkhoshansky (1966) *Supertraining*.

c. **Medico-Biological**—Some have already been discussed like massage, ultra-sound, heart, UV light, chiropractic and other spine manipulations.

On max effort day on Monday, which is 72 hours later, the intensity is 100 percent, and the volume of a barbell lift is low. It looks like a contest; one lift at around 90 percent, and one just under or just over an all-time best. Then, take one smaller jump.

An individual's level of preparedness will decide if he breaks his all-time record or not. Remember to switch a major barbell exercise each week, and always vary the volume and intensities per work out.

Let's not forget nutrition. Adequate protein, vitamins, and minerals are essential. Take advantage of everything at your disposal. Even a small walk can help restore the body for the next workout or aid in shedding a few pounds.

Remember, relaxation can play a large role in restoration. You all know that Westsiders believe in three-week waves for strength, but some findings (Medvedev, 1980) take into account the athlete or lifter as physical bio-cycles lasting 23 days, which corresponds with our three-week wave.

IVs for rehydration and chelation treatment for recovery are quite common at Westside Barbell and many professional teams. Pro Lo Therapy for increasing the size and strength of ligaments and tendons plus reducing pain in a particular area is also routinely implemented.

Oxygen injections into an injury are common among bicyclists. All of the above must be administered by a professional. Some form of restoration can be done every day. Remember some extreme recovery methods are taxing and can be substituted for a small workout. For more information, read the following: Siff and Yessis's (1992) *Sports Restoration*; Kurz's (2001) *Science of Sports Training;* and Siff's (1994) *Supertraining*.

4. **Small Workouts.**

A very natural way to recover from a hard workout is to do a small workout. While an extreme workout can take 72 hours to recover, a small workout can happen every 12 to 24 hours. They must be planned to fit the needs of the individual, and they can incorporate anything from strength training or some kind of flexibility, mobility, dexterity, endurance, hand and eye coordination, game strategy or whatever is needed to excel.

Never do a certain restoration GPP cycle that lasts longer than 23 days. The higher mental demands an individual places around himself, the shorter the restoration cycle. This information should help each person reach his strength and fitness potential.

At Westside, we carefully choose the exercises per workout, keeping over training in tack. Smaller workouts can occur 12 to 24 hours apart. Westside has followed the reasoning of Olympic caliber weight lifters as their heavy squat workouts are separated by 72 to 96 hours. This approach has Westside squatting on Friday with moderately high intensity and high volume.

If a lifter's lockout in the bench is weak, extra tricep work is needed. It's best to do light high rep work; one hundred reps in the push down three times a week at home can do wonders for tricep development. Doing 250 leg curls with five pound, 10 pound, or 20-pound ankle weights are super explosive and adds muscle mass as well as endurance. They can be accompanied with abdominal work. Band leg curls can also be implemented, consisting of two sets of 50 reps in the dorm or home. Performing 50 to 100 band Goodmonings can make a huge difference in building explosive power, muscular endurance, and muscle mass for lagging body parts. The ultra-high repetitions can build thickness in not only the muscles but also the soft tissue, ligaments, and tendons where KE is stored and transferred into explosive energy.

Hitting a speed bag or double end bag is good for hand and eye coordination; a heavy bag can be used for a great cardio workout, or hitting focus pads can be used to throw combinations. This type of work breaks the boredom of ball training. A short swim or walking in water up to the waste is excellent for restoration.

As discussed in the GPP chapter, pulling a light sled, walking with ankle weights, or wearing a weight vest is superb for restoration while gaining conditioning. Other restoration activities can encompass a small weight workout, using three sets of moderate dumbbells to squat, and on deadlift day, two sets of 15 reps of moderate weight for a light bench session—one very close and one very wide—can be performed. A sled can be pulled for the lower body, and on upper body days, two sets of reverse hypers with light weight for 15 reps can be completed. Along with the aforementioned exercises, perform two sets of push-ups on leg days, plus two sets of pull-ups, and finally, 100-500 Hindu squats on upper body day can be executed, remembering the reps depend on each individual's GPP.

I prefer to stay away from activities in the weight room that duplicate a sport. A strength coach is to make an individual as strong and quick as possible, ensuring he doesn't get hurt on the field. Lumbar injuries are common in football but not wrestling, why? There are countless hamstring injuries in football, why? Athletes train the hamstrings and stretch their hamstrings yet pull them, why? The coach neglects the lower back. That's why. They may be afraid to hurt a player; if that's the case, get a different job or learn how to train the lower back.

The old Soviets' coaches recommended 600 glute-ham raises a month as maintenance. That's only 20 a day. An individual can always do short 20 minutes on a treadmill by adding a weight vest, ankle weights and bands around your feet or other combinations. You could also walk or jog on foam, or in sand, when possible, or cross-country ski.

A Neuromuscular Therapist's View of the Reverse Hyper™
By John Quint NMT ART

My intent for writing this is very simple. I want people to understand and view the Reverse Hyper through my perspective. My first exposure to the Reverse Hyper was through the man who invented it, Louie Simmons. Louie's and my paths crossed when I began treating him over a year ago at the facility which he owns, Westside Barbell, in Columbus, Ohio. This facility is where some of the strongest athletes in the world come to train. Louie, with all of his experience, is a fountain of priceless information. I genuinely enjoy treating Louie, as it gives me the opportunity to ask him questions so that I can better understand his philosophy and perspectives on topics which interest me.

Working for a private medical practice full time, it is my job to explain in detail to patients what their issues are and what it is I am doing treatment-wise to help resolve and address those issues. When I treated Louie, I would do no different and explained what I was doing. It would always spark some very interesting topics and conversations depending on what it was I was treating him for on that day. The most interesting topic to me came up when I was treating his low back, and he explained to me that he broke his back years earlier. It was at a time when he was entering his prime in powerlifting, and he did not want to stop training due to this injury. Louie explained to me that out of necessity he invented a machine that enabled him to not only continue training, but also rehabilitated his spine so that he was able to continue his powerlifting career.

After finishing treatment on his low back, Louie took the time to show me around his facility. Obviously after the conversation we had, I needed to see this machine he had invented. I am not going to lie, I was highly skeptical and at first glance I was disappointed and not impressed with the machine I was looking at. Following the discussion we just had, my expectations were sky high, and when I laid my eyes on this simple-looking machine, it was a major let down. That is because I let my unrealistic expectations that Louie was going to show me some spectacular complex-looking machine cloud my thought process. It was just in my nature to assume that if there was a machine that could supposedly help rehab a complex issue like a broken back, you would need an equally complicated or even more sophisticated machine to do so, not the simple looking machine I was looking at.

Even with my initial disappointment, I remained open-minded as he explained this very simple looking machine to me. So that I was truly able to experience the movement and machine for myself, Louie coached me through a couple of sets until I could understand how to correctly use the machine. The trust I had in Louie's knowledge and advice on the machine trumped my initial disappointing visual impression of the machine, and I started to incorporate it into my training routine.

Immediately after incorporating this machine into my training, I began to experience not just the strength benefits, but also therapeutic benefits (decreased low pain/stiffness) of the reverse hyper. Before this machine, the only relief I would receive from my own low back pain was neuromuscular therapy treatment and active release technique. The relief that I received from those treatments was my motivation and reason for pursuing them as my career.

Just like the soft tissue treatment modalities that I currently practice (neuromuscular therapy and active release technique) sparked my interest enough that I pursed them as a career, the Reverse Hyper sparked my curiosity in much the same capacity. I knew that it would be extremely beneficial for both me as a therapist and equally beneficial to the patients whom I treat, to fully understand the effects of this machine on the spine and the soft tissue structures which surround the spine. So the following is my perspective of how the Reverse Hyper effects the spine.

The Iliopsoas, the "Hidden Prankster"

My experiences and interactions from working in the medical field have led me to believe that there is no muscle more misunderstood than what Dr. Janet Travell, MD refers to as "iliopsoas." Travell, author of the *Myofascial Pain and Dysfunction Manuals*, Personal Physician to President John F. Kennedy, and the pioneer of trigger-point medicine, appropriately named the *"iliopsoas"* in her manuals as the "Hidden Prankster." These manuals have been updated and are the bible for anyone who practices neuromuscular therapy like myself. She references the *"iliopsoas"* as a prankster in the sense that it is often times overlooked as the main source of low back pain. Looking at what she describes in her manuals as the *"iliopsoas"* and the multiple joints and path that it travels, as well as its attachment on the anterior (front) side of the spine, it is very easy to see and understand her reasoning.

Before we delve in any farther, I would like to address what Dr. Travell refers to as the *"iliopsoas,"*

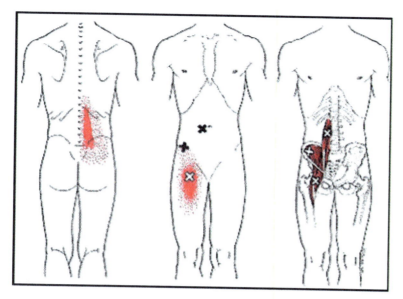

because it's very important to understand the anatomy involved. Dr. Travell's manuals were not written as anatomy textbooks or used in that manner. Rather they are medical manuals for treating myofascial pain and dysfunction. The manuals are organized into different parts depending on the referral pain pattern of the muscles. In that process she combined the two different muscles, the psoas and the iliacus, into one referral pain pattern and treatment section, called the "iliopsoas". However, it should be noted that the psoas and the iliacus are two separate muscles. Just like in treatment for low back pain where the psoas will receive the most attention, this article is no different and will primarily focus on the psoas.

Successfully relieving a patient from their myofascial pain and dysfunction through treatment requires the therapist to be very specific and focused on isolating and treating the soft tissue structures that are causing the patient's pain. Successfully understanding the positive effects of the Reverse Hyper on the spine in this article is no different; we need to be very specific in what we focus on and isolate the correct soft tissue structures to fully understand the effects on the spine. By isolating the "iliopsoas" and understanding its anatomy and function, it will enable us to understand the effects the Reverse Hyper has on the spine. Even though to most, this is a very unconventional way of understanding the effects that the reverse hyper has on the spine, to me and from my perspective as a neuromuscular therapist, it is makes perfect sense.

The objective of this article is to understand what Dr. Janet Travell refers to as the "iliopsoas". Through our understanding of the anatomy and functions, we will then be able to see the effects that the "iliopsoas" has on the spine. Once we understand the effects "iliopsoas" has on the spine, we can then change gears and focus on the Reverse Hyper's effects on the "iliopsoas." Once we are able to understand the Reverse Hyper's effects on the spine through understanding its effects on the "iliopsoas," you will then be able to see the effects the Reverse Hyper has on the spine through my perspective, which is my main objective for writing this.

So what is the iliopsoas? Anatomically, the iliopsoas is two separate muscles: the psoas and iliacus: There is a great deal of debate and varying opinions as to what exactly the functions of the psoas are, but there are no controversies about the anatomical attachments.

- The psoas is a multi-joint muscle, meaning it crosses multiple joints. The psoas crosses the spinal joint of thoracic vertebrae 12 and all the spinal joints of the lumbar vertebrae (thoracolumbar spine) into the hip joint.

- The "iliopsoas" is two separate muscles: the psoas and iliacus, which fascially blend together once the psoas travels distally (down) into the pelvis.
- The fibers of the psoas (pictured below) originate on the lateral (away from the midline of the body) and mostly anterior (front) surfaces of the vertebral bodies of T12 and L1-L5 and their associated intervertebral discs and attaches to the lesser trochantor of the femur (hip joint).
- The fibers of the iliacus originate in the iliac fossa (bowl of the pelvis), fascially blends with the psoas and attaches at the lesser trochantor of the femur (hip joint).
- The psoas and iliacus are curved muscles, meaning their muscle path (line of travel) is not a straight line, but curved.
- Muscles with a curved path wrap around bones or other tissues. In the case of the psoas, it wraps around the anterior (front) of the pelvis (iliopectineal rim of the pelvis).
- The psoas's attachments on all the spinal vertebrae are: mostly anterior (front) and lateral (away from the midline of the body) sides of the vertebrae (T12-L5) as well as their corresponding intervertebral discs.
- The psoas's insertion on the femur is located on the posterior (back) medial (inside) aspect of the lesser trochanter of the femur.

Other Anatomical Considerations

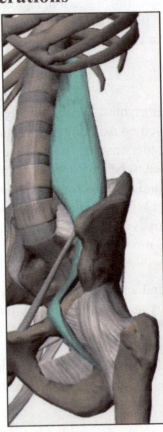

Illustration Angled view of the psoas that shows the full muscle path.

- At the point where the psoas travels distally (down), and begins to enter into the pelvis, where the interfaces of the iliacus and psoas muscles begin to fascially blend, it is the beginning of the psoas's myotendinous junction.
- The myotendinous junction is interface where the muscular tissues begins to transition into tendinous tissue. Functionally, it is the primary site of muscular force transmission.

- In conclusion, at the interface where the psoas and the iliacus first begin to fascially blend together to form the "iliospoas," the psoas is much more tendinous and the iliacus is much more muscular.

Muscle Fiber Considerations

Muscles are made up of different types of muscle fibers. We do not need to understand the different muscle types for the purposes of this article. We just need to know and understand the muscle fiber composition of the psoas and iliacus.

- The iliacus and psoas are considered postural muscles.
- Typical posture muscle are dominated by Type I, slow-twitch or "red" muscle fibers.
- Type I, slow-twitch muscle fibers are susceptible to pathological shortening or contracture.
- Individuals who are sedentary and/or are seated for prolonged periods of time as well as older people are very susceptible to this shortening of the psoas and iliacus.
- Generally posture muscles require regular soft tissue treatment in combination with stretching to maintain a healthy tone.

Up for Debate:

Some consider the psoas to be a fusiform muscle, meaning the belly (middle portion) of muscle is wider than both the origin and insertion. Others, including myself, consider the psoas to be a triangular muscle, much like the deltoid muscle. I came to this conclusion based on the work of Tom Myers. Tom Myers, a Certified Advanced Rolfer® and author of *Anatomy Trains (2001)*, stated that "The human psoas muscle makes a unique journey around the front of the pelvis. No other animal makes use of such a course for the psoas; in most quadrupeds (Illustrated right by Andrew Mannie), the psoas does not even touch the pelvis unless the femur is extended to its limits (6)."

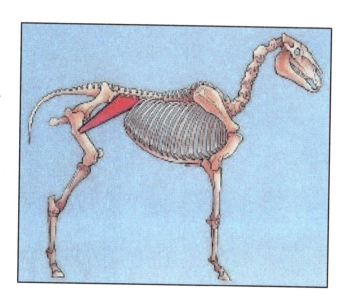

Tom Meyers furthers his argument of the psoas being a triangular muscle by stating that: "Humans have swung the pelvis, and indeed the entire spine, up vertically in such a way that the resting position of the standing hip is much more extended than your dog or cat would be comfortable with. The result for the human psoas is that it now is bent around the front of the hip joint, going forward from the femur to the iliopectineal rim of the pelvis, and then back from this edge to the spine (6)."

This article views the psoas muscle as Tom Meyers does, as a triangular muscle and not as a fusiform muscle.

It must be noted that the muscle fiber's path of travel in a triangular muscle is not parallel like the biceps muscle of your arm. Since the fibers are not parallel, but instead triangular in shape, they are going to have multiple different muscle path directions and therefore different lines of pull just like the deltoid muscle of your shoulder. Now that we have an anatomical understanding of what structures the psoas and iliacus articulate with, we will be able understand their path of travel from one attachment point to the other attachment point. This is also referred to as the muscle's path.

Muscle Path Considerations (Pictured below) *Forces exerted by the muscle are transmitted from one attachment site to another along a certain line of action, usually referred to as a **muscle path.***

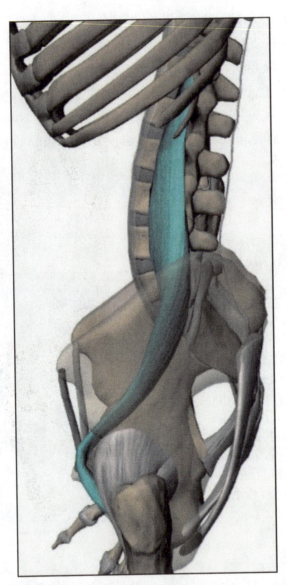

Pictured above: Side view of the psoas. Note how the muscle travels anterior (front) and distal (downward) to its attachment point on the posterior (back) side of the lesser trochantor of the femur.

- The fibers of the psoas originate at thoracic vertebrae 12, all the lumbar vertebrae and to their corresponding intervertebral discs.
- Starting at T12, the psoas travels distally (down) to its attachment site on the lesser trochanter of the femur (hip joint).

- When the psoas travels distally into the pelvis where the iliacus is located, it fascially blends to the iliacus, making the psoas now the "iliopsoas." However, they are still two different muscles.
- Once the psoas and iliacus fascially blend together, creating the "iliopsoas," the muscles continue their path distally (down), but now also travel anteriorly (towards the front of the body) to the anterior (front) ridge of the pelvis, where the muscle changes its path by curving and wrapping over the iliopectineal ridge (located on the front side of the pelvis) and changes its path once more and begins to travel posteriorly (towards the back of the body) and medial (towards the midline of the body) where it eventually attaches on the lesser trochantor of the femur.

Curved and Wrapped Muscle Path Considerations *(Pictured Right)*

- Muscles with a curved path wrap around bones or other tissues (9).
- When a curved muscle develops tension, the muscle tends to (a) bring the origin and insertion closer together and (b) straighten (9).
- Curved muscles exert forces not only along the muscle path but also laterally toward the inside (9).
- The mechanism is similar to what is happening when a bent rope is pulled at both ends: the rope tends to straighten (9).

Muscular Function and Biomechanics

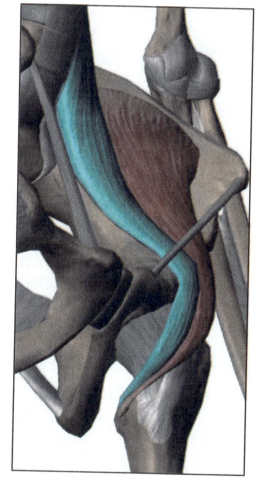

We can understand the definition of muscular function through our understanding of the definition of muscle path. As previously stated, ***the line of action*** from which forces are exerted and then transmitted by the muscle, from one attachment site to another, is ***muscle path*** (8). When the forces that are exerted and transmitted by the muscle from one attachment site to another create an action and therefore movement, **the action and movement created is the muscle's function.** Therefore, when a muscle concentrically contracts (shortens), it creates then exerts and transmits a force which pulls towards its center (between the muscles to two attachment sites). The concentric force (if it is great enough to overcome resistance), is exerted on the attachment sites and will pull (shorten) the two attachment sites towards each other. In most cases, the resistance force is the force of gravity.

Once the resisting force is overcome by a concentric muscular contraction (shortening), the attachment site of the muscle will move at the joint that is crossed by the muscle, creating the joint's actions. In a typical concentric contraction, only one of the two attachment sites moves. This is due in part because generally there is less resistance at one site in comparison to the other, enabling one of the attachment

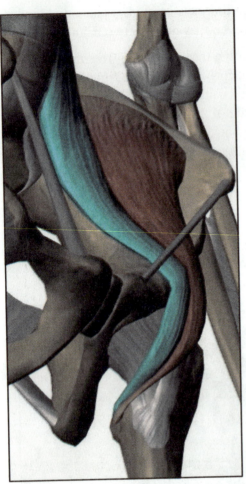

sites to move easier. However, it should be noted that in some cases, the resistance for each of the two attachment sites is approximately equal and both attachments will move. So in text, when a muscle's joint actions are listed, the muscle's concentric contraction joint actions are described.

Joint actions created by concentric muscular contractions are figured out by analyzing the muscle's path in relation to the joint/s that it crosses in route to its attachment sites. For example, if there is a concentric muscular contraction (shortening of the muscle) and muscle's path travels on the one side of the joint, it will create action on that side and at the joint. In contrast, if the muscle's path were traveling on the opposite side of the joint, it would create the opposite or antagonistic joint action. Joint actions therefore are motions or movements.

Pictured above: The psoas (blue) and iliacus (red) fibers curving and wrapping around the ridge of the pelvis as they travel to their distal attachment on the posterior (back) medial aspect of the lesser trochantor of the femur.

Furthermore, muscles function in tandem to create joint actions. When one muscle (agonist) concentrically contracts (shortens) it will exert and transmit a pulling force on its attachment sites. If there is enough force to overcome resistance, the joint action will occur. Joint action will occur because simultaneously the opposite (antagonist) muscle counterpart relaxes and will lengthen enabling motion at that joint. This simultaneous action of a contracting agonist muscle and a relaxing antagonist muscle powers all movements in the body.

Functions of the Psoas at the Hip Joint

Even with its mostly all anterior (front) attachments to the all lumbar vertebra and their corresponding intervertebral discs, the psoas muscle is viewed mostly as a muscle of the hip joint. This is due in large part because ***the only function of this muscle that is universally agreed upon is flexion of the thigh at the hip joint (2,3,8,9)***. Beyond this agreement, due to the ongoing debate anatomically of the psoas, there still remains a great deal of debate on the muscle's other functions, specifically at the spinal joints. Since we understand the multiple joints and its unique path to its attachments, it easy to see why so much is up for debate.

Functions of the Psoas at the Spinal Joints

To effectively understand the functions of the psoas at the spinal joints for the purposes of this article, I

Now to complicate things, notice above I said the fibers of the psoas are predominately on the anterior (front) side of the lumbar vertebra. Many researchers have concluded that a small majority of the fibers of the psoas are located on the posterior (back) of the lumbar vertebra (3,6). To understand the function of these posterior located fibers at the spinal joints, we are going to use the same simple approach that we used for the anterior fibers and conclude that the line of pull that these fibers are going to create is extension at those joints due to their attachment and muscle path.

To further complicate things, it must be mentioned the line of pull in both flexion and extension is not parallel. This is due to the fact that the psoas is a triangular muscle and therefore the line of force it has on the lumbar vertebrae will be at an angle.

In conclusion, the functions of the psoas at the spinal joints is both flexion and extension (3, 4, 6, 8), but more predominately flexion due to the large majority of anterior located fibers. Furthermore, we understand that the lines of pull created by both flexion and extension are angular and not in a straight line due to the muscle fibers being aligned in triangular fashion.

It should be very clear at this point that the more we learn about the psoas, the more confused we can become. Let's not lose focus on the purpose of this article though, to understand the effects the psoas has on the spine. *So from this section, the main point to take away is that the psoas is predominately going to create flexion at the lumbar spinal joints; however, since some of the fibers are located on the posterior (back) side, the psoas also has the ability to create extension at those spinal joints.*

How Does the Psoas have the Ability to Both Flex and Extend the Lumbar?

The lumbar portion of the spine is made of five vertebrae, each with their own segmental level and all which articulate to each other from top to bottom as L1-L5. At each lumbar vertebra, the attachment of the psoas will be at a different location. These different attachment locations of the psoas on the lumbar vertebrae are what enables the psoas to both flex and extend the spine.

Simply put, at one segment of the lumbar spine, the psoas attachment is going to be more anterior (front) and at another segment, the psoas attachment is going to be posterior (back). The differences in attachments of the psoas at the different segments of the lumbar spine are what enables the lumbar spine to both flex and extend at the same time. *For the purposes of this article, let's further simplify the effects that the psoas has on the spine and understand that more than the ability to just flex and extend the spine, the psoas has the ability to segmentally create movement between the lumbar spinal joints.*

The Psoas Creates Movement Segmentally

The human body is designed to move. Furthermore, movement in most every direction is very important to achieve for overall health. Movement works both the muscles and the joints. It stretches and strengthens soft tissue structures and promotes circulation. *The circulation promoted by the psoas, flexing and extending the lumbar spine segmentally, creates a pumping action of the nucleus pulposus so that nutrient supply to the intervertebral disc is significantly effected and improved (4).*

Psoas Functions as a Spine Stabilizer?

The functions of a muscle are generally defined by listing its concentric actions. Often times what is overlooked is the muscle's functions as a stabilizer, otherwise known as the muscle's isometric stabilization contraction functions. The stabilization function cannot be overlooked due to the fact that the characteristics needed for a healthy functioning joint is for it to be mobile, but also stable.

Some individuals in the medical field who have conducted extensive research on the psoas have concluded that the psoas's predominant function is as a spine stabilizer and not a flexor or extensor of the lumbar spine. This argument is very plausible and makes sense when we consider the many different opinions on the role the psoas has on the spine and to what extent it affects flexion and extension. It should be noted, like everything else about this muscle, this as well remains up for debate.

How Does the Psoas Stabilize the Spine?

When a muscles contracts it will create an action at a joint. As stated above, this is only one of the characteristics that defines a healthy functioning joint. The other characteristic is for the joint to be stable. The muscular contraction, which creates enough force to cause an action at a joint, is the same force that will stabilize the joint.

The psoas is viewed by some as a spinal stabilizer due to its obvious attachment on the spine. Remember the large majority of the psoas attaches to the anterior (front) side of the vertebrae, but we cannot forget about posterior (back) fibers. With the psoas having fibers on both the anterior (front) and posterior (back) of the lumbar vertebrae, it positions itself directly over the axes of motion (vertebrae). Therefore, when the force from the psoas contraction is transmitted into the spine, it pulls one vertebrae (lumbar spinal joint) into the other throughout the entire lumbar spine. This force that stabilizes the lumbar spine is a **compressive force**. It can be concluded that a compressive force throughout the lumbar spine means compression onto the corresponding intervertebral discs.

Psoas Contraction and Spinal Compression

As stated in the previous section, just how much of a role the psoas has in spinal stabilization is still up for debate. What we can state without a doubt is that the contraction of the psoas does create segmental spinal compression at each of the segments of lumbar vertebrae. This compression force will be transmitted upon the corresponding intervertebral discs, which will stabilize the lumbar region. However, it should be understood that the greater the compressive force transmitted to the intervertebral discs, the greater chance for injury to the discs.

McGill states: "Caution is advised when training this muscle due to the substantial spine compression penalty that is imposed on the spine when the psoas is activated (2)."

Carol Oatis, PT, Ph.D., expands on the previous statement to come to the conclusion that low back pain that occurs with hip flexion is due to the psoas contracting and transmitting compression throughout the lumbar spine (1). ***Based on the explanations and evidence provided, we can easily conclude*** *that compressive forces are applied to the intervertebral discs when the psoas is contracted.*

The Psoas' Effect on Spinal Alignment

Musculature effects spinal alignment. If a muscle that attaches to the spine is tight and restricted, it is going to negatively effect spinal alignment in an unhealthy way. With the psoas being the largest and most proximal muscle to the lumbar and thoracic spine, it will have a major effect on the spinal alignment if it is tight and restricted. "A deteriorated psoas ... chronically flexes the body at the level of the inguinal region, so that it prevents a truly erect posture," wrote Ida Rolf (7).

The effect will be felt and noticed the most when the individual with a tight and restricted psoas stands upright. Decreased range of motion, function and restriction in the psoas will cause a chain of events. First the tight and restricted psoas is going to pull both the thoracic and lumbar spine down and forward (from where it attaches on the spine to its distal attachment on the lesser trochantor of the femur). This down and forward pull is going to force the stabilization muscles on the posterior (back) side in both the back and hip (quadratus lumborum, erector spinae, piriformis, and gluteals) to respond and counterbalance this restriction. The counter balance is going to cause major compensation in biomechanics, segmental spinal compression and low back pain.

We need to understand the effects of a tight and restricted psoas on spinal alignment. However, due to the focus of this article, which is being able to understand the Reverse Hyper's effects on the spine through understanding its effects on the psoas, it should be stated that when performing the reverse hyper motion, the set up (described in detail later, open chain movement) does not enable the psoas to have this effect on the lumbar spine. This is due to the fact that the spine will be stabilized on the pad and the individual is not standing upright.

Psoas Conclusions

I have presented a great deal of information regarding the psoas and its effects on the spine. I must note there remains a significant amount of information, purposely left out, so that it does not distract the reader from the intent of this article.

The information and explanations provided in the sections above about the psoas are intended to enable the reader to not only understand the psoas, but to understand the effects the psoas has on the spine. Once those effects are understood, then it will be very easy for the reader to understand the effects the Reverse Hyper has on the spine through effecting the psoas. Below is a bullet point summary of those effects:

- It is universally agreed upon that the psoas functions as a flexor of the hip joint (2, 3, 8, 9).
- The psoas has the ability to both flex and extend the lumbar spinal joints (create movement) (3, 4, 6, 8).
- The ability to both flex and extend the lumbar spinal joints is due to the psoas having both ante-

rior (front) and posterior (back) attachments at the lumbar spinal joints.

- The fibers of the psoas are predominately anterior (front). Therefore, when the psoas is contracted or in a shortened state in a closed chain setting, it is going to pull the lumbar spine forward and down.
- The forward and downward pull in a closed chain setting created by a tight and/or restricted psoas will cause spinal compression of the intervertebral discs.
- With both anterior (front) and posterior (back) attachments at the lumbar spinal joints, it places the psoas fibers directly over the vertebra, enabling it to create segmental spinal compression of the lumbar vertebra and transmitting that force onto the intervertebral discs.
- **The argument over how much flexion and extension the psoas has on the spinal joints should not be our focus for the intent of this article. Rather, the focus should be that the psoas creates movement between the lumbar spinal segments.**
- Movement works both muscle, joints and the soft tissue structures that articulates to them (tendons, ligaments, fascia, etc.)
- Movement stretches and can strengthen these soft tissue structures (4).
- Movement promotes circulation (4).
- **The promoted circulation effect due to movement of the lumbar spinal joints through movement of the psoas, creates a pumping action of the nucleus pulposus so that nutrient supply to the intervertebral disc is significantly effected and improved (4).**

Biomechanics and Function of the Psoas in Open Chain and Closed Chain Settings

In order to understand the effects of the Reverse Hyper on the psoas, we must understand the difference between open chain movements and closed chain movements.

Generally when described in text, motions of the spine caused by the psoas are usually only considered in closed chain settings. In the case of the psoas, a closed chain setting is when the foot is planted on the ground. With the foot in contact with the ground, it makes the lower extremities immobile and therefore once motion is initiated the pelvis will move at the hip joint. Any motion created in this setting of the lower extremity in contact with the ground is considered a "closed chain" setting and movement.

In the setting and motion of the Reverse Hyper, the lower extremity and foot is mobile and is not in contact with the ground. This makes it an "open chain" setting and motion for the psoas, due to the fact that the upper spine is a fixed attachment and the lower extremities are mobile and not in contact with the ground. Since this article is focusing on the effects that the Reverse Hyper has on the psoas, the main focus will be to understand the effects the psoas has on the spine in an open chain setting and motion.

Now that it is understood that the Reverse Hyper positions the psoas in an "open chain" setting, we know that it will also create an open chain motion. Below are two different examples to better understand the effects the psoas has on the spine when there is motion in an open chain setting.

Example 1:

An individual is lying supine (face up) on a table. The individual contracts (shortens) the psoas bilaterally, causing the thighs to go into flexion at the hip joint and fixating the spine to the table. This flexion of the thighs will force the pelvis to begin to tilt posteriorly (back) at the lumbosacral joint (where the lumbar vertebrae 5 and the sacrum articulate). The lumbosacral joint only allows for several degrees of motion until the joint reaches its max range of motion. Once the contractual force of the psoas causes the lumbosacral joint to reach its maximal range of motion, the contractual force will continue up into the lumbar spine. When contraction on the psoas reaches the lumbar spine, it will move each lumbar vertebra into flexion relative to the vertebra that it is superior (above) to.

Simplifying Example 1 so that we can understand it for the context of this article: the individual is supine (face up), with the upper spine fixated on the table, creating an open chain setting for the psoas. Thigh flexion at the hip joint occurs due to the contraction of the psoas. The end effect that the psoas contraction has on the spine in this setting and hip flexion motion is that once the contraction reaches the spine, there is a sequential flexion of the lumbar vertebra. *Therefore, in an open chain setting when the psoas shortens and causes thigh flexion at the hip, the effect on the spine is sequential flexion of the lumbar vertebra.*

Example 2 (Reverse Hyper Example):

An individual is lying prone (face down) on a table. The spine is fixated and the lower extremities are mobile and not touching the floor, putting the hips in a flexed position at 90 degrees. The individual contracts (shortens) the gluteals, erector spinae and hamstrings bilaterally, causing the thighs to go into extension at the hip joint. This extension of the thighs will force the pelvis to begin to tilt anteriorly (forward) at the lumbosacral joint (where the lumbar vertebrae 5 and the sacrum articulate). The lumbosacral joint only allows for several degrees of motion until the joint reaches its max range of motion. Once the contractual force of the gluteals, erector spinae and hamstrings causes the lumbosacral joint to reach its maximal range of motion, the contractual force will continue up into the lumbar spine. When contraction reaches the lumbar spine, it will move each lumbar vertebra into extension relative to the vertebra that it is superior (above) to.

Simplifying Example 2 so that we can understand it for the context of this article: the individual is prone (face down), with the upper spine fixated on the table and the lower extremities mobile and bilateral hip flexion at 90 degrees, creating an open chain setting for the psoas. However in this example, instead of the psoas contracting (shortening), it is lengthening due to its antagonists contracting. It should be noted, however, that at the start, the psoas is not in a neutral position, but is in a shortened position. As we learned from Example 1, this shortened position of the psoas will put the lumbar vertebra into slight flexion.

Once the motion starts due to the effect of the gluteals, erector spinae and hamstrings contacting (shortening), the effect this has on the spine in this setting and motion is that once the contraction forces of these muscles reach the spine, there is a sequential extension of the lumbar vertebra due to psoas lengthening. This is due to the biomechanics of how muscles function in tandem, as stated earlier. Therefore, in an open chain setting when the psoas lengthens, the effect on the spine is sequential extension of the lumbar vertebra.

Both examples 1 and 2 are occurring in opposite sequence when an individual performs a correct repetition using the Reverse Hyper. The individual will either start in the same starting position as described in Example 2, or the in ending position described in Example 1, or whichever example is easier for you to understand. At the end of the repetition, the individual once again will either be in the end position described in Example 2 or in the starting position described in Example 1, or whichever example is easier for you to understand.

Of course, it should be noted the main difference that we need to understand is the set-up between Example 1 and 2. In Example 1, the individual is supine (face up) and in Example 2 the individual is prone (face down). However, both are open chain settings for the psoas. This set up is not without purpose. In example 1, the set up is to give the biomechanical advantage to the iliospoas, so that we can understand the muscle's effects on the spine when it is contracting or in a shortened position.

Remember, the focus of this article is to understand the effects the psoas has on the spine. Example 1 shows those effects on the spine when the psoas is in a maximal contracted (shortened) position. The shortened position of the psoas just so happens to be the starting position to perform a Reverse Hyper repetition, with the exception that the individual would be prone (face down) in order to be able to perform a repetition with the Reverse Hyper. By facing the individual prone (face down) on a pad that ends just in front of the hip joint, it will fixate the upper spine while at the same time enabling the lower extremities to be mobile, but starting with at least 90 degrees of hip flexion (shortened psoas position), with the ability to go into even greater hip flexion. This positioning gives full range of motion to the psoas in both flexion and extension while at the same it time takes away its biomechanical advantage against its antagonists.

Now that the differences in set-up for the above examples are understood, it should be noted that those differences in set-ups do not change the effects that the psoas has on the spine. Those effects on the spine being full flexion of the lumbar vertebra in sequence with posterior tilt of the lumbosacral joints when the psoas contracts (shortens) bringing the thighs into hip flexion. When the psoas is lengthened, bringing the thighs into hip extension, due to its antagonist contracting (shortening), extension of the lumbar vertebra in sequence with anterior tilt of the lumbosacral joints is the effect on the spine. These two motions are performed in sequence when an individual is performing a repetition with correct form on the Reverse Hyper. Therefore, the effects that the psoas has on the spine, as described above, are the effects that the reverse hyper has on the spine as well. So we are able to understand the Reverse Hyper's effects on the spine through understand the psoas's effects on the spine.

Do Not Get Distracted By Flexion or Extension of the Lumbar Spine and Who Cares About Traction?

It is easy to get distracted by exactly what the effects are on the spine via the psoas when performing the Reverse Hyper. I was for quite sometime, and I am sure many reading this article will be as well. It is very hard to digest all the information provided here, and I honestly believe it can distract us from the main point that really matters, in my opinion. The main point that I hope readers will understand after reading this has nothing to do with biomechanics, anatomy, etc. All those are needed for me to make my case for this article, but as stated earlier, all those facts and examples easily distract us.

The main point to understand is that the Reverse Hyper creates movement within the lumbar spine. And that:

- Movement works both muscles, joints and the soft tissue structures that articulates to them (tendons, ligaments, fascia, etc.)
- Movement stretches and can strengthen these soft tissue structures (4).
- Movement promotes circulation (4).
- The promoted circulation effect due to movement of the lumbar spinal joints through movement of the psoas, creates a pumping action of the nucleus pulposus so that nutrient supply to the intervertebral disc is significantly effected and improved (4).

Traction is passive. There is no movement. We get into a machine or use a device and it lengthens our spine. How much effect can traction have on the spine and intervertebral discs with no movement present? It has to be minimal at best. All the characteristics stated above that occur with movement are not present when an individual uses a traction device. Do not get me wrong. *In the correct setting, traction can be a very useful modality.*

However, we cannot compare a traction only device to the reverse hyper for obvious reasons.

Biomechanics of the Psoas's Antagonists When Performing the Reverse Hyper

The Reverse Hyper example (Example 2), which was described in the previous section, enables us to understand the open chain setting of the Reverse Hyper and its effects on the psoas. Since this article deals with the Reverse Hyper's effects on the psoas, the effects the reverse hyper has on the psoas's antagonist should be at least mentioned. The effects the reverse hyper has on the psoas's antagonists will in turn have an effect on the psoas.

Simply stated, the reverse hyper is a movement in a setting (open chain) which isolates the psoas's antagonists (gluteals, erector spinae and hamstrings) in a concentric contraction. The concentric contraction does not just strengthen the antagonist muscles. The antagonists muscles concentric contraction will force the psoas to be inhibited (forced to relax) via the law of reciprocal inhibition. While the psoas is relaxed, due to reciprocal inhibition, the motion and setting of the Reverse Hyper will also cause it to lengthen.

Based on what we know, we can clearly state that Reverse Hyper is the most efficient and effective way to exercise the psoas's antagonists. The result of this movement will have a positive effect on the psoas due to the fact that the exercise allows for the individual to not only relax and lengthen the psoas, but strengthen its antagonist muscles at the same time.

The Reverse Hyper: Therapeutic Exercise for Individuals with Low Back Pain

From our understanding of biomechanics and muscular function, we understand that in Example 2 (the Reverse Hyper example), the distal attachment of the psoas is being taken away from its attachments at the thoracic and lumbar spine. This is the case, because as we know muscles function in tandem, and as the psoas's antagonists contract (shorten), the psoas is forced to relax to enable extension at the hip joint (joint action), which in term lengthens the psoas. This is described in further detail in the above section.

We know through Dr. Travell's work that generally individuals who have low back pain will have some type of dysfunction with the psoas muscle and that treating this dysfunction should be a focus for successful treatment of their low back pain. Generally this dysfunction is that the psoas muscle is in a contracted, shortened and restricted position. Understanding this enables us to easily come to the conclusion that successful treatment of the psoas would take it out of its contracted, shortened and restricted state. The focus of treatment then would be to lengthen fibers of the psoas. For the purpose of this article, it should be reiterated, that at the end of contractual repetition of the Reverse Hyper, the psoas fibers are lengthened.

Understanding that the psoas is prone to this contracted and shortened position due to the majority of its fibers being slow twitch fibers, compounded with the fact that the majority of individuals spend most of their day in hip flexion (being seated, sleeping in the fetal position, etc.), it is easy to understand now both how and why the psoas becomes shortened. Just think about what you do as an example, and the amount of time that you are seated (hip flexion position) throughout the day. For most of us it is a large majority of our day.

After we are seated (hip flexion position) for a prolonged period of time, this causes the psoas to be shortened. Generally, low back pain is not felt just yet. Once the individual stands up, and lengthens the attachment points of the psoas (spine and femur), but the psoas itself remains short and restricted, the resulting action will be the pulling of the thoracic lumbar spine forward and down. Dr. Travell understood this concept and her understanding enabled her to convey the message and conclude that treating low back pain often requires successfully treating the psoas.

Understanding Dr. Travell's concept enables us to understand the therapeutic effects the reverse hyper has on the spine by effecting the psoas. The Reverse Hyper, however, does not treat the psoas, it effects the psoas. The motion of the Reverse Hyper is going to lengthen the psoas by forcing its antagonist muscles to contract. The movement created by the psoas lengthening is going to transmit movement in the lumbar spine. The movement transmitted into the lumbar spine is going to increase circulation by creating a pumping action that will effect and improve the nutrient supply to the intervertebral discs. Improved circulation and nutrient supply to the intervertebral discs can be clearly viewed as a therapeutic effect.

John Quint.

Reverse Hypers ™
By Louie Simmons

During large and small workouts, reverse hypers are always performed. Most consider them as a strength building exercise. While they do build extreme strength in the lower back, hips and hamstrings, it was first used to save the author and his long extensive career. Having a broken 5th lumbar vertebrae in 1973 that no one had a solution to repair, the author was forced to find his own way to continue his strength career. Every exercise he tried produced pain in the lower back. There was not one that didn't cause pain. No side bends, no back raises; a large part of his training that was too painful to do. When he exerted pressure on the ankles to raise the back, the pain was too much to bear. He could not find a cure.

One day while sitting in silence, emptying his mind it came to him. What if he reversed the action of the exercise by placing a platform on the safety pins of a power rack high enough to support the upper body, while hanging the legs off the support and not allowing the feet to touch the floor? The author raised his legs while keeping them straight to the rear concentrically as he arched the upper body and raised the legs, but not to a hyperextension position. After a few reps, no pain and he even felt a pumping sensation in the low back S1. By allowing the legs to swing, first by lowering them eccentrically, then forcing them under the platform and rounding the lower back, he gained much needed range of motion.

How was it possible that by reversing the action it relieved his back pain? When the torso was laying on the platform it caused a much higher Internal Abdominal Pressure (IAP) that results in pressure on the spine and intervertebral discs. This can be verified by the research by V.P. Sazonov (1985) as showed in V.M. *Zatsiorsky's* book *Science and Practice of Strength Training.*

Placing a pad under the abdomen will increase the IAP, which lessens the pressure on the discs. A weightlifting belt's primary use is to increase IAP to provide support against spinal deformation. Some muscles of the lumbar spine that lay underneath the large spinal erectors, like the epaxial muscles and the interspinales that connect the transverse processes of the vertebrae, are very difficult to work with normal exercises. Two methods are to stand with your back against a wall and press your lower back into the wall. If that is too difficult, try the exercise by laying face up and force the lower back into the table.

With the Reverse Hyper, it can be easy to lay on the machine as normal, place toes against plates and force the plates under the pad. It requires one to exert great pressure with the abdomen, that greatly increases IAP and builds all the underlaying muscles, tendons, ligaments and all soft tissues of the lower back. A person capable of squatting 500 pounds requires a total volume of 6,000 pounds. The Reverse Hyper poundage would be roughly 24,000 pounds, which shows how important reverse hypers are to the range of motion gain in the hamstrings and lower back.

Feet, Ankle, Knee and Hip Recovery

A simple pulling sled can eliminate or better yet prevent injuries of the hips, knee, feet, and ankles. By power walking a specific distance for your sport, it will build stronger feet, a problem for many track athletes. There is very little eccentric force while pulling a sled and it develops

the muscles that surround the joints. By attaching a belt around the waist and connecting a sled strap to it, pull the sled with long strides, touching the heel first and pull immediately causing the hamstrings, glutes and hip muscles to be developed. This action protects the joints.

Strong muscles are needed for joint protection. Forward, backwards and sideways must be done. The knee is stabilized by the calves below and the hamstrings above on each side. The sled work builds not only strong calves and hamstrings, but also the hips and glutes to protect the joints.

The author made an 821-pound squat, then suffered a complete rapture of the patellar tendon and recovered to squat 920 pounds at more than 50-years old, which ranked him 3rd in the world rankings that year. This has been done several times.

The greatest result: Jim Hoskinson's best contest squat was 774 pounds after repairing both patellar tendons and both quadriceps tendons. His rehab was to pull a sled one mile a day for five months and he squatted 500 pounds after nine months. He squatted 890 pounds after fully recovering. He squatted 1,107 pounds officially. All by sled walking.

Shoulder Rehab

The author also had a shoulder replacement. Within seven days he was using a broom stick to bench to his chest. Then, he started benching with a vibrating bar that had Kettlebells hung off it with rubber bands to cause more vibration. This resulted in a 300-pound benchpress in three months and he was able to bench press 505 pounds at 63-years-old.

These methods are proven to be very effective to first prehab or eliminate serious injuries or to rehab allowing you to fully recover and return to your sport. Start back slow and use an ART therapist to help you gain full range of motion in the muscles that surround the joint injury. Westside is very injury free because of these methods.

I hope I have given some applicable ideas. Two heads are better than one, so get together with other coaches and don't forget to get feedback from your athletes. I have found coaches' ideas and athletes' ideas differ significantly. Don't do the same small workouts over and over; they must be rotated constantly to avoid staleness. Workouts need to be made more difficult from year to year. A senior should not repeat what he did as a junior let alone as a freshman. A college career is in fact a multi-year training system, which is an Olympic cycle for some. It must be more and more satisfying and challenging to increase the sports performance of athletes.

At all times there must be some type of recovery and restoration participation by the athlete. The coach must properly control all aspects of his athletes training, technical, specific and general exercises, because without recovery all will fail.

The author would like the reader to review the restoration methods that kept the Westside machine going strong for more than 40 years. They are extensive—some quite common while others are almost unheard of. The author will tell you that these therapists are at the top of their field and have contributed much to his success as well as the entire Westside Club, and Westside certified gyms throughout the world.

Examples and Views from Strength Coaches Around the World
By Jon Davis, Owner and founder of Davis Training Systems

My experience training track athletes started about three years ago with a high school female hurdler who couldn't qualify for states. She worked only on technique for three years with her track coach and took three-tenths off her time. In six weeks, we decreased her hurdle time three-tenths and she qualified for states, giving her the opportunity to get a partial scholarship to FSU. Since then we have trained hurdlers, 100 m and 200 m sprinters.

My experience working with track athletes has proven that coaches rely heavily on genetics and nothing else. Genetics are useless if you are hurt. Many of the issues include improper warm-up protocols, strength training programs that are made up on the spot, weight training programs that are not specific to the individuals events, no real rehab program except rest and lack of education on how to make sprinters faster. Pre-season training begins with athletes jogging or running hills at a certain percentage. Why not get in the weight room? Instead, they use a vertimax and squats are performed on bosu balls, ad/ab squeezes with a yoga ball, leg press, and FMS just to name a few things that are being performed. This is a recipe for disaster.

I started training Curtis Mitchell, a 200-meter professional sprinter for Adidas, in July of 2012. Curt was coming off of injuries that kept him off the USA track team along with trying to qualify for the Olympics. His injuries ranged from a pulled hamstring, tendinitis, knee pain, ankle injury, calf pain, and IT band syndrome. We started slow and I based training off of a four-year plan, with the Olympics being the actual focus point. This past year the goals were to medal at World Championships, stay injury free and renew his contract.

We had Curt start with performing high rep leg curls and extensions. We fixed imbalances with sled dragging and reverse hyperextensions. He was so weak in his lower back, that he could barely do 50 pounds with a short strap for six to eight reps. We also used the fascial abrasive technique tool and fascial stretching.

We increased his work capacity, along with increasing all facets of strength. Reverse Hypers were performed four times per week. Also in the program were glute-ham raises, work on the inverse leg curl machine, and walks in the belt squat for time. Sled dragging was done two to four times per week. We used specific exercises for the start and the transition off the curve. Examples would be the power runner with bands and side bends with unbalanced weight. Jumps that we used were knee jumps, box jumps from foam and seated box jumps. Naturally, when Curt runs he prides himself in finishing the last 100, so we did not do a lot of multi jumps, but we will use these for the upcoming Olympics. We did exercises for time like dead lifts, the power runner with band tension, and sled drags.

We performed Max effort lifts ranging from one to six reps. Max effort lifts that we had him perform were front squats, belt squats, and the conventional deadlift from a deficit. His personal best is 500 pounds at a bodyweight of 178 pounds. Dynamic effort work was lower in percentages and weighted jumps were done.

When he first came to us, he said he was in great shape and that he can jump onto a 50-inch box. I laughed to myself because we have high school athletes of all sports that can do 50 plus. Towards the end of his training cycle before he left for Europe he was able to jump onto a 50-inch box with one leg. This was not planned and we were actually performing dynamic effort bench presses that day when Curt asked about one-legged box jumps and what was the highest that was performed in our gym. I told him 46 inches with one leg by Dartmouth wide receiver, Robbie Anthony. Curt said he could easily beat that and in our gym it is all about proving it, not talking about it. Let's just say he beat the record that day at 50 inches with one leg.

Perception of how good or how great you can be actually relies on how good someone believes in you and how you believe in yourself. All while "Experts" told Curt what he was doing was wrong, how lifting heavy weights will get him hurt and also how he was too lean at 3.4 percent body fat too early in the season. After only training with us for seven months, Curt set a personal best in the 200 meter and stayed injury free. He won a bronze medal, in dramatic fashion at the 2013 World Championships in Moscow, Russia, coming back from 7th place to finish 3rd against Usain Bolt and Warren Weir. This process with traveling overseas and not having a weight room made things very challenging at times, so bodyweight exercises with bands had to be used. Also, during this time he was training, his contract was being cut because he could not run due to injuries the previous two years. After training and setting a personal best, he was paid and he renewed his contract, something we take great pride helping athletes do.

You hear about track athletes being injured and that the next year they cannot qualify. This has to do with not educating athletes on how they should really be training. For example, to an athlete who boxes to get in shape, an athlete who has a list of injuries, but is performing Olympic lifts and hurdle jumps, by doing those exercises the weaknesses are so exposed. Why isn't anyone concerned about how the sprinter absorbs force? Why is everyone so worried about the glitz and glamour? The hurdle jumps they are already good at and the Olympic lifts don't build their base.

You have to look at what an athlete needs and look at what he does and how he moves and design a program to make him/her better. To me and after all my conversations with Louie, at the end of the day it shouldn't be too difficult to understand what most track athletes need. After all, they run in a straight line and turn left! Too often, people get caught up in emotions when training athletes. In the past six years, I have gotten emails and phone calls about what I should be doing with an athlete, and it's all wrong! Too many people milk their careers as coaches saying things like we don't do that because we don't train power lifters. Well, we have something in common. Neither do I! You have to learn to apply what you know in order to help an athlete achieve success and there is always a better way. I remember talking to Laura Phelps Sweatt, and she told me she would always be a student, as well as I am. Every day you learn from your athletes and what they go through mentally and physically. Sometimes what you have on paper cannot be done that day, due to the outside stressors of life. I think this gets lost at the upper levels at times; track athletes should not be getting injured as much as they do. It starts with proper training, planning of events and recovery.

Jon Davis
Owner and founder of Davis Training Systems
www.DavisTS.com; 407-331-3278

A Better Approach to Spinal Health Recovery and Performance
By D. R. Brian, Atlas Family Health Center

Louis Simmons and the Westside athletes have been using the services of Dr. Neidenthal for the past ten years. In addition to being a chiropractor, Dr. Neidenthal utilizes cutting edge, state-of-the-art upper cervical techniques and procedures. The Upper Cervical "Atlas" procedure offers patients a gentle and precise treatment for the correction of upper cervical subluxations.

The word "subluxation" comes from the Latin words meaning "to dislocate" (luxare) and "somewhat or slightly" (sub). A subluxation means a slight dislocation (misalignment) or biomechanical malfunctioning of the vertebral joints of the spine. These disturbances irritate nerve roots that branch off from the spinal cord and pass between each of the vertebrae. These irritations not only cause pain and dysfunction in muscle, lymphatic and organ tissue, but also produce neurologic imbalances in the normal body processes.

The Uniqueness of an Atlas Subluxation

Subluxation is a very common problem and may occur as a result of nominal trauma to an individual's head, neck or body. The Atlas is the first cervical vertebrae of the spine (C1). It is the vertebra that solely supports the head. Along with the Axis (C2) the Atlas provides the freely moving motions between the spine and the skull.

An Atlas subluxation often disrupts the nervous system and the communications between our brain and our body. The subluxation will cause a postural head tilt and unbalanced postural muscle tone that can begin to twist the spine into abnormal curves. The resulting lack of spinal center of gravity will begin weakening discs and can cause secondary nerve decline in other areas of the body. Every part of the body is influenced by spinal activity and alignment. In fact, 90 percent of the stimulation and nutrition to the brain is generated by the movement of the spine. When any small part in the spinal chain deviates from norm, gravity's effects are multiplied. Negative effects such as poor posture, muscle strain, disc problems, arthritis, pinched nerves and even disease result from posture that is a product of poor spinal health. Therefore, it is critical that all aspects of the spine are in place, intact, and capable of bearing the responsibility for the functioning of the rest of the body.

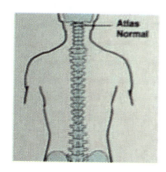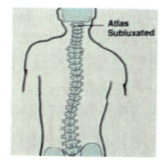

At Atlas Family Health Center, Dr. Neidenthal uses three-dimensional digital x-rays to obtain a clear image of your spine and a computer analysis of these x-rays provide the most accurate assessment the spinal misalignment. This can only be obtained by looking from all three dimensions, as shown by the photo below.

Three-Dimensional X-ray Series

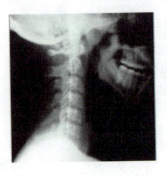 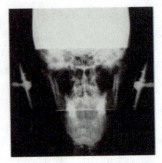 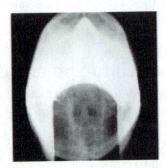

Precision X-ray Analysis

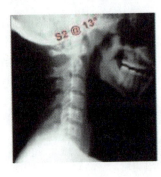 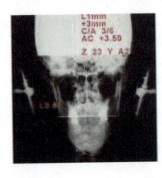 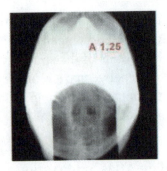

The x-rays show the doctor how severe the misalignment may be and forms basis of the tailored treatment each patient receives at Atlas Family Health Center using the Advanced Orthogonal protocol.

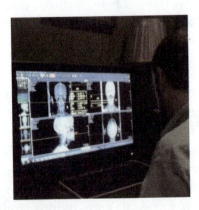

Following the determination of the precise misalignment the doctor will make a very specific adjustment based on the measurements taken from the x-rays. This is administered with an Advanced Orthogonal adjusting instrument through a painless and precise sound wave adjustment. Advanced Orthogonal sound wave adjusting minimizes patient discomfort while maximizing the accuracy of spinal correction.

Conclusion

With the increased accuracy of Upper Cervical Chiropractic, we have higher expectations for correcting your subluxations. The goal for spinal care should be to have your spine HOLD its own proper alignment for periods of time and require less adjusting. This is the difference between corrective care and simply relief care. Corrective care of our patients is the optimum goal of Atlas Family Health Center. For more information about how our services can help you achieve your health goals email drbrian@atlasfamilyhealthcenter.com or call 614-487-1905.

Pain Described
By Jerome Rerucha, Chiropractor

One of the most important considerations in physical training is to first remain injury free or in the event of prior injury, to promote recovery so the individual can maintain training. This is true when working with a novice, a collegiate athlete, a professional competitive athlete, a fitness enthusiasts or even the general public trying to maintain an active lifestyle. Whatever your role-- a personal trainer, strength and conditioning coach or clinician--pain and injury is a component that needs to be understood.

Pain is categorized as either acute (generally from a known cause or immediate trauma leading to injury) or chronic (long lasting). There are many subcategories or diagnoses under each of these main categories. We may feel the pain in our toes when we stub them, however the recognition, interpretation, and reaction to the pain occurs in the brain; not at the symptomatic area.

Awareness of pain happens when sensory neurons (special nerves throughout the body) react to pressure, vibration, trauma, heat, cold, and other stimuli. These neurons also respond to prostaglandins, histamine, and other chemicals released by injured or inflamed body tissue. The level of the sensation depends upon the strength of the stimulus and the total health (or lack thereof) of the body. When sensory neurons are stimulated, the nerves fire sending off messages that travel along the nervous system to the brain. Then, the pain information is rapidly evaluated, and sensations are interpreted. This complex reaction in the communication systems of the body protects us when there is a stressor (danger is a lil intense); when the protection due to the stress has passed, the brain is told to turn off the feeling of pain. If there is a problem in the communication system of the body; all of the neurological, chemical and emotional communication systems may not be able to tell the pain to stop.

Acute pain makes you aware of many problems in the body from torn ligaments to gallbladder attacks. At low levels, pain can motivate you to rest the injured area so that tissues can be repaired and additional damage can be prevented. Acute pain lets out a three-alarm warning when you accidentally put your hand on a hot stove or when it forces you to rest a sprained ankle. Frequently, traumatic pain is dealt with properly because the cause of trauma can be accurately identified and eliminated at which time the natural healing of the body can begin. Rest, Ice, Compression, and Elevation is commonly used effectively. For faster healing cold laser therapy, chiropractic care, acupuncture, Rolfing, soft tissue and other modalities can speed healing significantly and provide long term correction from some of the trauma that was encountered to the nervous system, skeletal system, fascia and muscles. Rehabilitation is very beneficial once the body can handle the excess physical stress of exercise.

Not all pain serves a useful function. While acute pain can alert us to a problem that needs immediate attention, in some cases pain lasts long after an injured area has healed. In other instances, pain may be in the form of a recurring backache, migraines (or other types of headaches), arthritis, and other disorders. This is referred to as chronic pain. Chronic pain may be a dull ache, sharp, stabbing, radiating, throbbing pain or any combination of these that seem to never subside or it may be experienced during certain times of the day and is lasting for more than six months. Pain may be localized at the site of an injury, or "referred" to another part of the body. Chronic pain may occur after a physical injury or surgery and continues after the normal healing period. Chronic pain can accompany many disease conditions such as fibromyalgia, headaches, neuropathy, depression, PMS, post-surgical pain syndrome, the accumulation of training stresses and many others. Chronic pain is a complex condition with a variety of causes. Remember, pain is only interpreted by the nervous system and identified by the brain. When pain persists, there is a lot of attention placed on the area of symptomatology, in a variety of ways depending on the type of specialist seen. Little effort is directed toward the retraining of lower motor neurons in order to ultimately change upper motor neuron activity in the brain, which inhibits the reflex pathways and Type C fibers that have become incorrectly programmed.

"Neuroplasticity" is a modern term to describe the remodeling of brain patterning; this includes pain. Neuroplasticity, also known as brain plasticity, referring to changes in the neural pathways and synapses that affect changes in behavior, environment and neural processes, as well as the changes resulting from bodily injury. Neuroplasticity has replaced the formerly-held position that the brain is a physiologically static organ, and explores how and in which ways the brain changes throughout life based upon what you do; this can be regenerative or degenerative.

Neuroplasticity occurs on a variety of levels, ranging from cellular changes due to learning, to large-scale changes involved in cortical remapping in response to injury. The role of neuroplasticity is widely recognized in healthy development, learning, memory, and recovery from brain damage; but I also recognize the correlation with elite fitness; not just clinical pathology.

During most of the 20th century, the consensus among neuroscientists was that brain structure is relatively immutable after a critical period during early childhood. This belief has been changed by findings revealing that many aspects of the brain remain plastic even into adulthood. Decades of research have now shown that substantial changes occur in the lowest neocortical processing areas, and that these changes can profoundly alter the pattern of neuronal activation in response to experience. This is why you can train your body to be strong, which can only happen after your nervous system is trained to be strong, within those pathways. This also applies to pain and visceral patterns. Neuroscientific research indicates that experience can actually change both the brain's physical structure (anatomy) and functional organization (physiology). Neuroscientists are currently engaged in a reconciliation of critical period studies demonstrating the immutability of the brain after development with the more recent research showing how the brain can, and does, change throughout life. Later on in this paper a brief explanation of patterning will be described. Many of you who are strong and injury free will say "I already do that" and that is not a coincidence.

Chronic pain is one of the most costly conditions in North America. Although pain is a major problem in this country, it is not treated compassionately or efficiently, and it is not just pain that is the problem. The side effects of chronic pain illnesses caused by a sedentary lifestyle, seclusion and depression and, in some cases, addiction to pain killers can be just as devastating as the pain itself. The estimated costs of direct medical expenses, lost income, lost productivity, compensation payments, and legal charges, are approximately *$90 billion a year.* 48 million Americans suffer from chronic pain. Over 21 million Americans routinely take prescription painkillers and also spend $3 billion on over the counter analgesics.

- More than 13 million Americans cannot perform routine activities because of pain.

- As many as 45 million Americans have chronic, severe headaches that can be disabling.

- Arthritis pain affects more than 40 million Americans each year.

- The majority of patients in intermediate or advanced stages of cancer suffer moderate to severe pain. More than 1.2 million new cases of cancer are diagnosed each year in the United States, and more than 550,000 people die from the disease.

- Fourteen percent of employees take time off from work because of pain.

- According to the National Institutes of Health (Harris et al. 1999), lower back pain is one of the most significant health problems in the United States, with back pain being the most frequent cause of physical impairment in people younger than 45 years of age: 65 to 80 percent of all people have back pain at some time in their life.

Although there are numerous types of injuries caused by countless circumstances, affecting the general public and athletes alike, we will concentrate on the #1 neuro-musculoskeletal injury in the world: back pain. The same principles apply when addressing any "systemic" weakness, asymmetry, inflexibility or improper functional (neurological) movement.

Back pain is the number one musculoskeletal problem in the world and the second most common reason for all visits to the doctors' office (#1 reason for the orthopedist). Low back pain primarily effects adults, ages 35 to 55, but may occur in children and adolescence. Approximately 75 percent of people in developed countries will experience low back pain at some time in their lives. The annual prevalence of low back pain in the U.S. is 15 percent to 20 percent of the population. Back pain is the second leading cause of absenteeism from work, after the common cold, and accounts for 15 percent of sick leaves. Back injuries cause 100 million lost days of work annually, and is the most costly for employers. Approximately one percent of the U.S. population is chronically disabled due to back problems and another one percent is temporarily disabled.

Signs and symptoms are centralized in the low back area and vary dependent upon the severity of the injury. Acute or chronic back pain symptoms can give indications as to the cause of the pain.

Many common symptoms are:
1. Paraspinal muscle spasms
2. Possible radiation of pain to the buttocks and into the lower extremities (sciatica)
3. Limited range of motion
4. Pain aggravated by motion and alleviated by rest
5. Severe pain leading to change in posture

Risk factors include:
1. More common in men than women
2. Common in those with high labor intensive jobs with a lot of repetitive bending

3. Obesity
4. Anatomical short leg (causing pelvic unleveling and spinal torqueing)
5. Trauma such as fractures, herniated discs, ligament sprain, muscle strain
6. Non-traumatic causes such as degenerative disc disease, inflammatory arthritis
7. Osteoporosis
8. Spondylolisthesis
9. Facet Syndrome
10. Sacral misalignments
11. Lumbar subluxations
12. Spinal Stenosis
13. Muscle imbalances
14. Visceral conditions (female cycle, colon, prostate, kidney, bladder)
15. Smoking

There are many causes of low back pain, from predisposed risk factors to acute injuries. These conditions can be divided into the broad categories of traumatic and non-traumatic.

Traumatic
- Micro traumas (jogging on hard surfaces, etc.)
- Macro traumas (car accident, impact traumas)
- Soft tissue sprain (ligaments), strain (muscular)
- Fractures
- Subluxations and dislocations
- Herniated discs
- Overexertion, fatigue (improper lifting)

Non-traumatic
- Arthritis
- Degenerative disc disease
- Side effects from medication (cholesterol lowering drugs)
- Sedentary life style
- Spinal structural imbalances (poor posture)

Low back pain can have many variables. Although, many individuals complain of localized symptoms, a successful program takes into account the health of the entire neuro-musculoskeletal-fascial system. Identifying weaknesses are important; however exercise or stretching isolated areas has proven to be ineffective, especially for long term relief. The body works together as a unit. Training the core strength of the body to achieve the ideal neutral posture, proper intersegmental motion, activating the nervous system and muscles synergistically to perform flexible, symmetrical functional movement creating a strong, healthy and pain free structure is the most effective method to reduce the incidence of low back pain (or any other injury) and also for those working for optimum performance.

Research has shown that those who suffer from back pain have a common imbalance throughout the musculoskeletal system. A normal spine has an ideal center of gravity from head carriage to the center of gravity over the pelvis. When people have a forward head tilt; for every one inch forward the head is held, there is a 100 percent increase in the weight of the head.

An article in *Spine,* the most renowned orthopedic medical journal in the world (September 15, 2005; 30 (18): 2024-9) which said "The impact of positive sagittal balance in adult spinal deformity," explains this concept accurately. The study used lateral full spine x-rays and measured overall spinal alignment with reference points from the center of the 7th cervical vertebra and the posterior-superior corner of the 1st sacral segment. A plumb line was then used to determine center of gravity and measure overall displacement and how this directly related to patients severity of symptoms of pain and overall decrease in health by also using (the standard form), the SF 36. They determined:

1. "All measures of health status showed significantly poorer scores as the C7 plumb line deviation increased (forward head carriage / body)."

2. "There was a high degree of correlation between positive sagittal balance and adverse health status scores, for physical health composite score and pain domain."

3. "There was clear evidence of increased pain and decreased function as the magnitude of positive sagittal balance (forward head carriage / body) increased."

This study shows that although even mildly positive sagittal balance is somewhat detrimental, severity of symptoms increases in a linear fashion with progressive sagittal imbalance (forward head carriage) per every 1 mm."

In addition to anterior head carriage, the pelvis commonly becomes "tipped" forward (referred to as lower cross syndrome) which creates further abnormal biomechanics and pressure and eventually leads to increased stress to the facets, injuries to the discs, vertebrae, ligaments and muscle imbalances. These mechanical stresses create pain signals throughout the nervous system and lock in a pattern of back pain (or injury to any area due to involvement throughout facial planes).

Poor daily habits promote an unhealthy lifestyle pattern beginning in childhood and continuing throughout the adult years. The flexor muscles of the body are overworked and the extensor muscles are severely under used. This cycle is created by young children in school sitting for extended periods during the growth and formative years. Children are not as active as in previous generations, relying on television and video games rather than proprioceptive dynamic activities.

In early adulthood we are "flexor conditioned." Many spend long hours sitting in the college classroom or at the desk jobs of corporate America. We have a labor force that performs repetitive bending (flexion) activities for many hours every day and who spend extended periods of time sitting in cars, commuting while doing nothing to offset this imbalanced lifestyle and promote proper health or recovery from injury. The physical imbalances are amplified by chemical imbalances of increased sugar/carbohydrates, energy drinks, supplements loaded with high fructose corn syrup, and improper ratios of essential fatty acids (ideal EFA 1.5: AA 1 ratio) all amplifying systemic inflammation. Further load the body up with artificial sweeteners (sucralose causes pain and stiffness and aspartame is a documented neurotoxin) and you have a physical and chemical crystal ball for pain, suffering and reoccurring injury.

Many patients/athletes report their acute injury was caused by a sneeze, or "throwing their back out tying their shoe" or "picking up a pencil from the floor." Although the injury effects are real and severe, taking a history and proper (functional) examination reveals many precipitating stresses and physical imbalances that led to the weakened condition which created the buckling injury. Even in the case of true acute injuries, such as car accidents and impact trauma, the focus of restoring spine stabilizing patterns to the whole musculoskeletal and nervous system is necessary for full, long-term recovery.

Poor biomechanics and repetitive stress also place an abnormal load on the muscles and the spine that leads to injury. Remember it is the muscles that stabilize and protect the spine and the nervous system (all synergistically working together) that drives proper communication. The spinal stabilizer muscles require:

1. Endurance to withstand the task of standing for hours and performing labor intensive, daily and athletic duties.
2. Strength to stabilize the core of the musculoskeletal system.
3. Flexibility to perform dynamic motion.
4. Balance to properly displace stress throughout the musculoskeletal system in an ideal weight bearing position
5. Increase in circulation accelerates tissue regeneration and recovery by bringing in nutrients and taking away metabolic by products.

A multidimensional evaluation and progressive program is optimum for any individual. For the purpose of this publication, however, we will only include some important points. Ideally each individual needs to be evaluated and a specific plan designed depending on asymmetry, injury or injuries involved.

Solutions: "If it is good for a strong person, it is good for a weak person. You just have to decrease the intensity so it is appropriate for the individual."

The body is designed to move to perform the normal activities of daily living. Elite athletes require more strength, endurance, balance, flexibility, mitochondrial output of ATP than the average person. Proper structural alignment is required to perform a task successfully and injury free. The average individual can perform normal daily activities with physical functional measurements far below those of the elite athlete. If either individual is physically unprepared (over time), the weakness will create an acute and possibly a chronic injury pattern.

Initially, in my professional career I was in the strength-coaching field where I gained valuable experience that gave me indispensable insight as I continued my education as a clinician. I have extensive background training both novice and elite athletes in a variety of sports and I became a competitive power lifter for 14 years. Understanding different body types, designing individual and team programs for specific physiological outcomes has helped me, as a clinician, to provide any necessary variable to help competitive athletes or the general public. Every day in practice or as I lecture to other clinicians, I use my extensive background in exercise physiology and the strength field.

Clinicians receive an extensive education in the basic sciences, which enables them to diagnose, within the scope of their license, and to use tools, such as x-ray, MRI, the knowledge to perform ortho/neuro exams and the like and to interpret clinical findings. All clinical exams are neutral exams, out of gravity. Some may want to claim that ortho/neuro tests are functional and that they are beneficial to a person with a physical injury. These exams are completely worthless when evaluating an uninjured individual and therefore cannot provide the benefit of being able to measure progress or to prevent a problem, in the first place, if you cannot detect predispositions to an injury.

Once a detailed analysis has been completed, as a clinician, it is your responsibility to "manage" the patient and to design a program for recovery. Some clinicians merely concentrate on and "manage" just the diagnosis, overlooking many possible contributing factors. Or minimally, some clinicians just "manage" the symptoms, often times achieving only a temporary solution to the overall condition. The majority of care relies on passive treatment applications: lying on a table to get adjusted, Rolfed, massaged, acupuncture or being hooked up to a variety of electrical stimulation devices, ice, heat, take this medication or a surgery is performed. I could write a book on patient success and the benefits and life changing results from many of these passive modalities that are appropriate and effective for treatment. There is no substitute for proper chiropractic adjustments for injured individuals or athletes training for peak performance with absolutely no injuries. The point to be made is this: passive treatment is only as good as the strength of the organism, injured areas have a compromised metabolism at the mitochondrial level. Many patients only want passive care and are unwilling participate in progressive activity for full recovery or better yet be proactive to prevent the predisposition in the first place. I have taught thousands of practitioners, from a variety of health specialties, over the years and the reality is many clinicians have "zero" experience or knowledge of movement let alone the knowledge of safe, effective exercises and stretches and other modalities to help correct the many problems seen by clinicians.

I compliment practitioners for the great work they currently perform; however, a great advancement for the future of any medical care is for clinicians to be aware of the benefits provided by the strength and conditioning industry and to integrate programs into their current services. There is a limit to the success from passive care. Without the knowledge of what can be achieved when integrating these various modalities of treatment, the next step (activation of proper movement) in the progression of treatment will not be achieved.

Strength and conditioning coaches and personal training have little to no experience in managing clients with a medical diagnosis. However, many are experts in movement and activation and teach proper exercise technique. For clinicians to have knowledge of strength, flexibility training, Kettlebells, bodyweight exercises, Olympic lifting, etc., would be invaluable in evaluating the injured patient.

Time and time again for every millimeter of flexibility improvement (to promote symmetry) and every small increment of strength that is gained, there is a linear progression of improvement even in the many individuals with chronic conditions. These positive results are greatly amplified when combining specific adjustments, low level laser therapy, soft tissue work or a wide variety of therapeutic options. When you have had the opportunity to work extensively on both average patients as well as elite athletes, it is amazing how physically incapable people become; being unable to even walk up stairs or get up off the floor unassisted. When entire professions are incapable of identifying improper functional movement and these imbalances and asymmetries are not addressed for a long period of time, they inevitably will manifest into chronic degenerative pathologies; even with common proper passive treatments being performed.

There are many beneficial strength exercises and rehabilitation variables. Let us focus on the pelvis and the importance of that center mass and how it applies—whether you are picking up a sack of groceries or you are an all pro offensive lineman—your center strength and function matters; and it effects the entire organism. An example of combining information between my personal and professional strength and conditioning career and clinical career is the use of the Reverse Hyper™ to produce significant physical improvement in those with debilitating conditions as well as use for elite athletic performance. I was first made aware of reverse hyperextension in the early 1990s. I was already competing at the national level and saw an article written by Louie Simmons in *Powerlifting USA*. The information made sense. Our gym got one and I have used it ever since. Already being a nationally ranked strength athlete, the first workout with the Reverse Hyper proved that all the good I was already doing did not achieve the results the Reverse Hyper did. Since that time it has become a standard part of all my training and treatment programs. It is an incredibly safe exercise in the hands of a qualified practitioner or strength and conditioning instructor. I have had severe pain patients with lumbar fusions and herniations perform the exercise achieving long term clinical success. While filming the lumbar –pelvic area with Digital Motion X-Ray using the Reverse Hyper, patients and clinicians can see what is happening at the spinal level, in real time, with these significant injuries and chronic post-surgical pain patients. These examples can be seen on my YouTube page on my website www.performancechirowellness.com.

I have used this exercise with many people with similar histories and have numerous testimonials about how it literally changed their life. The Reverse Hyper is something individuals can continue to use for themselves, without the need to rely on another person; self-empowerment is important for any long term success. As beneficial as this has proven to be, it amazes me how many personal trainers, strength coaches and self-proclaimed serious lifters / bodybuilders have never even heard of the Reverse Hyper and will try to defend what they do as working better. The explanation and x-ray graphics of the exercise speak for themselves, but the uniqueness of the exercises can only be experienced by using the Reverse Hyper machine itself (not re-creating the movement on an exercise ball or countertop and definitely not a hyperextension exercise). By placing appropriate resistance for the individual on the Reverse Hyper and performing the motion within the patient's initial capabilities, the clinical and performance potential becomes apparent.

The information below may benefit you in further understanding the injury process and some additional modes of treatment.

Static Decompression machines have been used for decades and have shown benefits to those suffering for back pain and who already have spinal degeneration.

Active Decompression, such as the reverse hyperextension exercise, takes the benefits of static decompression and includes the benefits of activating the nervous system, improving circulation and many tissue regeneration factors.

Many people have been through complete rehab sessions and even have had surgery and continue to have back pain. Others have their quality of life limited because they "know their limits" or were told "its old age and you will have to learn to live with it" and are destined for consistent degeneration and weight gain because they are unable to be active for fear of hurting themselves. In the majority of these pain patients, a proper understanding of the total problem was not identified, let alone explained, and no solution is provided.

Everyone has their weakened areas due to accumulated trauma from falls, car accidents, repetitive stress, sports injuries, muscle asymmetry, inflexibility, and dysfunctional movement patterns. A clinician can consider further metabolic factors such as improper EFA ratios, mitochondrial damage, chemical toxicities that tear down the physical structure and more. In every injury, every time, it is important to remember that it is the muscles that stabilize joints and are involved locally and globally by a neuro-musculo-skeletal-fascial system. If the muscles are not working properly, the joint is predisposed to an injury. If there is an existing injury, it promotes an inflammatory pain response throughout the nervous system (due to down regulation of muscle spindle fibers and lack of inhibition of Type C pain fibers). Muscles affect structure and structure affects muscles; prolonged stress on either of these systems fatigues (injures) the nervous system: specifically at the mitochondrial DNA level ("Mitochondrial DNA in Aging and Disease," *Scientific American;* Aug 1997 p. 40). When the nervous system can no longer compensate, physical breakdown of the body occurs. This breakdown is revealed by acute and chronic pain with degeneration to ligaments, cartilage, joints, triggers points and pulled muscles. All of these contributing factors apply to the science of "Mechanobiology."

"Mechanobiology and Diseases of Mechanotransduction"
Annals of Medicine 2003; 35(8), pp.564-577

Donald E Ingber, MD, PhD from the Vascular Biology Program, Departments of Surgery and Pathology, Children's Hospital and Harvard Medical School

The main goal of the article is to help integrate mechanics into our understanding of the molecular basis of physical and visceral disease. This article first reviews the key roles that physical forces, extracellular matrix and cell structure play in the control of normal development as well as in the maintenance of tissue form and function. The article explains insights into cellular mechanotransduction, the molecular mechanism by which cells sense and respond to mechanical stress [for many of us this is the application of proper exercise]. Re-evaluation of human pathophysiology in this context reveals that a wide range of diseases included within virtually all fields of medicine and surgery share a common feature: their etiology or clinical presentation results from abnormal mechanotransduction. "These new insights into mechanobiology suggest that many ostensibly unrelated disease share a common dependence of abnormal mechanotransduction."

There are many more important concepts that are described throughout the article that apply, not only to physical and visceral pathology, but also to taking a proactive approach in developing healthy athletes.

We can begin to safely and effectively correct the muscular imbalances, which will correct the global structural problems and therefore allow the nervous system to heal the pain response via retraining lower and upper motor neurons (neuroplastic changes). The Reverse Hyper is an invaluable asset toward building strength in the posterior kinematic chain, correcting muscular imbalances, remodeling fascia, increasing circulation and increasing intersegmental motion.

The muscular pattern that commonly needs to be corrected, starting from the pelvis:	
Short Muscles (need to stretch)	*Lengthened Muscles (need to contract)*
Iliopsoas	Gluteus Maximus
Quadriceps	Hamstrings/Gluteus Maximus
Tensor Fascia Latae	Gluteus Medius
Adductor group	Gluteus Medius
Erector Spinae	Transverse abdominalis, internal oblique
Gastrocnemius, soleus	Anterior Tibialis

The muscle imbalances and postural distortion extend to the upper body:	
Short Muscles (stretch)	*Lengthened Muscles (contract)*
Pectoralis Major	Rhomboid Group
Pectoralis Minor, Levator Scapulae, Teres Major, Upper Trapezius	Lower Trapezius, Serratus Anterior
Anterior Deltoid	Posterior Deltoid
Subscapularis, Teres Major, Latissimus Dorsi	Teres Minor, Posterior Deltoid, Infraspinatus
Sternocleidomastoid, Scalenes, Rectus Capitus	Longus Coli, Longus Capitus

It is the total pattern of all muscles working synergistically that determine spine stability, position, neurological patterning and ultimately functional movement and performance capabilities.

Another point that needs to be made is that intermuscular coordination between muscles groups is a must. The column on the left directly affects the column on the right and vice versa (agonist/antagonist relationship). When the right iliopsoas (hip flexor) is contracting, lifting the right leg up, the right gluteus maximus (buttock) is supposed to be relaxed or inhibited. When the right gluteus maximus is contracting, extending the right leg backward, the right iliopsoas is supposed to be relaxed or inhibited. This patterning is necessary throughout all the above muscle relationships. Those who have chronic and/or recurring pain commonly have anatomical imbalances as well as the muscle fascilitory and reflexive pathways firing improperly, which leads to muscles constantly turned off, others constantly spasm and then maintain instability and injury. The agonist/antagonist pattern above is further extended to the right upper quadrant and the left lower quadrant; neurological inhibition. The body's motor learning pattern must be trained and strengthened! A chiropractor that is trained in resetting neurological patterning can provide an accurate evaluation and correction with proper adjustments, soft tissue work, low level laser therapy and ultimately a strength and conditioning program retraining and strengthening the optimum pattern.

Proper motion is necessary to recover from chronic injuries. Many prescribed exercises place too much compression on the injured area or try to isolate an area of involvement instead of strengthening an entire area that works together naturally.

The Reverse Hyperextension has numerous advantages for those suffering from back pain.

1. There is no compression to the injured spine and discs. The motion of the reverse hyperextension actually "de-compresses" the spine and opens up the joint space on the forward swing phase.
2. The exercise is performed as an "active" therapy so there is an action potential throughout the nervous system and activation of muscle spindle fibers on the swing phase and the contraction phase. This action is retraining the nervous system to "close" the pain gate.
3. The Reverse Hyper increases circulation to the injured area by pumping cerebral spinal fluid, lymphatic fluid and blood to the area. Circulation is necessary to bring in repairing nutrients and eliminate waste products. This process is necessary for the muscles, tendons, ligaments, cartilage and the nervous system to heal.
4. The Inter-Vertebral Disc is an important component of the spinal column. Together the discs compose one third of the height of the column. The disc itself is made of collagen and cartilage. An important aspect of the disc is that it has a very poor blood supply. The only process by which it can receive nutrients is via imbibition. Imbibition refers to the exchange of fluid via movement. The Reverse Hyper "active decompression" exercise provides imbibition more than anything else I can provide my patients and clients with.

If you are suffering from back pain, your body has been in a degenerative and injured state for some time. The reverse hyperextension will help retrain and regenerate your body, no matter what your condition level is when you begin. Consistent use of the Reverse Hyper will allow progress to be made and will result in a decrease in symptoms if you follow these helpful guidelines.

- Start out cautiously! The Reverse Hyper is a very safe and effective exercise; however, your weak and injured low back is not used to having the joints, muscles, ligaments and bones move through normal range of motion or work together properly. Initially you are retraining the body and helping it relearn this process. This takes repetition, consistency and conservative progress. Beginning at a conservative level ensures long-term success and recovery.
- Initially, the full range of motion may not be possible with the Reverse Hyper in the forward swing phase. In addition, you may not be able to extend your legs up to the full extension (muscle contraction) phase. It is recommended to start with a short range of motion and gently increase as you warm up.
- In the beginning, patients and clients may feel muscle fatigue and some mild discomfort. This is normal and should not be mistaken for injury to the weakened area. As people age or for those with chronic back conditions; bone strength and muscle elasticity and tone tend to decrease. The discs begin to lose fluid and flexibility, which decreases their ability to properly distribute weight-bearing forces. Additionally, scar tissue does not have the strength or flexibility of normal tissue. A small effort performed more often is safer and more effective than too much effort in the beginning!

- Revaluate yourself at the end of every week for the first four weeks. You may be surprised at your progress and the general improvement in your symptoms and you may see increases in your range of motion, the number of repetitions and sets performed, as well as the amount of weight resistance being used during the exercise.

- A rehabilitation program using the Reverse Hyper is based on your current condition, consistency of use and continued increases in repetitions, sets of performing the exercise, and adding increased resistance to continually build your core strength and achieve a healthier, pain-free life. For those doing a complete strength and conditioning program, you don't fix the roof when it is raining. Implementing the Reverse Hyper into your program is one of the most beneficial, unique exercises you can ever do.

If you do have a diagnosed condition, it is always beneficial to have a practitioner than can coordinate a complete program and provide services that you cannot do for yourself. Chiropractic adjustments are proven to be one of the most beneficial treatments even when used only by themselves for people with chronic pain. Chiropractic is a form of treatment that seeks to return proper function to the nervous system: not just for putting bones back into place. There are numerous studies that prove chiropractic is one of the most effective and safest treatments for the elimination of pain. This is due to the fact that the spinal column has sensory receptors at the joints of the vertebrae (spinal bones) that transmit pain signals to the brain. If the bones are misaligned or not moving properly this creates improper neurological communication (subluxations) locally and globally throughout the body. Pain is a normal response to injury and instability of joints. The below research paper validates the effectiveness of the chiropractic adjustment, acupuncture compared to commonly prescribed drugs individually. Note: *Spine* is the number one orthopedic journal in the world.

"Chronic Spinal Pain: A Randomized Clinical Trial Comparing Medication, Acupuncture, and Spinal Manipulation," *Spine*, July 15, 2003; 28(L4): 1490-150

Treatment	Drugs Celebrex or Vioxx	Acupuncture	Chiropractic Adjustments
Years of chronic spinal pain	4.5 or 6.4	4.5 or 6.4	8.3
Percent asymptomatic within nine weeks	5%	9.4%	27.3%
Percent that suffered an adverse side effect	6.1%	0%	0%
Percent improvement in general health status	18%	15%	47%

Key Points of Study

In this study, the medication group had more patients' who experienced adverse side effect (6.1%) than recovered from their spinal complaints (5%).

Even though the chiropractic treatment group was the most chronic (8.3 years), 27.3 percent recovered with 18 spinal adjustments over a period of nine weeks, or less. This means that better than every fourth patient became asymptomatic with nine weeks or less with chiropractic adjustments, even though they had been chronic for more than eight years.

Chiropractic adjustments not only had the largest improvement in pain, but also had the largest improvement in removing any symptomatology (indigestion, headaches etc) of all standardized measurements of health status.

Because the patients had chronic spinal pain syndromes, it is unlikely that improvement resulted from "self-limiting" spinal pain, as could be the case with acute spinal pain.

Chiropractors are the only health care specialists who are trained in administering specific adjustments (not gross manipulations) to restore proper biomechanics and communication to help reduce and eliminate pain related to mechanobiology stresses.

Another unique modality worth mentioning is Low Level Laser Therapy (3LT), commonly known as LLLT. Most people are familiar with hot lasers that are used for surgical precision; low level lasers (cold lasers) are used for healing precision. 3LT is a form of phototherapy that involves the application of low power coherent light (below 25 mw qualifies as true LLLT) to injuries and lesions to stimulate healing. 3LT is not to be confused with Led Emitting Diodes (LED's) or "Infra-Red Light Therapy Devices. Erchonia Laser is the most researched and validated Low Level Laser in the world, having numerous FDA clearances and is published in many peer reviewed medical journals.

The effects of 3LT are photochemical/photobiological (cold), not thermal. During treatment of the tissue with the laser beam, an interaction between cells and photons takes place--a photochemical reaction. A very short explanation as to how this benefits athletes and patients is a photon provides an electron that passes through the electron transport chain of the mitochondria and increases the production of ATP (adenosine tri-phosphate). A further explanation involves how the process affects the valence electron and utilizes integrins that ultimately can have numerous physiological benefits throughout the body for recovery of athletes as well as a variety of needs of patient care. Since every cell in the body has mitochondria and the biological effects are well documented for a variety of uses (just type low level leaser therapy into www.pubmed.gov). Low Level Laser Therapy works when used alone, but if combined with exercise such as the Reverse Hyper, chiropractic and more the results are even more apparent.

Jerome Rerucha, Chiropractor

nutripedia@yahoo.com

ARP Wave Therapy
By Dan Fitchter

Westside members have used many types of therapy, but Accelerated Recovery Performance (ARP) Wave Therapy has proven to be very beneficial. ARP was developed by Dennis Thompson. Here at Westside ARP Wave Therapy has been used extensively on its members with great success. How does it work? Let's look at how it is used in athletes from high school to pros by using Dennis Thompson's advice along with Jay Schroeder, one of the nation's leaders in strength rehabilitation.

ARP has assisted in rehabilitating those with the following:

- Anyone in chronic pain
- Anyone with arthritis
- Anyone who has been told they are bone-on-bone and need joint replacement surgery.
- Anyone who has had joint replacement surgery and is still not back to activity without pain.
- Anyone who has had ANY orthopedic surgery and still not back to activity without pain.
- Anyone who has had a stroke.
- Anyone who has MS.
- Anyone who has a spinal cord injury.
- Anyone who has a neurological disease.
- Anyone who has been told they need spinal fusion surgery.
- Anyone who has a limited range of motion.

The Secret of ARP Wave

ARP uses direct current (DC) compounded with a high frequency double exponential patented background wave form. It allows for a deeper penetration of the direct current with no side effects. Above all, it produces little inhibitory protective muscle contractions allowing active range of motion during training or therapy. This allows for lengthening or eccentric actions to occur. This is a must during treatment.

ARP works faster than conventional rehab by eliminating the non-productive muscle responses to injury and by repairing injured cells and connective tissues and adding to blood flow. Dr. Andrew I Edelstein, CCEP, ARPP, explains how ARP works at its various intensities.

1. Level 1 increases blood supply with no muscle work. It works like a warm-up for sports activity.
2. Level 2 increases blood supply, muscle work, loosen muscles and help muscles that are in spasms.
3. Level 3 involves hard muscle work and is good for strengthening.

How the Practitioner uses ARP Wave

When the problem is found, the electrical stem pads are applied to the problem area and the muscle groups receiving treatment are pushed through a pre-determined range of motions. As the reps are performed the pain should diminish from the current. As the athlete can tolerate the discomfort, the current is increased at regular intervals. The athlete performs certain motions. It is important to increase currents to eliminate scarring of the tissue and the negative charge is diminished.

For Westside's ARP contact: Dan Fichter,

ARP Therapist

1-585-749-8636

The RECAST Approach to Strength Training for Short Track Speed Skating.

By JC Glauser and Phil Tremblay

When Louie approached us to write a few words on our approach to training international level short track speed skaters we couldn't refuse. What an honor. Hopefully our experience with the Russian National short track speed skating team and other international and national level speed skaters will stimulate strength coaches to dig deeper and strive to make all athletes stronger.

We believe that a complete analysis of the sport is crucial to understand the exact strength demands a strength coach needs to address in each athlete. There are many factors to keep in mind when analyzing your sport: sport specific functional maximal strength/endurance/power, speed-strength and strength-speed components, explosive strength, strength endurance, biomechanics and kinematics just to point out a few. You must first determine the exact optimal demands of your sport and then understand how to transfer them to the sport before possibly coaching.

Before setting foot in the gym a detailed injury history is essential to optimize progression and to avoid setbacks. An injured athlete will always compensate, greatly increasing the risk of injury. Strengthening weaknesses associated with/or causing injury will only speed up recovery, avoiding potential setbacks.

We can never over-emphasize the importance of individualized programs for maximum progression and safety. The risk-to-benefit ratio as it pertains to exercise selection, volume and intensity should always be considered. Style points of an exercise should never take precedence over the effectiveness and safety of another exercise.

Once a history is completed and measures are taken to address problematic areas, a structural and functional orthopedic profile of each athlete must be performed. Any restrictions that are not addressed will affect sport specific tremnique as well as the capacity to generate optimal strength. This will compromise the effectiveness of exercises selected because the athlete will not be able to perform them optimally.

The sport and the eventual exercises prescribed become the tests to determine if there are any mobility restrictions. Can the athlete perform the complete range of motion needed to perform the optimal sport technique (with perfect form and ease)? If not, sport-specific technique will never be proficient and lifts in the gym without proper mobility will lead to compensations and as previously mentioned, increased risk of injury. Mobility work and re-integration exercises (to re-educate the body and conserve needed mobility gains) will precede every workout until adequate mobility has been reached.

One of the biggest restrictions we see in speed skaters is at the ankle joint. Athlete's talocrural joint mobility is insufficient to maintain optimal kinematics at the sport's most demanding positions. Talocrurual joint improvements lead to immediate results on the ice. Skating techniques become more efficient even improving strength profile capacities on ice just by allowing ease in the movement.

After evaluation of the sport's specific strength weaknesses we knew that the introduction of Westside principles would lead to great results. From experience many athletes show large imbalances between anterior and posterior chains.

For years, off-ice training for speed skating focused mainly on the anterior chain. Yes, quads are essential to maintain the demanding positions of speed skating, but a powerful posterior chain and hip musculature will generate the horizontal line-of-force needed to propel you forward.

Introduction of the wide-stance box squat, which has increased recruitment of the adductors, hamstrings and glutes (essential for horizontal force production), over conventional squats lead to significant improvements in sport-specific performance. The box squat also alleviated lower back and knee torque loading, decreasing tension on areas that are highly solicited in speed skaters. A recent study by Swinton et al, demonstrated that compared to regular squats, power lifting box squats were easier on the lower back and produced a three-fold increase in the rate of force production. They also break the eccentric to concentric phase of the squat, which mimics the gliding phase speed skaters experience while skating.

Re-balancing the quad-to-hamstring ratio with proper box squats and other exercises such as inverse curls, pull thru, sling pulls and volume-appropriate sled work, as well as other supplemental exercises, lead to increased functional sport-specific maximums and relative strength without lower back and knee pains, which athletes were experiencing in the past. By increasing the strength of the hamstrings and adductors, athletes were able to reduce the anterior shifting of the tibia during the skating motion. Off-ice training resulted in fewer injuries and increased strength in athletes that were previously suffering from knee problems. It also helped them to increase their explosiveness safely.

Loading parameters were modulated individually using bar speeds calculated with a tendo unit (allowing us to modulate training intensities specific to each athlete's level of preparedness at every workout) addressing specific speed-strength or strength-speed weaknesses in order to achieve results that would be transferable to the ice. Since strength is measured in velocity, not weight, we could always adapt loading parameters in order to maintain optimal training sessions without compromising the athlete's general readiness/fatigue level as to not negatively affect further training sessions and on-ice sessions. We also calculated velocities on max effort days to avoid grinding and prioritize safety.

Using specific accommodating resistance, different specialty bars and specific bar speeds on dynamic training days allowed a greater carryover to sport specific weaknesses that we noticed in the preliminary evaluations. Chains were introduced first and were easier to control on speed days and also greatly improved squat technique for beginner-level lifters. As athlete's became more efficient the over-speed eccentrics of the bands and elimination of deceleration helped dynamic workouts immensely.

Westside's template of max-effort and dynamic trainings days allowed us to have significant strength gains without increasing athlete's body weight. Squat gains went upwards of three times body weight for some male skaters without any injury setbacks. Westside's 20 percent to 80 percent volume parameters allowed us to eliminate weaknesses and imbalances that were noticed during the max effort lifts (observing where athletes were breaking). Having the capacity to identify breaking and/or weaknesses under maximal loads paired with on-ice observations of weaknesses allowed us to individualize programs for optimal transferability to the sport.

Westside's emphasis on the accessory exercises especially for the lower back and all parts of the abdominals, but especially the obliques, was an integral part of the speed skaters training (adjusting loading intensities and volumes specific that day).

Louie's personal experience, intensive research and continuously testing new techniques have led to a continuously evolving Westside protocol. And the results speak for themselves. By implementing the Westside way we saw great progress in the weight room that transferred to on-ice success.

Is Your Fuel Source Actually Slowing You Down?

At RECAST we know that an individualized training plan is an integral part of what makes you stronger, but how efficiently your body works as a unit is probably equally if not more important.

How "clean" is your body? Are you firing at your full potential? Eugen Sandow, for a long time considered the worlds strongest man, said back in the late 1800s, "You can't have healthy muscles without first having healthy organs and glands."

Science has evolved since Eugen's statement and we are now able to prove he was right. Every organ has a referred muscle and body part. In the book *Applied Kinesiology Essentials: The Missing Link in Healthcare* by Cuthbert Walker (2013), Walker says,

> "the nervous system is the vital link between muscle and organ or glandular function. When improper nerve activity adversely influences an organ or gland, it can be observed by testing a specific muscle or muscle associated with the organ or gland. Pain generates reflex changes in muscle tone and it does not matter whether the painful source is an inflamed visceral organ or gland, a muscle, joint, tendon or ligament. The muscle will usually be weak but can be hypertonic."

The relationships between organs and muscles are well documented. The pancreas for example, responsible for sugar regulation (which has become a common problem in today's society because of a diet littered with sugar and sweeteners), is associated with the triceps and latissimus dorsi muscles. Improperly regulated sugar in a professional power lifter could lead to both the triceps and/or the latissimus dorsi being inhibited and not firing optimally. This could be a serious problem especially for the bench press. If you can't set yourself and/or fire your triceps, how can you expect to have a 900-pound bench? You'll have to compensate with other muscles, therefore diminishing your true potential.

The same goes for the liver, which is associated with the sternal part of the pectoral muscle. A diet full of toxins can overload the liver and lead to underperforming pectoral muscles.

A "clean" diet will ultimately have less of an adverse affect on your organs and glands allowing for a better functioning of your muscles.

You're probably asking yourself right now, "Do I eat clean?" This discussion would be endless and that's not our objective, but we want you to start questioning if what you're putting in your body is actually helping you.

Body weight for many sports is important. What if you carried significant amounts of extracellular fluid in your body? This specific defense mechanism of the body to get toxins out of the cells and dilute them in extracellular fluid, as to minimize their negative impact on the integrity and functioning of the cell, can add significant amounts of undesired weight. To make a specific weight class, or in a sport where relative strength is important, wouldn't you want to avoid any water retention? Even if you need to maintain a high weight to be stronger like power lifters, you want that weight to be helpful (optimal intra to extra cellular water ratio so that any extra weight is beneficial). Why carry extra weight in the form of toxins, which in the end make you slower, more fatigued and affect your recovery time.

Everybody will react differently to all types of foods, but avoiding the one's your body doesn't respond well to is crucial. Any inflammation in your body can cause inhibition or hypertonicity of certain muscles, so ingesting foods that your body can't tolerate will eventually cause an inflammatory response that could not only make you gain weight, retain water and lack energy, but also have the potential to inhibit muscles that are essential to your sports performance.

Swinton PA, Lloyd R, Keogh JW, Agouris I, Stewart AD. A *biomechanical comparison of the traditional squat, powerlifting squat, and box squat.* J Strength Cond Res. 2012 Jul;26(7):1805-16

RECAST Train right. info@recastperformance.com

info@recastperformance.com

FOR MORE INFORMATION DON'T HESITATE TO CONTACT US AT:

RECASTPERFORMANCE.COM

Rugby Training Using the Westside Barbell Conjugate Method
By Matias Bussi, Strength and Conditioning Coach from Argentina

As a young athlete training for Rugby, I always felt the old periodization methods had something wrong. In my sport I had to peak every Saturday throughout the eight months the season lasted. I couldn't afford to neglect any physical quality while training another because I needed all of them on the rugby field. I couldn't neglect my strength, speed or hypertrophy; I had to have them all, all year long. I trained like this for a couple of years while learning from some great coaches, but deep inside me I knew something was wrong that there had to be a better way to train.

While undergoing my degree in Physical Education at the university, I spent hours and hours searching for every article, blog and website with information regarding to strength training, my biggest passion. Most of the articles about strength mentioned a man called Louie Simmons and a place named Westside Barbell. Very quickly I realized there was something special about it, big squats, deadlifts, chains, bands, chalk, I loved it!!!

But that was not all. As I digged more and more into the Westside philosophy I started to understand what made this man and this place so different from the rest: the application of science to strength training. What makes Louie Simmons and Westside Barbell so special is that all the methods applied in training have scientific background and if they don´t have, not much time will go until someone proves that Louie was correct … once more.

One of Mr. Simmons most famous quotes is "strength training is physics, biomechanics and mathematics" as crazy as it may sound for some people. Every day that goes by I realize this is truer. Newton´s Laws of Motion have to be applied for optimal performance, every barbell, dumbbell or weight is affected by these laws. The correct technique in every exercise is crucial for injury prevention and to reach peak performance. Volume control is of upmost importance if you want to have an optimal training effect.

Besides the application of science per se, the thing that got me the most from the Westside method was the periodization system. It made sense immediately!!! Training all the physical qualities together in the same week, all year long, just as a team sport athlete needs. Rugby as most team sports or ball games are of unpredictable nature, you have to face ever-changing situations that might need very different physical qualities, so you can't afford to neglect one of them for a certain period of time. You need to be in peak performance the entire season, how could you know when to peak your athletes performance? The first couple of games, trough mid season, when? It is impossible to predict when to perfectly peak your athletes in this kind of sports, you have to acquire top form at the end of the pre-season and maintain it throughout the whole season.

Another reason why I fell in love with the Conjugate method is that it is a set a principles that evolve and adapt. It is not some fixed rules that you have to stick to them. The principles are flexible and adaptable to every circumstance; this method it gives you guidelines to find the correct answer for every situation. It forces you to think to go outside your comfort zone and look for the best answers for each situation. You have to find the correct tool for the job. What I am writing today may not be the same things I will be doing tomorrow with my athletes, but the same principles will still rule my training program.

In my opinion one of the biggest misconceptions of the conjugate method is the "train your weaknesses" principle. As simple as it sounds I found many coaches who can't seem to grasp it. The articles and the books only tell you the common weak areas, but that doesn't mean everyone has the same weak spots. You have to be very objective and analyze your true weaknesses and go make them a strength of yours. Your weakness can be anything that is keeping you from reaching optimal performance. It doesn't always have to be a muscular weakness. It could be GPP, flexibility, mental toughness, coordination, etc; every aspect of ultimate performance can and has to be addressed.

I find this and the 20/80 rule (for total training volume) very similar to rugby training and most of sports training. You don't play your sport all the time when you train it; sports training is not playing the sport every single training session. You compete/train, evaluate your performance and them go work on the weak points or what has to be corrected or even perfected for an optimal performance. In a rugby game it could be defense, tackling, ball handling, conditioning, kicking. It could be every facet of the game and many times more than one aspect on the game is trained in the week … just as with the conjugate system. As Louie answered many times when asked if the conjugate method is suited for sports training, the conjugate method is sports training because it uses the same frame of thought.

My rugby program for the off season consists of four days: Mondays, Tuesdays, Thursdays and Fridays. It's a modified Westside template because most players still engage in some kind of activity on Saturdays, so it was very difficult to get them to the gym. This split, although not optimal, is what works best for my rugby players. Monday is max effort lower body. Tuesday is dynamic effort upper body. Thursday is dynamic effort lower body and Fridays is max effort upper body. I have tried many variations of the weekly split, but I always come back to this one, which was the one that yielded the best results. Mostly I work with three-week waves for all exercises except for the max effort ones, which rotate on a weekly basis and once every four weeks are replaced with a Repetition effort day. Dynamic effort days are almost never replaced.

As Rugby is an unstable environment sport where the athlete has to adapt to the ever changing situations, I use a much wider pool of max effort exercises to rotate from, so as to get the players to strain in different situations and not to adapt to the same stimulus (as Louie quoted from Ben Tabachnik "to adapt to training is to never adapt"). Each week is a new challenge to overcome. Most of the time it's a one rep max, but we sometimes use three to five rep max according to how the athlete may feel and his training experience (to younger athletes I tend to prescribe more reps). The only pet peeve I have with max effort is letting my athletes fail; I like to get them used to succeed, not to fail. The training has to be optimal; there is no need to crush the athletes for the sake of getting a PR.

For upper body we rotate bars (Straight, Swiss, Football and fat), angles, grips, pin presses height, band tension and chain weight on a weekly basis. I prefer to use more full-range pressing. We very seldom use board presses and if we do we use it as an accessory exercise, although we do use the floor press regularly. For lower body we alternate a pull and a squat each week leaving Goodmonings as an accessory movement on max effort days. For the pulls we rotate stances, bar height, band tension and chain weight and for the squats we rotate bars, box heights, band tension, and chain weight and sometimes use also concentric-only movements.

Accessory movements for max effort lower body days, as mentioned earlier, would be some type of Goodmorning, RDL, stiff-legged deadlift or maybe a close-stance squat, free or to a box, for a heavy sets of three or five reps. After that it could be a single-leg movement like a lunge or sled variation followed by glute-hams or reverse hypers with a moderate to heavy weight for three to four sets of ten to fifteen reps. If the athletes feel a bit crushed they would use a lighter weight for sets of twenty or more reps. To finish the session we always do ab work and flexibility/mobility, and maybe more upper back or triceps, if needed.

For the dynamic lower body days, we will always start with a speed squat against some form of accommodating resistance and always to a box. The percentages used may vary from athlete to athlete, but as a rule, we start with 50 percent and then evaluate if we need to increase or reduce the percentages so the athlete can generate enough force. We mostly use doubles in the squat, but if the athlete is inexperienced he may do more reps per set but always following the indications of Prilepin's chart. The rest between sets: If training in teams is what takes the other athletes to squat and if training alone it goes from 20 to 40 seconds. After each three-week wave we rotate something: from type of bar, amount of accommodating resistance or box height. The squats most of the time are followed by speed pulls, also against some form of accommodating resistance; and always each new wave starts with something different (bar height, stance, accommodating resistance).

Dynamic effort in my opinion is one of the keys in athletic and rugby performance, although it is ignored by many coaches. "Many roads lead to Rome," but it will always be a better decision to take a road that is signaled on the map. The same is true for strength training. Science is the map and it will always be better to look at the map. Newton´s second Law of Motion is the key here, training your athletes to accelerate the bar as fast as possible to generate enough force (as in a max effort lift) for as many sets as prescribed will teach their CNS to fire the same way when they play Rugby. This type of force output is what the player does every time they tackle, take the ball to contact or enter a ruck; so in my opinion it is a wise thing to train it in the gym.

Next, for the special exercises to perfect technique and address weaknesses, a direct posterior chain exercise is performed: Glute-ham variations (angle or weight) or reverse hypers, with lighter weight than on max effort day, but for more reps per sets (something around 20 to 30 reps). This is followed by power walking with a sled using moderate weight for six to eight trips 30 meters for a posterior chain variation. After that, maybe another sled exercise like sideways or backward dragging could be added for another three trips of the same or longer distance. Like every other day, the last part of the workout is abs and flexibility/mobility work with some upper back/read delt or triceps exercises, if needed.

On max effort upper body days, after the main exercise we use a dumbbell/Kettlebell pressing variation for three to four sets with moderate to heavy weight to work the chest and arms. I prefer having my athletes use the same style of bench pressing with the dumbbell/Kettlebell pressing, upper back tight, elbows tucked and no hand rotation. I found this variation less stressful on the shoulder, which is an injury prone body part for rugby players so any less stress is beneficial. The next exercise depending on each athlete most important weaknesses could be a lat or triceps exercise. For the triceps on max effort days I tend to prescribe a bar exercise with heavier weights and less total reps. It could be a JM Press or any type of extensions to the throat, forehead or behind the head. This is always superseded with light, but very strict, pushdowns on a band or a pulley. The lat exercise is going to be some form of heavy row: standing barbell rows, rows on a machine or inverted rows with bodyweight or more. Also here we use a lot of variations such as changing grips, angles, using bands, etc, anything that makes the exercise harder or overloads a specific portion of the lift. This exercise could be replaced by some form of pull-up or chip-up for the athletes that need to work on their relative strength. The last part of the workout is going to be a superset including biceps, rear delts, abs and grip work. If needed some light reverse hypers could be added.

On the speed days for upper body we rotate mainly between bench pressing, explosive pushups or med ball throws. The bench pressing is always performed with some kind of accommodating resistance and the percentages range from 40 percent to 60 percent depending on the athlete. Also sets and reps vary according to the athletes lifting experience. Newer guys use more reps per set and less total sets. The normal range for sets and reps goes from nine to 15 sets of three to five reps. This is the same kind of rep/set scheme we use with the explosive pushups; for the throws we would use a scheme similar to the jumps.

During the season our main objective is to keep the athlete injury free and in top rugby shape throughout the most part of the year. So this means the sessions are much more flexible than on the off-season where strength training is the main priority. During the season each session is planned according to how the athlete feels upon arriving to the gym: players only train full throttle if they feel/are recovered enough. During this part of the year I mainly use a three-day-a-week split, a lower body dynamic effort session, an upper body dynamic effort session and a mixed repetition effort session where we target specific weaknesses. If they don't have any lower body injury they will do a dynamic effort lower body session on Mondays, or as far away from the game as possible, involving speed squats (always to a box) and maybe speed pulls. How many sets and reps depends on the athlete, but anything from six to 12 sets of two to four reps in the squat and 10 to six sets of one to two pulls. After that is a couple of accessory exercises such as glute-hams, Reverse Hypers, sled work and always abs and flexibility work at the end of the session.

The upper body session would consist of some form of speed bench press against bands on chains, during the in-season as shoulders get beat up from all the tackling. The athletes mainly use the football bar or the Swiss bar, which are less stressful on the shoulders. They could also do some variation of explosive push-ups or med ball throw. After that comes some kind of light pressing movement, either with dumbbells or Kettlebells rotating angles every week, or push-ups also changing body angle for two to three sets of submaximal reps. This set of pressing movement could be super setted with some form of light upper back work such as band pull-aparts. Next, depending on the athletes' weaknesses, they'll do triceps work or lat work. For triceps in season we use more dumbbell or Kettlebells exercise as they are less stressful. The sets four to six are almost always high rep from 12 to 20 range and every set is followed by some kind of light, but strict triceps extension with a band or a pulley. Most of the time lat work would consist of some kind of rowing motion; we use almost every rowing exercise to strengthen the upper back. We always try to do twice as much work for the lats than the chest. Lately we started using a lot more pull-up/chin-up variation with our bigger guys trying to increase their relative strength. To finish the session there is a superset for three sets with bicep, rear delts, abs and grip exercises. Last activity of the session is flexibility/mobility work.

The repetition effort session would be even more specific for each player's needs, but you will always find a lot of ab exercises and mobility exercises. Another staple in this kind of session could be ultra-high rep (100 to 300) triceps pushdowns on a band or 100 to 200 leg curls with bands or two to five kg ankle weights.

As a side note, I want to thank Mr. Simmons for introducing me to sled work, one of the most versatile pieces of equipment ever made. With a simple sled you can train the entire body for strength, speed and conditioning—it's an all-in-one toll. Louie many times said, and he is totally right, that you don't have much time to train your athletes, so why not use a piece of equipment that trains more than one physical quality at a time. Sled dragging is a huge part of my rugby program, especially during the season when I don't want my athletes to get sore from strength training. The almost inexistent eccentric pounding of the sled allows us to get enough training volume without taking too much from our athletes. For the lower body we drag sled in every direction, with ankle weights, weights vests, holding dumbbells, doing sport specific movement, etc; variations are endless. For the upper body we do all kinds of presses, rows, external rotations, etc; in many different positions so as to duplicate rugby movements.

Jump training is a big part of our training program. We use jumping to boxes alongside med ball throws to develop explosive power in our athletes; we almost never use Olympic lifting because I feel the cost-benefit relationship is too high. Most athletes can't perform them with correct technique. It takes too long to teach them correctly and in my opinion puts unnecessary stress on the athletes shoulder, elbows and wrists. Throughout the year we jump twice almost every week rotating different forms of jumping to a box: standing jumps with bodyweight, with resistance (weight vests, ankle weights, dumbbells, Kettlebells and combos), from a seated position, with one step, with a sport-specific movement before; and from the knees: for distance, for height, with resistance, barbell on back, cleaning a barbell, snatching a barbell, split stance and combos of everything. Occasionally we also do long jumps from the standing position, but more for an evaluating purpose. I prefer to jump always to a box as the impact forces, especially with heavy athletes, are reduced comparing to jumping and landing.

As with max effort exercises we have record for each jump variation, for explosive power development we jump between 75 percent and 85 percent of the existing record in three-week waves increasing the percentages by five percent each week. If we are going for a new record we use a similar progression as with max effort lifts using no more than three jumps at 90 percent or above. When training for explosive power development we stick with Verkshoransky recommendations of 30 to 40 jumps per session, mostly using three or four sets of ten jumps at 75 percent to 85 percent of the existing record. This is done twice a week during the off-season and one or two if possible during the season. Jumps are done generally before the main movement on lower body days as warm up and CNS primer, but can also be done last on the workout so as to train explosive power endurance.

Recovery is one of the most important parts of our rugby program; we know that training is mostly recovering from the stimulus rather than the stimulus itself, so we place a big emphasis on recovering well after each session. As general means for recovery after the games, ice baths and hot showers are used combined with compression gear. The next couple of days massage and light exercise, like swimming, biking or jogging, are also used. Some athletes like getting chiropractic or osthepathic adjustments monthly. Nutrition for recovery and performance is worked outside the gym with the individual specialist each athlete works with.

The most important aspect of recovery we try to make our athletes embrace is sleeping enough for good recovery. People in Argentina and in most Latin American countries have a tendency to go to bed late at midnight (dinner time in most houses in around 9 pm) and wake up early in the morning to start activities back again, so getting seven hours of sleep is almost a miracle. That is aggravated in young athletes who stay awake to almost sunrise playing around with the computer or TV. It is a tough job to make them understand how important sleeping is, and even more important to stress that sleeping during the day is not even near in recovery possibilities as sleeping at night.

Training Collegiate Athletes For Maximal Results
By Jerry Shreck, Head Strength Coach, Bucknell Univerity

The strength and conditioning industry has changed a lot over the years. There are so many different approaches and philosophies that a strength coach can apply today. I speak at many strength and conditioning conferences each year and I've often said that if we took a dozen strength coaches and asked them all to lay out their off-season programs for basketball; all those programs would have similarities and differences. Although their approaches and philosophies may differ their goals are all the same, to get an athlete stronger and more powerful while keeping them injury free for the practices and competition.

When I first entered the field as a young strength and conditioning coach, I actually thought I knew a lot. I quickly realized that I did not know even remotely a third of what I needed to learn and know to become a good or at least an applicable strength coach. I made many mistakes along the way and I still make some mistakes today, but I try to focus on learning from those mistakes versus being discouraged by the mistakes that I make.

Hi, my name is Jerry Shreck and I'm a Division I strength conditioning coach at the collegiate level. I currently work at Bucknell University, which is a small Division I school in Central Pennsylvania. I am also a certified and licensed Athletic Trainer and although I do not work as an Athletic Trainer, it has proven to benefit me well in this career choice. You may or may not have ever heard of me and that's why thought it might be smart to take a few seconds to give a little background information about me and what I'm about.

When I first got out of college I was hired at a sports medicine center and was contracted to a high school in the coal region area of Central Pennsylvania. This was a pretty big high school and their sports programs were taken very seriously within the community. I was brought on to be their first-ever athletic trainer to take care of athletic injuries and be on the sidelines for their sports programs. I quickly became their first-ever strength and conditioning coach as well because they did not have anyone to work in their weight room and the student athletes of the sports programs really needed guidance and direction. Working both as the head athletic trainer and head strength coach of this high school taught me many lessons about work ethic and what it takes to work long hours to be successful.

Three years later I was given an opportunity to move up to the Division I level as a full-time athletic trainer. I took this position because of the pay increase and the opportunity to get to the next level being a Division I University. I quickly found out when I got to the university level that the school had no full-time strength coach and many of these teams had no direction in the weight room. It did not take long before I was working with a team and it got catchy and before I knew it I was working seven athletic teams providing them with programs and meeting with them voluntarily in the weight room to train them. Again this helped me build the foundation of work ethic. I found myself in the weight room before 6 am and leaving in the evening sometimes after 10:30 pm from covering a sporting event.

Again, I was given an opportunity and in the right place at the right time when the university decided to upgrade its facilities and build a varsity weight room with the idea of hiring a full-time strength and conditioning coach. Head athletic trainer, Mark Keppler, encouraged me to apply for the position as he saw that it was my true passion to be in the weight room and it was not my passion to be a full-time athletic trainer. To make a long story short, I did apply and I have been the head strength conditioning coach ever since.

My background in athletic training and my passion for athletics has led me over the years to try and develop strength and conditioning programs to not only enhance the athletes' abilities for increased potential, but also to maximize injury prevention training techniques. All of this has led me to many years of research—reading and contacting professionals in the field to gain knowledge and collaborate information into a training system, which I have devised. This has led to many contacts over the years including Louie Simmons from Westside barbell, hence the reason why I am now being given an opportunity to present some information in this book that you're reading today. I have never really been intimidated by reaching out and contacting individuals in their field of expertise and trying to find information that I want to learn or gain from that I can apply to my own training principles for my athletes. As I mentor younger strength coaches or strength interns, I often tell them not to be intimidated by people in this field; they're only humans, reach out and contact them. There is a wealth of knowledge out there and the knowledge that I have gained over the years by asking is priceless, but they will only help you if you reach out to them.

I am a believer in sharing information and passing along training information principles to the younger generation, as this will only strengthen our profession. This led me to develop my own website called varietytrainer.com. This site was developed to share information about injury prevention techniques and principles of training athletes for maximal results. This is more for athletes, sport coaches, and strength coaches. Many strength coaches now seek me out across the country for my injury prevention techniques that I've developed by gaining knowledge and experience over the years. I truly believe in giving back and providing information. This is why I'm truly honored to be part of this book and share some of my information with you. I am mainly going to generalize and try to get you to think a little bit and hopefully stimulate you to go out to do research on your own. Most of the information that I'm going to present can be found in greater detail on my website.

I am responsible for overseeing two weight rooms at Bucknell University with 27 athletic teams and a very small staff of strength and conditioning coaches. I get many volunteers who want to gain experience and learn the techniques that we apply at Bucknell. We also get interns from surrounding colleges looking to gain experience towards their college credits for graduation. Many people think the life of the strength conditioning coach at the collegiate level is not glamorous. We get up before dawn and usually go home when the sun is already down. A typical week involves working five to seven days covering 60 to 70+ hours during this time. We are overworked, understaffed and underpaid, but I love it and I wouldn't trade it for the world. I've never worked a traditional job, the "9 to 5," so I don't know what it's like to have time off like most people around the world. Luckily, I have a very understanding and loving wife.

With 27 varsity athletic teams and over 700 participating athletes, the different sports require different skills, but they all require strength and power. The top priority of the strength coach should be to provide injury prevention for athletes. I have often said it does not matter how big, fast, strong, or how powerful I can get an athlete; if they are injured, they cannot participate and are useless for their team.

I've never really had one training philosophy for training athletes. Maybe it's because I get bored easily or maybe I'm always trying to improve. I've told people that I follow a Russian conjugate training style, but really it's a hybrid of many different styles with a Russian conjugate background base.

I don't follow standard western periodization models, but I do training in cycles or in little phases. Most of my phases last three to five weeks before I'm ready to make a change. No one phase in the training cycle at the collegiate level is perfect. There are so many things to take precedence like NCAA time restraints, coaches changing schedules, practices themselves, finals, and athletes going home at certain times of the year. This creates a training atmosphere that is not necessarily perfect; so being able to adapt is a necessity at this level. Typically I'm given one full hour for most training sessions. Knowing the number of athletes of teams that will be in the weight room at the same time will many times dictate the volume of work that can actually be accomplished in a training phase for that program for that day.

All of my athletes will start each work out with a dynamic warm-up. This will get the body warmed up and the central nervous system excited for activity. I learned long ago that as a strength coach we are not training muscles; if that is your thought process you will not be a successful strength coach. We are training the neurological system to be responsive.

After their dynamic warm-ups are done my athletes will do injury prevention exercises. These will address the smaller intrinsic muscles of the shoulder, hip, and ankle and are normally done with small bands of theraband tubing. We will also address proprioception exercises this time. Many strength coaches many times overlook these and I believe this to be a big mistake. I have always learned that the most important exercises should be done first in any work out.

I will next address the core through series of weighted exercises that will hit the abdominal low back and many other areas of the trunk and torso. These are normally done in a standing position.

In some phases or on certain days of a teams program, the next step would be implementing GPP or general physical preparedness exercises. These are exercises that will raise one's work capacity. These are typically bodyweight exercises done explosively or some low-grade plyometric movements. I will also use some training implements such as tires, sleds, kettle bells, and plyo boxes. These are normally timed portions of the workout.

Now we get to the meat and potatoes of the program, the emphasis lifts. These are multi-muscle group or big muscle group lifts that require coordination, strength, and power. These would include squats, bench press, pulling exercises, and triple extension movements like Olympic lifts. The sets, reps, and volume of this area of the program will be determined basically on the needs of the team and time of year the team in question is in.

Once the emphasis lifts have been completed we move into the area of the program called the supplemental lift area. These are lifts or exercises that are typically sport specific in nature or what addresses the athletes weak links that have been identified during the emphasis lifts.

Let's stop here for a moment and discuss weak link areas of the body. This is where a strength coach can really make big gains with an athlete and their injury prevention. The old saying goes you are only as strong as the weakest link in the chain. This is also true in any person's body and we all have weak links that need addressing. Now there are systems out there today we can buy and implement that you can run each athlete through individually to try to determine if there are muscle imbalances, flexibility issues, or muscle weaknesses. The main problems I see with systems like this is that they tend to be a little overpriced or expensive and they're extremely time-consuming. Both problems—the cost and the time—result in an expectation that you won't have the opportunity to purchase these if you work at any university such as the one I work at. It is just not feasible with the number of athletes and the small staff that I have. Strength coaches must develop a keen eye to be able to identify an athlete's imbalances and weak links. Just by watching the athlete perform a heavy back squat or heavy bench press can tell you a lot about the weak links in an athlete. During each and every workout the athlete is under constant evaluation. It is a strength coach's duty to address and identify these weak link areas. By not addressing these weak link areas you may be encouraging greater muscle imbalances, greater potential for injuries, and lessening the potential for increased strength and power gains. Unfortunately, I believe this is where the educational system and strength and conditioning industry fails our students who are going through it in college. It is important for older strength coaches to teach younger strength coaches these skills and stress the importance of them. Weak link exercises are key in the success of an athlete's development.

After the weak link exercises have been completed, I again will address the core of the body. This is the trunk area that would include abdominal, low back, hip flexor, and glute regions. Sometimes this will be done with bodyweight exercises in a circuit style fashion or again addressing the area with weighted core work in the application of rotational work, anti-rotation work, or stabilization work.

All training workouts will end with some type of recovery work in the form of static stretching, band stretching, foam rolling, or a combination of them. I am a huge believer in doing some form of stretching particularly static stretching at the end of a weight training session. But I also believe that band stretching is a superior form of stretching to increase range motion in an athlete's body.

So let's recap what a typical day for my athletes looks like in the weight room: They first complete their dynamic warm-up, which would be followed with their injury prevention exercises, core routine, GPP or small low-grade plyometrics. We then enter into our main emphasis muscle exercises, then onto our supplemental lifts. We address the core again, followed with some type of static or stretching routine. This has been the layout of my weight training routine for athletes for the last couple of years and it has worked out and been very successful.

Any work outside of the weight room usually consists of form running, speed training, footwork, and deceleration to acceleration work. I do not usually focus on conditioning my athletes due to the low number of strength coaches. Our attention is directed towards the weight room. I personally think that their coach can handle the conditioning drills that many times I will supply for them; anyone can run a stopwatch and blow whistle. Over the years I've come to realize that one of the biggest factors in an athletes training outside the weight room has to deal with learning how to decelerate the body properly. Deceleration training is vitally important to me in an athlete's development. If we cannot land from a jump, stop from a full sprint, or make a cut properly, the body will be in a position to injure itself and also is not in a position to maximize the acceleration principles that are in place. It has been said by many strength coaches that if an athlete cannot decelerate properly they will never reach their true maximal potential to accelerate properly, or be explosive, and maintain balance on the playing field or on the court. I have studied deceleration training techniques by many strength coaches over the years and have developed a training system and properties that have nearly eliminated ACL tears with my athletes, greatly decreasing the number of injuries that we once saw.

I think most coaches and athletes are now aware that training the posterior chain is a necessity if you want to be successful in sports and athletics. Fifteen years ago the main concentration I saw with incoming freshmen and athletes was focusing on the hamstring area of the posterior chain. There was a lot of talk about the ratio between the quad and the hamstring muscles and the amount of output that was being generated between the two. Over the last couple of years, I do not personally believe that the hamstring is a major indicator of potential for injury or something we need to make the main focus of our programs. Training the hip complex is much more superior of an area to be putting your focus on as a strength and conditioning coach or an athlete who is training to prevent injuries and maximize their potential.

The main focus should be placed on increasing the range of motion of the hip flexor and getting greater neurological output out of the glute muscles. Today's youth sit more now than ever before and between sitting at a computer, school, texting, TV remotes, and playing video games. I believe that we are seeing an increase in shortening of the hip flexors in today's youth. This is detrimental to an athlete because if the hip flexors are in a shortened position this will inhibit the amount of activity that the glutes will want to produce naturally or during an athletic performance. If this is the case, this will make you be more quad dominant in their athletic positions on the field. When an athlete is more quad dominant they are automatically placed in a higher category for injury particularly to the knee area. This is where deceleration training becomes so vital outside of the weight room to maximize the potential of the athlete and decrease the percentage of injury to occur.

The strength coach, sport coach, or athlete should be focused on doing certain drills that can enhance the development of the hips and the neurological firing patterns of the glutes so that they become the more dominant muscle group going into deceleration and back into acceleration. I have spent years of research working on this and presenting this at conferences, and strength and conditioning clinics and it always amazes me when coaches tell me that they don't make this a focus of the training and they are stunned at the thought process of doing some of the simple techniques that I present at these conferences and clinics. Remember again that all athletic movements are executed by the motor systems of the brain through the neuromuscular connection. This is why it is important to focus on certain drills to get this neurological adaptation. Being able to stabilize the joints through athletic movements when an athlete is going one hundred percent is of vital importance for decreasing the potential for injury.

Since I do make a focus of presenting ideas and examples of injury prevention, I would like to now give you some examples of how you can implement injury prevention techniques directly in the weight room with the emphasis lifts in your training program.

Accommodating resistance training has really taken the level of potential for training athletes to a new level. There are many ways to apply accommodating resistance training into your workouts. Training with chains by hanging chains off of a barbell has been a staple in many weight rooms for years. As the weight rises, and the links of the chain come off the floor, the weight increases as the lifter is trying to stand up or press; thus requiring the body to recruit more muscle fibers going through the full range of motion. This is a dramatic increase in potential for athletic performance instead of just moving weight with a certain number of motor neurons excited. Being able or having the ability to recruit more activity in the muscle during the neuromuscular connection through range of motion is awesome. This was taken one step further when Dick Hartzel invented jump stretch bands that now are common staple in most weight rooms thanks to Louie Simmons presenting them to the world and in the training techniques that they apply at Westside Barbell. As I write this small passage for this book, I have not personally read the book or haven't seen the book prior to writing what I'm writing and sharing with you, but I'm sure that these principles are probably well covered in this book so I'm not going to dive into them and the impact they can make in athletics.

Louis Simmons has done a lot for the world in regards to training and reaching maximal potentials and there are two pieces of equipment that I believe he has developed to be the ultimate for the strength conditioning industry that most coaches may not be utilizing. They are his Reverse Hyper and his Belt Squat Machine.

When I first saw Louie's Reverse Hyper machine I'll admit, I wasn't very impressed. I am not much of a machine guy. I am a free weight guy and I believe free weight training has more benefits to offer an athlete. It was not until I got on a reverse hyper and actually trained with it a little bit and practiced with it myself before I could fully understand what it was that this machine has the potential to accomplish.

I use the Reverse Hyper for two main applications. First, for strength and power development of the posterior chain of the athlete. Second, for traction properties and decompression of the spine. I use the Reverse Hyper machine in my programs as either an emphasis lift or as a supplemental lift depending on it's application.

As an emphasis lift, I use the Reverse Hyper either by loading it up with very heavy weight for 10 to 14 reps or I will use the machine to promote high-volume training with sets of up to 20 to 40 reps at a time. When I use the Reverse Hyper as a supplemental lift I typically do it and partner it up on our heavy squat day or heavy deadlift day and I use it as a rehab or a pre-hab tool in decompressing the spine. When I use this to decompress the spine I usually go with a moderate to lighter weight and we swing it for reps just to alleviate pressure and allow the swing to provide traction on the spine. Most of my athletes really enjoy the feeling they get after coming off the Reverse Hyper, saying how well their low back feels. I personally have had some low back injuries through my years of personal training and I have found this machine to be a blessing in disguise as my back has never felt better after using this for multiple years now. I also believe that in the future you're going to see the Reverse Hyper found in many rehab settings across this country and with different, various applications for rehab. I am not sure that even Louie completely understands the impact that this machine has made in a positive way across the athletic world and in the training of athletes.

The Belt Squat Machine is Louie's other piece of equipment that I use in the training of my athletes and in a sick demented way, I think I am secretly in love with this piece of equipment. When I was thinking about purchasing this piece of equipment and getting it for the varsity weight room, I wanted to learn everything I could know about it to make sure that it was the right piece of equipment that I was looking for. I traveled on two separate occasions to Westside Barbell, which for me is about nine hours of travel just to get there one way. I wanted to train on Louie's Belt Squat Machine and have Louie run me through the exercises to be done on this piece of equipment. I have already mentioned previously the importance of training the hip complex. This machine will hit hip complex, particularly the glutes and smaller intrinsic muscles of the hip, like no other machine or exercise I have ever used before. There are many applications of how to utilize this machine in either your emphasis or in your supplemental lift areas of a weight training program. The Belt Squat Machine can target everything from strength training of maximal potential output, to generalized conditioning, to high endurance power training. If you have someone with herniated discs or a back problem that is a genetic trait, this machine gives you great options to increase their abilities to gain strength in the lower body that otherwise they may not be able to gain by not being able to do traditional squat or dead lift movements.

In my professional opinion every weight room should have both a Reverse Hyper and Belt Squat Machine if they truly want to maximize the potential for their athletes and their lifters. I know that this is a very bold statement, but I truly believe that these are great pieces of equipment that can add a benefit to any weight room.

Attaining results is the primary reason for strength coaches in any weight room, but truth be told even the best weight training program will only produce so many results. What happens outside the weight room really determines the best results for any program. The athletes' recovery after workouts is vital and it will determine the results you actually get from the weight training sessions. There are many different recovery methods out there so I'm going to cover a few that I have our athletes do.

I should not have to say this, but nutrition is probably the biggest factor in your results. Most athletes have a very poor diet especially when they get to the college level and they're exposed to an open cafeteria to go in and eat whatever they want and as much as they want. Making it a priority to educate the athlete on how to eat and what to eat so they can maximize their potential results is vital in any training program. Luckily at my school we have a full-time sports nutritionist that is a huge asset to us. Her name is Tanya Williams and she is outstanding. Tanya meets and talks to all of our athletic teams in the beginning of the fall semester each year and she counsels athletes on a weekly basis and monitors their nutrition programs to give them the food choices to maximize the results. Never underestimate the power of sound nutritional habits. Remember, you are what you eat.

At the Division I level supplementation in athletics is a popular subject. Whenever an athlete asks me about supplements the first thing I ask them is "Did you have breakfast today?" What did you eat? What time did you eat it? If they didn't eat a breakfast that morning or did not eat it before 8 am, then this is the starting point of our conversation. Supplements should never be taken in place of poor nutrition or a bad diet. The role of a coach should always be educating your student athlete on the proper ways to eat first before there's any talk of supplements. There are supplements that will help, so I'm not totally bashing the supplement industry because some do work. At the college level we can supply some of our athletes with a protein carbohydrate mix on a ratio that is within NCAA standards and is compliant with the NCAA. I personally do not recommend my athletes taking a lot of supplements. I council them and send them to Tanya to learn about how to eat properly and get the right caloric intake in first. If my athletes feel they need to take more supplementation, I encourage them to come talk to me about it prior to them taking it. I always want to make sure that it's NCAA compliant and if they are taking a supplement they need to know how to use it properly. Creatine is still a very popular supplement in the athletic community and one that I do believe to be positive for an athlete. If my athlete chooses to take creatine, I will always recommend them to cycle it. I typically will recommend no more than five grams per day for a cycle of six weeks on and two weeks off. After three cycles, I tell them to take at least one full month off from any creatine supplementation. This allows the body to naturally re-regulate its own creatine production. Again, a clean diet with the right nutritional benefits and a surplus of calories is always the best option.

When it comes to athletics, stretching is a priority. Before any practice or any training session we always have our athletes do a dynamic stretching program. After their activity we encourage them to do a static stretching program or sometimes we utilize jump stretch bands. I personally recommend the use of bands over static most times. I like the bands because you can use them in static positions and/or you can use them dynamically through movement. A great way to get an athlete to believe in the bands is first have them do a standing reach or sitting reach to get a general measurement as to their level of flexibility. Then have them do a static stretching routine and take it again, you'll find that they'll be a slight increase in range motion and the athlete will say they feel little better. Follow that up with a band stretching routine and have them take the measurements again. Usually the measurements will increase by more than two inches. This is a great selling point to the athlete as they can definitely feel the benefits of the bands and see it with visible proof that the bands increased their range of motion greatly. When doing this, usually you will have never have a problem getting them to stretch with bands again.

Myofascial release (massage) or rolling out with a foam roller, tennis ball, or lacrosse ball has gained in popularity greatly over the last few years. When I first started learning about myofascia release using the foam roller, I didn't really buy into it. I thought it was a waste of time and it would take up too much time to do in our already narrow window of opportunities for training. I quickly found out I was totally mistaken and should have more of an open mind when it comes to new training principles and philosophies. I now have foam roller racks that hold up to seven foam rollers in the varsity weight room that we use with our athletes post workout. We encourage the athletes to use the foam rollers after the stretching routine. We also use the foam roller sometimes before the workouts to loosen up and get the body ready to operate movement more correctly. I have instructed some athletes for certain areas of their bodies that need to foam roll prior to every lifting routine. I have found that using myofascial release techniques can greatly decrease some athlete's limitations. I know this is true for myself as well as I am not as young as I used to be. Foam rolling prior to the workout has been a major benefit for me. It can be beneficial to use before and/or after workouts.

If you have access to a swimming pool, this can be a great resource to use for active recovery. The hydrostatic properties of the water in the pool can really help decrease the inflammation that was produced from the previous days work out. Just letting an athlete move around in chest or neck deep water can really help in alleviating tension, increase mobility in the joints, and improve blood flow throughout the body.

Pool workouts in general can be a great addition to any strength and conditioning program for an athlete. In chest-deep water, do a dynamic warm-up routine, sprinting, and a jumping routine to help develop potential for power output. Take an athlete into the deep water and have them do straight up sprint work. This alone takes the pressure off the knees, but allows them to get some good cardiovascular and power endurance; some people would even consider this over-speed training. Swimming laps and changing up your swimming strokes is another way to increase blood flow to the body and getting the muscles ready to recover from a heavy lift day. With the right applications this could also be considered GPP work or raising one's work out capacity.

I also recommend the use of a contrast bath or shower for my athletes. At my university we are lucky enough to have a hydrotherapy area that has two giant whirlpool tubs deep enough for our athletes to submerge themselves up to their neck. Contrast therapy is using a hot and cold source and applying each for time. My recommendation is for an athlete to start in the hot tub for one minute and then move to the cold tub for one minute and they will repeat this up to six minutes. I will then tell them to keep repeating the cycle but do it at 30-second bouts for up to another six to eight minutes completing the total time of 12 to 14 minutes of contrast bath. I want them to end in the cold tub and then get out of the water and relax for the next six to 10 minutes allowing the body to re-regulate and rewarm itself up naturally to normal status.

I then want them to do a static stretching routine to loosen the body up and really aid in recovery. If they do not have time to do a contrast bath they can always have the option of doing a contrast shower in the locker room. This will be done a little differently with the thought process that they will not be stretching afterwards and going directly to class. As they're showering I want them to start in hot water for one minute and then go to cold for 30 seconds. They will repeat this sequence the entire time they're taking a shower while washing their hair and bodies. This will also result in a systemic response to the body increasing blood flow to the tissues that were just worked. Unlike doing the contrast bath, I encourage them when taking a contrast shower to end with hot water for up to two minutes before getting out and drying off to get ready for their day. The times that I've come up with for the contrast bath and the Contra shower are merely times that I have done myself and felt like I had the best results from.

Results will vary with athletes from any training program to any recovery model. The constant that has stood through the test of time for any coach who is training athletes is to show the athlete that you generally care for their well-being. If you're just there to beat them up and collect a paycheck they will see right through that. An athlete must trust and create a bond with their coach and when you have developed this trusting bond you will have success with your lifting program and your athletes.

Jerry Shreck, BS, ATC/L, NCSF-CPT

Coach Shreck is the Head Strength & Conditioning Coach and Fitness Facilities Coordinator at Bucknell University in Lewisburg, Pennsylvania. Jerry is also the Head Strength Coach for Bucknell's club power lifting team. He has coached the Men's Basketball team to several Patriot League Championships and a first-ever advance to the 2nd round of the NCAA tournament in 2005 and then repeated this significant feat again in 2006. He has also been featured in *Men's Health Magazine* as the second best men's basketball Cardio Challenges in the country. Coach Shreck was regularly featured in *Real Solution's* Magazine with articles such as "Expert Training Tips and Injury Prevention." Jerry contributes to many strength and fitness websites and is a questions & answer expert of several professional fitness forums. He is a speaker at numerous National Strength & Conditioning Conferences each year and is featured monthly on CCN Channel 8 News Fitness segments. Coach Shreck has coached all levels of athletes from Jr. High School up to professional athletes. His main interest is in Division I collegiate athletics. His free training website www.varietytrainer.com constantly gets great reviews for the information he shares. He is an innovator of several training styles and is sought out by many professionals for his injury prevention techniques. www.varietytrainer.com, www.totalcoreforathletes.com

The Benefits of Sled Dragging

By Daniel Di Pasqua, Head Strength Coach - Melbourne Storm Rugby League Team.

For the development of speed, strength and power, Louie's training system and principles far exceed any method of physical preparation for the athlete that I have seen. Louie's system of percent training, conjugated periodization and special strength development has lead to performance increases with all our athletes.

In particular, the use of sled dragging has become a staple in our programs.

We use the sled for several reasons:

- Loads posterior chain without spinal compression
- High transfer to sports field activities (acceleration)
- Prehab and rehab tool for all lower limb injuries
- Joint conditioning of ankles, knees, hips
- Increase muscle mass of posterior chain
- Active recovery/restorative.

In contact sports, you must work around all the aches and pains that are a given in your sport. Sled dragging offers a way to do this. We have had experienced athletes gain lean muscle mass in their legs in-season as confirmed through the use of Dexa scans, by the implementation of sled dragging. Depending on how you load the sled, it can be used for many different applications from strength development, hypertrophy to restorative. We have seen tremendous results with this very simple tool and it should be a staple in all strength programs that value speed, strength and power development.

In elite sports, only the strong survive. As a strength coach I am always looking for the best and most effective methods to train our athletes. I consider Louie's training system and methods fundamental in the development of explosive athletes for all sports and must be implemented to reach the top.

His training methods are proven at the elite level of powerlifting and also in my experience, proven in sports preparation.

Daniel Di Pasqua

Head Strength Coach - Melbourne Storm Rugby League Team.

BSc. Exercise Science.

MS. Exercise Science (Strength & Conditioning)

di01@hotmail.com

Conjugate System Is Program Cornerstone

Josh Bush, MS, SCCC, CSCS, USAW SP

Human Performance Specialist, Army 7th Special Forces Group, Eglin Air Force Base

I have been a Strength and Conditioning Coach in a variety of environments, the majority of which at the collegiate level. Most recently I have served as the Head Strength and Conditioning Coach at Morgan State University for eight years. Throughout my career, I've studied multiple philosophies and disciplines, but have found none comparable to the Conjugate System. For the last six years I've used this philosophy as the cornerstone of my program and have seen measurable success.

At Morgan State University this past off-season, we had five short weeks to get the team strong, explosive, and in shape. Through the hard work of my staff and players, the team bought into our program, which utilized the conjugate method, which led to big gains in a very short time. The team had the following lifting schedule during this period:

- Mondays: Max Effort Bench Press
- Tuesdays: Max Effort Squat or Deadlift
- Wednesdays: Off
- Thursdays: Dynamic Effort Bench
- Fridays: Dynamic Effort Box Squats.

To demonstrate how I implemented the conjugate system into Football's five-week off-season program, we will first discuss max effort pressing days, which occurred on Mondays. Upon initial testing, average bench press was a very weak 290 pounds. After the five-week off-season, the average bench press went up to 315 pounds. During each week of the five weeks, we rotated bars and worked up to 100 percent of the players' max with that specific exercise. Each week's exercise is as follows:

- Week 1—Fat Bar Floor Press.
- Week 2—Swiss Bar Press.
- Week 3—2-Board Press.
- Week 4—Rep Effort with the Bamboo Bar for 3 sets of as many reps as possible with the same weight for all 3 sets.
- Week 5—Fat Bar Floor Press again for a PR.

Each week after working the players up to a max for that day on a special exercise, the accessories included bamboo pressing for high reps, dumbbell tricep work, band press downs, high rep shrugs, shoulder and scapula work, and core work. Dynamic benching occurred 72 hours following max effort press day. We used sling shots to teach the players to pull the bar apart and so they could handle a little more weight with speed since strength is internal. All sets below were with Tendo Unit Weightlifting

Analyzers attached to the bar measuring average velocity with a standard of at least .80 m/s every set and every rep for it to count.

- Week 1 was at 60 percent without accommodating resistance for three reps and eight sets rotating grips.
- Week 2 at 47 percent with mini band tension for five reps and six to eight sets rotating grips.
- Week 3 at 52 percent with mini band tension for five reps and six to eight sets rotating grips.
- Week 4 at 57 percent with mini band tension for five reps and six sets rotating grips.
- Week 5 again at 60 percent without accommodating resistance for three reps and eight sets. This week was a huge confidence boost when compared to Week 1 average velocity numbers on the Tendo units.

Tuesdays were max effort squat or deadlift day.

- Week 1—Ultra Wide Sumo Straight Leg Deadlifts
- Week 2—Safety Bar Box Squat
- Week 3—Cambered Bar Box Squat
- Week 4—Ultra Wide Sumo Straight Leg Deadlifts
- Week 5—Safety Bar Box Squat

Each week after the players worked up to a max for that day on a special exercise, they would power clean or squat clean from the floor and perform overhead squats. The accessories would consist of box step-ups with Kettlebells, single leg RDL's, glute-ham raises with band stomps, and lots of core work.

Box squatting days occurred on Fridays, 72-hours after our max effort day. The football team came back with a very weak squat average of 350 pounds and a power clean average of 245 pounds. After just five weeks of implementing the conjugate system, squat average improved to 410 pounds and the power clean average improved to 270 pounds. With every set we utilized our Tendo Unit Weightlifting Analyzers and measured average velocity. We set a standard of at least .80 average velocity for every rep and every set. The following training methods were used to obtain fast results:

- Week 1: Dynamic box squats with 50 percent for two reps and 14 sets and with no accommodating resistance and no more than a 60-second rest interval. Accommodating resistance was not used during Week 1 to allow greater focus on technique and speed.
- Week 2: 45 percent plus average (green) band tension for 18 sets of two.
- Week 3: 50 percent plus average (green) band tension for 18 sets of two.
- Week 4: 55 percent plus average (green) band tension for 12 sets of two.
- Week 5: 50 percent with no accommodating resistance for 8 sets.

On Fridays after box squatting, the team power cleaned from blocks, followed by front squats. Throughout the five weeks the team cycled through use of reverse hypers, high rep band Goodmornings, ultra high rep ankle weight leg curls, Kettlebell walking lunges, and of course, core work of all kind. If you have any questions about this article or anything else you can contact me at jbush.7SFG@gmail.com.

Strength Matters in MMA
By Eddie Wineland, UFC Bantamweight

"Anyone that says strength doesn't matter in MMA isn't fighting at the highest level. Your strength, both physical and mental is what you are going to rely on when that door closes, and I have never been stronger since I adopted the WSBB methods into my training. Besides that and above all else Westside has taught me to train optimally! To train as an athlete, both in the weight room and on the mat…! I will win, I may lose, but I will always, ALWAYS, step into the octagon stronger and more ready than any opponent standing in front of me."

What does Westside's ART Specialist Say?
By John Quint NMT, Active Release Technique Practitioner

Soft Tissue Injuries

Soft tissue refers to muscles, tendons, ligaments, fascia, discs, nerves, and joint capsules in the body. Therefore, a soft tissue injury would include an injury to any of these structures, which cover our bodies from head to toe. Soft tissue injuries generally fall into the categories of a sprain, strain, contusion, repetitive strain injury, tendonitis, or bursitis. Injuries of the soft tissue are generally poorly understood and therefore improperly treated.

Due to the lack of understanding of soft tissue injuries combined with less than optimal treatment methods, soft tissue injuries are a major cause of pain and disability in today's society. If the injury cannot be properly diagnosed, then it cannot be properly treated and resolved. Working in the medical field, I see on a daily basis people living in pain and dysfunction due to the inability to properly diagnose their soft tissue injures, coupled with the inability to apply proper treatment to resolve it.

Injuries to soft tissue structures has a widespread effect on both function and performance of muscles, joints, ligaments, tendons, connective tissue, the central nervous system, and the circulatory system. The residual scar tissue that is formed as a result of an injury to a soft tissue structure will restrict movement of the tissue, which in turn results in the development of abnormal and dysfunctional movement and motion patterns due to the body compensating and working around these restrictions. Compensation leads to dysfunction and altered biomechanics that will generally create further structural imbalances and put the individual at a higher risk for further injury.

The buildup of scar tissue and the residual effects that it can have due to the altered biomechanics from compensation can last for years, even after what seems to be a resolution of the initial injury. Due to the improper diagnoses and treatment of soft tissue injuries, they have become very prevalent in today's society, and most people suffer the lingering effects of past injuries like altered movement patterns and biomechanics without conscious awareness of their impact on their daily function and performance.

Injury Cycle

When the body is subjected to injury, it undergoes numerous changes including altered biomechanics (gait and motion patterns), the inability for the internal soft tissue structures to translate with each other correctly and efficiently, decreased circulation and blood flow to injured areas due to tissue restriction and scar tissue build up, and these are just a few examples. As you can see, it can be a snowball effect and generally is due to the inability to properly treat and diagnose these soft tissue injuries. More times than not, people believe their injury is or was resolved; however, if it was not properly treated with function and mobility restored to the soft tissues, then the altered biomechanics and motion patterns as well as some of the other issues mentioned above will continue to linger and affect daily function and mobility.

Do not assume that external forces are all that is needed for there to be an injury to any of the soft tissue structures. More often than not, a great deal of pain and dysfunction is not from the initial injury, but from how the body adapts to deal with it. Some of the residual after-effects from an injury to a soft tissue structure include:

Inflammation: The body responds to inflammation by laying down scar tissue in an attempt to stabilize the area so it is able to continue to function, even though proper function will now be altered due to the scar tissue preventing the soft tissue structures from translating over each other correctly.

Adhesion and Fibrosis: Soft tissue structures are supposed to translate or glide internally with each other; however, once the injury cycle begins and inflammation is present, it creates an environment where scar tissue is being built up to continue to support the injured area. Skeletal muscle is generally divided into three layers: superficial (close to the surface), intermediate (between the superficial layer and deep layer) and deep (the deepest layer of soft tissue). Along with all the other soft tissue structures mentioned above (tendons, ligaments, nerves, etc.), these soft tissue structures are all designed to translate or glide about each other for optimal and smooth function and biomechanics. When scar tissue is being laid down, it binds these layers of soft tissue together and prevents the internal movement or translation of these tissues layers across each other. When the lack of translation of these tissues is accompanied by continued repetitive actions, the result is an increase in friction between the internal layers of soft tissue, resulting in an increase of inflammation and therefore the formation of more scar tissue.

Increased Internal Friction, Pressure and Tension: When soft tissue structures are adhered together, friction, pressure and tension are all drastically increased. For some soft tissue injuries, all that is needed is a decrease in the internal translation of soft tissue structures to initiate the inflammation and adhesion fibrosis injury cycle. This cycle then can put an individual at a much greater risk for an acute injury. This is why I stated earlier that you should not assume that external forces are needed to create or initiate an injury cycle.

Decreased Circulation: When internal pressure is increased, it decreases the circulation to those soft tissue structures. The decreased circulation limits the amount of nutrients, blood and lymphatic flow, and oxygen that the tissues need in order to maintain function. It is essential to increase circulation for soft tissue injuries to be resolved so that they can have the nutrients that are needed to heal.

Cellular Hypoxia: The decreased circulation due to increased pressure will decrease the amount of oxygen that can be delivered to the soft tissue. Decreased oxygen (hypoxia), along with the other effects listed above, is one of the main causes of the formation and buildup of fibrotic scar tissue between the internal layers of soft tissue.

Shorten Tight Muscle Tissues: Muscles are designed to behave much like rubber bands. When a muscle is optimally functioning without knots or restrictions and the muscle has internal tissue translation, it has the ability to store, release, absorb, and recycle energy. The ability to absorb energy enables the muscle to help prevent a great deal of injuries by having the ability to absorb an external force that can cause injury. Once the formation of scar tissue begins, they lose a great deal of their ability to act like rubber bands and absorb energy, making them very susceptible to further injury.

Weak Muscle Tissues: As mentioned earlier, muscles are designed to behave much like rubber bands, which enables them to store, release and absorb energy. When muscles become tight, they lose much of this ability, which in turn makes them weak. Instead of functioning like a rubber band, they now function more like a rope that is tied down at both ends. The only issue is this rope is tied down tightly to two or more boney landmarks via a tendon attachment, which now due to the increased tension is going to cause an increase in pressure and friction in and between tendons, causing further damage to those soft tissue structures.

Tissues that are Compressed Together

- Inhibit the function of nerves
- Reduce lymphatic flow
- Decrease blood flow
- Creates cellular hypoxia
- Increase the formation of adhesion and scar tissue

Many of the effects listed above, when combined with continued altered motion can cause chronic irritation to the soft tissue structures resulting in an increase in everything described above. The combination of all or even a couple of the effects listed above generally leads to *increased friction and pressure between the layers of soft tissues, which in turn leads to micro tears within those effected soft tissue structures.*

Function and performance are based upon optimal biomechanics without compensation. Without optimal biomechanics, balance and coordination are altered, forcing the body into compensation and creating muscular imbalances that often lead to injuries.

Effective treatment, management and rehabilitation of soft tissue injuries necessitate knowledge and understanding of phases of tissue healing.

The Phases of Remodeling of Soft Tissue Healing:
Phase I - Inflammation

Acute inflammation, also referred to as swelling, generally lasts for approximately 72 hours, but can last longer and is the first phase of soft tissue healing. Inflammation accompanied by pain from the injury characterizes this phase. This is the body's reaction as a result of the soft tissue structures being damaged. The damage impacts the tissues, and the inflammation creates internal pressure, particularly on the capillaries, resulting in decreased blood flow and oxygen to the area.

Phase II - Regeneration

The regeneration phase starts after the inflammation phase and can last up to six months or more. The regeneration phase begins once the capillaries can be restored back to normal function and they begin to supply the injured tissues with the blood flow and oxygen needed to deliver the healing substances and nutrients to begin to heal the tissue. Once oxygen and blood flow are restored, collagen will begin to be laid down where the gaps are in the injured soft tissue structure. Unfortunately, the collagen tissue that is being laid down is not only weaker but stiffer, which in turn decreases the functionality of that tissue and makes it less elastic. Therefore, as touched on earlier, instead of being able to act like a rubber band that can store, absorb and release energy, it functions more like a rope.

It should be noted that if receiving proper treatment with the combination of correct exercises during this phase, it will make this new tissue not only stronger, but the collagen tissue will be laid down in the same direction as the tissue being repaired. Without treatment and exercise during this phase, the tissue will be laid down in random patterns, making it more susceptible to re-injury, and the tissue will not be as strong.

Phase III - Remodeling

The final phase is the remodeling of soft tissue, which can last up to a year or longer. During this phase, collagen fibers are remodeled and increase in size, diameter and strength to increase the functional capabilities in the once injured and now healing region. Corrective motion and exercise should be continued and increased during this phase as the amount of remodeling is directly related to the forces that are applied to the tissue. Collagen is remodeled to withstand the forces and stresses that are placed upon it during this important phase. If the injured person is performing corrective motions and exercise coupled with soft tissue treatment, the remodeling will lead to a full and complete recovery of the injured tissue. If the combination of corrective motion and exercise with soft tissue treatment is not introduced and maintained during this phase, it will be a much longer recovery time, and the chance for re-injury will be significantly higher.

It should be noted that the combination of soft tissue treatment and corrective motion and exercise should be incorporated directly after the inflammation phase and sustained throughout all of the stages listed above. Also light stretching during Phase II and III is particularly important for restoring range of motion and flexibility as well as improving function and biomechanics.

Treatment of Soft Tissue Injuries

Active Release Technique® (ART®)

"ART is a patented, state of the art soft tissue system/movement based massage technique that treats problems with muscles, tendons, ligaments, fascia and nerves. Headaches, back pain, carpal tunnel syndrome, shin splints, shoulder pain, sciatica, plantar fasciitis, knee problems, and tennis elbow are just a few of the many conditions that can be resolved quickly and permanently with ART. These conditions all have one important thing in common: they are often a result of overused muscles."

ART is a non-invasive, hands-on, biomechanics based, soft-tissue technique which locates and breaks up adhesions and scar tissue. As touched upon earlier, adhesion and scar tissue build-up is the primary cause of pain, stiffness, weakness, compensation, and altered biomechanics that are generally associated with soft-tissue injuries. Treatment through ART restores function and internal translation to the layers of soft tissue, and increases circulation and neurological function.

The goal of ART treatment:

- Reestablish optimal tissue texture, decrease tension, and restore function and movement.
- Reestablish internal translation to the soft tissue structures
- Restore strength and flexibility to skeletal muscle tissue
- Break up and release soft-tissue restrictions (adhesions and scar tissue)

What ART Treatment is like:

"Every ART session is actually a combination of examination and treatment. The ART provider uses his or her hands to evaluate the texture, tightness and movement of muscles, fascia, tendons, ligaments, and nerves. Abnormal tissues are treated by combining precisely directed tension with very specific patient movements."

"These treatment protocols — over 500 specific moves — are unique to ART. They allow providers to identify and correct the specific problems that are affecting each individual patient. ART is not a cookie-cutter approach."

Http://www.activerelease.com. Active Release Techniques®, 2010. Web. 23 June 2013. http://www.activerelease.com/what_patients.asp>.

For more information or to locate an ART-certified proved near you, visit www.activerelease.com.
John Quint

Other Restoration Thoughts
By Louie Simmons

I highly recommend the Precision Neuromuscular Therapy. It's a process of measuring for postural distortion caused by muscle imbalances, which can lead to a functional deficit and restricted range of motion. This procedure addresses tissues involved in trigger point formation or secondary referred pain sensations. PNMT also focuses on muscles that entrap nerves i.e. median nerve entrapment with carpal tunnel muscles can cause misalignment and even compression of the nerves leaving the spine. More information can be found at www.stillpointtherapy.com.

Chiropractic and detraction devices can help in restoration. Chiropractic adjustments really need to be implemented, especially for the neck. Proper spinal alignment can eliminate some hamstring pulls and help relieve IT band tightness. Heavy squats and Goodmonings could cause trauma to the upper back, causing pain, weakness, and numbness in the fingertips consequently affecting grip.

I recommend the Palmer School of Chiropractic's and the Chicago School of Chiropractic Medicine. Chiropractic diagnosis is essential for top sports performance. To learn more, read Siff and Yessis's (1992) *Sports Restoration and Massage.*

Of course, there are many supplements that aid in recovery. Review the nutrition chapter of this book.

Water is a means of recovery. Saunas, hot tub, ice baths, being sprayed with a high pressure hose, contrast baths, hot and cold, ice packs, heating pad moist and dry are all examples of water recovery techniques. Having a good rapport with therapists is vital.

One needs adequate recovery to reach his or her potential. Optimal time is 72-hours between extreme workouts.

Restoration can and should be low intensity. Walking is great restoration, but as the saying goes, I like to kill two birds with one stone. During the morning workout, I pull a light sled with 45 pounds to 90 pounds for six to ten trips of 60 yards. This may be for lower body by walking forward, backward and sideways. Also, the sled can be implemented for upper body, targeting all muscle groups. An individual will suffer from accommodation if he continues the same work at the same intensity and volume. Variance can be added by walking with ankle weights and a weight vest for two miles. This takes no more than 20 minutes a day, but provides a different intensity through sled walking. Periodically, rotate to a special non-motorized treadmill with a weight vest or ankle weight resistance. This is much more intense training for a minute to 20 minutes of work compared to walking outside. Many more steps are done per minute on the special treadmill. Another option is wheel barrow walking. Walking forward or backward like a rickshaw is great for overall conditioning.

Don't underestimate Kettlebell work. I have cleaned 16 kg for 15 minutes, switching continuously from left to right arm. I consider this a type of restoration. Alternating arm snatches with light Kettlebells, which is something that can be executed for at least five minutes. I have cleaned a 24 kg Kettlebell for five minutes, which is a strength endurance workout, but too taxing for restoration. Although they are intertwined, don't be confused between the two. Kettlebells are a great tool to develop muscular strength, muscular mass, strength endurance, cardio, flexibility coordination, and mobility. Kettlebells are great for prehab and rehab, and like Kettlebells, Indian clubs are great conditioners and great for range of motion for the shoulder rotators. The cleans are internal-external rotation on every rep. Find a certified Kettlebell instructor in your area.

Swimming is also a great form of restoration. The resistance is, of course, the water. I can't swim, but I do 200 to 500 kick steps in a pool, much like V. Alekseev who would do 1,000 per day for hips and abs strength to prevent injury. Other varieties would be doing 300 tricep push-downs during the week outside the gym by placing a light band over a door at home. Perform 100 reps at a time for a total of 300 reps.

Leg curls with bands or ankle weights should be done as well. I have mentioned several times about Diane Guthrie doing 250 leg curls a day with 10-pound ankle weights. She stopped doing them for a period and hurt her leg muscles. She started the leg curls again and eliminated her injury.

Track Notes—Sled Work for Speed Development

As you can see, Westside's approach with a sled is to use a methodical style to develop the posterior chain, which in turn builds stronger muscles to run faster. For pure strength, walking on the heels will work much like calf/ham/glute raises. Power walking on the balls of the feet is, of course, more technically sound to actual sprinting. This is with heavy weights, sometimes up to 225 pounds for strength and strength endurance. But what did top sprint coaches do with a weight sled and how much? Thanks to www.jimsonleespeedendurance.com. He gives insight to the training systems of two great sprint coaches, Stephen Francis and Glen Mills. Because we utilize sled work as much as possible, what did these two coaches do to improve acceleration and how? Its hill sprints and weight training, but six months of sled work. The average weight for men is 50 pounds and for women it's 22 pounds. Westside uses much more for the purpose of building the sprinters' muscles for sprinting and also for eliminating, decelerating and maintaining maximal velocity as a heavy sled makes each step as powerful as the next. Coach Francis uses a much lighter weight sled for improving acceleration in the first 30 minutes. While the 50 pounds for men and 22 pounds for women appears light, the normal is 10 percent of bodyweight, and you must remember the Jamaican's are far from normal. No sand work. Francis says it stresses the quads too much. A lot of prehab and good health is the first priority. Francis does lots of work on grass to avoid shin splints. It does no good to concentrate on speed or speed endurance if you lack good biomechanics. You must master the blocks and many other aspects that contribute to sprinting the greatest.

Contrast Method

A very experienced strength coach understands how effective contrast training can be. Try four trips of 60 meters with a heavy power sled workout, where each step is methodical, but powerful. Then drop the weight on the sled to 45 pounds and 25 pounds for women on the direction of the Jamaican coaches. For acceleration this is the contrast method in action. A coach must know all strength and sports training methods and when to combine methods to insure your athlete reaches his or hers greatest. All my lifting and coaching career played the odds. Pick the best nutrition, gear, prehab and rehab techniques as well and, most importantly, pick members that are physically proportioned to do the immense volume and have the mental state to not only reach the top but also beyond human limits.

To raise your mark as a coach I highly suggest that you learn the proven techniques of Bob Winter and Stephen Francis. What Coach Winter accomplished is unbelievable. As a coach, you must constantly gain knowledge of all aspects of your sport. However, remember an athlete may sometime in the future become a coach, so learn about your sport and always ask questions. If you don't receive a qualified answer, seek a new and more experienced coach. One coach everyone must admire is Glen Mills. The coach of Usain Bolt is one to follow.

I use the conjugate system for all sports including track and field. This allows all from a novice to an elite athlete to constantly break new training records all year round. This is a major plus for all. Every time my girls train they break some type of record, with weights, jumping, and short sprinting with several different weights or endurance work of many types. When you are used to breaking records you expect to break some record everyday. It becomes constant. Winning can be taught by constantly breaking records.

- Louie Simmons

References

(1) Oatis, C.A. (2004). Kinesiology: The mechanics & pathomechanics of human movement. Baltimore: Williams & Wilkins.

(2) McGill, S. (2007). Low back disorders: Evidence-based prevention and rehabilitation. Champaign Livingstone or Elsevier.

(3) Muscolino, J. (n.d.). Psoas Major Function. Learnmuscles.com - Anatomy, Physiology, and Kinesiology Books and Workshops with Dr. Joseph E. Muscolino. Retrieved 4/1/2014, from http://www.learnmuscles.com

(4) Muscolino, J. (n.d.). To Flex or Extend?. Learnmuscles.com - Anatomy, Physiology, and Kinesiology Books and Workshops with Dr. Joseph E. Muscolino. Retrieved 4/1/2014, from http://www.learnmuscles.com

(5) Myers, T.W. (2009). Anatomy trains: Myofascial meridians for manual and movement therapists (2nd ed.). Edinburgh: Churchill Livingstone of Elsevier.

(6) Myers, T. (2001, April 1). The Opinionated Psoas, Part 2. Massage Therapy: Everybody Deserves a Massage. Retrieved April 1, 2014, from http://www.massagetherapy.com

(7) Rolf I. Rolfing: re-establishing the natural alignment and structural integration of the human body for vitality and well-being. Healing Arts Press, 1989.

(8) Simons, D. G., & Travell, J. G. (1999). Travell & Simons' myofascial pain and dysfunction: the trigger point manual (2nd ed.). Baltimore: Williams & Wilkins.

(9) Zatsiorsky, V. M., & Prilutsky, B. I. (2012). Biomechanics of skeletal muscles. Champaign, IL: Human Kinetics. 19 Pictured: Angled view of the psoas which shows the full muscle path.

CHAPTER 11 – AGE AND LONG-TERM PLANNING

CHAPTER 11 – AGE AND LONG-TERM PLANNING

When should young athletes start training? How should they be trained? What effect does weight training have on youth?

In the United States, boys can start playing sports at eight or nine years of age. They are given a baseball or football, and let the games begin. This, of course, is with no General Physical Preparedness (GPP). Only sports specific skills are first taught or Specialized Physical Preparedness (SPP). Because young athletes are not physically prepared, this is all wrong. They must first raise flexibility, strength, speed, coordination, endurance and other motor skills, such as balance and raising oxygen consumption. GPP should start with jumping rope, which teaches rhythm and timing while building the thighs, ligaments and tendons. This is important for rebounding or the stretch reflex response.

A young athlete or novice must have good coaches. Notice that I said "coaches," not "coach." When an athlete reaches a higher level, it does not mean he can coach. At Westside, we have many great lifters who rose from nothing to greatness. As I taught the Westside training system to our lifters, they were learning what constitutes good form, what volume to use, and what exercise is best for a particular body type. In essence, I educated them to lift as well as to coach. Every lift is thoroughly monitored at Westside, and we constantly analyze each other before something becomes a problem.

It is important for beginners to learn everything about training. At meets, our new lifters all have good form, which is not the case with most beginners at meets. We insist new lifters squat wide and bench close, ensuring that the correct muscle groups are developed. Those muscle groups encompass the posterior chain—the hamstrings, glutes, calves, and spinal erectors. Someone with little knowledge usually tries to build the quads to increase his squat or running capacity, but this reduces hip flexion. In strength training, a reduction in hip flexion results in difficulty reaching a parallel position in the squat and destroys the lockout in the deadlift.

A strong child is a coordinated child. Pre-athletes should do short sprints of five to 10 yards plus some at 30 and 60 yards. Adding jumping on a trampoline builds coordination as well as strong legs; also, lots of jumping at optimal box heights is beneficial, but never jump down. Other exercises that should be implemented include the following: push-ups, sit-ups, lightened pull-ups, jumping over obstacles not only forward, but side-to-side and any activities such as rope climbing, tumbling, non-competitive wrestling, riding bikes, short sprints and longer leisure riding. Light Kettlebells work for hand and eye coordination by letting go then catching the Kettlebells. The light weight and low intensity work in high volume re-enforces muscles, ligaments and tendon development. Start with the basics of throwing and catching balls because this determines the child's attitude for a particular sport. An individual must learn to skate before playing hockey.

Mothers or fathers should not choose the sport, but let the child decide. Let an expert help develop the child's ability to play a sport that he has an aptitude for. Not everyone can be a world champion, but an individual's chances can be increased. Because children are constantly growing and the body dimensions are always changing, they should stretch. Progress should be tracked in all exercises including the long jump and triple jump. Can he squat with a broom stick overhead? And with a very wide or very narrow grip? How strong are the abs? What sport does he talk about most? How are his eating habits? Is the child overweight or underweight? All these factors must be monitored without putting pressure on the child. He must learn to achieve satisfactory grades while picking and participating in a sport. Also, motivation cannot be forgotten.

Beginners should learn proper form first and then add chains and later bands. There should be no extreme training, like circa-max squatting until an individual can squat three and a half times his bodyweight. Light equipment should be mastered first and then graduate to stronger gear. An individual should lift in positive federations or he will be frozen in time just like some federations are. There is no reason a beginner should not start with an advanced system. Everyone sends his son to Bobby Knight's basketball camp, and I've seen lots of athletes come and go. Don't be one of those. If a lifter starts correctly, he won't incur injuries, fail to make progress, or be forced to stop.

Westside teaches correct form and how to raise GPP and SPP while increasing work capacity. Other fundamentals of Westside include the following: how to educate others, when to wear stronger gear, how to separate different types of training and to know the effect of a particular training load while finding the proportionate training load that matches maximum strength, and how to organize training for an annual goal.

I suggest reading books like *Jonathan Livingston Seagull* and Jack London's *The Call of the Wild*. In *Jonathan Livingston Seagull*, the shining seagull lands some distance from Jonathan, and in a blink of an eye, he is standing next to Jonathan, who is startled to say the least. Jonathan says, "How did you do that?" And the enlightened gull responds, "Perfect speed is being there, it's all in your mind and as your imagination goes, so goes your potential to overcome." Normal people only give normal results. An individual's goal must always be to strive to do the spectacular. Coaches should sense the child's needs, not their own.

The training for boys and girls can start at 10 years of age. This is the beginning of a long-term training plan. At 10, they must learn what learning is. I recommend an average of 200 hours a year, which is four hours a week. Don't limit the sports training to one sport, and don't force the child, but encourage him to play other ball sports other than just his favorite sport. From ages 11 through 14, a child must improve technical skills in sports of all kinds as well as weight training. With all the machines available, a coach who can teach proper lifting techniques for barbell and dumbbell exercises is critical. All physical qualities must improve year by year. Of course, look for improvements in a sport where the child shows the most improvement. Is the child learning to compete? How is his concentration? How well can she run from five-yard to 10-yard sprints to running 200, 400 and 600 meters? Is he going to be in the right sport for his muscular fiber?

All skills must show improvement as the child matures from 15-years-old to 17-years-old. At 17 he must choose a sport to specialize. The ratio of sports training must tilt toward the sport, but GPP still plays a great role in sport's excellence. More attention should be paid to the physical qualities that lack in the young sportsman, and the least amount of focus should be placed on what he excels at without disrupting the sports performance.

The training of young boys and girls is far advanced in European training centers. Training as early as five includes running, jumping, throwing, catching as well as hopping or jump roping, balancing and flexibility. These physical abilities must be taught very young or it makes it difficult to learn later. The more physical activities one can learn will increase the synaptic connections between brain cells. (Black, 1990)

First and foremost, physical fitness must be raised. Physical fitness is the ability to perform everyday tasks without an excess of energy and to enjoy the tasks chosen. The coach must stress upon the child to be proficient at many sporting tasks while raising speed, flexibility, balance and strength of all types. Muscular endurance, cardio endurance and body composition increasing limb movement are all important.

Teach coordination first with many drills such as throwing, catching, jumping, landing, and running drills for short and moderate distances. There is far too much to learn about training boys and girls at early ages. There are many experts on the subject, but considered reading the works by esteemed authors like Jozef Drabik, PhD who wrote *Children and Sports Training* (1996) and L.S. Dvorkin who wrote *Weightlifting and Age* (1992, Bud Charniga Jr. copyright).

Perhaps one of the most important studies of age and training was conducted on Naim Suleymanoglu, a Bulgarian weightlifter who at 10-years-old was allowed to train at the main training center along with world champions, while living in a boarding house. At 22 kg he lifted 25 kg. It was normal for weightlifting to start at 13-years-old, but Naim changed that for good. He became open world champion at 15-years-old. This was unheard of. He immediately changed what was right and wrong about the training of our young. Maybe you can develop the next pocket Hercules. A coach is like an archers bow, and the young athlete is like the arrow. If the arrow doesn't leave the bow correctly there is little chance of hitting the training target over. Consider reading *Naim Suleymanoglu The Pocket Hercules,* by Yazan Enver Turkileri.

Age and Weight Training

At what age should one begin weight training? Are there dangers to the growth plates? The lifters of the former Soviet Union set over 1,000 world records since 1946. They had a well-planned youth development program. Top coaches, sports scientists plus medical and physical communities were involved in L.S. Dvorkin *Weightlifting and Age* (1989) and A.S. Medvedev's *Fundamentals of a Multi-Year System of Training Jr. Weightlifting* (1989).

I. Kurachenkov ran a very complex study on the effects of weightlifting and age. In two studies of weightlifters ranging from 14-years-old to16-year-olds, it was found that neither the development of the osteomotor apparatus nor height was affected. The results were similar to swimmers. He also noted the weight-bearing activities did not cause pathological changes to the spine, but on a positive note, these activities strengthened the muscular core set and had a positive effect on posture. In conclusion, shorter people make better weightlifters, but lifting weights does not make a person shorter.

The author, Louie Simmons, with no former coaching, cleaned and jerked 260 pounds at 14-years-old and had an unofficial deadlift of 475 pounds at 155 pounds bodyweight. He believes his early success came from his job as a mason laborer, where he carried blocks upstairs, mixing mortar on the job. This was in 1960 with hardly any labor laws to contend. Today, the same author is supplying you with a plan specifically for improving sports performance. A pyramid is only as tall as its base; this is simply mathematics as so is the loading.

Though the Bulgarian system was very successful, it was very selective in its athletes. Many succeeded in the circa-max style of training with the emphasis on six exercises; however, even more failed including former world champions. This system was based on what the top lifter could handle. The great Naim Suleymanoglu was one such guinea pig who could control almost any load placed upon him. Unfortunately, many of his training partners could not manage the physical demands or more importantly the emotional stress. The Soviet's developed young lifters to become world and Olympic championships by developing the lifters' physical qualities.

The Westside system is a combination of both, plus the near circa-max training of the Bulgarian team where Naim's mean training weight was 87 percent. Westside's mean training weight on speed day is 80 percent. The author was highly influenced by the Russian style training that uses the conjugate system by constantly changing special exercises with a variety of accommodating resistance. Using the system of loading devised by A.S. Prilepin, he found lifts at 70 percent was 12 to 24 with 16 being optimal, and 80 percent for 10 to 20 lifts with 15 being optimal, and 90 percent was four to 10 lifts with seven lifts being optimal. The reps for three to six at 70 percent; two to four at 80 percent and one to two lifts at 90 percent intensity.

To the novice, this may not mean much, but it led to A.S. Medvedev's tremendous success with the Soviet's team. A.S. Medvedev's works changed everything I thought about weight training because I realized it is physics, bio-mechanics and mathematics. It does not matter if a person is 14-years-old or 60-years-old, and it does not matter if he can squat 900 pounds or 300 pounds because it is a mathematical formula based on strength. A 900-pound individual lifts 70 percent or 630 pounds just as fast as a 300-pound squatter lifts his 70 percent or 210 pounds.

This system provides a structure to train optimally according to one's max strength. No more will the weaker lifter over train while trying to keep up with a stronger lifter or a stronger lifter train down to a weaker lifter's level. Excessive reps at a pre-determined percentage that are no longer producing maximum force production can be eliminated. This system was made and formulated from Soviet weightlifters, so it can be used for all classical lifts, snatch, clean-jerk, squat, bench press and deadlifts. It can even be implemented for determined resistance while jumping on a box by calculating the height of the box max instead of maximal weight in a certain lift. Consequently, speed strength is best performed with weights in the 75 percent to 85 percent range in a three-week wave. This is a simple math formula based on an individual's max strength level on a particular lift or specialty bar or on a box jump. Fitness level is a significant part of the equation. A fast pace must accompany the sub-maximal lifts that are intended for explosive and speed strength training.

Studies from the former Soviet Union on junior weight lifting is somewhat incomplete. Although they have broken more than 1,000 world records, their information on junior weight lifters was slow coming. Even up to the 1970s, they considered weight lifting an adult sport. L.S. Dvorkin's *Weightlifting and Age* reveals that only 16-year-olds and 17-year-olds could compete in the 1950s, and in the late 1960s, 15-year-olds were allowed to participate (Roman, 1988).

In 1953, Al Kurachenkov did an in-depth study on 14-year-olds to 16-year-olds. There was no noticeable disruptive development of the osteomotor apparatus and height was not affected. No doubt the greatest junior weight lifter of all time was Naim Suleymanoglu, the great Bulgarian who later moved to Turkey because of his exploits. He was the only weightlifter to break records on first attempts. While the Bulgarians were starting junior weight lifters at 13-years-old, he was selected at 10-years-old to train with adult weight lifters who were European and world record holders, who lived in the same house. He first had to pass a physiological and psychological test. The Bulgarians only chose model sportsmen who passed an anatomical test, having correct proportions for the weight class or sport. Naim was the youngest to start a real weight lifting program; he was so talented the country started a scientific research study on 11-year-olds and 12-year-olds, and they added more than 50 percent to the weightlifting budget to not lose young athletes. This study would include looking into growth issues as well as addressing cardiovascular questions. Thank goodness they did. It was found that the GPP would be an essential part of the success of the experiment. Because many leading weightlifting experts could not believe what they were watching, they were astonished to say the least. Naim was world champ at 15-years-old. How could this happen? Change, that's how.

Einstein said people hate change, but without change, there would be no progress. Enver Turkileri was largely responsible for the success of Naim's system. All may not know of it because the true system was not to be disclosed entirely for fear that other countries would use the same system with their vast numbers of young weight lifters. Nevertheless, this was remarkable to say the least. The information was taken from Turkileri's *Naim Suleymanoglu: The Pocket Hercules* because no one could duplicate Naim's success. Why is that? The United States is constantly using a Bulgarian training system with no success at all. We must develop someone like Naim, not have one dropped in our lap.

What about training loads? There have been many studies about optimal training loads. M.Y. Yakovlev ran studies about the perfect training loads in 1927, and his findings concluded the 2/3's of a max single was best (Dvorkin, 1992). As years go by, various authors have found more and more sophisticated programs. For example, 80 percent weights in classical lifts 50 percent of the time followed by small and moderate weights in special exercises for individual muscle groups. There are three primary methods to develop strength:

The Dynamic Method
Lifting a non-maximal weight with the highest attainable speed

Maximal Effort Method
Lifting a maximal weight with no time limit

Repetition to Near Failure Method

This is used at Westside with small or special exercises, such as: glute/ham raise, Reverse Hyper® s, weight chains, tricep exercises, abs exercises, sled pulling, and the like. (Zatsiorsky, 1995).

Just as many renowned coaches and sports scientists such as A.K. Melinikov, B.E. Podskotsky, A.S. Medvedev, R.A. Roman and many others, concluded that a certain method of loading at certain age groups 12-year-olds to 14-year-olds, 15-year-olds to 16-year-olds and 17-year-olds to 18-year-olds had certain needs, I also found the younger the lifter, the greater base he must have. This training was for weight lifters who were constantly adding the number of classical lifts until they reached an elite status, and 50 percent of their training consisted of special exercises.

Westside's system found any age can perfect form in the classical lifts in the squat, bench, and deadlift and also the snatch and clean by performing primarily special exercises. This is part of the conjugate system. Westside never does regular squats, but rather box squats. Deadlifting is not executed off the floor without some accommodating resistance; however, rack pulls and box squats are employed on a regular basis. Consequently, a sumo puller pulls mostly conventional and a conventional puller trains sumo, most often in an ultra-wide sumo stance. For benching, speed days use 40 percent to 50 percent of a one rep max with some means of accommodating resistance. One or two times a year is when someone does an actual lift in the gym; other regular powerlifts are completed only at contests where it counts.

I prefer to have 12-year-olds to 14-year-olds pull sleds to build all the squatting, running and jumping muscles. To achieve strength and conditioning simultaneously, lower and upper body exercises need to be employed. Examples of lower body movements include sled pulls, forward, backward, sideways between the legs, with ankle weights, weight vests or both. A heavy sled is versatile; it can be used for max effort work, a supplemental workout, or even extra workouts. Additional strength and conditioning exercises include the following: lots of rope climbing, push-ups, chin-ups, sit-ups, leg raises, box jumps, bounding, and standing long jumps over an obstacle. Combine this with a basic well balanced diet and plenty of rest.

Working with a young sprinter and several ball players, I found their sports activities formed a GPP background. The athlete must want to participate in the chosen sport, which must be up to the child, not the parent or guardian.

Now that an individual is able to start a loading program, a 14-year-old can do the same workouts as an adult. Just remember to do the optimal amount of lifts. I have guided the career of 14-year-olds who later became ranked number one worldwide in two divisions in the total. One of them being Dave Hoff, an open world record holder at 22 years, and the other was the youngest at the time in 1995, Kenny Patterson. It does not matter if someone squats 200 pounds or 1,000 pounds; the Westside loading is based on a one rep max. It's simple mathematics. An individual is simply asked to do the correct amount of volume based off his max. Looking at the graphs, it is evident how simple it is to control volume to train optimally at one's strength level or how to change volume by changing bars that have their own maxes.

The first graph exhibits an example of one's combined max lifts on three different styles of squatting. Note: the percent is the same, the bar speed would be the same, about .8 m/s, but the volume varies at the same percent.

1A.

500 back squat	50%	250 lb.
350 front squat	50%	175 lb.
250 overhead squat	50%	125 lb.

Common bar speed .8 m/s

It is essential to know the maximal and minimal number of lifts for explosive strength of 40 percent to 60 percent. Speed strength is 70 percent to 80 percent, and maximal strength is 90 percent and above. If an individual trains significantly above or below the recommendations, the training effects are diminished.

1B.

40% no less than 24 and no more than 48
50% no less than 24 and no more than 48
60% no less than 20 and no more then 40
70% no less than 12 and no more then 24
80% no less than 10 and no more then 20
90% no less than 4 and no more then 10

I highly recommend doing the optimal number of lifts per training session. The goal is to move the prescribed weight at the fastest rate possible. When repetitions go beyond the number of Prilepin's recommendations or my own, Louie Simmons, bar speed suffers and so will force production.

The Optimal Lifts

Percent	Reps	Lifts
40%	4-8	36
50%	3-6	36
60%	3-6	30
70%	3-6	18
80%	2-4	15
90%	1-2	4-7

Some individuals are not as explosive, or they lack proper GPP. These individuals may have to train at five percent lower to obtain proper bar speed to acquire a special strength. Others may have to take longer rests between sets. All things such as GPP, endurance, the development of speed strength qualities, raising maximal strength as well as strength endurance and explosive strength must be equal through the conjugate system.

Starzynski, T. & Sozanski, H. *Explosive Power and Jumping Ability for all Sports.* Island Pond, VT: Stadium Publishing, (1995).

Suleymanoglu, N. & Turkileri, Y. *The Pocket Hercules.* Livonia Mi.: Sportivny Press, (1997).

Tabalhnik, B. & Papanov, V. Sprinters from the G.D.A. Leg Kaya Atletika. Soviet Sports Review. 8:16-18. (1987).

Turkuleri, E. Naim Suleimanoglu: *The Pocket Hercules.* Livonia Mi.: Sportivny Press, (2004).

Verkhoshansky, V.M. *Fundamentals of Special Strength Training in Sports.* Livonia Mi.: Sportivny Press, (1997).

Verkhoshansky, Y.V. *Programming and Organization of Training.* Livonia Mi.: Sportivny Press, (1985).

Viru, Atko. *Adaptation in Sports Training.* (1995).

A. Charniga, Jr. *Weightlifting Yearbook.* Trans. Livonia Mi.: Sportivny Press, (1985).

A. Charniga, Jr. *Weightlifting Yearbook.* Trans. Livonia Mi.: Sportivny Press, (1983).

A. Charniga, Jr. *Weightlifting Yearbook.* Trans. Livonia Mi.: Sportivny Press, (1981).

A. Charniga, Jr. *Weightlifting Yearbook.* Trans. Livonia Mi.: Sportivny Press, (1980).

S.H. Westing. European Journal of Applied Science. (1988).

Winter, Bud & Lee, Jimson *The Rocket Sprint Start.* USA: Bud Winter Enterprises, (2011).

Winter, Bud *SO YOU WANT TO BE A SPRINTER.* USA: Bud Winter Enterprises, (2010).

Winter, Bud *RELAX and WIN.* USA: Bud Winter Enterprises, (2012).

Yessis, M. *Biomechanics and Kinesiology of Exercise.* Michigan: Ultimate Athletic Concepts, (2013).

Yessis, M. *Secrets of Soviet Sports Fitness and Training.* Michigan: Ultimate Athletic Concepts, (1987).

Yessis, M. Soviet Sports Review. Volume 19, Number 2 Michigan: Ultimate Athletic Concepts, (1984).

Yessis, M. Soviet Sports Review. Volume 19, Number 3 Michigan: Ultimate Athletic Concepts, (1984).

Yessis, M. *Soviet Sports Review. Volume 20, Number 1* Michigan: Ultimate Athletic Concepts, (1985).

Yessis, M. *Soviet Sports Review. Volume 20, Number 2* Michigan: Ultimate Athletic Concepts, (1985).

Yessis, M. *Soviet Sports Review. Volume 20, Number 3* Michigan: Ultimate Athletic Concepts, (1985).

Yessis, M. *Soviet Sports Review. Volume 20, Number 4* Michigan: Ultimate Athletic Concepts, (1985).

Yessis, M. *Soviet Sports Review. Volume 21, Number 3* Michigan: Ultimate Athletic Concepts, (1986).

Yessis, M. *Soviet Sports Review. Volume 21, Number 4* Michigan: Ultimate Athletic Concepts, (1986).

Yessis, M. *Soviet Sports Review. Volume 22, Number 1* Michigan: Ultimate Athletic Concepts, (1987).

Yessis, M. *Soviet Sports Review. Volume 22, Number 2* Michigan: Ultimate Athletic Concepts, (1987).

Yessis, M. *Soviet Sports Review. Volume 22, Number 4* Michigan: Ultimate Athletic Concepts, (1988).

Yessis, M. *Soviet Sports Review. Volume 24, Number 1* Michigan: Ultimate Athletic Concepts, (1989).

Zatsiorsky, V.M. *Science and Practice of Strength Training.* Champaign, IL: Human Kinetics, (1995).

It is essential to know the maximal and minimal number of lifts for explosive strength of 40 percent to 60 percent. Speed strength is 70 percent to 80 percent, and maximal strength is 90 percent and above. If an individual trains significantly above or below the recommendations, the training effects are diminished.

1B.

40% no less than 24 and no more than 48
50% no less than 24 and no more than 48
60% no less than 20 and no more then 40
70% no less than 12 and no more then 24
80% no less than 10 and no more then 20
90% no less than 4 and no more then 10

I highly recommend doing the optimal number of lifts per training session. The goal is to move the prescribed weight at the fastest rate possible. When repetitions go beyond the number of Prilepin's recommendations or my own, Louie Simmons, bar speed suffers and so will force production.

The Optimal Lifts

Percent	Reps	Lifts
40%	4-8	36
50%	3-6	36
60%	3-6	30
70%	3-6	18
80%	2-4	15
90%	1-2	4-7

Some individuals are not as explosive, or they lack proper GPP. These individuals may have to train at five percent lower to obtain proper bar speed to acquire a special strength. Others may have to take longer rests between sets. All things such as GPP, endurance, the development of speed strength qualities, raising maximal strength as well as strength endurance and explosive strength must be equal through the conjugate system.